Twice Ten: An Introduction to Poetry

Twice Ten: An Introduction to Poetry

Chad Walsh and Eva T. Walsh

Chad Walsh

Writer-in-Residence
Beloit College

Eva T. Walsh

formerly of Rockford College

John Wiley & Sons, Inc., New York · London · Toronto

Library of Congress Cataloging in Publication Data:

Main entry under title:

Twice ten.

Includes bibliographies.
1. American poetry—Explication. 2. English poetry—Explication. 3. American poetry—History and criticism. 4. English poetry—History and criticism. 5. American poetry. 6. English poetry. I. Walsh, Chad, 1914– II. Walsh, Eva.
PS306.T9 821'.008 75-29311
ISBN 0-471-91923-3

Printed in the United States of America

10 9 8 7 6 5 4 3 2 1

Cover & Book Design by Angie Lee

For Howard and Marion Munford

To Stephen G. Perine for his assistance in the preparation of the Instructor's Manual to accompany this text.

Preface to the Student

We agree with Robert Frost—poetry *is* important. It may be true, as W. H. Auden insisted, that poetry "makes nothing happen" in the world of the commonplace, that it does not send the stock market up or down or elect presidents. But poetry does invite us into a dimension of life that we would otherwise miss.

We all live with language, but poetry is a special way of using language. It is a special angle of vision that helps us to see ourselves, others, and the whole universe in a different way.

Poets often have a special sensitivity to the shape of things to come. For instance, who in the early 1920s (except the poets and other artists) foresaw the breakup of traditional patterns of civilization? Who captured that sense of desolation best? The answer is certainly T. S. Eliot in *The Waste Land* and *The Hollow Men* (page 354). Who is speaking for us today—seeing beyond our chaos? The answer is, again, the poets. If we want to know what is actually going on in the world, we must listen to the poets. But this is a special kind of listening—and that is what this book is all about. From poets like Blake, Yeats, Eliot, Auden, and Ginsberg we learn to see the world differently, to recognize patterns of the future as well as of the present and the past.

Really learning how to read poetry offers such great rewards that a life without it is sadly impoverished. In poetry there is tremendous mental stimulation. There is also an intense aesthetic satisfaction. The patterns of poetry—stanza forms, rhythm, the way language is used, the musical qualities—all of these are a rich banquet. Also, poetry is not ashamed to be emotional. This makes it doubly precious in a period like our own. Most educational systems put emphasis on reason, logic, and common sense. There is nothing wrong with these goals, but they need to be balanced by a sense of wonder and beauty. Poetry restores the intuition of mystery that we had as children and lost in adulthood.

Poetry can also, as Yeats believed, impose some kind of order and pattern on the chaos of the world. We can perhaps find no real meaning or unity in the world today—but a poem that takes the ordinary words of the language and out of them creates order and meaning gives us some clue about the necessity of the arts. It even gives us faith that some patterns—man created, perhaps—are possible.

And finally, through art, and especially through the experience of really encountering a poem, wrestling with it, probing it, responding to it—interpreting it for ourselves—we share in some small measure the creative process that the poet went through. "Men work together," Frost insisted. We may never write a memorable poem, but as we make someone else's poem our own by probing its depths, we understand a little of what the creative process is all about. For the moment, at least, we escape the tyranny of the humdrum, and realize that man's uniqueness rests in his ability to be a creator.

All of this may sound pretentious. We don't mean it to be. We only urge you to begin this book with an open mind, a sense of expectancy. If you land at the end with a thud, part of it will be your inadequacy and part of it ours—but don't blame the poets.

Publisher's Note to the Instructor

Twice Ten: An Introduction to Poetry is based on the belief that the best way to teach poetry is to single out a small number of poets and to explore them in depth. Up to the present, no one-volume text with adequate analytic and critical apparatus, and a sufficient number and variety of poets, has been available for this approach.

This book presents ten poets in detail. Each chapter is equivalent to a separate casebook, with first a brief biographical sketch, and then a short treatment of the special characteristics of the poet's work. Next come half a dozen poems, explicated in detail, often with considerable use of major literary criticism. Finally, two or three poems are more briefly treated, followed by a short anthology of poems for further study, and a highly selective bibliography.

Following the ten chapters on individual poets, there is an anthology of an additional ten, with each poet represented by about ten pages. The instructor and student thus have twenty poets represented by enough work so that each can be explored in depth.

The poets are selected with variety in mind. They range from the 17th century to the present. They are as diverse in technique, subject matter, and tone as John Donne, Allen Ginsberg, and A. E. Housman.

Twice Ten: An Introduction to Poetry opens new possibilities for teaching students to explore the world of poetry. It is suitable for "introduction to poetry" courses, genre courses, sophomore literature, general humanities, and any freshman English course that emphasizes a literary approach.

C.W.
E.T.W.

Acknowledgments

With Special Thanks:

To our students, who helped write this book more than they realize.

To our colleagues, at Beloit College, Rockford College, and far away, who made available their insights, doubts, and affirmations when we called on them for advice.

To Alan Perlis, in particular, for his great help on the Stevens chapter (any deficiencies remaining are ours, not his).

To our friend, Dolores Reppert, patient and accurate at the typewriter.

And to two of our daughters, Madeline Hamblin and Alison, who faithfully typed what their parents had written.

C.W.
E.T.W.

Contents

Twice Ten: An Introduction to Poetry

Poets

John Donne

His Life

John Donne (born 1572) was a younger contemporary of Shakespeare—yet it is hard to imagine two poets more different in their angle of vision and sense of language. His father died when he was four, and his mother remarried the same year. On the maternal side he came from a long line of professing Catholics and his mother saw to it that his education reinforced the tenets of that faith. This early training led to some of Donne's later difficulties. He had a brilliant mind, a sharp wit, and a driving ambition to get ahead in the secular world of the English court, a goal impossible for a Catholic.

Ever since Henry VIII, the Catholic Church and the Church of England had been enemies. During the reign of Elizabeth severe restrictions were imposed. Catholics were not allowed degrees at Oxford or Cambridge and advancement at court was out of the question. In many instances, when they persisted in their allegiance to Rome, they faced exile, confiscation of their property, or imprisonment, as happened to the third husband of Donne's mother. Donne's family background made him constantly suspect. It was thus inevitable that his mind and heart should wrestle with the competing claims of the two churches.

Donne's personal qualities were such that, despite the ambiguities of his religious stance, he began to be noticed and admired. He became known as a young man about town, and in 1597 he entered the service of the Lord Keeper, Sir Thomas Egerton. The way seemed opened for the secular success his talent merited and his whole being craved. But Donne was an impulsive and passionate man, and in December of 1601 he secretly married young Anne More. The validity of the marriage was questioned; Donne was imprisioned and he was promptly dismissed by Egerton. Though the civil court upheld the legality of the marriage and Donne was released from prison, any hope of a career at court seemed doomed.

The young Donnes had a difficult financial struggle for many years. Without the help of loyal friends the situation would have been even more desperate. Yet there is no evidence that Donne found in his relationship with Anne anything but deep devotion and support. She died in 1617—worn out with childbearing at the age of thirty-three. It was a devastating loss for Donne and he never remarried.

Meanwhile, for a number of years he still hoped to get some kind of advancement at court, but each time he sought a position his hopes were dashed. Nonetheless, his brilliance was widely recognized. He had patrons among the powerful and his poetry was circulating in manuscript. During this period he also came to accept the validity of the Church of England and to recognize that the only official advancement open to him lay through ordination and service in the Church. For a long time he resisted such a career, but in 1615 he was finally ordained and appointed a royal chaplain.

To say that he went into the ministry for worldly reasons is to exercise a judgment that is beyond us more than 300 years later.[1] As we read the *Holy Sonnets* we see Donne's struggle to reach God; we experience the conflicting claims of Rome and Canterbury; we explore the dichotomy between faith and reason which must have torn him apart at times. All in all, we can only honor a commitment painfully arrived at, and which in the end did give him peace and fulfillment. In 1621 Donne was installed as Dean of St. Paul's in London and became famous as a great preacher as well as a poet. His sermons were published, as were his private "devotions," one of which contains the famous passage that is often quoted by readers who have read nothing else of Donne's: "No man is an Iland, intire of it selfe; every man is a peece of the Continent, a part of the maine . . . And therefore never send to know for whom the bell tolls; It tolls for thee."

Even before his ordination his contact with the powerful had led him to certain enriching experiences, though not to the career he so longingly sought. For instance, he received an honorary M.A. from Oxford in 1610, and in 1612 he went on an extended tour of Europe with Sir Robert and Lady Drury, serving as sort of secretary-companion. Upon his return he moved his family into a house at Drury House in London, closer to the center of political activity. In 1614 he even served for a time in Parliament.

Donne's last years were spent in the service of St. Paul's, in preaching at court, revising his sermons and, happily, amassing some of the worldly goods that had been in such short supply during his younger days.

He died in 1631 and was buried in St. Paul's. Though the first collection of his poetry was not published until 1633, his reputation among his contemporaries was high. Changing tastes in the late 17th and 18th centuries led to a reevaluation of his reputation and a feeling that the complexity of his language and the audacity of his wit amounted to nothing more than riddles. The late 19th and early 20th centuries were periods of new interest in what has been called metaphysical poetry and in Donne especially. In this century, T. S. Eliot and the New Criticism were largely responsible for enhancing Donne's reputation. Today he is ranked as one of the major poets in the English language. Perhaps by exploring some of his poems in depth we can understand the pull, power, and paradoxes of his genius.

[1] For a penetrating study of this complex question, see Robert S. Jackson, *John Donne's Christian Vocation* (Evanston, Ill.: Northwestern University Press, 1970).

The Poet and His Poetry

Donne is conventionally labeled a "metaphysical poet," a term invented after his time. Scholars and critics apply it to certain 17th century poets to characterize qualities they share in common. The poets most frequently singled out are Donne, Herbert, Grashaw, and Vaughan, but here our concern is entirely with Donne. As you read him, you can make certain deductions about the characteristics of his poetry. For instance, what strikes you as you read the following poem?

The Flea

Marke but this flea, and marke in this,
How little that which thou deny'st me is;
It suck'd me first, and now sucks thee,
And in this flea, our two bloods mingled bee;
Thou know'st that this cannot be said
A sinne, nor shame, nor losse of maidenhead,
Yet this enjoyes before it wooe,
And pamper'd swells with one blood made of two,
And this, alas, is more then wee would doe.

Oh stay, three lives in one flea spare,
Where wee almost, yea more then maryed are.
This flea is you and I, and this
Our mariage bed, and mariage temple is;
Though parents grudge, and you, w'are met,
And cloystred in these living walls of Jet.
Though use make you apt to kill mee,
Let not to that, selfe murder added bee,
And sacrilege, three sinnes in killing three.

Cruell and sodaine, hast thou since
Purpled thy naile, in blood of innocence?
Wherein could this flea guilty bee,
Except in that drop which it suckt from thee?
Yet thou triumph'st and saist that thou
Find'st not thy selfe, nor mee the weaker now;
'Tis true, then learne how false, feares bee;
Just so much honor, when thou yeeld'st to mee,
Will wast, as this flea's death tooke life from thee.

Of course, the language and the spelling seem somewhat archaic, but this is superficial. The language was modern in Donne's time, and even today all the words are familiar. As for the subject of the poem, it is obviously love, despite the title.

And it is here that one of the chief characteristics of metaphysical poetry strikes you—the use of outrageous "conceits" (refer to Glossary for the definition of this technical term) to express such a concept as love. Who would think of writing a love poem using a flea, of all things, as the chief image to persuade the lady that in yielding to her lover she will lose no honor, since the blood of both has already met and mingled in the flea?

Try reading the poem aloud. You will discover a roughed-up meter which seems nearer to the rhythm of common speech than to the smooth flow of the usual Elizabethan love lyric. Donne was deliberately trying to get away from the trite conventions of Elizabethan love poetry—the overly regular rhythm, the simpering shepherdesses and wistful shepherds, the stale references to the classical muses, the general artificiality of a poetry that treated love as a stylized game. Donne was, in fact, deliberately writing poetry that in the context of his time was shockingly "modern." "The Flea" summons up in the reader's imagination no pleasant images. But the very outrageousness of its imagery makes a blunt point effectively and without evasion.

We do Donne an injustice, however, if we take "The Flea" as representative of his work. In most of his love poems—although the same audacious imagery persists—the emotions are deeper and are cast in more intellectual terms. This is evident in several poems shortly to be considered.

There is also another quality in Donne's poetry that seems almost as shocking as the flea metaphor, and that is his constant mixing of secular and religious imagery, so that lovers are canonized or their bones are viewed as religious relics. Or else the church is compared to a whore because she is open to all–or in another poem God ravishes (rapes) Donne.

We spoke a while back about the intellectual images used in Donne's love poetry. Examples from "A Valediction Forbidding Mourning" (p. 27) illustrate this. He speaks of "the trepidation of the spheares" (meaning the movement of the concentric spheres supposed to support the planets) and he uses the famous compass imagery where he compares his wife to the fixed foot of the common compass used in geometry and himself to the foot that moves. Donne had a far ranging and inquisitive mind and the new science—particularly the Copernican theory of the solar system—intrigued him. His poetry is full of references to both the old (Ptolemaic) and the new astronomy.

In general, Donne uses whatever will suit the purposes of a particular poem–science old and new, the rhythm of common speech, a mixture of the holy and the profane, intellectual concepts or a flea to express states of emotion. All of these, taken together, produce a complex and exciting poetry that may seem almost a riddle, but at its best is fresh and provocative.

Perhaps we can sum all this up by quoting from Joan Bennett's *Four Metaphysical Poets*:[2]

[2] New York: Vintage Books, 1960. Originally published 1934, second edition 1953, pp. 5, 6, 15.

> . . . . The word "metaphysical" refers to style rather than to subject matter, but style reflects an attitude to experience. Experience to the metaphysical poets was, as it were, grist to an intellectual mill. . . .
> . . . . The peculiarity of the metaphysical poets is not that they relate, but that the relations they perceive are often more logical than sensuous or emotional, and that they constantly connect the abstract with the concrete, the remote with the near, and the sublime with the commonplace.
> . . . . The metaphysical poets demand a continual breakdown of mental habits—experiences which have been kept apart in the mind are suddenly yoked together. This often occasions what seems like obscurity in a poem, but is really only an obstruction in the reader's mind. . . .

One other comment before we study certain of Donne's poems in more detail. The idea of death haunts his work. This is not, of course, unique to metaphysical poets; the consciousness of "time's winged chariot" has hovered over the work of many great poets. But perhaps it is enhanced in Donne because of his Christian commitment—his fears, but still more his growing conviction that the mercy of God would finally grant him eternal life in the company of the blessed. We should remember, too, that death was faced more openly and realistically in earlier centuries, and there were few families that had not suffered all too often the sudden intruder. Several of Donne's children died, two of them in the same year; two were stillborn, and as we have seen, his wife died at the relatively young age of thirty-three, after the birth of her twelfth child. Hence uncertainty of life, its ephemeral and transitory character, was embedded in Donne's awareness.

Poems

There is no standard, cut-and-dried method to explore a poem. Sometimes a knowledge of the poet's life and historical period will shed light. At other times, awareness of a psychological dimension in the poem or a recognition of archetypal themes is illuminating. Most of all, close attention to the way the poem is put together, and its use of language, image, and symbol is helpful. (For an explanation of these four frequently used approaches, see *traditional approach, psychological approach, archetypal approach,* and *formalistic approach* in the Glossary.)

The reader, experiencing a poem he has not read before, needs to be an opportunist, going at the poem from various angles and finding by trial-and-error the approaches that will yield insights. All this will be illustrated in the discussions of the ten poets who constitute the main part of this book.

First, one of Donne's simpler love poems:

The Anniversarie

All Kings, and all their favorites,
All glory' of honors, beauties, wits,
The Sun it selfe, which makes times, as they passe,
Is elder by a yeare, now, then it was
When thou and I first one another saw:
All other things, to their destruction draw,
Only our love hath no decay;
This, no to morrow hath, nor yesterday,
Running it never runs from us away,
But truly keepes his first, last, everylasting day.

Two graves must hide thine and my coarse,
If one might, death were no divorce.
Alas, as well as other Princes, wee,
(Who Prince enough in one another bee,)
Must leave at last in death, these eyes, and eares,
Oft fed with true oathes, and with sweet salt teares;
But soules where nothing dwells but love
(All other thoughts being inmates) then shall prove
This, or a love increased there above,
When bodies to their graves, soules from their graves remove.

And then wee shall be throughly blest,
But wee no more, then all the rest.
Here upon earth, we'are Kings, and none but wee
Can be such Kings, nor of such subjects bee;
Who is so safe as wee? where none can doe

Treason to us, except one of us two.
True and false feares let us refraine,
Let us love nobly,' and live, and adde againe
Yeares and yeares unto yeares, till we attaine
To write threescore, this is the second of our raigne.

What use is a biographical approach here? Perhaps not very much, except as a matter of curiosity. One might do research and find the identity of the lady favored by Donne's attentions, but this would not add much to the poem. It is the sort of poem that any man (if he had the sensibility of John Donne) might write about his beloved.

Some knowledge of history does add a dimension of understanding. The opening stanza, with its reference to "All Kings, and all their favorites is used in a context suggesting the passage of time—"The Sun it selfe, which makes times, as they passe, / Is elder by a yeare. . . . " To a 17th century reader, any mention of courtiers would suggest their tenuous status; a Walter Raleigh could be in favor one day, and headless the next. The threatening nature of time, which brings decay and destruction in its wake, is implied at the very start of the poem.

A knowledge of Elizabethan and Jacobean history would also help the reader respond to the images of royalty scattered throughout the poem—references to kings, princes, and subjects. To a person of Donne's time, a king was not just a president dressed in ermine instead of gray flannel. Something mythic enveloped him; as an ideal he was a universal father to his people, divinely commissioned to be the agent of God the Father on a portion of this globe. Thus the aura of ultimate justice, ultimate meaning hovered about him, in theory if less often in fact. The realm of the divine came to one focus in church and to another at the king's court.

Finally, some passing familiarity with the ways the English language has changed is helpful. In "The Anniversarie" the words mostly have the same meanings as at present, and the grammar is not too difficult, although sometimes the word order is a little odd, as in the line where the verb is put last —"When thou and I first one another saw." The main problem for the moment is Donne's wild spelling, a trait he shared with Shakespeare and, indeed, with most people up to the 18th century, when the standardizers set to work on orthography. You have to get accustomed to seeing *reign* spelled *raigne*, and *corse* (archaic form of *corpse*) spelled *coarse*. The spelling *then* is also confusing, for with Donne it often means *than*. These matters of spelling, however, are superficial problems; one soon learns to figure them out almost intuitively. Any that give real trouble can be looked up in the Oxford English Dictionary (OED or OD) or an annotated edition of Donne.

The general idea of "The Anniversarie" is easily summarized. The poem celebrates love that has endured for a year, and prophesies that it will survive triumphantly beyond the grave. The theme of the passage of time runs through the whole poem. Everything, even kings, even the sun who daily marks the passing of time, is a year older. Only this love is timeless; it exists in a kind of eternity: "Running it never runs from us away, / But truly keepes his first, last, everlasting day."

Observe the division into three stanzas. You will soon find that this is not arbitrary. The stanzas function here something like themes in a musical composition. Stanza one states the triumphant survival of love in a world growing older day by day. Stanza two concedes that the lovers are not literally immune to time and decay. They too will die. Stanza three reverts to the affirmations of the first stanza.

This way of looking at the poem is a little better than a plain paraphrase. At least it brings out the movement of the poem—the progression from simple celebration of earthly love, to acknowledgment of age and death waiting even for perfect lovers, to the final resolution where the power of love to transcend time and decay is again proclaimed and brings the poem to an end. The poet, in the middle stanza, has taken into account the common sense objections of the reader—"But won't they die and their love come to an end?"—and has answered them in the final stanza.

The reader now has a kind of road map. But how does he enter into the landscape of actual poetic experience? One way is to examine the mental pictures the "map" creates in the imagination.

The first stanza is dominated by two images of splendor. One is "all Kings," in the setting of a royal court. The other image of splendor is the sun. It is a heavenly equivalent to the King in his court, creating time by functioning as the means of reckoning time. The sun, however, is not itself immune to time. No matter how splendid anything may be, it moves inevitably toward decay. The exception is love.

In the second stanza, the poet gives the devil his due. He admits that on the everyday, realistic level, he and his beloved are subject to the ravages of time.

> Alas, as well as other Princes, wee,
> (Who Prince enough in one another bee,)
> Must leave at last in death, these eyes, and eares,
> Oft fed with true oathes, and with sweet salt teares;

Their bodies will die. But their souls are wholly filled with love. "All other thoughts" are *inmates*—temporary lodgers, not permanent residents of the soul.

The second stanza reintroduces the note of hope toward the end, preparing the way for the affirmations of the last stanza. The lovers, upon death, when body and soul part, will discover (*prove*) a still greater love.

The first stanza was dominated by bright colors. A golden radiance seems to suffuse the picture of the royal court and the majestic sun. The second stanza has more of a grayness to it, and is filled with somber words: graves, coarse (corse), death, divorce, teares, bodies.

What strikes you about the last stanza is that it makes little use of color. Instead, it concentrates on ideas, and has a kind of abstract transparency about it. This is because the final stanza is here intended to tie together the loose threads and apparent contradictions that were presented, mostly in vivid imagery, earlier in the poem.

What does the poem say? That after death, they will continue together in heaven, happy, but no happier than the other blessed souls who inhabit heaven. Meanwhile, they inhabit the earth, and they are kings. Indeed, more than kings. A king is vulnerable to treason and assassination. The lovers inhabit a world of two, and they can be injured only if one turns traitor to the other. A second year has begun. "This is the second of our raigne," the poet states as though he were a king issuing a proclamation. "Let us love nobly," he exhorts his beloved, "and adde againe / Yeares and yeares unto yeares, till we attaine / to write threescore."

In an effective poem, the verse form contributes to the total effect, strengthening and deepening the impact of the thought and imagery. "The Anniversarie" is written in iambic rhythm, but not so regular as to become monotonous. The first line, "All Kings, and all their favorites," flows smoothly enough as iambic, but there are many deliberate irregularities scattered through the poem, like the third line—"The Sun it selfe, which makes times, as they pass"—where the first two feet (The Sun itselfe) are smooth iambic, but the rest of the line departs from iambic and is irregular like the rhythm of actual conversation.

The poem is written in rhyming couplets, except that at the end of each stanza, four lines rhyme together, imparting an extra emphasis to these concluding lines. It is interesting to note that each four-line section expresses a complete thought.

1. If Donne were writing this poem today, what kind of imagery do you think he might use in place of the references to kings and their courts? See if you can create modern phrases to replace "All kings, and all their favorites" and "Who is so safe as we, where none can do / Treason on us, except one of us two?"

2. Does the grotesque imagery of "The Flea" make it a less serious love poem than "The Anniversarie"? Give reasons for your opinion.

The foregoing discussion of one famous love poem may suggest how much complexity can go into the expression of a frequent enough human experience. But Donne is more than a poet celebrating human love. His gift was many-faceted, and he evolved into one of the most powerful of all religious poets.

His period of stress, when he was wrestling with doubt and faith, was particularly fruitful. You will find no smug and easy orthodoxy in these poems. Rather, they depict a passionate and honest mind at work, trying to resolve ultimate questions of meaning.

As Helen Gardner has pointed out in her excellent discussion of Donne's religious poetry, his "Holy Sonnets" were written in a well-established tradition of religious meditation. The method for such meditations had been extensively treated by a variety of writers, most systematically by St. Ignatius Loyola, founder of the Jesuit order. Remember that Donne's early religious training was Catholic. Although he later gave his allegiance to the Church of England, he retained a sensibility profoundly shaped by the Catholic tradition.

It was a tradition in which man was man and God was God, and only God's Grace and intervention could bridge the gulf. As Helen Gardner says of these sonnets:[3]

> No other religious poems make us feel so acutely the predicament of the natural man called to be the spiritual man. None present more vividly man's recognition of the gulf that divides him from God and the effort of faith to lay hold on the miracle by which Christianity declares that the gulf has been bridged.

Sonnet 5 will illustrate the peculiar intensity of these poems.

I Am a Little World

I am a little world made cunningly
Of Elements, and an Angelike spright,
But black sinne hath betraid to endlesse night
My worlds both parts, and (oh) both parts must die.
You which beyond that heaven which was most high
Have found new sphears, and of new lands can write,
Powre new seas in mine eyes, that so I might
Drowne my world with my weeping earnestly,
Or wash it if it must be drown'd no more:
But oh it must be burnt; alas the fire
Of lust and envie'have burnt it heretofore,
And made it fouler; Let their flames retire,
And burne me ô Lord, with a fiery zeale
Of thee' and thy house, which doth in eating heale.

In form, the poem is a sonnet. The first eight lines, the octet, conform to the rhyme pattern of the Petrarchan sonnet, as contrasted with the Shakes-

[3] *John Donne*: *The Divine Poems* (Oxford: Clarendon Press, 1952), p. xxxi.

pearean. The rhyme scheme is: *abbaabba.* Taking advantage of the freedom traditionally allowed in the last six lines, the sestet, of a Petrarchan sonnet, Donne uses the somewhat uncommon rhyme scheme: *cdcdee.* The flow of thought in this particular sonnet does *not* correspond with the patterning of the rhyme scheme. For example, in many Petrarchan sonnets the octet represents the presentation of an idea or emotion, and the sestet in some way modifies or resolves it. Here the break between the two halves of the poem does not affect the presentation of ideas. The last line of the octet is "Drown my world with my weeping earnestly," which is not even the end of a sentence. The effect throughout the poem is that of passionate thoughts and feelings pouring out without regard to the formal structure of the poem. On the other hand, the fact that the poem does have a strict form provides a foil for the uninhibited outpouring of thought and feeling. A car veering this way and that along a highway is more dramatic than one doing the same thing on a level and unmarked field.

The language presents no special problems, except the word *spright,* a variant of spirit. Donne does assume, however, that his readers are deeply versed in the Bible, acquainted with science and geographical exploration, and familiar with popular beliefs. "You which beyond that heaven which was most high / Have found new spheares, and of new lands can write" is a reference to the astronomers discovering new stars, and the earthly explorers mapping a new hemisphere. "Or wash it if it must be drown'd no more" echoes God's promise when, after the Great Flood, He made a covenant with Noah: "And I will establish my covenant with you; neither shall all flesh be cut off any more by the waters of a flood; neither shall there any more be a flood to destroy the earth." (Genesis 9:11) "But oh it must be burnt" refers to the popular belief that the "end of the world" would be accomplished by fire. The phrase, "a fiery zeal / Of Thee and Thy house" paraphrases "For the zeal of thine house hath eaten me up." (Psalm 69:9)

In the first line, Donne is toying with a common idea of the time—that a human being is a kind of small-scale universe—"I am a little world made cunningly." (expertly or ingeniously) The *little world* is not all of one piece. It is an unstable combination of the physical and the spiritual. Sin has corrupted both parts of the little world. In fact, *both* parts must die. The physical body dies literally and the spirit must die to sin and be reborn by God's Grace and mercy. Donne pleads for the gift of repentance and cleansing, asking the astronomers and explorers to provide adequate tears for his eyes—or if the age of deluges is past (God's promise to Noah), then at least to "wash" his "world" (his being) and make it pure. But if the age of deluges is over, the time of universal fire lies in the future. The *little world* has experienced the fires of lust and envy previously. Now it requires the divine fire, which cleanses and heals as it destroys.

Some of the symbols used in this poem have more than one meaning. *Water* suggests drowning, but also cleansing, rebirth, and new life. *Fire* suggests destruction but also a drastic cleansing, perhaps followed by new life. (In the legend of the phoenix, rising periodically from the flames, fire is the prelude to resurrection.) The symbolic overtones of fire are strengthened by many passages from the Bible. There is the story of the burning bush and Moses' awareness of God's presence. There is the tale of the three young men in the fiery furnace saved by their faith and God's help.

The use of water and fire imagery thus carries complex implications of destruction, cleansing, and rebirth. The water imagery is used first, perhaps because it is gentler. The poem seems to say that water is not enough, that only the complete destruction, cleansing, and rebirth provided by fire is adequate to deal with the "black sin" that infects "My world's both parts."

The fire is one "which doth in eating heal." To a person of Donne's period—and particularly to Donne, strongly influenced by Catholic teaching—this would almost inevitably carry a further connotation—the bread of Holy Communion. The communicant, partaking of the sacrament, is united with Christ and thereby the act of eating is a healing of man's alienation from the ultimate. The fire symbolism thus implies the restoration of spiritual health and communion.

1. How do you react to the lines, "Powre new seas in mine eyes, that so I might / Drowne my world with my weeping earnestly?" Are these lines poetically effective? Is the language overdone?

2. Helen Gardner has written:[4]

> There is an ecstasy of joy and an ecstasy of grief in his love poetry; in his divine poetry we are conscious almost always of an effort of will. In the "Holy Sonnets" there is passion and longing, and in the Hymns some of the 'modest assurance' which Walton [Donne's first biographer] attributed to Donne's last hours, but there is no rapture.

Is there any note of rapture in "I am a Little World"? Do you agree with Gardner or not?

To Donne, the "sacred" and the "secular" worlds were not two watertight compartments of experience. Each moves in and out of the other; each can be a symbol for the other. A relatively light-hearted example is "The Relique," in which he talks of a Platonic love relation in the language customarily applied to the saints.

[4] *John Donne: The Divine Poems,* p. xxxv.

The Relique

When my grave is broke up againe
Some second ghest to entertaine,
(For graves have learn'd that woman-head
To be to more then one a Bed)
And he that digs it, spies
A bracelet of bright haire about the bone,
Will he not let'us alone,
And thinke that there a loving couple lies,
Who thought that this device might be some way
To make their soules, at the last busie day,
Meet at this grave, and make a little stay?

If this fall in a time, or land,
Where mis-devotion doth command,
Then, he that digges us up, will bring
Us, to the Bishop, and the King,
To make us Reliques; then
Thou shalt be'a Mary Magdalen, and I
A something else thereby;
All women shall adore us, and some men;
And since at such time, miracles are sought,
I would have that age by this paper taught
What miracles wee harmelesse lovers wrought.

First, we lov'd well and faithfully,
Yet knew not what wee lov'd, nor why,
Difference of sex no more wee knew,
Then our Guardian Angells doe;
Comming and going, wee
Perchance might kisse, but not between those meales;
Our hands ne'r toucht the seales,
Which nature, injur'd by late law, sets free:
These miracles wee did; but now alas,
All measure, and all language, I should passe,
Should I tell what a miracle shee was.

Donne's fascination with death and graveyards sets the scene here. Cemeteries were customarily located in churchyards. Since the space was limited, old graves were often dug up to make room for new "guests"—a situation familiar enough to anyone who recalls the burial of Ophelia in *Hamlet.* The religious references of the poem have to do with the cult of relics, much practiced by the Catholic Church and rejected by Protestants. The last three lines of the first stanza refer to the popular belief that on Judgment Day, when the general resurrection takes place, the bodies of the risen must seek out the places where they left any part of themselves in order to be complete. The lady would come running to his grave to reclaim her "bracelet of bright hair," and they would thus be assured of meeting again.

Perhaps, the poet suggests, the gravedigger will leave the grave in peace, recognizing that the bracelet of bright hair is a device to reunite them. On the other hand, the opening of the grave might take place during a superstitious period, and the gravedigger would leap to the conclusion that he had discovered a martyr's grave. "Then he that digges us up, will bring / Us, to the Bishop, and the King / To make us Reliques." Well, the poet says, if you want saints, I'll provide you with the official evidence—the miracles we accomplished.

The final stanza lists the miracles of platonic love. The two loved, but in a purely spiritual way. True, they kissed each other as a token of greeting on meeting and parting, but this was like shaking hands; they did not kiss at other times. They obeyed the moral law (which has been superimposed upon nature). These were their miracles, but they are nothing compared to the miracle she was in herself. By this point, the poem has enumerated more than enough miracles to justify formal canonization for the two lovers.

1. What do you consider the most striking line in the poem? Why?

2. The tone of the poem depends a great deal on particular phrases and lines. Example the following carefully (use the Oxford Dictionary if uncertain of meanings) and explain the effect of each. Then discuss the overall tone of the poem:

(a) (For graves have learn'd that woman-head / To be to more then one a Bed)

(b) All women shall adore us, and some men.

(c) What miracles wee harmelesse lovers wrought.

(d) Yet knew not what we lov'd.

(e) Difference of sex no more wee knew, / Then our Guardian Angells doe.

(f) Our hands ne'r toucht the seales, / Which nature, injur'd by late law, sets free.

The next poem demonstrates that attitudes toward language can vary from one period to another. Today, the average person has been taught to groan when he hears a pun. The device is associated with an outrageous sense of humor, and invites the audience's mock reproof. In the time of Shakespeare and Donne the pun could be used for humor, but also was used to make a serious point, by suggesting the previously unrealized connection between two things ordinarily considered separate.

In "A Hymne to God the Father," Donne seems to be making a pun on his last name, as well as on the word *sun.*

A Hymne to God the Father

Wilt thou forgive that sinne where I begunne,
  Which is my sin, though it were done before?
Wilt thou forgive those sinnes through which I runne,
  And do them still: though still I do deplore?
    When thou hast done, thou hast not done,
      For, I have more.

Wilt thou forgive that sinne by which I wonne
  Others to sinne? and, made my sinne their doore?
Wilt thou forgive that sinne which I did shunne
  A yeare, or two: but wallowd in, a score?
    When thou hast done, thou hast not done,
      For I have more.

I have a sinne of feare, that when I'have spunne
  My last thred, I shall perish on the shore;
Sweare by thy selfe, that at my death thy Sunne
  Shall shine as it shines now, and heretofore;
    And, having done that, Thou haste done,
      I have no more.

The fifth line of stanzas one and two can mean either "When thou hast finished, thou hast not finished," or "When thou hast finished, thou hast not Donne." Then, in the last stanza, an affirmative twist is given. The fifth line can mean either "And, having done that, Thou hast finished," or "And, having done that, Thou hast Donne."

The movement of the poem from uncertainty and apprehension to affirmation is also carried by the last line of each stanza. The first and second stanzas have the same last line, filled with apprehension—"For I have more." Then in the last stanza the concluding lines change to the hopeful "I have no more."

The poem, then, is a prayer of confession for "that sinne" (Original Sin, the consequence of Adam's and Eve's disobedience, and shared by all mankind) plus the individual sins of Donne. The special sin of which he is guilty is revealed in the last stanza—"a sinne of feare." So he throws himself upon the mercy of the compassionate Christ, with another pun, praying that "thy Sunne" ("thy sun" and "thy Son") will continue to shine, bringing mercy and forgiveness.

The use of the punning has made possible a compression and compactness that would be hard to achieve in any other way. The accidental circumstance that the poet's name is pronounced like the word, *done,* may have given him the opening for the poem. At least, once he finished the first stanza, he had established the punning possibility, and inevitably would think of ways to extract the full measure of poetic meaning from it. The pun on sun/son has a by-product in that an aura of golden radiance, the splendor of the sun, now seems to surround Christ, the son of God—who is, according to the New Testament, the *light* of the world.

1. The language is rather plain here. Why do you think the poet chose to make it so?

2. Why do you think the last two lines of each stanza are shorter than the first four?

3. What effect is created by having the same rhymes run through all three stanzas?

Donne has provided many scholarly battlegrounds for critics who are intent on interpreting his poems. One of the most debated is "A Valediction of Weeping," which has been called "That fiendishly ingenious poem.[5]

A Valediction of Weeping

Let me powre forth
My teares before thy face, whil'st I stay here,
For thy face coines them, and thy stampe they beare,
And by this Mintage they are something worth,
For thus they bee
Pregnant of thee;
Fruits of much griefe they are, emblemes of more,
When a teare falls, that thou falls which it bore,
So thou and I are nothing then, when on a divers shore.

On a round ball
A workeman that hath copies by, can lay
An Europe, Afrique, and an Asia,
And quickly make that, which was nothing, *All,*
So doth each teare,
Which thee doth weare,
A globe, yea world by that impression grow,
Till thy teares mixt with mine doe overflow
This world, by waters sent from thee, my heaven dissolved so.

[5] J. B. Leishman, *The Monarch of Wit* (New York: Harper Torchbooks, 1965, 1966), p. 175. His discussion is well worth reading. Still more provocative is William Empson, *Seven Types of Ambiguity,* second edition (Cleveland and New York: Meridian Books, The World Publishing Company, 1955), pp. 158-65. Some of Professor Empson's insights are incorporated into the discussion here.

O more then Moone,
Draw not up seas to drowne me in thy spheare,
Weepe me not dead, in thine armes, but forbeare
To teach the sea, what it may doe too soone;
Let not the winde
Example finde,
To doe me more harme, then it purposeth;
Since thou and I sigh one anothers breath,
Who e'r sighes most, is cruellest, and hasts the others death.

The occasion of the poem is a farewell (*vale* is Latin for farewell; *diction* comes from *dicere,* 'to say'). Very likely it was written when Donne was obliged to make a prolonged trip to the Continent.

"Metaphysical poetry" often compares very unlike things. In the first stanza, tears and coins are compared. They resemble in being round. But the tears can also reflect the face of his beloved. Thus they are coined; they are no longer round blobs, but are like disks of metal that have been stamped into coins. Implied in the comparison is thoughts of royalty. One of the most jealously defended perogatives of a king or queen was the exclusive right to mint coins, and the monarch's likeness was usually stamped on the coin. The first few lines of stanza one are therefore saying that "As long as I'm with you, your face, reflected in my tears, makes them valuable coins. But when you and I are far apart, my tears will lose their value; they can no longer bear your image, for you will not be there to be reflected."

The second stanza begins with a vivid picture of a mapmaker pasting the continents on a ball. He creates a world. By analogy, each tear that bears your image is a complete world. But your tears, mixed with mine, overflow and inundate the world, destroying my happiness.

The poet continues in the last stanza—you are more than moon, more than a satellite to your earth. You are the world itself. Do not weep, for if you do the ocean my decide to follow your example, and destroy me on my voyage to the Continent.

The final pair of lines is particularly rich in implication. There is the suggestion of at least three meanings: (1) we are so united that we "sigh one anothers breath," (2) sighing is perilous, for the sea may follow its example and turn dangerous, (3) sighing was thought in Donne's time to shorten life; hence, to sigh "one anothers breath" is to threaten the life of the other.

This poem may seem an involved and complex way of describing a relationship. Your first impulse might be so ask, "Why can't he say it simpler?" Perhaps the answer to that is—try to do it.

Like many poems, this one can on one level be reduced to a flat statement —perhaps something like "I can't stand being separated from you." Poetry, however, is the art of probing beneath the obvious, and finding ways to express, in a fresh manner, nuances that escape through the coarse meshes of everyday prose. Anyone who reads this poem is likely at some future time to find himself thinking about relations that had not occurred to him before—such as here the mysterious analogy between very large and very small things.

Finally, the poetic structure is worth a brief examination. The three stanzas are in the same nine-line stanza form. The characteristic that strikes you first is the pattern made by the short and long lines. Then, if you diagram the rhyme scheme, you discover that while short lines usually rhyme with short, and long with long, there is a deliberate exception in each stanza (lines one and four are of different length, but rhyme). Perhaps this prevents the poem from seeming too mechanically put together.

The rhyme scheme of each stanza is as follows (short lines are indicated by lower-case letters, long ones by capitals): *aBBAccDDD.* The way the first four lines rhyme—*aBBA*—has a circular quality, the fourth line linking back with the first. But then the stanza begins marching straight ahead with definite strides—a rhymed couplet (*cc*) followed by three lines rhyming together (*DDD*). Thus each stanza starts out slowly and tentatively, and then seems to acquire a sense of direction, moving emphatically toward the final three lines rhyming together.

The last line of each stanza is also extra long—seven feet. This seems to accentuate the sense of finality, and to stress the meaning conveyed in that particular line.

1. Look up *pregnant* in the multi-volume Oxford Dictionary and make a list of the meanings it had in Donne's time. Does this list throw any additional light on the poem?

2. Are the things that the poem associates with tears (coins, emblems, a round ball, map, the world, the moon, the seas, the wind) completely arbitrary? Or can you show in each case some natural connection?

3. Compare the way weeping is used in this poem with its use in "I am a Little World."

4. Compare the form of this poem with that of "The Anniversarie," and show how the differences in form contribute to the differing effect of the two poems.

In "The Relique," we examined a poem that uses religious imagery to speak of human love. In "The Canonization," Donne is doing the same thing again. (Canonization, in the Catholic Church, is the long, complicated process by which a deceased person is officially declared a saint, worthy of special veneration.)

Rather than discussing it, we choose to reprint Cleanth Brooks' discussion.[6] Professor Brooks is one of the most eminent "New Critics" and specializes in a "close reading" of poems. His treatment of "The Canonization" may suggest ways that you can approach other poems by Donne—or by any author, for that matter.

First, the poem. Read it carefully and determine how you would interpret it, then go on and read Brooks' explication.

The Canonization

For Godsake hold your tongue, and let me love,
Or chide my palsie, or my gout,
My five gray haires, or ruin'd fortune flout,
With wealth your state, your minde with Arts improve,
Take you a course, get you a place,
Observe his honour, or his grace,
Or the Kings reall, or his stamped face
Contemplate, what you will, approve,
So you will let me love.

Alas, alas, who's injur'd by my love?
What merchants ships have my sighs drown'd?
Who saies my teares have overflow'd his ground?
When did my colds a forward spring remove?
When did the heats which my veines fill
Adde one more, to the plaguie Bill?
Soldiers finde warres, and Lawyers finde out still
Litigious men, which quarrels move,
Though she and I do love.

Call us what you will, wee'are made such by love;
Call her one, mee another flye,
We'are Tapers too, and at our owne cost die,
And wee in us finde the'Eagle and the dove.
The Phoenix ridle hath more wit
By us, we two being one, are it.
So, to one neutrall thing both sexes fit.
Wee dye and rise the same, and prove
Mysterious by this love.

[6] *The Well Wrought Urn* (New York: Harcourt, Brace and Company, 1947), pp. 10-17, from Chapter 1, "The Language of Paradox." The entire chapter, which is replete with insights into the nature of poetry, is reprinted in Frank Kermode, ed., *Discussions of John Donne* (Boston: D.C. Heath and Company, 1962).

Wee can dye by it, if not live by love,
And if unfit for tombes and hearse
Our legend bee, it will be fit for verse;
And if no peece of Chronicle wee prove,
We'll build in sonnets pretty roomes;
As well a well wrought urne becomes
The greatest ashes, as halfe-acre tombes,
And by these hymnes, all shall approve
Us *Canoniz'd* for Love.

And thus invoke us; You whom reverend love
Made one anothers hermitage;
You, to whom love was peace, that now is rage,
Who did the whole worlds soule extract, and drove
Into the glasses of your eyes
So made such mirrors, and such spies,
That they did all to you epitomize,
Countries, Townes, Courts: Beg from above
A patterne of your love!

Cleanth Brooks' explication follows:

. . . The basic metaphor which underlies the poem (and which is reflected in the title) involves a sort of paradox. For the poet daringly treats profane love as if it were divine love. The canonization is not that of a pair of holy anchorites who have renounced the world and the flesh. The hermitage of each is the other's body; but they do renounce the world, and so their title to sainthood is cunningly argued. . . .

. . . a reading of the poem will show that Donne takes both love and religion seriously; it will show, further, that the paradox is here his inevitable instrument. . . .

The poem opens dramatically on a note of exasperation. The "you" whom the speaker addresses is not identified. We can imagine that it is a person, perhaps a friend, who is objecting to the speaker's love affair. . . . To use the metaphor on which the poem is built, the friend represents the secular world which the lovers have renounced.

Donne begins to suggest this metaphor in the first stanza by the contemptuous alternatives which he suggests to the friend:

. . . Chide my palsie, or my gout,
My five gray haires, or ruin'd fortune flout. . . .

The implications are: (1) All right, consider my love as an infirmity, as a disease, if you will, but confine yourself to my other infirmities, my palsy, my approaching old age, my ruined fortune. . . . (2) Why don't you pay attention to your own welfare—go on and get wealth and honor for yourself. What should you care if I do give these up in pursuing my love.

The two main categories of secular success are neatly, and contemptuously epitomized in the line

Or the Kings reall, or his stamped face . . .

Cultivate the court and gaze at the king's face there, or, if you prefer, get into business and look at his face stamped on coins. But let me alone.

This conflict between the "real" world and the lover absorbed in the world of love runs through the poem; it dominates the second stanza in which the torments of love, so vivid to the lover, affect the real world not at all —

What merchants ships have my sighs drown'd?

It is touched on in the fourth stanza in the contrast between the word "Chronicle" which suggests secular history with its pomp and magnificence, the history of kings and princes, and the word "sonnets" with its suggestions of trivial and precious intricacy. The conflict appears again in the last stanza, only to be resolved when the unworldly lovers, love's saints who have given up the world, paradoxically achieve a more intense world. . . .

But before going on to discuss this development of the theme, it is important to see what else the second stanza does. For it is in this second stanza and the third, that the poet shifts the tone of the poem, modulating from the note of irritation with which the poem opens into the quite different tone with which it closes.

Donne accomplishes the modulation of tone by what may be called an analysis of love-metaphor. . . . This second stanza, he fills with the conventionalized figures of the Petrarchan tradition: the wind of lovers' sighs, the floods of lovers' tears, etc. . . . The implication is that the poet himself recognizes the absurdity of the Petrarchan love metaphors. But what of it? The very absurdity of the jargon which lovers are expected to talk makes for his argument: their love, however absurd it may appear to the world, does no harm to the world. The practical friend need have no fears: there will still be wars to fight and lawsuits to argue.

The opening of the third stanza suggests that this vein of irony is to be maintained. The poet points out to his friend the infinite fund of such absurdities which can be applied to lovers:

Call her one, mee another flye,
We'are Tapers too, and at our owne cost die. . . .

For that matter, the lovers can conjure up for themselves plenty of such fantastic comparisons: *they* know what the world thinks of them. But these figures of the third stanza are no longer the threadbare Petrarchan conventionalities; they have sharpness and bite. The last one, the likening of the lovers to the phoenix; is fully serious, and with it, the tone has shifted from ironic banter into a defiant but controlled tenderness.

The effect of the poet's implied awareness of the lovers' apparent madness is to cleanse and revivify metaphor; to indicate the sense in which the poet accepts it, and thus to prepare us for accepting seriously the fine and seriously intended metaphors which dominate the last two stanzas of the poem.

The opening line of the fourth stanza,

Wee can dye by it, if not live by love,

achieves an effect of tenderness and deliberate resolution. The lovers are ready to die to the world; they are committed; they are not callow but confident. (The basic metaphor of the saint, one notices, is being carried on; the lovers in their renunciation of the world, have something of the confident resolution of the saint. By the bye, the word "legend"—

. . . if unfit for tombes and hearse
Our legend bee —

in Donne's time meant "the life of a saint.") The lovers are willing to forego the ponderous and stately chronicle and to accept the trifling and insubstantial "sonnet" instead; but then if the urn be well wrought, it provides a finer memorial for one's ashes than does the pompous and grotesque monument. With the finely contemptuous, yet quiet phrase, "halfe-acre tombes," the world which the lovers reject expands into something gross and vulgar. But the figure works further; the pretty sonnets will not merely hold their ashes as a decent earthly memorial. Their legend, their story, will gain them canonization; and approved as love's saints, other lovers will invoke them.

In this last stanza, the theme receives a final complication. The lovers in rejecting life actually win to the most intense life. This paradox has been hinted at earlier in the phoenix metaphor. Here it receives a powerful dramatization. The lovers in becoming hermits, find that they have not lost the world, but have gained the world in each other, now a more intense, more meaningful world. Donne is not content to treat the lovers' discovery as something which comes to them passively, but rather as something which they actively achieve. They are like the saint, God's athlete:

Who did the whole worlds soule contract, and drove
Into the glasses of your eyes. . . .

The image is that of a violent squeezing as of a powerful hand. And what do the lovers "drive" into each other's eyes? The "Countries, Townes," and "Courtes," which they renounced in the first stanza of the poem. The unworldly lovers thus become the most "worldly" of all.

The tone with which the poem closes is one of triumphant achievement, but the tone is a development contributed to by various earlier elements. One of the more important elements which works toward our acceptance of the final paradox is the figure of the phoenix, which will bear a little further analysis.

The comparison of the lovers to the phoenix is very skillfully related to the two earlier comparisons, that in which the lovers are like burning tapers, and that in which they are like the eagle and the dove. The phoenix comparison gathers up both: the phoenix is a bird, and like the tapers, it burns. We have a selected series of items: the phoenix figure seems to come in a natural stream of association. "Call us what you will," the lover says, and rattles off in his desperation the first comparisons that occur to him. The comparison to the phoenix seems thus merely another outlandish one, the most outrageous of all. But it is this most fantastic one, stumbled over apparently in his haste, that the poet goes on to develop. It really describes the lovers best and justifies their renunciation. For the phoenix is not two but one, "we two being one, are it"; and it burns, not like the taper at its own cost, but to live again. Its death is life: "Wee dye and rise the same . . . " The poet literally justifies the fantastic assertion. In the sixteenth and seventeenth centuries to "die" means to experience the consummation of the act of love. The lovers after the act are the same. Their love is not exhausted in mere lust. This is their title to canonization. Their love is like the phoenix.

. . . the sexual submeaning of "die" does not contradict the other meanings: the poet is saying: "Our death is really a more intense life"; "We can afford to trade life (the world) for death (love), for that death is the consummation of life"; "After all, one does not expect to live *by* love, one expects, and wants, to die by it." But in the total passage he is also saying: "Because our love is not mundane, we can give up the world"; "Because our love is not merely lust, we can give up the other lusts, the lust for wealth and power"; "because," and this is said with an inflection of irony as by one who knows the world too well, "because our love can outlast its consummation, we are a minor miracle, we are love's saints. . . . "

I submit that the only way by which the poet could say what "The Canonization" says is by paradox. More direct methods may be tempting, but all of them enfeeble and distort what is to be said. This statement may seem the less surprising when we reflect on how many of the important things which the poet has to say have to be said by means of paradox: most of the language of lovers is such—"The Canonization" is a good example; so is most of the language of religion—"He who would save his life, must lose it;" "The last shall be first." Indeed, almost any insight important enough to warrant a great poem apparently has to be stated in such terms. Deprived of the character of paradox with its twin concomitants of irony and wonder, the matter of Donne's poem unravels into "facts," biological, sociological, and economic. . . . Well, what happens to Shakespeare's lovers, for Shakespeare uses the basic metaphor of "The Canonization" in his *Romeo and Juliet*? In their first conversation, the lovers play with the analogy between the lover and the pilgrim to the Holy Land. Juliet says:

For saints have hands that pilgrims' hands do touch
And palm to palm is holy palmers' kiss.

Considered scientifically, the lovers become Mr. Aldous Huxley's animals, "quietly sweating, palm to palm."

For us today, Donne's imagination seems obsessed with the problem of unity; the sense in which the lovers become one—the sense in which the soul is united with God. Frequently, as we have seen, one type of union becomes a metaphor for the other. It may not be too far-fetched to see both as instances of, and metaphors for, the union which the creative imagination itself effects. For that fusion is not logical; it apparently violates science and common sense; it welds together the discordant and the contradictory. Coleridge has of course given us the classic description of its nature and power. It "reveals itself in the balance or reconcilement of opposite or discordant qualities: of sameness, with difference; of the general, with the concrete; the idea, with the image; the individual, with the representative; the sense of novelty and freshness, with old and familiar objects; a more than usual state of emotion, with more than usual order. . . . "It is a great and illuminating statement, but is a series of paradoxes. Apparently Coleridge could describe the effect of the imagination in no other way.

1. Are there any places where you think Brooks is overinterpreting the poem? Explain.

2. Do you find the sensibility of the poem strange and different from your own? If so, in what ways?

3. Pick out examples of imagery from the poem that you have found in other poems by Donne. Decide in each case whether they have the same connotations, or different ones.

4. Why do you think Donne often writes of earthly love in religious terms, and of religion in terms of earthly love?

For an extreme example of sexual imagery used to speak of religious truth, consider this poem:

Show Me Deare Christ

Show me deare Christ, thy spouse, so bright and cleare.
What, is it she, which on the other shore
Goes richly painted? or which rob'd and tore
Laments and mournes in Germany and here?
Sleepes she a thousand, then peepes up one yeare?
Is she selfe truth and errs? now new, now'outwore?
Doth she,'and did she, and shall she evermore
On one, on seaven, or on no hill appeare?
Dwells she with us, or like adventuring knights
First travaile we to seeke and them make love?
Betray kind husband thy spouse to our sights,
And let myne amorous soule court thy mild Dove,
Who is most trew, and pleasing to thee, then
When she'is embrac'd and open to most men.

The basic imagery is established by the first line. In Christian devotional language, the Church is often pictured as the "Bride of Christ." The question posed by the poem is—How can we recognize the true bride? There is the bride who "Goes richly painted"—the Roman Catholic Church. There is the rival bride, "rob'd and tore," who "Laments and mournes in Germany and here" —the Protestant Church. The line "On one, on seaven, or on no hill appeare?" refers to Mount Moriah (site of Solomon's temple), Rome with its seven hills, and flat Geneva (the latter a center of Protestantism).

In the last six lines, the language of secular love takes over.

1. Does the phrase, "adventuring knights," call up any memories of stories you have read? What does it suggest in the context of this poem?
2. What happens to the concept of marital fidelity in the last four lines?
3. How does the poem answer the question of "What is the true Church?"

Next a poem that you may find interesting to compare with "A Valediction of Weeping":

A Valediction Forbidding Mourning

As virtuous men passe mildly'away,
  And whisper to their soules, to goe,
Whilst some of their sad friends doe say,
  The breath goes now, and some say, no.

So let us melt, and make no noise,
  No teare-floods, nor sigh-tempests move,
T'were prophanation of our joyes
  To tell the layetie our love.

Moving of th'earth brings harmes and feares,
  Men reckon what it did and meant,
But trepidation of the spheares,
  Though greater farre, is innocent.

Dull sublunary lovers love
  (Whose soule is sense) cannot admit
Absence, because it doth remove
  Those things which elemented it.

But we by'a love, so much refin'd,
  That our selves know not what it is,
Inter-assured of the mind,
  Care lesse, eyes, lips, and hands to misse.

Our two soules therefore, which are one,
  Though I must goe, endure not yet
A breach, but an expansion,
  Like gold to ayery thinnesse beate.

If they be two, they are two so
  As stiffe twin compasses are two,
Thy soule the fixt foot, makes no show
  To move, but doth, if the'other doe.

And though it in the center sit,
  Yet when the other far doth rome,
It leanes, and hearkens after it,
  And growes erect, as that comes home.

Such wilt thou be to mee, who must
  Like th'other foot, obliquely runne.
Thy firmnes makes my circle just,
  And makes me end, where I begunne.

The poem was apparently written by Donne shortly before he departed for a long stay on the Continent. It is presumably colored by his feeling for his wife, whom he was not to see again for a long period of time. However, the poem makes perfectly good sense if one imagines the lover and his lady to be products of the poetic imagination.

1. Make two lists—one of words and phrases associated with true lovers, one of words and phrases relating to the "laity." How does the mixture function in this poem?

2. The first three stanzas seem built around the contrast between sound and silence. How does this prepare the reader for the rest of the poem?

3. What does the image of "gold to a ayery thinnesse beate" say about the quality of the relationship between the speaker and his beloved?

4. Express in prose everything that is implied by the image of the twin compasses.

5. Why did Donne use *two* images—gold and compasses?

Finally, we present a brief anthology of Donne's poems, with no special aids. In reading them, think about the poems you have already studied, and what you have learned about Donne's style of poetry. If particular words trouble you, look them up in the Oxford Dictionary.

Elegie: Going to Bed

Come, Madam, come, all rest my powers defie,
Until I labour, I in labour lie.
The foe oft-times having the foe in sight,
Is tir'd with standing though he never fight.
Off with that girdle, like heavens Zone glittering,
But a far fairer world incompassing.
Unpin that spangled breastplate which you wear,
That th'eyes of busie fooles may be stopt there.
Unlace your self, for that harmonious chyme,
Tells me from you, that now it is bed time.
Off with that happy busk, which I envie,
That still can be, and still can stand so nigh.
Your gown going off, such beautious state reveals,
As when from flowry meads th'hills shadowe steales.
Off with that wyerie Coronet and shew
The haiery Diadem which on you doth grow:
Now off with those shooes, and then softly tread
In this loves hallow'd temple, this soft bed.
In such white robes, heaven's Angels us'd to be
Receavd by men: thou Angel bringst with thee
A heaven like Mahomets Paradice, and though
Ill spirits walk in white, we easly know,
By this these Angels from an evil sprite,
Those set our hairs, but these our flesh upright.
  Licence my roaving hands, and let them go,
Behind, before, above, between, below.
O my America! my new-found-land,
My kingdome, safeliest when with one man man'd,
My Myne of precious stones: My Emperie,

How blest am I in this discovering thee!
To enter in these bonds, is to be free;
Then where my hand is set, my seal shall be.
  Full nakedness! All joyes are due to thee,
As souls unbodied, bodies uncloth'd must be,
To taste whole joyes. Jems which you women use
Are like Atlanta's balls, cast in mens views,
That when a fools eye lighteth on a Jem,
His earthly soul may covet theirs, not them:
Like pictures or like books gay coverings made
For lay-men, are all women thus array'd.
Themselves are mystick books, which only wee
(Whom their imputed grace will dignifie)
Must see reveal'd. Then since that I may know;
As liberally, as to a Midwife shew
Thy self: cast all, yea, this white lynnen hence,
There is no pennance due to innocence:
  To teach thee I am naked first; why than
What needst thou have more covering then a man?

The Sunne Rising

Busie old foole, unruly Sunne,
Why dost thou thus,
Through windowes, and through curtaines call on us?
Must to thy motions lovers seasons run?
Sawcy pedantique wretch, goe chide
Late schoole boyes, and sowre prentices,
Goe tell Court-huntsmen, that the King will ride,
Call countrey ants to harvest offices;
Love, all alike, no season knowes, nor clyme,
Nor houres, dayes, moneths, which are the rags of time.

Thy beames, so reverend, and strong
Why shouldst thou thinke?
I could eclipse and cloud them with a winke,
But that I would not lose her sight so long:
If her eyes have not blinded thine,
Looke, and to morrow late, tell mee,
Whether both the'India's of spice and Myne
Be where thou leftst them, or lie here with mee.
Aske for those Kings whom thou saw'st yesterday,
And thou shalt heare, All here in one bed lay.

She'is all States, and all Princes, I,
Nothing else is.
Princes doe but play us; compar'd to this,
All honor's mimique; All wealth alchimie;
Thou sunne art halfe as happy'as wee,
In that the world's contracted thus.
Thine age askes ease, and since thy duties bee
To warme the world, that's done in warming us.
Shine here to us, and thou art every where;
This bed thy center is, these walls, thy spheare.

The Funerall

Who ever comes to shroud me, do not harme
Nor question much
That subtile wreath of haire, which crowns my arme;
The mystery, the signe you must not touch,
For 'tis my outward Soule,
Viceroy to that, which then to heaven being gone,
Will leave this to controule,
And keepe these limbes, her Provinces, from dissolution.

For if the sinewie thread my braine lets fall
Through every part,
Can tye those parts, and make mee one of all;
These haires which upward grew, and strength and art
Have from a better braine,
Can better do'it; Except she meant that I
By this should know my pain,
As prisoners then are manacled, when they'are condemn'd to die.

What ere shee meant by'it, bury it with me,
For since I am
Loves martyr, it might breed idolatrie,
If into others hands these Reliques came;
As 'twas humility
To'afford to it all that a Soule can doe,
So, 'tis some bravery,
That since you would save none of mee, I bury some of you.

Death Be Not Proud

Death be not proud, though some have called thee
Mighty and dreadfull, for, thou art not soe,
For, those, whom thou think'st, thou dost overthrow,
Die not, poore death, nor yet canst thou kill mee;

From rest and sleepe, which but thy pictures bee,
Much pleasure, then from thee, much more must flow,
And soonest our best men with thee doe goe,
Rest of their bones, and soules deliverie.
Thou'art slave to Fate, chance, kings, and desperate men,
And dost with poyson, warre, and sicknesse dwell,
And poppie,'or charmes can make us sleepe as well,
And better then thy stroake; why swell'st thou then?
One short sleepe past, wee wake eternally,
And death shall be no more, Death thou shalt die.

Batter My Heart

Batter my heart, three person'd God; for, you
As yet but knocke, breathe, shine, and seeke to mend;
That I may rise, and stand, o'erthrow mee,'and bend
Your force, to breake, blowe, burn and make me new.
I, like an usurpt towne, to'another due,
Labour to'admit you, but Oh, to no end,
Reason your viceroy in mee, mee should defend,
But is captiv'd, and proves weake or untrue,
Yet dearely'I love you, and would be lov'd faine,
But am betroth'd unto your enemie,
Divorce mee,'untie, or breake that knot againe,
Take mee to you, imprison mee, for I
Except you'enthrall mee, never shall be free,
Nor ever chast, except you ravish mee.

SELECTIVE BIBLIOGRAPHY

At the end of each chapter a short, selective bibliography is included for the benefit of the student who wishes to learn more about the particular poet and his work. Highly specialized books, of little relevance to the the reader at this stage, are omitted. Many of the works listed have further bibliographies that will aid the student who wishes to explore a poet's work in depth.

The edition of Donne's poetry used in this text is John T, Shawcrosse, ed., *The Complete Poetry of John Donne* (New York: Doubleday and Company, Inc., 1967).

A. Alvarez, *The School of Donne* (London: Chatto, 1961).

R. C. Bald, *John Donne: A Life* (New York and Oxford: Oxford University Press, 1970).

Joan Bennett, *Four Metaphysical Poets* (New York: Vintage, 1960).

Cleanth Brooks, *The Well-Wrought Urn: Studies in the Structure of Poetry* (New York: Harcourt-Brace, 1947).

T. S. Eliot, *Selected Essays: 1917-1932* (New York: Harcourt, 1932).

Helen Gardner, ed., *John Donne: A Collection of Critical Essays.* Twentieth Century Views (Englewood Cliffs, N.J.: Prentice-Hall, 1962).

Robert Jackson, *John Donne's Christian Vocation* (Evanston, III.: Northwestern University Press, 1970).

J. B. Leishman, *The Monarch of Wit* (New York: Harper & Row, Torch book, 1966).

Louis Martz, *The Poetry of Meditation* (New Haven: Yale University Press, 1954).

Milton Rugoff, *Donne's Imagery: A Study in Creative Sources* (New York: Russell and Russell, 1962).

Rosamund Tuve, *Elizabethan and Metaphysical Imagery* (Chicago: Chicago University Press, 1947).

Leonard Unger, *Donne's Poetry and Modern Criticism* (Chicago: Chicago University Press, 1950).

Helen White, *The Metaphysical Poets: A Study in Religious Experience* (New York: Macmillan, 1936, 1962).

William Blake

His Life

William Blake was born in London in 1757, the son of a hosier who never earned more than a modest living. The boy was a solitary child and a natural visionary; he was given to catching sudden glimpses of a world beyond the familiar, visible one. When he innocently recounted his visions at school, he was commanded to stop lying. Stubbornly insisting that he was telling the truth, he was promptly expelled. This abrupt termination of his formal education did not doom him to ignorance. He became amazingly well-read on his own, and his wide range of knowledge is revealed in his poetry.

Very early in life Blake's aptitude for art was evident. He went for a time to drawing school. In his early teens he was apprenticed to an engraver. He also studied for a while at the Royal Academy, but seethed in rebellion against the pedantic instructional methods and the teachers' emphasis on someone like Rubens rather than the titanic Michelangelo. During this period of his life he found time to do a number of engravings—the craft by which he subsequently made his meager living.

In 1782 he married a young woman named Catherine, who was so illiterate she could not sign her name. Blake proved a patient and tender husband. He taught his wife to read, and she worked faithfully at his side to the end of his life.

There has been speculation but no firm proof that the marriage proved a disappointment to Blake, first because Catherine could not follow him in his intellectual and visionary quests, and second because no children were born to them—and Blake was devoted to children. From Catherine's viewpoint, Blake must have been a bewildering and at times a difficult husband. In particular, there was a period when he wanted to put into practice some of his theories about freedom within marriage. He refrained only because she was so upset. Blake was no superficial sensualist, but he believed the human spirit must be free, not fenced in by a marriage contract.

In 1784 Blake's father died. Blake and Catherine moved next door to the family and set up a joint shop. His brother, Robert, whom Blake dearly loved, lived with them. The latter's death in 1787 was a devastating blow to Blake. Afterward he often felt the spiritual presence of Robert, and even talked with him "in vision." In one of these visions Robert revealed to Blake a new printing process which the poet-engraver subsequently employed.

Meanwhile, Blake was thinking and writing and making engravings for his various poems. And the winds of change were shaking the larger world about him. This was a time when new concepts about democracy and the rights of man were stirring the world and arousing new longings and hopes. The American Revolution had occurred when Blake was a young man, and the mightier force of the French Revolution was moving to its climax during his middle age. Blake went through a period under the influence of friends like Thomas Paine,

Priestley, and Godwin (Mary Shelley's stepfather) when it looked as though the new vision of man would literally create a heaven on earth. It was a time of great excitement and optimism, and a faith in human possibilities that was shared by poets as diverse as Wordsworth and Shelley. The dream was eventually shattered in the brutality and carnage which were an aftermath of the French Revolution. But even if utopia were not to be, Blake became convinced that the world of eternity impinges on the temporal world, and that men must not be mired down in the morass of mere reason and materiality.

Blake, before the French Revolution, was working out his ideas in poems. Toward the close of 1788 he had completed *Songs of Innocence.* He decided to produce the book with a separate design which he would etch to illustrate each poem. It was at this point that Robert's spirit appeared and gave him the clue to the method.

As you read some of the lyrics from this collection they appear—at first glance—deceptively simple. No complicated verse forms, no metaphysical conceits, no difficult words. They seem to express the innocence, the simplicity, and the directness of a child's world where guilt, corruption, and revolt are almost unknown. There is a kind of crystal purity about these poems—and Blake often said that children could read and understand them.

The *Songs of Experience* appeared in 1794. It is clear that Blake wanted his readers to see the two books as a unity. He bound them into one volume, and as we read them, we see that many of the poems in the second volume are parallel to or an antithesis of so many of the earlier poems. Examples: the two introductions; "The Lamb" and "The Tyger"; the two "Holy Thursday" poems; the two poems called "Nurse's Song"; etc.

Blake's life on the surface was fairly uneventful, though it is obvious the spiritual and mental world he inhabited was profound. He always had very limited means. Although many influential people were aware of his work, fewer and fewer seemed to care about it as his life wore on. He continued to earn his living as an engraver. Perhaps the only real break in his external life occurred when in 1800 he was introduced to William Hagley, a dilettante in the arts, who had ample resources and who suggested that Blake and his wife move to Felpham in Sussex to be near him while he produced work for Blake to illustrate. Thus Hagley really served as Blake's patron. This arrangement lasted for three years. Blake became increasingly unhappy because Hagley wanted him to do illustrations which were banal and nothing but drudgery. Inevitably the relationship ended, and the Blakes returned to London to live out the rest of their days close to poverty.

In Blake's imagination the relation was so shattered that Hagley assumed the role of a devil. There was, though, a moment of high drama during this period when a soldier accused Blake of treasonous remarks and he was hauled into court. To Hagley's credit, he provided a stout defense for Blake, who was finally acquitted.

For a period after his return to London, Blake apparently passed through a time of great spiritual anguish and despair. But he continued to write, to do his engravings, and to work out his ideas in his prophetic poems.

His final years were lived in obscurity, though he had his scattered admirers. In 1818 he met John Linnell who recognized Blake's genius and intensity and also introduced him to his own circle of friends. These were young men, mostly artists, who were able to respond to Blake. In 1825 Henry Crabb Robinson met Blake, realized the uniqueness of the man, and for the next two years—until Blake's death—he kept detailed notes on conversations with him. On the first meeting he said to himself: "Shall I call him Artist or Genius—or Mystic or Madman? Probably he is all."

Linnell in 1825 commissioned him to illustrate Dante's *Divine Comedy.* The poet-engraver, aged 68, set about teaching himself Italian so he could do a more conscientious job of illustrating—but never lived to finish the project. He died August 12, 1827, and Catherine followed him four years later.

How can one find a label for his lifelong mental state? W. H. Auden once said in a conversation, "Blake was dotty but not batty." Certainly, the poet-engraver managed the practicalities of life with little outside help; he was also a major figure in both literature and engraving. In his visionary way, he reached and expressed insights that most of us are not mad enough—or perhaps sane enough—to reach by ourselves.

The Poet and His Poetry

Here, then, is a poet whose mental life was rich, complicated, and—from some viewpoints—bizarre. The attempt to determine "influences" has been much pursued by literary scholars. Some have suggested, for instance, that Blake's father was fascinated by the Swedish mystic, Swedenborg, and may have passed this interest along to his son. The matter is debatable. If indeed Blake shows some trace of this influence, it is not predominant. It seems safer to assume that many of Blake's ideas came to him from his own thinking and visions, no doubt supplemented by his reading, in the Bible most of all.

In a short survey it is not possible to go into great detail about Blake's philosophic system, and a full command of this is not needed unless the reader is dealing with the long prophetic poems. Still, certain aspects of the system should be discussed here, as background for the poems to be analyzed. Such a work as "The Mental Traveller" would be completely opaque without some knowledge of Blake's thought.

Though Blake created mythic characters like Urizen, Orc, and Los, most of his basic ideas are biblical in origin and deal with familiar concepts such as the fall of man, redemption, the meaning of Christ, etc. Blake did not use these concepts in any standard way. He reshaped them and rejected traditional interpretations. His heterodoxy led him to interesting conflicts at times. For example, he greatly admired Milton, but felt that the poet had misinterpreted Satan in *Paradise Lost.* In his own poem on Milton, Blake tries to point out the errors of the earlier poet.

For the purpose of dealing with the shorter poems, only a few of Blake's concepts need to be explored. Basic to *Songs of Innocence* and *Songs of Experience* is the conviction that, in order to reach the higher innocence or redemption, man must first move from a state of original innocence into the world of experience. He must "fall" into the material world. From his understanding of this fall comes rebirth or a state of higher innocence. *The Book of Thel* best represents this idea. Thel can never achieve rebirth because she refuses to accept the fall into the world of matter.

Blake said, "Without contraries is no progression." At the root of his thinking is this idea of necessary opposites—the spiritual and the material, good and evil, man and woman, heaven and hell, life and death, Christ and Satan.

The poet identified human imagination with God. It was through the power of the imagination that the unity of all life could be perceived. The thin veil that divides this ordinary world from the eternal realm is swept aside.

Blake railed against the restraints imposed on man by the manacles of institutions—the laws of the state, the priestcraft of the Church, the emphasis on reason and common sense which stamped out the visionary faculty. His trinity of contempt consisted of Newton, Bacon, and Locke, whose views—it seemed to Blake—dominated the world with an emphasis on reason, a mechanistic view of the universe, and a colorless God conceived in terms of Deism. The world of the unholy trinity of thinkers was constricted, legal, passionless. It made a mockery of the relations between the sexes and effectively cut man off from that eternal world and the unity of life in which his redemption was finally possible.

Blake was assuredly an original thinker.[1] He understood human psychology far better than most men of his time. Although he repudiated institutions—and the Church in particular—he turned to the figure of Christ for understanding and inspiration. His love of Christ was a constant throughout his life, but not Christ as the traditional Church viewed Him. Blake saw the Old Testament as the rule of law, and the religion which Christ preached was not law but a way of vision which led to the Kingdom of Heaven, with love the only rule. It was Christ the revolutionary who found response in Blake. Once Crabbe Robinson asked Blake about his views on the divinity of Christ. Blake's reply was that He was the Son of God—"and so am I and so are you." To Blake, Christ realized the unity of man in God and taught men how to achieve that unity more fully than anyone else.

Blake was not interested in the Old Testament God—or perhaps it is more accurate to say he waged unremitting war against Him. Nor did the traditional "Thou shalt nots" of Christian teaching appeal to him. According to Harold Bloom[2] "Blake's God possesses no powers that differ in kind from the highest human gifts, for Blake's God is 'the real man, the imagination which liveth for ever.'"

In a letter written in 1802—apparently after an intense spiritual agony—Blake wrote:[3] "I am again Emerged into the light of day; I still & shall to Eternity Embrace Christianity and Adore him who is the Express image of God."

As E. D. Hirsch expresses it:[4] "It is ourselves—'the human form'—that we love in 'heathen, turk, or jew' and it is at the same time God. Blake's equation of divine and human love implies a genuine love of God, for love is ultimately the sense of identity we feel with others, whether men or Gods."

Northrup Frye states it succinctly when he says,[5] "The identity of God and man is for Blake the whole of Christianity." And finally Bernard Blackstone

[1] Special thanks to Northrop Frye for his perceptive treatments of Blake. Many of his insights are incorporated in our discussions.

[2] *The Visionary Company* (Ithaca: Cornell University Press, 1971), p. 6.

[3] Quoted in Bernard Blackstone, *English Blake* (London: Cambridge University Press, 1949), p. 114.

[4] *Innocence and Experience: An Introduction to Blake* (New Haven: Yale University Press, 1964), pp. 193-94.

[5] Northrop Frye, "Blake's Treatment of the Archetype," in John E. Grant, ed., *Discussions of William Blake* (Boston: D. C. Heath and Company, 1961), p. 11.

points out that the concluding section of Blake's *The Everlasting Gospel* shows us[6] "Jesus as the complete revolutionary. He mocked the Sabbath, He turned fishermen into divines and so upset the social order, He destroyed the idea of sin. He attacked war and injustive. He scorned His parents, and sent His seventy disciples into the world 'against Religion & Government'. He was a vagrant and a friend of prostitutes and publicans. He died on the gibbet as a common criminal." From all this it is quite evident that Blake's understanding was far removed from 18th-century orthodoxy.

Since imagination was the highest faculty of man and enabled him to view the world with the eyes of vision, and since it was found most prominently in art, Blake assigned to the arts a supreme value. One must remember also that he was not only a poet but an engraver—one of the few persons who have been equally great in two art forms.

In recent years, Blakean scholars have made us realize that not only was Blake a supreme poet and engraver, he was also a profound thinker[7] who carefully worked out in methological and archetypal terms a complete cosmology. Though we do not have to go into Blake's archetypes in detail, we do need to recognize that no historical-biographical—or even formalistic—approach to his work is going to be very rewarding. All the prophetic works deal with archetypes, and archetypal patterns move through the earlier poetry also—for instance, in "Tyger," "Ah! Sun-Flower," and "The Mental Traveller."

At this point, Northrup Frye's definition of archetypes may be helpful:[8] "By an archetype I mean an element in a work of literature, whether a character, an image, a narrative formula, or an idea, which can be assimilated to a larger unifying category."

In his vision of reality, Blake saw not only contraries but also had a perception of what life could be without the "man-made manacles" of institutions and priestcraft. He perceived these as fetters fashioned to imprison men in the commonplace. He viewed the institution of marriage as one such a fetter because it was a device that society used to bind and limit men; as a consequence, the possessiveness of marriage destroyed any genuine relationship. At the same time, Blake saw the sexual act as a uniting of two contraries, as a way most people can imaginatively glimpse Eden; he was talking, in his plea for freedom, not about casual lust but genuine love.

To sum up this discussion of Blake. We have touched on his concept of contraries, his view of innocence and experience, his attitude toward Christ, his belief in the power of the imagination, his hatred of institutions, his use of archetypes, and his belief in vision. It remains to see how all this operates in his poetry.

[6] *English Blake,* p. 381.

[7] His influence continues to grow. The recent "God is dead" movement in theology was based to a considerable extent on Blake's convictions and intuitions.

[8] Grant, p. 15.

A good starting point is to consider the "Introduction" to *Songs of Innocence* and the "Introduction" to *Songs of Experience:*

Introduction (to Songs of Innocence)

Piping down the valleys wild
Piping songs of pleasant glee
On a cloud I saw a child.
And he laughing said to me.

Pipe a song about a Lamb;
So I piped with merry chear,
Piper pipe that song again—
So I piped, he wept to hear.

Drop thy pipe thy happy pipe
Sing thy songs of happy chear,
So I sung the same again
While he wept with joy to hear

Piper sit thee down and write
In a book that all may read—
So he vanish'd from my sight.
And I pluck'd a hollow reed.

And I made a rural pen,
And I stain'd the water clear,
And I wrote my happy songs
Every child may joy to hear

Introduction (to Songs of Experience)

Hear the voice of the Bard!
Who Present, Past, & Future sees
Whose ears have heard,
The Holy Word,
That walk'd among the ancient trees.

Calling the lapsed Soul
And weeping in the evening dew;
That might controll,
The starry pole;
And fallen fallen light renew!

O Earth O Earth return!
Arise from out the dewy grass;
Night is worn,
And the morn
Rises from the slumberous mass.

Turn away no more:
Why wilt thou turn away
The starry floor
The watry shore
Is giv'n thee till the break of day.

The first "Introduction" certainly presents no difficulties. The language is straightforward. The rhyme scheme is a familiar one—the poem is in four-line stanzas; the even lines always rhyme; the odd lines rhyme part of the time. The rhythm is a little more unusual. It is basically trochaic tetrameter (´ ˘ | ´ ˘ | ´ ˘ | ´ ˘) but the final unstressed syllable is dropped:

Pípiňg | dówn thě | válleÿs | wíld

It is a very regular rhythm, sharply accentuating the separation of line from line, and in fact is reminiscent of many nursery rhymes. Try reciting "Twinkle, Twinkle, Little Star," and you will discover it has the same beat.

There is a good deal of alliteration on the letter *p,* helping further to give the quality of a child's rhyme to the poem. The sentence structure is simple and direct. And from beginning to end, the child motif is emphasized. The poem begins with a visionary child, commanding the poet to write. The poem ends with a dedication of the poems to "Every child."

This "Introduction" sets the stage for the other poems in *Songs of Innocence.* It demonstrates the sure mastery of craft that is subsequently shown. The poem is tightly controlled, but with such ease that it sounds as spontaneous as a nursery rhyme. A key symbol for innocence, the lamb, is presented—and, of course, the lamb is also a Christian symbol for Christ. The idea of a reed pipe on which these songs are played makes one think of the great god Pan, the deity of wildernesses and shepherds. The tears are of joy and the songs are to be happy ones, written not in store-bought ink but ink that is made of clear water colored with natural dye. Moreover, the songs must be those that all can read and even a child can understand. The total picture is that of a world of joy and innocence. It glows with the colors of an Eden before the fall.

1. The word *hear* is repeated a number of times. Why?

2. The poet is inspired by a child "On a cloud." In succession he then plays on the pipe, sings songs, writes them down. Suppose lines five-nine (about piping) were deleted. Apart from the violence done to the structure of the third stanza, how would this change the effect of the poem?

Now what about the "Introduction" to *Songs of Experience*? Here we enter a different world. The very form of the verse itself makes us aware of this. The poem is written in five-line stanzas, which is in itself unusual with Blake. The line length varies, with the second and fifth lines longer than the others. The rhyme scheme also is more complicated—abaab. All in all, the poem lacks the dancing, simple quality of the other. There is nothing of the nursery rhyme about it. About all the two introductions have in common is that they each have twenty lines. In the second one, the world has darkened; the innocent clarity of childhood has been engulfed by the sad exile of the adult banished from Eden. The call now is not to celebrate the innocent paradise but to reclaim it on a higher level.

1. Why is the soul lapsed? And from what?

2. Why does Blake use the word *bard* instead of *poet* (apart from the half rhyme)?

3. Explain: starry pole, fallen fallen light, starry floor, watry shore.

The directly following poem, "Earth's Answer," may give some retrospective clues. In addition, all that you know about Blake and his system of thought should help.

EARTH'S Answer

Earth rais'd up her head,
From the darkness dread & drear.
Her light fled:
Stony dread!
And her locks cover'd with grey despair.

Prison'd on watry shore
Starry Jealousy does keep my den
Cold and hoar
Weeping o'er
I hear the Father of the ancient men

Selfish father of men
Cruel jealous selfish fear
Can delight
Chain'd in night
The virgins of youth and morning bear.

Does spring hide its joy
When buds and blossoms grow?
Does the sower?
Sow by night?
Or the plowman in darkness plow?

Break this heavy chain,
That does freeze my bones around
Selfish! vain,
Eternal bane!
That free Love with bondage bound.

This poem is also written in five-line stanzas like the second "Introduction," but the rhyme scheme is less regular. "Earth's Answer" obviously deals with the forces that imprison the earth and its inhabitants, jealousy in particular. Love has been bound on earth, imprisoned on the "watry shore" by jealousy. As several commentators have pointed out, earth is doubly imprisoned, by jealousy and by the God of the Old Testament—"the Father of the ancient men / Selfish father of men / Cruel jealous selfish." Here Blake strikes out at the kind of religion that emphasizes moral prohibitions and stifles spontaneity.

You will recall the discussion of Blake's system of thought, and his belief that man must "fall" into experience—the material world—and then subsequently extricate himself into a higher state of innocence. The interlude of "experience" cannot be bypassed. The danger is that the individual may be satisfied with experience and remain mired in mere materiality.

In "Earth's Answer," the Bard has heard the holy word and knows that time and eternity are contiguous, that life is a unity. But he knows also that the soul chained by the material world and, especially, by jealousy is unable to break through to that greater vision, the higher innocence.

Though the poem paints a grim picture of man's imprisonment, it is shot through with hope. The earth *can* be redeemed, the lapsed soul can rise. By listening to the Bard, who has heard the holy word, man can learn not to turn away but rather, through imagination, to attain vision and inhabit the world of eternity.

1. What is the indirect reference to the book of Genesis?

2. Make two lists of words: (1) those suggesting unpleasant things, and (2) those suggesting pleasant things. Which list has the more "technological" flavor? Why?

We are ready now to examine a seemingly simple but intellectually complex poem, "The Tyger." But as a background to it, a brief glance at "The Lamb" may be useful:

The Lamb

Little Lamb who made thee
Dost thou know who made thee
Gave thee life & bid thee feed.
By the stream & o'er the mead;
Gave thee clothing of delight,
Softest clothing wooly bright;
Gave thee such a tender voice,
Making all the vales rejoice!
Little Lamb who made thee
Dost thou know who made thee

Little Lamb I'll tell thee,
Little Lamb I'll tell thee!
He is called by thy name,
For he calls himself a Lamb:
He is meek & he is mild,
He became a little child:
I a child & thou a lamb,
We are called by his name.
Little Lamb God bless thee.
Little Lamb God bless thee.

Like "The Tyger," it is a poem of questions. These are posed in the first stanza, but then (unlike "The Tyger") they are answered in the next stanza. The world of the lamb is clear and limpid; love surrounds him, and the blessing of God his Creator is his. In this poem we see only the gentleness of God—the identification of Jesus and the lamb.

A much more terrifying and complex universe is presented in the companion poem:

The Tyger

Tyger Tyger, burning bright,
In the forests of the night;
What immortal hand or eye,
Could frame thy fearful symmetry?

In what distant deeps or skies
Burnt the fire of thine eyes!
On what wings dare he aspire?
What the hand, dare sieze the fire?

And what shoulder, & what art,
Could twist the sinews of thy heart?
And when thy heart began to beat,
What dread hand? & what dread feet?

What the hammer? what the chain,
In what furnace was thy brain?
What the anvil? what dread grasp,
Dare its deadly terrors clasp?

When the stars threw down their spears
And water'd heaven with their tears:
Did he smile his work to see?
Did he who made the Lamb make thee?

Tyger, Tyger burning bright,
In the forests of the night:
What immortal hand or eye,
Dare frame thy fearful symmetry?

This poem is apparently simple, but actually is very complex. It is a good example of the way that a poem may contain circles-within-circles and say much more than appears on a quick, first reading. Let us look at it in detail and see what we find when we go beyond the description of a magnificent, beautiful, and dangerous beast.

Even on a first reading the suspicion arises that this is not *just* a wild animal in a zoo or jungle. Perhaps you intuitively leap to a conclusion, deciding that the tiger represents, say, the forces of evil in the universe, or perhaps the powers of nature. At that point you are turning literary critic, and entering a realm where—as you have probably discovered already—a variety of approaches is possible, and the experts differ on which are the most useful.

For example, the formalistic critics (sometimes called "New Critics," though they are no longer new) emphasize each poem as an autonomous work of art, and insist that biographical or historical background rarely helps in understanding a poem. Each poem must stand on its own feet and not derive its meaning from outside factors. Other critics insist with equal vehemence that the life of a poet and the period in which he flourished profoundly shape his work, and that often a poem cannot be clearly understood without taking these facts into consideration. Yet other critics, the Freudians in particular, look for psychoanalytic themes beneath the language of poetry. Still others find the archetypal approach the most fruitful. For instance, Huckleberry Finn's raft would be an archetype of the earthly Paradise, and his struggle to escape town life would be the reluctance to leave an innocent world and inhabit a corrupt one. You may wish to try these four approaches.

But a word of warning at this point. It is usually a mistake to get too analytic and "critical" too soon. The initial thing is to read and reread the poem without any critical presuppositions. Open yourself to it. Let it get inside you. See what spontaneous concept you have of the poem's meaning.

Let's say you have read "The Tyger" several times, responded to it in an almost wordless way, and that it seems to you the poem is simply a vivid and picturesque description of a magnificent beast. Shouldn't this possibility at least be considered, before launching forth in the depths of archetypal or Freudian criticism?

It should be. A poem does not necessarily have layer on layer of significance.

How can you be sure that you are right or wrong about "The Tyger?" The one general approach is to use *consistency* as a touchstone. If you have an interpretation of a poem and it is not contradicted by any part of the poem, there is at least the presumption that you may be on the right track. Can your interpretation of "The Tyger" stand up to this test?

The tentative assumption that "The Tyger" is solely about a flesh-and-blood tiger begins to break down when you notice some lines apparently referring to another being: "Did he who made the Lamb make thee?"—"What immortal hand or eye, / Dare frame thy fearful symmetry?" and several earlier references. It looks as though the poem deals with a creator who made the tiger, as well as with the beast himself.

There is thus more to the poem than the tiger, but the reader is right to insist that the tiger, in all his jungle splendor, is central. To convert the tiger immediately into mere symbol—say, of the atomic bomb or the Pentagon—is to lose the rich concreteness of the poem. The challenge is to keep the tiger in all his splendid junglehood, but discover what shadings of meaning radiate from him.

We do not pretend that the following brief interpretation is original—it is partly the work of many scholars, partly insights that evolved across the breakfast table when talk turned to Blake. Perhaps no one will accept it in all its details. But at least it illustrates some of the approaches that can prove useful in reading poetry.

To begin with, as we have already emphasized, the poem is about a tiger, a flesh-and-blood tiger. But the poem goes beyond the mere tiger. In large part, this is done by a series of questions—"What immortal hand or eye, / Could frame thy fearful symmetry?" etc. Are these questions merely rhetorical, or are they serious? And might the answer be "No" as well as "Yes?" Or are there alternatives to simple "Yes" and "No"?

If the poem has its obscurities, they are not due to difficult language; the vocabulary is very simple. Perhaps any obscurity is connected with the allusions. In the first stanza, everthing is clear enough—or is it? The "immortal hand" suggests God, but it would be premature to be certain. In the second stanza, as we move into the depths of the poem, doubts and complexities arise. If you are at all familiar with Greek mythology, you will undoubtedly think of the story of Prometheus—a god who disobeyed Zeus and stole fire from heaven in order the save the race of men whom Zeus had resolved to destroy. Is it possible that the creation of the tiger involves some act of rebellion, one god pitted against another?

In stanzas three and four, Greek myth once more may play a part. The reference might be to the legend of Haephastus—the god who was a smith; hence the reference to "What the hammer? what the chain, / In what furnace was thy brain? / What the anvil?" It may be significant that Haephastus, like Prometheus, was disobedient to Zeus, and that he was thrown bodily out of heaven, an event that lamed him permanently.

At this point it appears that the world in "The Tyger" is obviously in the process of creation, things are not fixed and static, and some kind of rebellion is involved throughout.

Thus, we come to the fifth stanza with Christian references this time. Obviously there has been some great cataclysm—"When the stars threw down their spears." Is there any Christian myth that is consistent with what has gone before in the poem? One thinks of Lucifer—the angel who refused to obey God, and as a consequence was hurled from heaven.

Did God smile to see "his work?" Could he have created *both* the Lamb and the tiger? (And the Lamb, of course, is both the animal and the "Lamb of God," Christ.)

If God created the tiger, did he do it directly, or indirectly by creating beings—Prometheus, Haephastus, Lucifer—capable of paying him the supreme compliment of asserting a will of their own by bringing the tiger into being? Are the rebels really aspects of God himself?

One thing is certain—the supposition that Blake is referring to the God-Lucifer relation in the fifth stanza is greatly strengthened by the bit of biographical information mentioned previously—that Blake was strongly influenced by Milton, and the latter was fascinated by the Satan figure when he wrote *Paradise Lost.*

The final stanza seems at first a simple repetition of the first, but with one all-important change. The would *could* in the last line has been replaced by *dare.*

At this point, it is a good idea to reread the poem again, in its entirety, and determine what overall response you have to it. Then you can ask yourself—what does the poem and all this discussion of it, add up to? Clearly it is a poem about the nature of God as much as one about tigers. Some knowledge about Blake's own concept of God is helpful. The poet was spontaneously drawn toward Christ as a revolutionary figure. His attitude toward God the creator was more mixed; he tended to view this God as a cosmic tyrant.

Anyway, the poem seems to be saying that God not only could, but does—directly or indirectly—create both the lamb and tiger, and that the tiger symbolizes those forces in the universe that either defy the creator himself or express the savage aspect of his creativity. There may also be the implication that the beings created by God pay him the highest compliment when they refuse to be his dutiful puppets.

This is not the only way to interpreting the poem. Some take the tiger as a symbol of evil—though if this is done, the meaning of evil has to be enlarged to encompass vitality, self-respect, freedom—and ceases to be evil in any ordinary sense of the word. Certainly, and in any case, the poem as a whole deals primarily with the nature of God. But since it is a poem rather than a theological treatise, it poses more questions than it answers, and leaves the reader with the persistent ambiguities that draw him back again and again.

At this point you may have decided that reading poetry at any depth requires a basic knowledge of Greek mythology and the Bible as minimum equipment. And it is true that this knowledge helps. On the other hand, if your education has been strictly "modern," your situation is still not hopeless. You can still get a good deal out of most poems that use classical mythology and biblical lore, although you are ignorant of the precise allusions. Take "The Tyger." Perhaps the idea of fire makes you think of various modern theories of creation, in particular the "big bang" hypothesis. Does that distort the poem? Not necessarily, since it operates on several levels and with built-in ambiguities. Or perhaps, along with many who have read the poem, you see the reference to "the stars threw down their spears" as the Crucifixion. (Even a person who has never read the New Testament has heard of this event!) Is this too far-fetched? Again, not necessarily. There is a kinship between Christ and the mythological Prometheus. Each is a scapegoat figure, striving to save mankind.

The odds are that if you read the poem on your own, without a good background of mythology and Bible, you would come to an understanding compatible with the more elaborate interpretation. But acquaintance with myth and Biblical lore would certainly enrich, and bring into sharper focus, your response to the poem.

The experience of digging deep into a poem, it needs to be emphasized, is not a dry, pedantic thing. The farther you go, the more you follow on the tracks of the poet himself. When you read, and reread, a poem, you share something of the wonder of the poet-creator bringing into existence a new inhabitant of the universe, his poem. The more intensely you can share and relive his experience, the deeper your response and reward will be.

1. This poem is written in the same "Twinkle twinkle little star" rhythm that we found in the first "Introduction." But it rhymes by couplets instead of abab. Why do you think Blake chose couplets for this particular poem?

2. Discuss the role of the fifth stanza—characteristics that set it apart from the rest of the poem, and also ways in which it modifies your response to the poem as a whole.

3. Discuss how the feeling of the poem is conditioned by the following

phrases: burning bright, forests of the night, immortal hand or eyes, fearful symmetry, deadly terrors.

Although we cannot go into Blake's "prophetic works," we should at least consider one of his longer poems. One that has attracted a legion of commentators is given below.

The Mental Traveller

I traveld thro' a Land of Men
A Land of Men & Women too
And heard & saw such dreadful things
As cold Earth wanderers never knew

For there the Babe is born in joy
That was begotten in dire woe
Just as we Reap in joy the fruit
Which we in bitter tears did sow

And if the Babe is born a Boy
He's given to a Woman Old
Who nails him down upon a rock
Catches his shrieks in cups of gold

She binds iron thorns around his head
She pierces both his hands & feet
She cuts his heart out at his side
To make it feel both cold & heat

Her fingers number every Nerve
Just as a Miser counts his gold
She lives upon his shrieks & cries
And she grows young as he grows old

Till he becomes a bleeding youth
And she becomes a Virgin bright
Then he rends up his Manacles
And binds her down for his delight

He plants himself in all her Nerves
Just as a Husbandman his mould
And she becomes his dwelling place
And Garden fruitful seventy fold

An aged Shadow soon he fades
Wandring round an Earthly Cot
Full filled all with gems & gold
Which he by industry had got

And these are the gems of the Human Soul
The rubies & pearls of a lovesick eye
The countless gold of the akeing heart
The martyrs groan & the lovers sigh

They are his meat they are his drink
He feeds the Beggar & the Poor
And the wayfaring Traveller
For ever open is his door

His grief is their eternal joy
They make the roofs & walls to ring
Till from the fire on the hearth
A little Female Babe does spring

And she is all of solid fire
And gems & gold that none his hand
Dares stretch to touch her Baby form
Or wrap her in his swaddling-band

But She comes to the Man she loves
If young or old or rich or poor
They soon drive out the aged Host
A Beggar at anothers door

He wanders weeping far away
Untill some other take him in
Oft blind & age-bent sore distrest
Untill he can a Maiden win

And to allay his freezing Age
The Poor Man takes her in his arms
The Cottage fades before his sight
The Garden & its lovely Charms

The Guests are scatterd thro' the land
For the Eye altering alters all
The Senses roll themselves in fear
And the flat Earth becomes a Ball

The Stars Sun Moon all shrink away
A desert vast without a bound
And nothing left to eat or drink
And a dark desart all around

The honey of her Infant lips
The bread & wine of her sweet smile
The wild game of her roving Eye
Does him to Infancy beguile

For as he eats & drinks he grows
Younger & younger every day
And on the desart wild they both
Wander in terror & dismay

Like the wild Stag she flees away
Her fear plants many a thicket wild
While he pursues her night & day
By various arts of Love beguild

By various arts of Love & Hate
Till the wide desart planted oer
With Labyrinths of wayward Love
Where roams the Lion Wolf & Boar

Till he becomes a wayward Babe
And she a weeping Woman Old
Then many a Lover wanders here
The Sun & Stars are nearer rolld

The trees bring forth sweet Extacy
To all who in the desart roam
Till many a City there is Built
And many a pleasant Shepherds home

But when they find the frowning Babe
Terror strikes thro the region wide
They cry the Babe the Babe is Born
And flee away on Every side

For who dare touch the frowning form
His arm is withered to its root
Lions Boars Wolves all howling flee
And every Tree does shed its fruit

And none can touch that frowning form
Except it be a Woman Old
She nails him down upon the Rock
And all is done as I have told

It is easy to become discouraged when confronting this poem and the variety of interpretations that have been offered. As Bernard Blackstone Remarked:[9] "'Mental Traveller' is an extremely cryptic poem in quatrains; as to its meaning, one reader's guess seems as good as another's."

We make no attempt at a detailed analysis here, but all the same, the poem is not a complete puzzle. On the basis of what we now know about Blake's thought and poetry, we should be able to penetrate the poem in some depth.

[9] *English Blake,* p. 131.

It is a cliché to observe that this is a cyclical poem—apparently the process that goes on continually repeats itself. If the earth is the realm of the Mental Traveler, and the "I" of the poem is the Bard of the first "Introduction," then he is observing what happens in the world of experience where contraries exist —a world where the sexes are not unified, jealousy and hatred dominate, and the pursuit of Mammon comes to nothing. Each generation undergoes the same painful process. The note of hope and redemption found in the first "Introduction" is missing.

Perhaps this needs to be spelled out in more detail. We cannot go into Blake's private symbolism, but the poem yields additional meaning even without that. The Babe is born, surrounded by Christ and Promethean analogies. When the Babe is nailed to the rock, both heroic figures are evoked. We have seen that Blake regards Christ as the expression of the ultimate, divine possibilities of man. Hence, the Babe comes into the world of experience with the ability to redeem the fallen world. What happens? He is caught in the "mind-forged manacles" and bound. The old woman can represent everything that blocks imagination and vision—institutions, marriage, priestcraft, restraint. She ultimately corrupts the Babe. He gives himself to her and the material world she represents. His ability to redeem the world or even to save himself is lost. He is condemned to the endless repeating pattern of the cycle of experience.

A full explication of the poem would require a familiarity with Blake's mythology as developed in the prophetic poems. (Orc, for example, is a bound Titan, sometimes pictured as an infant seeking to escape his mother's domination.) But short of that, the following quotations may give you some additional insights. Both discussions are worth looking up and reading in their entirely.

> . . . . This poem, as its last stanza suggests, describes a cycle, and while this cycle is not exclusively the cycle of history, the latter is the central form of it. Here the infant Orc begins as a rock-bound Prometheus in subjection to an old woman. At puberty he tears loose from the rock and copulates with the old woman, who grows younger as he grows older and becomes his wife or emanation. As Orc declines, his imaginative achievements are completed into a single form or "Female Babe," which is then to be used by other imaginations, just as an appletree sheds its fruit for others to eat. But a plant in its old age begins to scatter seeds, which fall into the fertile ground of another virgin mother and enter the place of seed again. Here the male principle tends to become younger and the female more aggressive and maternal. Orc, now Urizen, (symbolizing Eden), dies a seed's death as the world becomes "a dark desart all around," and eventually re-enters the world of Generation as a reborn Orc.[10]
>
> —Northrop Frye

[10] *Fearful Symmetry: A study of William Blake* (Boston: Beacon Press, p. 229.)

. . . . The traveler is speaking as if he has returned from a journey into the fallen world, which is *also* a land of men, though considerably different from the eternal land of men. In the first place, this land is also a land of "female wills." Elsewhere Blake emphasizes his belief that in the fallen world there is an unnatural (Blake inverting the language, would say "natural") division of the sexes into male and female wills or selfhoods. By this, Blake does not mean that there are no sexes. But "sexual" in Blake denotes a fallen condition, resulting in the aloofness of the emanation, which in time causes man to become a spectre of himself. The result is a negation of the true relationship between man and the emanation. In the second place, the things seen and heard, like the things seen and heard in the poem "London," are "dreadful"—so dreadful that "cold Earth wanderers" have never known them. This statement suggests a distinction between mental travelers (the speaker is a mental traveler) and wanderers or "weak travelers." The "cold Earth wanderers" are not simply, as Sutherland implies, people of the fallen world who have never seen the land of archetypal forms that the traveler describes. It is more precise to say that their utter submersion in the cold stultification of materialism has made them unable to see or "know" the truth about their own condition.[11]

—Hazard Adams

1. What is the function of the following lines? (a) "She lives upon his shrieks & cries / And she grows young as he grows old" (lines 19-20). (b) "Full filled all with gems & gold / Which he by industry had got" (lines 31-32). (c) "For as he eats & drinks he grows / Younger & younger every day" (lines 73-74). (d) "They cry the Babe the Babe is Born / And flee away on Every side" (lines 95-96). (e) "And none can touch that frowning form / Except it be a Woman Old? (lines 101-02).

2. Bearing in mind the quotations from Frye and Adams, reread the poem and discuss the ways in which it describes an eternal cycle.

Now for a few poems more briefly treated.

London

I wander thro' each charter'd street,
Near where the charter'd Thames does flow.
And mark in every face I meet
Marks of weakness, marks of woe.

[11] *William Blake: A Reading of the Shorter Poems* (Seattle: University of Washington Press, 1963, pp. 87-88.)

In every cry of every Man,
In every Infants cry of fear,
In every voice: in every ban,
The mind-forg'd manacles I hear

How the Chimney-sweepers cry
Every blackning Church appalls,
And the hapless Soldiers sigh,
Runs in blood down Palace walls

But most thro' midnight streets I hear
How the youthful Harlots curse
Blasts the new-born Infants tear
And blights with plagues the Marriage hearse

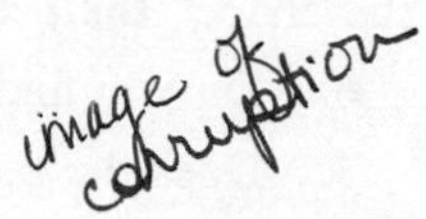

1. How does this poem reflect the radical thought and sensitized social conscience of the French Revolution?

2. What does *charter'd* mean in the context of the poem? (Look it up in the Oxford dictionary, if you are uncertain.)

3. Why do you think the chimney sweeper is chosen as a symbol of oppression? (Why not a child working in a factory or coal mine?)

I Saw a Chapel All of Gold

I saw a chapel all of gold
That none did dare to enter in
And many weeping stood without
Weeping mourning worshipping

I saw a serpent rise between
The white pillars of the door
And he forcd & forcd & forcd
Down the golden hinges tore

And along the pavement sweet
Set with pearls & rubies bright
All his slimy length he drew
Till upon the altar white

Vomiting his poison out
On the bread & on the wine
So I turnd into a sty
And laid me down among the swine

1. Is there any theme or attitude in this poem that reminds you of any other poems by Blake? Explain the similarity.

2. Does the chapel symbolize anything? If so, what?

3. Does the serpent symbolize anything? If so, is the connotation favorable or disagreeable, or both?

4. In the context of the whole poem, how do you take the lines—"All his slimy length he drew / Till upon the altar white / Vomiting his poison out / On the bread & on the wine"?

5. In the light of the concluding two lines, what is the poem saying about the chapel, the people outside, and the serpent?

6. Do you find any mythological or Biblical allusions? Explain them.

7. Does the poem in any way reflect the period in which it was written?

8. Can you give this poem a sexual interpretation? (*Touchstone:* principle of consistency.)

And now some additional poems. In reading them, bear in mind the themes and attitudes you have already found in Blake's poetry.

Holy Thursday

Twas on a Holy Thursday their innocent faces clean
The children walking two & two in red & blue & green
Grey headed beadles walkd before with wands as white as snow
Till into the high dome of Pauls they like Thames waters flow

O what a multitude they seemd these flowers of London town
Seated in companies they sit with radiance all their own
The hum of multitudes was there but multitudes of lambs
Thousands of little boys & girls raising their innocent hands

Now like a mighty wind they raise to heaven the voice of song
Or like harmonious thunderings the seats of heaven among
Beneath them sit the aged men wise guardians of the poor
Then cherish pity, lest you drive an angel from your door

THE Chimney Sweeper

A little black thing among the snow:
Crying weep, weep, in notes of woe!
Where are thy father & mother? say?
They are both gone up to the church to pray.

Because I was happy upon the heath,
And smil'd among the winters snow:
They clothed me in the clothes of death,
And taught me to sing the notes of woe.

And because I am happy, & dance & sing,
They think they have done me no injury:
And are gone to praise God & his Priest & King
Who make up a heaven of our misery.

The Divine Image

To Mercy Pity Peace and Love,
All pray in their distress:
And to these virtues of delight
Return their thankfulness.

For Mercy Pity Peace and Love,
Is God our father dear:
And Mercy Pity Peace and Love,
Is Man his child and care.

For Mercy has a human heart
Pity, a human face:
And Love, the human form divine,
And Peace, the human dress.

Ah! Sun-flower

Ah Sun-flower! weary of time,
Who countest the steps of the Sun:
Seeking after that sweet golden clime
Where the travellers journey is done.

Where the youth pined away with desire,
And the pale Virgin shrouded in snow:
Arise from their graves and aspire,
Where my Sun-flower wishes to go.

Mock on Mock on Voltaire Rousseau

Mock on Mock on Voltaire Rousseau
Mock on Mock on tis all in vain
You throw the sand against the wind
And the wind blows it back again

And every sand becomes a Gem
Reflected in the beams divine
Blown back they blind the mocking Eye
But still in Israels paths they shine

The Atoms of Democritus
And Newtons Particles of light
Are sands upon the Red sea shore
Where Israels tents do shine so bright

SELECTIVE BIBLIOGRAPHY

The edition of Blake's poetry used in this text is David V. Erdman, ed., with commentary by Harold Bloom, *The Poetry and Prose of William Blake* (Garden City, N. Y.: Doubleday, 1965, 1970).

Hazard Adams, *William Blake: A Reading of the Shorter Poems* (Seattle: University of Washington Press, 1963).

G. E. Bentley, Jr., *Blake Records* (New York: Oxford, 1969).

Bernard Blackstone, *English Blake* (London: Cambridge University Press, 1949).

Harold Bloom, *The Visionary Company* (Ithaca and London: Cornell Paperback, 1971). Not confined to Blake.

———, *Blake's Apocalypse* (New York: Doubleday, 1963).

C. M. Bowra, *The Romantic Imagination* (Cambridge, Mass: Harvard University Press, 1949). Not confined to Blake.

Jacob Bronowski, *William Blake: A Man Without a Mask* (Harmondsworth, England: Penguin [Pelican], 1954). Reissued as *William Blake and the Age of Revolution* (New York: Harper & Row, 1965).

S. Foster Damon, *William Blake, His Philosophy and Symbols (Boston: Houghton Mifflin, 1924; Gloucester, Mass.: P. Smither, 1958).*

David Erdman, *Blake: Prophet Against Empire* (Garden City, N. Y.: Doubleday Anchor, 1969).

Northrop Frye, *Fearful Symmetry, A Study of William Blake* (Boston: Beacon Press, 1962).

Robert Gleckner, *The Piper and the Bard* (Detroit: Wayne State University Press, 1959).

John Grant, ed., *Discussions of William Blake* (Boston: D.C. Heath and Co., 1961).

Jean H. Hagstrum, *William Blake, Poet and Painter* (Chicago: University of Chicago Press, 1964).

E. D. Hirsch, Jr., *Innocence and Experience: An Introduction to Blake* (New Haven: Yale University Press, 1964).

Raymond Lister, *William Blake: An Introduction to the Man and His Work,* Foreword by G. E. Bentley, Jr. (New York: Ungar, 1968, 1970).

Morton D. Paley, ed., *Twentieth Century Interpretations of Songs of Innocence and of Experience* (Englewood Cliffs, N. J.: Prentice-Hall, 1969).

Mark Shorer, *William Blake, The Politics of Vision* (New York: Holt, 1946).

Mona Wilson, *The Life of William Blake* (London: E. Hart-Davis, 1927, 1948).

Robert Browning

His Life

Robert Browning was born on the outskirts of London in 1812, into a solid, middle-class family. His father, though connected with banking, had many scholarly and artistic interests, and apparently decided from the outset that his son was to be a literary genius. Browning's mother came of a Nonconformist background and her brand of evangelical Christianity had a great impact on him, although indecisive arguments have been waged as to whether Browning in his maturity could be called an orthodox Christian. Certainly he had a period under the influence of Shelley when he bordered on atheism, but he later repudiated such extreme ideas.

The fact that he came of Nonconformist stock shut the doors of Oxford and Cambridge to him, just as years before they had been shut to Donne because of his Catholicism. Since Browning's father was comfortably well-off and had an amazing library of wide-ranging books, it was in his home that Browning's main education took place. He went to a private school for his early training and had a very short period at the University of London just as it opened, but his education largely was under the aegis of his father and his own curiosity. This helps to explain where he got so much unusual information, particularly about historical but not very well known personages which he used in his poetry. In addition, he had the advantage of traveling on the continent and even getting as far as St. Petersburg, the present-day Leningrad. All of these experiences fed his poetry.

In fact, although Browning became known to the literary world in his twenties with the publication of three long poems, *Pauline, Paracelsus* and *Sordello,* his early literary career did not really prosper, especially after the appearance of *Sordello*, which baffled those few who bothered to read it. Consequently, he had a period when he attempted to be a dramatist, chiefly because of his friendship with the actor William Macready. But the plays were commercial failures, and Browning was supported by his indulgent father until he was well over thirty.

In spite of the fact that his literary reputation seemed aborted, Browning kept on writing. Here and there were appreciative responses, among them Elizabeth Barrett, an invalid and a recluse who was becoming rather well known as a poet herself. She was six years his senior. First they corresponded, then Browning called on her and fell in love with her immediately. Although there were many obstacles to be overcome, not the least of them her tyrannical father, he finally persuaded her, frail health and all, to elope with him. They went to Italy and settled in Florence where they lived for the remainder of their married life. Her health improved remarkably, she bore him a son, and meanwhile she continued to write. The English public responded to her work, especially her long poem *Aurora Leigh*, and during their married years her reputation was far greater than his.

After her death in 1861, Browning could no longer bear to live in Italy. He and his son returned to England. Slowly Browning's work gained a wider audience, but for many years he lived in the shadow of Tennyson, who was then poet laureate, and who seemed to touch the spirit of the age more profoundly than Browning. The latter was viewed as being obscure, and his poems, dealing so often with abnormal psychology, bewildered readers, or offended their sense of what poetry should be.

However, his reputation did grow and as he aged he became known as a philosophic poet, almost a prophet. In the 1880s Browning Societies sprang up all over England composed of people interested in his work and committed to explaining it to the uninitiated. Unfortunately many of them were more interested in Browning as prophet or guru rather than as poet, and they extracted philosophic nuggets from his work, an act of homage that did not help his reputation with succeeding generations.

In the 20th century, especially from the late twenties on, interest in Browning diminished. In a world of vast wars and depressions, he seemed too sunny a poet, too unaware of evil in the world, too sturdily sure of what he believed. Somehow his modernity in language and his psychological interests seemed to escape most of the New Critics who shaped so much of the mid 20th century response to poetry. And, of course for a time, any mention of Victorianism—and Browning was a Victorian—produced a negative reaction.

The interest in Browning was more on certain aspects of his life, especially his courtship of Elizabeth Barrett. The play and later the movie, *The Barretts of Wimpole Street,* entranced audiences, and everyone knew about Elizabeth's dog, Flush. Certainly Browning's love for Elizabeth was the central passion of his life. But long before he met her he had begun to find his poetic voice, and his central beliefs were already established. He outlived her by more than a quarter century, dying in 1889. What many think is his greatest work (and certainly he did), *The Ring and the Book,* was written after her death.

His relationship with Elizabeth strengthened his conviction that love in all its aspects was the motive force in the world, but he did not share her interest in spiritualism, nor her complete dedication to the cause of Italian independence. For her part, she was not altogether happy with the dramatic emphasis in his poetry nor his fascination with morbid characters. All this does not diminish the relationship they had. It tremendously enriched both their lives. But it remains true that he had pretty much found his voice before he married and that what he owed to Elizabeth lay more in the realm of emotional depth and fulfillment than in any way she shaped his poetry.

The Poet and His Poetry

The poet Shelley was probably Browning's greatest poetic influence, though in later years, when he realized how badly Shelley had treated his first wife, his enthusiasm for Shelley waned. Browning's rhetoric, however, seems completely his own. Though he was a failure as a dramatist, he did learn from his contact with the theater that he was essentially a dramatic poet. He specialized in the dramatic monologue. Some of his finest poetry takes that form; for instance, "My Last Duchess," "Andrea Del Sarto," "Fra Lippo Lippi," and "The Bishop Orders His Tomb." In the dramatic monologue he was able to portray his men and women without intruding into the poetry in his own person. The characters—many with twisted personalities—reveal themselves to the reader by their actions and their speech. Browning, long before the 20th century, stressed psychological problems, was fascinated by the abnormal, and his poetry centers on the complexities of the human psyche. In this he seems far in advance of his age.

But he was also a product of his time. One facet of the Victorian era—in spite of Darwin and blows religion received from science—was a belief in the perfectability and the potential of man. Browning shared some of this optimism, based on his religious beliefs. This is not the place to argue his exact religious position, although certainly the influence of his early training reasserted itself after his bout with atheism. He apparently did not question the existence of a personal God, and he viewed the world with all its color and joy and pain as a place of "soul-making" so that even evil and adversity had purpose. As William O. Raymond states it.[1]

> A deep conviction of the infinite potentialities of the soul, its transcendental origin and immortal destiny, is a primary element in his self-consciousness. Linked with this is a belief that the purpose of life is a continuous striving to surpass the limitations imposed upon the soul by the finite conditions of time and sense . . . The limitations imposed on man by the imperfect conditions of his earthly existence are a school of discipline intended to serve the end of spiritual growth.

Or as Edwin Muir[2] succinctly puts it, Browning saw four truths that were the cornerstones of his world—"These four truths or affirmations, which depend upon and follow from each other, are—the uniqueness of personality, the imperfection of human life, the desire of the imperfect being for perfection, and the presence of God."

He also never doubted that love was the ultimate force in the universe. This

[1] William O. Raymond, *The Infinite Moment and Other Essays in Robert Browning* (Toronto: University of Toronto Press, second edition, 1965), pp. 161-62.

[2] Edwin Muir, *Essays on Literature and Society* (The Hogarth Press, 1949), p. 103.

conviction appears in poem after poem from *Paracelsus,* written when he was twenty-three, to *The Ring and the Book.* His relationship with Elizabeth Barrett further confirmed it. By love he meant human love and God's love—both *eros* and *agape.* Whether he viewed the Incarnation as a unique event is immaterial—certainly he believed that God's love, to be understood, had to be translated into human terms, whether in the life of Christ or any human being who lives in terms of love. It is this belief, that ultimately the world is in God's hands, that love triumphs and evil serves a purpose, that accounts for many 20th-century readers' disenchantment with Browning. He seems too sure and too sunny for a century that has confronted global war on an unprecedented scale, that has experienced the bestiality of which man is capable, and that lives in the shadow of a nuclear or ecological catastrophe.

Browning's verse forms, especially the monologues, are very modern. They try to catch the cadences of ordinary speech—he is almost a novelist in verse. His poetry does not abound in the compression, the verbal fireworks, or the wit that is so characteristic of Donne. He seems best when he is working in long poems with their stress on the quirks of the human personality. Certainly his interest in psychological nuances is modern, and it is interesting to realize how carefully Browning probed the relationship between men and women. At times he is very "un-Victorian" as in the attitude toward illicit love that he expresses in "The Statue and the Bust."

In addition to the relationship between men and women, he frequently explores the tension between art and life, or in Stevens' terms the relationship between imagination and "things as they are."

Browning knew a great deal about painting as well as music, and a number of his poems deal with artists or musicians as central characters. In "Fra Lippo Lippi," for example, he couples a belief in art with a joyous and sensuous response to the physical world. "Andrea del Sarto" came into being because a friend of Browning's wanted a photograph of the painting the artist did of himself and his wife, which hung in the Pitti Palace, a Florentine art gallery. Since one was not available, Browning wrote the poem to fill the gap, though he also relied on a biography of the artist to flesh the poem out.

Among the poems about musicians are "A Toccato for Galuppi" and "Abt Vogler". In the latter he is analyzing the effect of music and how it differs from the other arts. According to William De Vane,[3] "nowhere else in his poetry does Browning come so near Plato in conception as in the concluding lines of the ninth stanza":

> Therefore to whom turn I but to thee, the ineffable Name?
>   Builder and maker, thou of houses not made with hands:
> What, have fear of change from thee who art ever the same?

[3] William Clyde DeVane, *A Browning Handbook* (New York: F. S. Crofts & Co.), p. 258. A very useful book for its explications of individual poems.

Doubt that thy power can fill the heart that thy power expands?
There shall never be one lost good: What was, shall live as before;
The evil is null, is nought, is silence implying sound;
What was good shall be good, with, for evil so much good more;
On the earth the broken arcs; in the heaven a perfect round.

It is difficult to imagine any major 20th-century poet who could express so unqualified an optimism. Perhaps this passage illustrates some of our difficulties with Browning in spite of his modern sense of language and his interest in abnormal psychology.

Browning can rough up his language, use common speech, let his characters reveal themselves in ways that may remind us of Frost. But his style is more narrative and dramatic than strictly poetic. Modern poetry—at least until recently, with the rise of the Beats—has led us to take delight in complicated language, in the brilliant metaphor, in intense compression. Many readers have been brought up to think that metaphysical poetry is the ultimate in poetry. And Browning is very far from "metaphysical" in his work. Perhaps we do him an injustice when we do not see him for what he mainly was—a writer who used the techniques of the novel in the form of poetry. And surely we can respond to his intense and probing interest in men and women even though we may not be able to accept all his philosophic premises.

Finally, his relatively straightforward use of language is not too different from strong tendencies one finds in recent poets as diverse as Philip Larkin, Robert Creeley, and Allen Ginsberg. Just possibly Browning—in his own way—is more "modern" than we have realized.

Some of Browning's qualities as a poet are illustrated by one of his shorter and simpler poems, "Evelyn Hope":

Evelyn Hope

I

Beautiful Evelyn Hope is dead!
  Sit and watch by her side an hour.
That is her book-shelf, this her bed;
  She plucked that piece of geranium-flower,
Beginning to die too, in the glass;
  Little has yet been changed, I think:
The shutters are shut, no light may pass
  Save two long rays thro' the hinge's chink.

II

Sixteen years old when she died!
  Perhaps she had scarcely heard my name;
It was not her time to love; beside,
  Her life had many a hope and aim,
Duties enough and little cares,
  And now was quiet, now astir,
Till God's hand beckoned unawares,—
  And the sweet white brow is all of her.

III

Is it too late then, Evelyn Hope?
  What, your soul was pure and true,
The good stars met in your horoscope,
  Made you of spirit, fire and dew—
And, just because I was thrice as old
  And our paths in the world diverged so wide,
Each was nought to each, must I be told?
  We were fellow mortals, nought beside?

IV

No, indeed! for God above
  Is great to grant, as mighty to make,
And creates the love to reward the love:
  I claim you still, for my own love's sake!
Delayed it may be for more lives yet,
  Through worlds I shall traverse, not a few:
Much is to learn, much to forget
  Ere the time be come for taking you.

V

But the time will come,— at last it will,
When, Evelyn Hope, what meant (I shall say)
In the lower earth, in the years long still,
That body and soul so pure and gay?
Why your hair was amber, I shall divine,
And your mouth of your own geranium's red—
And what you would do with me, in fine,
In the new life come in the old one's stead.

VI

I have lived (I shall say) so much since then,
Given up myself so many times,
Gained me the gains of various men,
Ransacked the ages, spoiled the climes;
Yet one thing, one, in my soul's full scope,
Either I missed or itself missed me:
And I want and find you, Evelyn Hope!
What is the issue? let us see!

VII

I loved you, Evelyn, all the while.
My heart seemed full as it could hold?
There was place and to spare for the frank young smile,
And the red young mouth, and the hair's young gold.
So, hush,—I will give you this leaf to keep:
See, I shut it inside the sweet cold hand!
There that is our secret: go to sleep!
You will wake, and remember, and understand.

One notes first of all the language. There is a certain plainness and lack of "poetic" quality about it. "Beautiful Evelyn Hope is dead!" the poem begins, the simple statement of plain fact. "Sit and watch by her side an hour." The language has a transparent quality. The reader's attention does not focus on words but sees *through* them, as through a window, to observe the setting and the event.

The form of the poem, too, does not call attention to itself. Each stanza consists of two quatrains that rhyme *abab*: the meter is mostly iambic tetrameter, though with a good many variations to keep the rhythm close to that of ordinary conversation. Again, the form seems to point beyond itself to what is being said, the actual situation, the theme of the poem.

The human situation is summarized by two lines—"Sixteen years old when she died!" and "I was thrice as old." A middle-aged man, a teenaged girl. Immediately the inquisitive reader wonders whether an actual Evelyn lived, and died at the age of sixteen, and whether the poet Browning had an October-and-April passion for her. The answer, if found, would be humanly interesting, but not poetically vital. It may be that Evelyn was a figment of the poet's imagination, or a composite of all the charming teenage girls he had encountered. And it may be that Browning was not speaking in an autobiographical way in this poem; possibly he is wearing a mask, adopting a persona, while a little drama is acted out: the encounter between a living middle-aged man and a dead teenage girl. To appreciate the poem, one does not need to know whether "Evelyn Hope" reflects some infatuation in the life of a particular poet named Robert Browning.

The situation has something of the archetypal about it. What middle-aged man has not felt a sudden catch in his throat as a beautiful teenage girl goes past and the world seems freshened and renewed? Who has not daydreamed of some magic way to cancel the gap of years and be at one with her? But the poem begins after the idle daydreams are over. The girl is dead. Edgar Allen Poe's recipe for perfect beauty is fulfilled: a beautiful woman dead.

The descriptive details individualize Evelyn a little, but only a little. She is not so much a particular girl in this poem as an idealized picture of young girlhood. Her mouth is like a geranium blossom, she has a "sweet white brow," her soul is "pure and true," and the "good stars met in your horoscope, / Made you of spirit, fire and dew." Her hair is amber, tending toward gold. She does not sound like a particular girl with a street address and quirks of temperament, but fancy's picture of a young girl, any young girl, when viewed wistfully from the perspective of advancing years.

But the poem is more than an idealized portrait. It wrestles with the question of whether differences in age are ultimately final, and whether death itself is the concluding word on all human relationships. "Is it too late then, Evelyn Hope?" the speaker in the poem asks. "Each was nought to each, must I be told? / We were fellow mortals, nought beside?"

"No, indeed!" the poet insists, and bases his hopes on God who "is great to grant, as mighty to make, / And creates the love to reward the love." One life is not the only life, the speaker insists. He pictures a succession of lives, one reincarnation after another, a common enough idea in Platonic thought and many strands of Oriental philosophy. After their many lives, and with whatever experience and wisdom they have gained along the way, they will meet again, this time not to part.

The one symbolic touch in the poem seems to be in the last stanza: "I will give you this leaf to keep: / See, I shut it inside the sweet cold hand: / There that is our secret: go to sleep! / You will wake, and remember, and understand." The token carried into the other world as a reminder of human ties is a common folklore theme; the poem suddenly vibrates with archetypal implications at this point.

1. Why do you think Browning used these particular phrases? (a) "Beginning to die too." (b) "Save two long rays thro' the hinge's chink." (c) "Much

is to learn, much to forget." (d) "Why your hair was amber, I shall divine." (e) "Ransacked the ages."

2. Does the poem depict a kind of static reunion, in which nothing has changed except that the girl is alive again? Or has the meaning of the relation changed during the period of many lives that intervenes?

Some students of Browning have detected in "Evelyn Hope" a strain of abnormal psychology. Perhaps they are suspicious of the age gap and the preoccupation with the beauties of death. The matter is debatable, but there is hardly any doubt that "Porphyria's Lover" deals with a kind of love that specialists in abnormal psychology would find interesting.

Porphyria's Lover

The rain set early in to-night,
  The sullen wind was soon awake,
It tore the elm-tops down for spite,
  And did its worst to vex the lake:
I listened with heart fit to break.
When glided in Porphyria; straight
  She shut the cold out and the storm,
And kneeled and made the cheerless grate
  Blaze up, and all the cottage warm;
  Which done, she rose, and from her form
Withdrew the dripping cloak and shawl,
  And laid her soiled gloves by, untied
Her hat and let the damp hair fall,
  And, last, she sat down by my side
  And called me. When no voice replied,
She put my arm about her waist,
  And made her smooth white shoulder bare,
And all her yellow hair displaced,
  And, stooping, made my cheek lie there,
  And spread, o'er all, her yellow hair,
Murmuring how she loved me—she
  Too weak, for all her heart's endeavour,
To set its struggling passion free
  From pride, and vainer ties dissever,
  And give herself to me for ever.
But passion sometimes would prevail,
  Nor could to-night's gay feast restrain
A sudden thought of one so pale
  For love of her, and all in vain:
  So, she was come through wind and rain.
Be sure I looked up at her eyes
  Happy and proud; at last I knew

Porphyria worshipped me; surprise
  Made my heart swell, and still it grew
  While I debated what to do.
That moment she was mine, mine, fair,
  Perfectly pure and good: I found
A thing to do, and all her hair
  In one long yellow string I wound
  Three times her little throat around,
And strangled her. No pain felt she;
  I am quite sure she felt no pain.
As a shut bud that holds a bee,
  I warily oped her lids: again
  Laughed the blue eyes without a stain.
And I untightened next the tress
  About her neck; her cheek once more
Blushed bright beneath my burning kiss:
  I propped her head up as before,
  Only, this time my shoulder bore
Her head, which droops upon it still:
  The smiling rosy little head,
So glad it has its utmost will,
  That all it scorned at once is fled,
  And I, its love, am gained instead!
Porphyria's love: she guessed not how
  Her darling one wish would be heard.
And thus we sit together now,
  And all night long we have not stirred,
  And yet God has not said a word!

This is a poem in which the restrained language and matter-of-fact tone are set in counterpoint with the violence of the story. When the murder occurs, it is prefaced with the simple statement. "I found / A thing to do," as though a moderately difficult problem in geometry has been solved by a happy inspiration. The murder, however, has been foreshadowed and the reader is prepared to accept it as psychologically probable.

In the first place, the rather "Gothic" nature description at the beginning of the poem suggests violence. "The rain set early in to-night, / The sullen wind was soon awake, / It tore the elm-tops down for spite / And did its worst to vex the lake." The speaker is in a tense state, with "heart fit to break." The cottage seems isolated from the social world. What goes on there is entirely between Porphyria and her lover, and perhaps God—but the last line later comments "God has not said a word!"

The two characters seem almost tongue-tied. Porphyria, who glides in like a ghost fleeing the storm, busies herself with making a fire. She takes off her outer garments, sits down beside the man, speaks to him. He keeps his silence.

She makes timidly amorous gestures. She confesses her pity for his longing and acknowledges her love; she is ready at last to yield to his entreaties. The man keeps his silence.

Thus far the poem seems to be building up to a happy consummation. But a sinister, abnormal tone has already been created by the weather, Porphyria's gliding way of entering the cottage, the strange immobility of her would-be lover. The moment he yearned for has come; she is ready to give herself completely. But the man seems paralyzed. Instead of advancing confidently and quickly to the consummation, he ponders:

> Be sure I looked up at her eyes
>   Happy and proud; at last I knew
> Porphyria worshipped me; surprise
>   Made my heart swell, and still it grew
>   While I debated what to do.

The moment he has longed for is at hand, but now that it has come, the normal consummation somehow seems inadequate. Perhaps he feels that this moment must be made eternal; time must stop. Perhaps his ego cannot be satisfied by mere love and mere sex. The poem does not say. The lover is with his beloved who is "Perfectly pure and good." She is his for the taking. He ponders. He finds "A thing to do."

The murder has an intensely esthetic quality to it. He doesn't remove his belt and strangle her with that; nothing but a strand of her golden hair is adequate. She closes her eyes as the bud of a flower is closed. When he opens her lids again, the blue eyes are laughing as though alive. Now at last the lover is liberated to make love in his own fashion. With the perfect (because dead) woman completely at his mercy, he assaults her with burning kisses, puts her head to rest upon his shoulder, and spends a happy night.

1. Pick out all the words or phrases that seem to point toward the lover's abnormal psychological condition. If you have any familiarity with psychiatry, how would you diagnose him? Give reasons.

2. Why do you think the final line is included?—"And yet God has not said a word!" Can it be interpreted more than one way *in the context of this poem*?

The next poem is part III of a sequence called "Bad Dreams."

Bad Dreams: III.

This was my dream: I saw a Forest
  Old as the earth, no track nor trace
Of unmade man. Thou, Soul, explorest—
  Though in a trembling rapture—space
Immeasurable! Shrubs, turned trees,
Trees that touch heaven, support its frieze
Studded with sun and moon and star:
While—oh, the enormous growths that bar
Mine eye from penetrating past
  Their tangled twine where lurks—nay, lives
Royally lone, some brute-type cast
  I' the rough, time cancels, man forgives.

On, Soul! I saw a lucid City
  Of architectural device
Every way perfect. Pause for pity,
  Lightning! nor leave a cicatrice
On those bright marbles, dome and spire,
Structures palatial,—streets which mire
Dares not defile, paved all too fine
For human footstep's smirch, not thine—
Proud solitary traverser,
  My Soul, of silent lengths of way—
With what ecstatic dread, aver,
  Lest life start sanctioned by thy stay!

Ah, but the last sight was the hideous!
  A City, yes,—a Forest, true,—
But each devouring each. Perfidious
  Snake-plants had strangled what I knew
Was a pavilion once: each oak
Held on his horns some spoil he broke
By surreptitiously beneath
Upthrusting: pavements, as with teeth,
Griped huge weed widening crack and split
  In squares and circles stone-work erst.
Oh, Nature—good! Oh, Art—no whit
  Less worthy! Both in one—accurst!

What is the poem saying? Browning, like many Victorian poets, often summarizes quite explicitly the main meaning of a poem. Here he provides a clue at the end:

Oh, Nature—good! Oh, Art—no whit
  Less worthy! Both in one—accurst!

As we have seen, the rival claims of "life" (or nature) and "art," and the difficulty of reconciling them, are 19th-Century preoccupations and themes that weave in and out of Browning's poetry. He put the problem most often in the contrast of life and art, though sometimes, as in this poem, it seems to be nature and art. And the only conclusion he can reach here is that each is good and proper in its own right, but destructive to the other when they come together.

The first stanza describes a primeval forest magnificent beyond depiction, and free of human contagion unless one grants honorary humanity to the ape-man (some brute-type cast / I' the rough) who wanders in the perfect forest. The second stanza depicts a perfect city, whose creators seem to have discreetly withdrawn so as not to mar its perfection. Here, again, the reader is invited to contemplate something that is completely right in and of itself.

Then comes the final stanza—"the last sight was the hideous!" The City and the Forest, "each devouring each." They are like matter and antimatter, mutually destructive on contact.

1. In the poem, what qualities of the Forest and the City are singled out to emphasize the particular perfection that each has?

2. Have you ever experienced in yourself the conflict between life and art, nature and civilization, etc.? What form did it take? Were you able to reconcile the competing claims?

3. If you want to see this work in a wider context, read "Bad Dreams" in a collected Browning. There are four poems, dealing with the relation between a husband and wife whose marriage is close to dissolution. You may come to feel that "Bad Dreams: III"—while still a poem about nature and art—also serves symbolically to differentiate the attitudes of the husband and wife.

Browning, as we have seen, had an intense interest in music, painting, and sculpture. This is reflected in some of his best known poems. One, in celebration of music and its powers to link heaven and earth, is "Abt Vogler." Vogler is an almost forgotten German composer (1749-1814), who in his day was celebrated as an organist, and famous particularly for his ability to improvise. He traveled widely, and his pupils carried his techniques as far as England; Browning learned music from one of the disciples. Vogler was also famous for inventing a small, portable organ, called the orchestrion. Browning attributes to the poet an intense spirituality, perhaps a larger portion than he possessed in real life.

Browning always associated music, the most abstract of the arts, with architecture, the most tangible. To him music was a kind of momentary architecture, aspiring toward heavenly absolutes. The quest for a spiritualized perfection runs through the poem, along with a recognition that—in this present life at least—it can be achieved only fleetingly, and that the familiar world quickly resumes its sway.

The analogy of music and architecture is stated at the very beginning of the poem— " . . . the structure brave, the manifold music I build," followed by a long description of musical composition as a form of architecture. The ecstatic ascent into heaven or the realm of Platonic Absolutes is climaxed at the end of stanza IV: "For earth had attained to heaven, there was no more near nor far." The unity of all things, all experiences, is made manifest. The revelation is savored for several stanzas, with diminishing intensity. By stanza VIII the composer admits: "Well, it is gone at last, the palace of music I reared." The momentary perfection is fading into the common light of day. What has been its meaning? In stanza IX the speaker turns to "the ineffable Name" and proclaims his faith that "There shall never be one lost good!" The vision may come and go, wax and wane, but the final word of reality is affirmation of the highest to which mortals can aspire.

The concluding stanzas continue the diminishing effect, the gradual movement back into ordinary life, but a life illumined by memories of ecstasy and perfection. The struggle to reach the Absolute has not been a waste of energy and spirit.

Browning is often singled out as a poet peculiarly interested in dramatizing philosophic and metaphysical questions, and "Abt Vogler" is one of his most striking achievements in this endeavor. It is also a dramatic monologue, building up an impression of the composer by the words he speaks while at the keyboard.

In reading "Abt Vogler," it is well to keep in mind the basic movement of the poem—from earth to heaven and back to earth. Bear also in mind that to Browning the striving for the almost unattainable for a value in itself, whether or not permanent success was achieved.

Finally, one comment on style. We previously pointed out that Browning typically writes in fairly simple language and with natural sentence structures. In this poem, a deliberate elevation of diction and sentence structure seems to be sought. Browning evidently felt he was dealing with an elevated subject, and wanted it to be expressed in language of a certain majesty and formality.

Abt Vogler

(After he has been extemporising upon the musical instrument of his invention.)

I

Would that the structure brave, the manifold music I build,
  Bidding my organ obey, calling its keys to their work,
Claiming each slave of the sound, at a touch, as when Solomon willed
  Armies of angels that soar, legions of demons that lurk,
Man, brute, reptile, fly,—alien of end and of aim,
  Adverse, each from the other heaven-high, hell-deep removed,—

Should rush into sight at once as he named the ineffable Name,
And pile him a palace straight, to pleasure the princess he loved!

II

Would it might tarry like his, the beautiful building of mine,
This which my keys in a crowd pressed and importuned to raise!
Ah, one and all, how they helped, would dispart now and now combine,
Zealous to hasten the work, heighten their master his praise!
And one would bury his brow with a blind plunge down to hell,
Burrow awhile and build, broad on the roots of things,
Then up again swim into sight, having based me my palace well,
Founded it, fearless of flame, flat on the nether springs.

III

And another would mount and march, like the excellent minion he was,
Ay, another and yet another, one crowd but with many a crest,
Raising my rampired walls of gold as transparent as glass,
Eager to do and die, yield each his place to the rest:
For higher still and higher (as a runner tips with fire,
When a great illumination surprises a festal night—
Outlining round and round Rome's dome from space to spire)
Up, the pinnacled glory reached, and the pride of my soul was in sight.

IV

In sight? Not half! for it seemed, it was certain, to match man's birth,
Nature in turn conceived, obeying an impulse as I;
And the emulous heaven yearned down, made effort to reach the earth,
As the earth had done her best, in my passion, to scale the sky:
Novel splendours burst forth, grew familiar and dwelt with mine,
Not a point nor peak but found and fixed its wandering star;
Meteor-moons, balls of blaze: and they did not pale nor pine,
For earth had attained to heaven, there was no more near nor far.

V

Nay more; for there wanted not who walked in the glare and glow,
Presences plain in the place; or, fresh from the Protoplast,
Furnished for ages to come, when a kindlier wind should blow,
Lured now to begin and live, in a house to their liking at last;
Or else the wonderful Dead who have passed through the body and gone,
But were back once more to breathe in an old world worth their new:
What never had been, was now; what was, as it shall be anon;
And what is,—shall I say, matched both? for I was made perfect too.

VI

All through my keys that gave their sounds to a wish of my soul,
All through my soul that praised as its wish flowed visibly forth,
All through music and me! For think, had I painted the whole,
Why, there is had stood, to see, nor the process so wonderworth:

Had I written the same, made verse—still, effect proceeds from cause,
  Ye know why the forms are fair, ye hear how the tale is told;
It is all triumphant art, but art is obedience to laws,
  Painter and poet are proud in the artist-list enrolled:—

VII

But here is the finger of God, a flash of the will that can,
  Existent behind all laws, that made them and, lo, they are!
And I know not if, save in this, such gift be allowed to man,
  That out of three sounds he frame, not a fourth sound, but a star.
Consider it well: each tone of our scale in itself is nought;
  It is everywhere in the world—loud, soft, and all is said:
Give it to me to use! I mix it with two in my thought:
  And, there! Ye have heard and seen: consider and bow the head!

VIII

Well, it is gone at last, the palace of music I reared;
  Gone! and the good tears start, the praises that come too slow;
For one is assured at first, one scarce can say that he feared,
  That he even gave it a thought, the gone thing was to go.
Never to be again! But many more of the kind
  As good, nay, better perchance: is this your comfort to me?
To me, who must be saved because I cling with my mind
  To the same, same self, same love, same God: ay, what was, shall be.

IX

Therefore to whom turn I but to thee, the ineffable Name?
  Builder and maker, thou, of houses not made with hands!
What, have fear of change from thee who art ever the same?
  Doubt that thy power can fill the heart that thy power expands?
There shall never be one lost good! What was, shall live as before;
  The evil is null, is nought, is silence implying sound;
What was good shall be good, with, for evil, so much good more;
  On the earth the broken arcs; in the heaven, a perfect round.

X

All we have willed or hoped or dreamed of good shall exist;
  Not its semblance, but itself; no beauty, nor good, nor power
Whose voice has gone forth, but each survives for the melodist
  When eternity affirms the conception of an hour.
The high that proved too high, the heroic for earth too hard,
  The passion that left the ground to lose itself in the sky,
Are music sent up to God by the lover and the bard;
  Enough that he heard it once: we shall hear it by-and-by.

XI

And what is our failure here but a triumph's evidence
  For the fulness of the days? Have we withered or agonised?
Why else was the pause prolonged but that singing might issue thence?
  Why rushed the discords in but that harmony should be prized?

Sorrow is hard to bear, and doubt is slow to clear,
Each sufferer says his say, his scheme of the weal and woe:
But God has a few of us whom he whispers in the ear;
The rest may reason and welcome: 'tis we musicians know.

XII

Well, it is earth with me; silence resumes her reign:
I will be patient and proud, and soberly acquiesce.
Give me the keys. I feel for the common chord again,
Sliding by semitones, till I sink to the minor,—yes,
And I blunt it into a ninth, and I stand on alien ground,
Surveying awhile the heights I rolled from into the deep;
Which, hark, I have dared and done, for my resting-place is found,
The C Major of this life: so, now I will try to sleep.

One difficulty in writing poetry about music is that there is nothing to *see,* except perhaps the musician seated at his instrument. An interesting aspect of the poem is the way Browning translates music into visual images—"palace of music," etc. You might try rereading the poem with this in mind, and make a list of all the visual images that express the impact of music.

But this is preeminently a poem of ideas, a philosophic poem. As you think about it further, certain key ideas begin to emerge. They are embodied in the experience of music but are not confined to it. A sort of harmonious blending of Platonic metaphysics and Christian idealism seems to control the thought of the poem, brought to a point by the last two lines of stanza IX: "What was good shall be good, with, for evil, so much good more; / On the earth the broken arcs; in the heaven, a perfect round."

1. Taking the last quotation as one key to the poem, show how other lines fit in with it by preparing for the statement or amplifying it.

2. Read the last line of each stanza, and comment on the meaning (in the context of the total poem) of any that particularly strike you.

3. What is the significance of the poem ending with a reference to "The C Major of this life"?

As was pointed out earlier, Browning tried his hand at playwriting. He was a commercial failure, but the experience sharpened his sense of the dramatic and helped prepare him for what many regard as his most characteristic works, the dramatic monologues (or "dramatic romances," as Browning called some of them).

In Browning's dramatic monologues the "cast" may be more than one, but only one speaks. The other "actors," if any, are seen—perhaps accurately, perhaps with distortion—through the eyes of the speaker; the reader must "read between the lines" and deduce their personality, appearance, even their actions from clues given by the speaker. The speaker himself is usually at some crucial moment in his life. What he says may reveal his past as well as his present and his thoughts about the future. Often he reveals more of himself than he consciously intends; sometimes he unintentionally presents a different picture of himself from the one he is trying to project. The dramatic monologues tend to be highly probing psychological studies. Often they dramatize themes that constantly interested Brown: the relation of man and woman, the completing claims of arts and life, success and failure, for example.

One of Browning's earliest monologues, a model of compression and implication, is "My Last Duchess." In this short poem the speaker, a Italian duke at the time of the Renaissance, is engaged in formal negotiations to win a new duchess to replace the earlier one who disappeared under mysterious circumstances. Some kind of official negotiator from the bride's family is with him to work out the details of the transaction. The personality of the last Duchess emerges glowingly even when screened through the disapproving words of the Duke. The Duke himself seems a person of complete self-confidence and sangfroid. He as good as admits that the last Duchess disappeared (into a grave? a convent?) at his command. Perhaps he is warning the envoy that he should instruct the future bride to be more selective with her smile. In the midst of reminiscences about the last Duchess, and some plain talk about the size of the dowry, the Duke reveals himself as an esthete, displaying his art treasures to the envoy. He seems a man absolutely in control of himself, capable of controlling others (except perhaps his first wife), and in control of every situation.

As you read the poem, notice all the lines that tell you something about the personality of the Duke.

My Last Duchess

The speaker is the Duke of Ferràra,
an art patron of the Renaissance.

Ferràra

That's my last Duchess painted on the wall,
Looking as if she were alive. I call
That piece a wonder, now: Frà Pandolf's hands
Worked busily a day, and there she stands.
Will't please you sit and look at her? I said
"Frà Pandolf" by design, for never read
Strangers like you that pictured countenance,
The depth and passion of its earnest glance,
But to myself they turned (since none puts by
The curtain I have drawn for you, but I)
And seemed as they would ask me, if they durst,

How such a glance came there; so, not the first
Are you to turn and ask thus. Sir 'twas not
Her husband's presence only, called that spot
Of joy into the Duchess' cheek: perhaps
Frà Pandolf chanced to say "Her mantle laps
Over my lady's wrist too much," or "Paint
Must never hope to reproduce the faint
Half-flush that dies along her throat": such stuff
Was courtesy, she thought, and cause enough
For calling up that spot of joy. She, had
A heart—how shall I say?—too soon made glad,
Too easily impressed; she liked whate'er
She looked on, and her looks went everywhere.
Sir, 'twas all one! My favour at her breast,
The dropping of the daylight in the West,
The bough of cherries some officious fool
Broke in the orchard for her, the white mule
She rode with round the terrace—all and each
Would draw from her alike the approving speech,
Or blush, at least. She thanked men,—good! but thanked
Somehow—I know not how—as if she ranked
My gift of a nine-hundred-years-old name
With anybody's gift. Who'd stoop to blame
This sort of trifling? Even had you skill
In speech—(which I have not)—to make your will
Quite clear to such an one, and say, "Just this
Or that in you disgusts me; here you miss,
Or there exceed the mark"—and if she let
Herself be lessoned so, nor plainly set
Her wits to yours, forsooth, and made excuse,
—E'en then would be some stooping; and I choose
Never to stoop. Oh sir, she smiled, no doubt,
Whene'er I passed her; but who passed without
Much the same smile? This grew; I gave commands;
Then all smiles stopped together. There she stands
As if alive. Will't please you rise? We'll meet
The company below, then. I repeat,
The Count your master's known munificence
Is ample warrant that no just pretence
Of mine for dowry will be disallowed;
Though his fair daughter's self, as I avowed
At starting, is my object. Nay, we'll go
Together down, sir. Notice Neptune, though,
Taming a sea-horse, thought a rarity,
Which Claus of Innsbruck cast in bronze for me!

1. What are the values by which the Duke appears to live?

2. The Duke mentions a number of activities of his late wife that displeased him. What do they all have in common?

3. The dramatic monologue has been popular with many 20th-century poets. Can you think of an example, and compare it with "My Last Duchess"?

4. Do you get any idea of the kind of relationship that exists between the Duke and the envoy? How would you describe it?

5. Why are rhymed couplets used here instead of the line Browning more often used (blank verse)?

"My Last Duchess" is a very clear-cut dramatic monologue. Far more complex and psychologically subtle—and very much longer—is "Andrea del Sarto." This monologue grew out of Browning's fascination with the Italian Renaissance, the artistic temperament, and the whole tortured question of success and failure. In the poem, Browning singles out certain facets and traits of the painter, and shows his relationship to his wife, the amorous "cousin," and to other painters of the time.

Andrea is depicted, quite accurately, as a flawless craftsman, but lacking in ultimate passion and daring. The whole monologue has a gray tinge to it. Some fundamental weakness holds Andrea back from the highest achievements. This quality makes him a half-willing pawn to the imperious demands of his beautiful but unscrupulous wife. It makes him incapable of the final rush of will and energy needed for the greatest art.

It is interesting to observe Andrea as he sometimes turns to self-pity and makes excuses for his failure to achieve greatness; then observe him in his moments of cold clarity when he sees himself for the weak person he actually is. One almost believes he is relieved to have a tyrannical and money-mad wife; it gives him a good excuse to concentrate on profitable (and artistically easy) commissions, and to forget about art for art's sake. There is more than a small streak of masochism in his nature; he even seems to derive vicarious pleasure from the circling presence of the "cousin." Among the unspeaking characters in the monologue are the titanic artists who have reached heights forever beyond Andrea; they haunt him like an accusing artistic conscience.

Andrea is imprisoned by the beauty of his wife's body, but knows at the same time that he is a failure as a husband, just as he is a relative failure as an artist. His weakness, perhaps, is as much a moral one as a simple lack of drive.

Andrea Del Sarto

(Called "the faultless painter.")

But do not let us quarrel any more,
No, my Lucrezia; bear with me for once:
Sit down and all shall happen as you wish.

You turn your face, but does it bring your heart?
I'll work then for your friend's friend, never fear,
Treat his own subject after his own way,
Fix his own time, accept too his own price,
And shut the money into this small hand
When next it takes mine. Will it? tenderly?
Oh, I'll content him,—but to-morrow, Love!
I often am much wearier than you think,
This evening more than usual, and it seems
As if—forgive now—should you let me sit
Here by the window with your hand in mine
And look a half-hour forth on Fiesole,
Both of one mind, as married people use,
Quietly, quietly the evening through,
I might get up to-morrow to my work
Cheerful and fresh as ever. Let us try.
To-morrow, how you shall be glad for this!
Your soft hand is a woman of itself,
And mine the man's bared breast she curls inside.
Don't count the time lost, neither; you must serve
For each of the five pictures we require:
It saves a model. So! keep looking so—
My serpentining beauty, rounds on rounds!
—How could you ever prick those perfect ears,
Even to put the pearl there! oh, so sweet—
My face, my moon, my everybody's moon,
Which everybody looks on and calls his,
And, I suppose, is looked on by in turn,
While she looks—no one's: very dear, no less.
You smile? why, there's my picture ready made,
There's what we painters call our harmony!
A common greyness silvers everything,—
All in a twilight, you and I alike
—You, at the point of your first pride in me
(That's gone you know),—but I, at every point;
My youth, my hope, my art, being all toned down
To yonder sober pleasant Fiesole.
There's the bell clinking from the chapel-top;
That length of convent-wall across the way
Holds the trees safer, huddled more inside;
The last monk leaves the garden; days decrease,
And autumn grows, autumn in everything.
Eh? the whole seems to fall into a shape
As if I saw alike my work and self
And all that I was born to be and do,
A twilight-piece. Love, we are in God's hand.
How strange now, looks the life he makes us lead;
So free we seem, so fettered fast we are!

I feel he laid the fetter: let it lie!
This chamber for example—turn your head—
All that's behind us! You don't understand
Nor care to understand about my art,
But you can hear at least when people speak:
And that cartoon, the second from the door
—It is the thing, Love! so such things should be—
Behold Madonna!—I am bold to say.
I can do with my pencil what I know,
What I see, what at bottom of my heart
I wish for, if I ever wish so deep—
Do easily, too—when I say, perfectly,
I do not boast, perhaps: yourself are judge,
Who listened to the Legate's talk last week,
And just as much they used to say in France.
At any rate 'tis easy, all of it!
No sketches first, no studies, that's long past:
I do what many dream of, all their lives,
—Dream? strive to do, and agonise to do,
And fail in doing. I could count twenty such
On twice your fingers, and not leave this town,
Who strive—you don't know how the others strive
To paint a little thing like that you smeared
Carelessly passing with your robes afloat,—
Yet do much less, so much less, Someone says,
(I know his name, no matter)—so much less!
Well, less is more, Lucrezia: I am judged.
There burns a truer light of God in them,
In their vexed beating stuffed and stopped-up brain,
Heart, or whate'er else, than goes on to prompt
This low-pulsed fortright craftman's hand of mine.
Their works drop groundward, but themselves, I know,
Reach many a time a heaven that's shut to me,
Enter and take their place there sure enough,
Though they come back and cannot tell the world.
My works are nearer heaven, but I sit here.
The sudden blood of these men! at a word—
Praise them, it boils, or blame them, it boils too.
I, painting from myself and to myself,
Know what I do, am unmoved by men's blame
Or their praise either. Somebody remarks
Morello's* outline there is wrongly traced,
His hue mistaken; what of that? or else,
Rightly traced and well ordered; what of that?
Speak as they please, what does the mountain care?
Ah, but a man's reach should exceed his grasp,

* One of the Apennines.

Or what's a heaven for? All is silver-grey
Placid and perfect with my art: the worse!
I know both what I want and what might gain,
And yet how profitless to know, to sigh
"Had I been two, another and myself,
Our head would have o'erlooked the world!" No doubt.
Yonder's a work now, of that famous youth
The Urbinate who died five years ago.
('Tis copied, George Vasari sent it me.)
Well, I can fancy how he did it all,
Pouring his soul, with kings and popes to see,
Reaching, that heaven might so replenish him,
Above and through his art—for it gives way;
That arm is wrongly put—and there again—
A fault to pardon in the drawing's lines
Its body, so to speak: its soul is right,
He means right—that, a child may understand.
Still, what an arm! and I could alter it:
But all the play, the insight and the stretch—
Out of me, out of me! And wherefore out?
Had you enjoined them on me, given me soul,
We might have risen to Rafael, I and you!
Nay, Love, you did give all I asked, I think—
More than I merit, yes, by many times.
But had you—oh, with the same perfect brow,
And perfect eyes, and more than perfect mouth,
And the low voice my soul hears, as a bird
The fowler's pipe, and follows to the snare—
Had you, with these the same, but brought a mind!
Some women do so. Had the mouth there urged
"God and the glory! never care for gain.
The present by the future, what is that?
Live for fame, side by side with Agnolo!
Rafael is waiting: up to God, all three!"
I might have done it for you. So it seems:
Perhaps not. All is as God over-rules.
Beside, incentives come from the soul's self;
The rest avail not. Why do I need you?
What wife had Rafael, or has Agnolo?
In this world, who can do a thing, will not;
And who would do it, cannot, I perceive:
Yet the will's somewhat—somewhat, too, the power—
And thus we half-men struggle. At the end,
God, I conclude, compensates, punishes.
'Tis safer for me, if the award be strict,
That I am something underrated here,
Poor this long while, despised, to speak the truth.
I dared not, do you know, leave home all day,

For fear of chancing on the Paris lords.
The best is when they pass and look aside;
But they speak sometimes; I must bear it all.
Well may they speak! That Francis, that first time,
And that long festal year at Fontainebleau!
I surely then could sometimes leave the ground,
Put on the glory, Rafael's daily wear,
In that humane great monarch's golden look,—
One finger in his beard or twisted curl
Over his mouth's good mark that made the smile,
One arm about my shoulder, round my neck,
The jingle of his gold chain in my ear,
I painting proudly with his breath on me,
All his court round him, seeing with his eyes,
Such frank French eyes, and such a fire of souls
Profuse, my hand kept plying by those hearts,—
And, best of all, this, this, this face beyond,
This in the background, waiting on my work,
To crown the issue with a last reward!
A good time, was it not, my kingly days?
And had you not grown restless . . . but I know—
'Tis done and past; 'twas right, my instinct said;
Too live the life grew, golden and not grey,
And I'm the weak-eyed bat no sun should tempt
Out of the grange whose four walls make his world.
How could it end in any other way?
You called me, and I came home to your heart.
The triumph was—to reach and stay there; since
I reached it ere the triumph, what is lost?
Let my hands frame your face in your hair's gold,
You beautiful Lucrezia that are mine!
"Rafael did this, Andrea painted that;
The Roman's is the better when you pray,
But still the other's Virgin was his wife—"
Men will excuse me. I am glad to judge
Both pictures in your presence; clearer grows
My better fortune, I resolve to think.
For, do you know, Lucrezia, as God lives,
Said one day Agnolo, his very self,
To Rafael . . . I have known it all these years . . .
(When the young man was flaming out his thoughts
Upon a palace-wall for Rome to see,
Too lifted up in heart because of it)
"Friend, there's a certain sorry little scrub
Goes up and down our Florence, none cares how,
Who, were he set to plan and execute
As you are, pricked on by your popes and kings,
Would bring the sweat into that brow of yours!"

To Rafael's!—And indeed the arm is wrong.
I hardly dare . . . yet, only you to see,
Give the chalk here—quick, thus the line should go!
Ay, but the soul! he's Rafael! rub it out!
Still, all I care for, if he spoke the truth,
(What he? why, who but Michel Agnolo?
Do you forget already words like those?)
If really there was such a chance, so lost,—
Is, whether you're—not grateful—but more pleased.
Well, let me think so. And you smile indeed!
This hour has been an hour! Another smile?
If you would sit thus by me every night
I should work better, do you comprehend?
I mean that I should earn more, give you more.
See, it is settled dusk now; there's a star;
Morello's gone, the watch-lights show the wall,
The cue-owls speak the name we call them by.
Come from the window, love,—come in, at last,
Inside the melancholy little house
We built to be so gay with. God is just.
King Francis may forgive me: oft at nights
When I look up from painting, eyes tired out,
The walls become illumined, brick from brick
Distinct, instead of mortar, fierce bright gold,
That gold of his I did cement them with!
Let us but love each other. Must you go?
That Cousin here again? he waits outside?
Must see you—you, and not with me? Those loans?
More gaming debts to pay? you smiled for that?
Well, let smiles buy me! have you more to spend?
While hand and eye and something of a heart
Are left me, work's my ware, and what's it worth?
I'll pay my fancy. Only let me sit
The grey remainder of the evening out,
Idle, you call it, and muse perfectly
How I could paint, were I but back in France,
One picture, just one more—the Virgin's face,
Not yours this time! I want you at my side
To hear them—that is, Michel Agnolo—
Judge all I do and tell you of its worth.
Will you? To-morrow, satisfy your friend.
I take the subjects for his corridor,
Finish the portrait out of hand—there, there,
And throw him in another thing or two
If he demurs; the whole should prove enough
To pay for this same Cousin's freak. Beside,

What's better and what's all I care about,
Get you the thirteen scudi for the ruff!
Love, does that please you? Ah, but what does he,
The Cousin! what does he to please you more?

I am grown peaceful as old age to-night.
I regret little, I would change still less.
Since there my past life lies, why alter it?
The very wrong to Francis!—it is true
I took his coin, was tempted and complied,
And built this house and sinned, and all is said.
My father and my mother died of want.
Well, had I riches of my own? you see
How one gets rich! Let each one bear his lot.
They were born poor, lived poor, and poor they died:
And I have laboured somewhat in my time
And not been paid profusely. Some good son
Paint my two hundred pictures—let him try!
No doubt, there's something strikes a balance. Yes,
You loved me quite enough, it seems to-night.
This must suffice me here. What would one have?
In heaven, perhaps, new chances, one more chance—
Four great walls in the New Jerusalem,
Meted on each side by the angel's reed,
For Leonard, Rafael, Agnolo and me
To cover—the three first without a wife,
While I have mine! So—still they overcome
Because there's still Lucrezia,—as I choose.

Again the Cousin's whistle! Go, my Love.

1. Point out specific places in the poem where Andrea reveals more than he realizes.

2. Pick out passages dramatizing the ambivalence of his attitude toward his wife.

3. What clues does Browning give the reader that it is not totally the force of circumstances that prevents Andrea from being a great artist?

4. Make a list of *colors* and *shapes* mentioned in the poem, and discuss how they serves the purposes of the poem.

5. Discuss ambiguities (revealed through Andrea's words) in the painter's attitude toward other people.

"The Statue and the Bust" is a narrative, not a monologue, but it has many of the psychological and moral preoccupations found in Browning's monologues. Indeed, it has a strong thematic resemblance to "Andrea del Sarto," for both poems are explorations of weakness—the inability to rise to the heights of art in one case, and inability to risk all for love in the other.

Victorian England was shocked on a moderately large scale by "The Statue and the Bust," for it pictures a situation in which marital fidelity in a vice and weakness, and adultery would have been a virtue. The shock was due to a failure to recognize what should long have been clear in Browning's poetry—his insistence that love is the ultimate virtue, and that it must be judged not by legalities but by the intensity and honesty of the emotion itself. In "The Statue and the Bust," a man and a woman recognize the existence of this kind of love spiritually uniting them, daydream about making their lives together, but constantly delay doing anything about it, and finally settle into the routine of the proper and the humdrum.

The poem can be studied as the fading of a dream, as coming to terms with timidity, conventionality, whatever one wishes to call it. Browning here, as in "Andrea del Sarto," indirectly praises courage and decisiveness by portraying their opposites.

The Statue and the Bust

There's a palace in Florence, the world knows well,
And a statue watches it from the square,
And this story of both do our townsmen tell

Ages ago, a lady there,
At the farthest window facing the East
Asked, "Who rides by with the royal air?"

The bridesmaids' prattle around her ceased;
She leaned forth, one on either hand;
They saw how the blush of the bride increased—

They felt by its beats her heart expand—
As one at each ear and both in a breath
Whispered, "The Great-Duke Ferdinand."

That self-same instant, underneath
The Duke rode past in his idle way,
Empty and fine like a swordless sheath.

Gay he rode, with a friend as gay,
Till he threw his head back—"Who is she?"
—"A bride the Riccardi brings home to-day."

Hair in heaps lay heavily
Over a pale brow spirit-pure—
Carved like the heart of a coal-black tree,

Crisped like a war-steed's encolure*—
And vainly sought to dissemble her eyes
Of the blackest black our eyes endure.

And lo, a blade for knight's emprise
Filled the fine empty sheath of a man,—
The Duke grew straightway brave and wise.

He looked at her, as a lover can;
She looked at him, as one who awakes:
The past was a sleep, and her life began.

Now, love so ordered for both their sakes,
A feast was held that selfsame night
In the pile which the mighty shadow makes.

(For Via Larga is three-parts light,
But the palace overshadows one,
Because of a crime which may God requite!

To Florence and God the wrong was done,
Through the first republic's murder there
By Cosimo and his cursed son.)

The Duke (with the statue's face in the square)
Turned in the midst of his multitude
At the bright approach of the bridal pair.

Face to face the lovers stood
A single minute and no more,
While the bridegroom bent as a man subdued—

Bowed till his bonnet brushed the floor—
For the Duke on the lady a kiss conferred,
As the courtly custom was of yore.

In a minute can lovers exchange a word?
If a word did pass, which I do not think,
Only one out of the thousand heard.

That was the bridegroom. At day's brink
He and his bride were alone at last
In a bedchamber by a taper's blink.

Calmly he said that her lot was cast,
That the door she had passed was shut on her
Til the final catafalk repassed.

The world meanwhile, its noise and stir,
Through a certain window facing the East,
She could watch like a convent's chronicler.

* A horse's mane.

Since passing the door might lead to a feast,
And a feast might lead to so much beside,
He, of many evils, chose the least.

"Freely I choose too,' said the bride—
"Your window and its world suffice,"
Replied the tongue, while the heart replied—

"If I spend the night with that devil twice,
May his window serve as my loop of hell
Whence a damned soul looks on paradise!

"I fly to the Duke who loves me well,
Sit by his side and laugh at sorrow
Ere I count another ave-bell.

" 'Tis only the coat of a page to borrow,
And tie my hair in a horse-boy's trim,
And I save my soul—but not tomorrow"—

(She checked herself and her eye grew dim)
"My father tarries to bless my state:
I must keep it one day more for him.

"Is one day more so long to wait?
Moreover the Duke rides past, I know;
We shall see each other, sure as fate."

She turned on her side and slept. Just so!
So we resolve on a thing and sleep:
So did the lady, ages ago.

That night the Duke said, "Dear or cheap
As the cost of this cup of bliss may prove
To body or soul, I will drain it deep."

And on the morrow, bold with love,
He beckoned the bridegroom (close on call,
As his duty bade, by the Duke's alcove)

And smiled "Twas a very funeral,
Your lady will think, this feast of ours,—
A shame to efface, whate'er befall!

"What if we break from the Arno bowers,
And try if Petraja, cool and green,
Cure last night's fault with this morning's flowers?"

The bridegroom, not a thought to be seen
On his steady brow and quiet mouth,
Said, "Too much favour for me so mean!

"But, alas! my lady leaves the South;
Each wind that comes from the Apennine
Is a menace to her tender youth:

"Nor a way exists, the wise opine,
If she quits her palace twice this year,
To avert the flower of life's decline."

Quoth the Duke, "A sage and a kindly fear.
Moreover Petraja is cold this spring:
Be our feast to-night as usual here!"

And then to himself—"Which night shall bring
Thy bride to her lover's embraces, fool—
Or I am the fool, and thou art the king!

"Yet my passion must wait a night, nor cool—
For to-night the Envoy arrives from France
Whose heart I unlock with thyself, my tool.

"I need thee still and might miss perchance.
To-day is not wholly lost, beside,
With its hope of my lady's countenance:

"For I ride—what should I do but ride?
And passing her palace, if I list,
May glance at its window—well betide!"

So said, so done: nor the lady missed
One ray that broke from the ardent brow,
Nor a curl of the lips where the spirit kissed.

Be sure that each renewed the vow,
No morrow's sun should arise and set
And leave them then as it left them now.

But next day passed, and next day yet,
With still fresh cause to wait one day more
Ere each leaped over the parapet.

And still, as love's brief morning wore,
With a gentle start, half smile, half sigh,
They found love not as it seemed before.

They thought it would work infallibly,
But not in despite of heaven and earth:
The rose would blow when the storm passed by.

Meantime they could profit in winter's dearth
By store of fruits that supplant the rose:
The world and its way have a certain worth:

And to press a point while these oppose
Were simple policy; better wait:
We lose no friends and we gain no foes.

Meantime, worse fates than a lover's fate,
Who daily may ride and pass and look
Where his lady watches behind the grate!

And she—she watched the square like a book
Holding one picture and only one,
Which daily to find she undertook:

When the picture was reached the book was done,
And she turned from the picture at night to scheme
Of tearing it out for herself next sun.

So weeks grew months, years; gleam by gleam
The glory dropped from their youth and love,
And both perceived they had dreamed a dream;

Which hovered as dreams do, still above:
But who can take a dream for a truth?
Oh, hide our eyes from the next remove!

One day as the lady saw her youth
Depart, and the silver thread that streaked
Her hair, and, worn by the serpent's tooth,

The brow so puckered, the chin so peaked,—
And wondered who the woman was,
Hollow-eyed and haggard-cheeked,

Fronting her silent in the glass—
"Summon here," she suddenly said,
"Before the rest of my old self pass,

"Him, the Carver, a hand to aid,
Who fashions the clay no love will change,
And fixes a beauty never to fade.

"Let Robbia's craft so apt and strange
Arrest the remains of young and fair,
And rivet them while the seasons range.

"Make me a face on the window there,
Waiting as ever, mute the while,
My love to pass below in the square!

"And let me think that it may beguile
Dreary days which the dead must spend
Down in their darkness under the aisle,

"To say, 'What matters it at the end?
I did no more while my heart was warm
Than does that image, my pale-faced friend.'

"Where is the use of the lip's red charm,
The heaven of hair, the pride of the brow,
And the blood that blues the inside arm—

"Unless we turn, as the soul knows how,
The earthly gift to an end divine?
A lady of clay is as good, I trow."

But long ere Robbia's cornice, fine,
With flowers and fruits which leaves enlace,
Was set where now is the empty shrine—

(And, leaning out of a bright blue space,
As a ghost might lean from a chink of sky,
The passionate pale lady's face—

Eyeing ever, with earnest eye
And quick-turned neck at its breathless stretch,
Some one who ever is passing by—)

The Duke had sighed like the simplest wretch
In Florence, "Youth—my dream escapes!
Will its record stay?" And he bade them fetch

Some subtle moulder of brazen shapes—
"Can the soul, the will, die out of a man
Ere his body find the grave that gapes?

"John of Douay shall effect my plan,
Set me on horseback here aloft
Alive, as the crafty sculptor can,

"In the very square I have crossed so oft:
That men may admire, when future suns
Shall touch the eyes to a purpose soft,

"While the mouth and the brow stay brave in bronze—
Admire and say, 'When he was alive
How he would take his pleasure once!'

"And it shall go hard but I contrive
To listen the while, and laugh in my tomb
At idleness which aspires to strive."

So! While these wait the trump of doom,
How do their spirits pass, I wonder,
Nights and days in the narrow room?

Still, I suppose, they sit and ponder
What a gift life was, ages ago,
Six steps out of the chapel yonder,

Only they see not God, I know,
Not all that chivalry of his,
The soldier-saints who, row on row,

Burn upward each to his point of bliss
Since, the end of life being manifest,
He had burned his way thro' the world to this.

I hear you reproach, "But delay was best,
For their end was a crime."—Oh, a crime will do
As well, I reply, to serve for a test,

As a virtue golden through and through,
Sufficient to vindicate itself
And prove its worth at a moment's view!

Must a game be played for the sake of pelf?
Where a button goes, 'twere an epigram
To offer the stamp of the very Guelph.

The true has no value beyond the sham:
As well the counter as coin, I submit,
When your table's a hat, and your prize a dram.

Stake your counter as boldly every whit,
Venture as warily, use the same skill,
Do your best, whether winning or losing it,

If you choose to play!—is my principle.
Let a man contend to the uttermost
For his life's set prize, be it what it will!

The counter our lovers staked was lost
As surely as if it were lawful coin:
And the sin I impute to each frustrate ghost

Is—the unlit lamp and the ungirt loin,
Though the end in sight was a vice, I say.
You of the virtue (we issue join)
How strive you? *De te, fabula!**

1. What impressions do you get of the personality of the two main characters?

2. According to the poem, why do they constantly put off the consummation of their love?

* Concerning thee, this tale.

3. Is there any indication early in the poem that they will fail to come together?

4. What is the symbolism of "the statue" and "the bust"?

Now we include another poem, treated more briefly. As so often with Browning, it deals with man and woman in intricacy of relationships.

The Last Ride Together

I

I said—Then, dearest, since 'tis so,
Since now at length my fate I know,
Since nothing all my love avails,
Since all, my life seemed meant for, fails,
  Since this was written and needs must be—
My whole heart rises up to bless
Your name in pride and thankfulness!
Take back the hope you gave,—I claim
Only a memory of the same,
—And this beside, if you will not blame,
  Your leave for one more last ride with me.

II

My mistress bent that brow of hers;
Those deep dark eyes where pride demurs
When pity would be softening through,
Fixed me a breathing-while or two
  With life or death in the balance; right!
The blood replenished me again;
My last thought was at least not vain:
I and my mistress, side by side
Shall be together, breathe and ride,
So, one day more am I deified.
  Who knows but the world may end to-night?

III

Hush! if you saw some western cloud
All billowy-bosomed, over-bowed
By many benedictions—sun's
And moon's and evening-star's at once—
  And so, you, looking and loving best,
Conscious grew, your passion drew
Cloud, sunset, moonrise, star-shine too,
Down on you, near and yet more near,
Till flesh must fade for heaven was here!—
Thus leant she and lingered—joy and fear!
—Thus lay she a moment on my breast.

IV

Then we began to ride. My soul
Smoothed itself out, a long-cramped scroll
Freshening and fluttering in the wind.
Past hopes already lay behind.
  What need to strive with a life awry?
Had I said that, had I done this,
So might I gain, so might I miss.
Might she have loved me? just as well
She might have hated, who can tell!
Where had I been now if the worst befell?
  And here we are riding, she and I.

V

Fail I alone, in words and deeds?
Why, all men strive and who succeeds?
We rode; it seemed my spirit flew,
Saw other regions, cities new,
  As the world rushed by on either side.
I thought,—All labour, yet no less
Bear up beneath their unsuccess.
Look at the end of work, contrast
The petty done, the undone vast,
This present of theirs with the hopeful past!
  I hoped she would love me; here we ride.

VI

What hand and brain went ever paired?
What heart alike conceived and dared?
What act proved all its thought had been?
What will but felt the fleshly screen?
  We ride and I see her bosom heave.
There many a crown for who can reach.
Ten lines, a statesman's life in each!
The flag stuck on a heap of bones,
A soldier's doing! what atones?
They scratch his name on the abbey-stones.
  My riding is better, by their leave.

VII

What does it all mean, poet? Well,
Your brains beat into rhythm, you tell
What we felt only; you expressed
You hold things beautiful the best,
  And pace them in rhyme so, side by side.

'Tis something, nay 'tis much: but then,
Have you yourself what's best for men?
Are you—poor, sick, old ere your time—
Nearer one whit your own sublime
Than we who never have turned a rhyme?
  Sing, riding's a joy! For me, I ride.

VIII

And you, great sculptor—so, you gave
A score of years to Art, her slave,
And that's your Venus, whence we turn
To yonder girl that fords the burn!
  You acquiesce, and shall I repine?
What, man of music, you grown grey
With notes and nothing else to say,
Is this your sole praise from a friend,
"Greatly his opera's strains intend,
Put in music we know how fashions end!"
  I gave my youth; but we ride, in fine.

IX

Who knows what's fit for us? Had fate
Proposed bliss here should sublimate
My being—had I signed the bond—
Still one must lead some life beyond,
  Have a bliss to die with, dim-descried.
This foot once planted on the goal,
This glory-garland round my soul,
Could I descry such? Try and test!
I sink back shuddering from the quest.
Earth being so good, would heaven seem best?
  Now, heaven and she are beyond this ride.

X

And yet—she has not spoke so long!
What if heaven be that, fair and strong
At life's best, with our eyes upturned
Whither life's flower is first discerned,
  We, fixed so, ever should so abide?
What if we still ride on, we two
With life for ever old yet new,
Changed not in kind but in degree,
This instant made eternity,—
And heaven just prove that I and she
  Ride, ride together, for ever ride?

1. What is the actual situation at the beginning of the poem?
2. Has it changed—or is it viewed in a different way—at the end?

3. What questions about the meaning of life does this poem pose? What answers does it give?

4. Which other Browning poems does this remind you of? For what reasons?

The remaining poems are to be read on your own. Look for attitudes and situations that you have come to associate with Browning.

Prospice

Written in the autumn following Mrs. Browning's death.

Fear death?—to feel the fog in my throat,
    The mist in my face,
When the snows begin, and the blasts denote
    I am nearing the place,
The power of the night, the press of the storm,
    The post of the foe;
Where he stands, the Arch Fear in a visible form,
    Yet the strong man must go:
For the journey is done and the summit attained,
    And the barriers fall,
Though a battle's to fight ere the guerdon be gained,
    The reward of it all.
I was ever a fighter, so—one fight more,
    The best and the last!
I would hate that death bandaged my eyes and forbore,
    And bade me creep past.
No! let me taste the whole of it, fare like my peers
    The heroes of old,
Bear the brunt, in a minute pay glad life's arrears
    Of pain, darkness and cold.
For sudden the worst turns the best to the brave,
    The black minute's at end,
And the elements' rage, the fiend-voices that rave,
    Shall dwindle, shall blend,
Shall change, shall become first a peace out of pain,
    Then a light, then thy breast,
O thou soul of my soul! I shall clasp thee again,
    And with God be the rest!

*A Toccata of Galuppi's**

I

Oh Galuppi, Baldassaro, this is very sad to find!
I can hardly misconceive you; it would prove me deaf and blind;
But although I take your meaning, 'tis with such a heavy mind!

II

Here you come with your old music, and here's all the good it brings.
What, they lived once thus at Venice where the merchants were the kings,
Where Saint Mark's is, where the Doges used to wed the sea with rings?

III

Ay, because the sea's the street there; and 'tis arched by . . . what you call
. . . Shylock's bridge with houses on it, where they kept the carnival:
I was never out of England—it's as if I saw it all.

IV

Did young people take their pleasure when the sea was warm in May?
Balls and masks begun at midnight, burning ever to mid-day,
When they made up fresh adventures for the morrow, do you say?

V

Was a lady such a lady, cheeks so round and lips so red,—
On her neck the small face buoyant, like a bell-flower on its bed,
O'er the breast's superb abundance where a man might base his head?

VI

Well, and it was graceful of them—they'd break talk off and afford
—She, to bite her mask's black velvet—he, to finger on his sword,
While you sat and played Toccatas, stately at the clavichord?

VII

What? Those lesser thirds so plaintive, sixths diminished, sigh on sigh,
Told them something? Those suspensions, those solutions—"Must we die?"
Those commiserating sevenths—"Life might last! we can but try!"

VIII

"Were you happy?"–"Yes."–"And are you still as happy?"–"Yes. And you?"
–"Then, more kisses!"–"Did *I* stop them, when a million seemed so few?"
Hark, the dominant's persistence till it must be answered to!

IX

So, an octave struck the answer. Oh, they praised you, I dare say!
"Brace Galuppi! that was music! good alike at grave and gay!
I can always leave off talking when I hear a master play!"

* Galuppi: Italian composer (1706-1785).

X

Then they left you for their pleasure: till in due time, one by one,
Some with lives that came to nothing, some with deeds as well undone,
Death stepped tacitly and took them where they never see the sun.

XI

But when I sit down to reason, think to take my stand nor swerve,
While I triumph o'er a secret wrung from nature's close reserve,
In you come with your cold music till I creep thro' every nerve.

XII

Yes, you like a ghostly cricket, creaking where a house was burned:
"Dust and ashes, dead and done with, Venice spent what Venice earned.
The soul, doubtless, is immortal—where a soul can be discerned.

XIII

Yours for instance: you know physics, something of geology,
Mathematics are your pastime; souls shall rise in their degree;
Butterflies may dread extinction,—you'll not die, it cannot be!

XIV

As for Venice and her people, merely born to bloom and drop,
Here on earth they bore their fruitage, mirth and folly were the crop:
What of soul was left, I wonder, when the kissing had to stop?

XV

Dust and ashes!" So you creak it, and I want the heart to scold.
Dear dead women, with such hair, too—what's become of all the gold
Used to hang and brush their bosoms? I feel chilly and grown old.

Incident of the French Camp

I

You know, we French stormed Ratisbon:
  A mile or so away,
On a little mound, Napoleon
  Stood on our storming-day;
With neck out-thrust, you fancy how,
  Legs wide, arms locked behind,
As if to balance the prone brow
  Oppressive with its mind.

II

Just as perhaps he mused "My plans
  That soar, to earth may fall,
Let once my army-leader Lannes
  Waver at yonder wall,"—

Out 'twixt the battery-smokes there flew
  A rider, bound on bound
Full-galloping; nor bridle drew
  Until he reached the mound.

III

Then off there flung in smiling joy,
  And held himself erect
By just his horse's mane, a boy:
  You hardly could suspect—
(So tight he kept his lips compressed,
  Scarce any blood came through)
You looked twice ere you saw his breast
  Was all but shot in two.

IV

"Well," cried he, "Emperor, by God's grace
  We've got you Ratisbon!
The Marshal's in the market-place,
  And you'll be there anon
To see you flag-bird flap his vans
  Where I, to heart's desire,
Perched him!" The chief's eye flashed; his plans
  Soared up again like fire.

V

The chief's eye flashed; but presently
  Softened itself, as sheathes
A film the mother-eagle's eye
  When her bruised eaglet breathes;
"You're wounded!" "Nay," the soldier's pride
  Touched to the quick, he said:
"I'm killed, Sire!" And his chief beside
  Smiling the boy fell dead.

Epilogue

At the midnight in the silence of the sleep-time,
  When you set your fancies free,
Will they pass to where—by death, fools think, imprisoned—
Low he lies who once so loved you, whom you loved so,
  —Pity me?

Oh to love so, be so loved, yet so mistaken!
  What had I on earth to do
With the slothful, with the mawkish, the unmanly?
Like the aimless, helpless, hopeless, did I drivel
  —Being—who?

One who never turned his back but marched breast forward,
  Never doubted clouds would break,
Never dreamed, though right were worsted, wrong would triumph,
Held we fall to rise, are baffled to fight better,
          Sleep to wake.

No, at noonday in the bustle of man's worktime
  Greet the unseen with a cheer!
Bid him forward, breast and back as either should be,
"Strive and thrive!" cry "Speed,—fight on, fare ever
          There as here!"

SELECTIVE BIBLIOGRAPHY

The edition of Browning's poetry used in this text is Robert Browning, *Selected Poetry,* Introduction by Horace Gregory (New York, etc.: Holt, Rinehart and Winston, 1956). This edition contains most of Browning's more famous poems, with the exception of very long ones. It is based on Augustine Birrell, ed., *The Complete Poetical Works of Robert Browning,* new edition with additions (New York: Macmillan, 1915).

Leonard Burrows, *Browning the Poet, An Introductory Study* (Nedlands, Western Australia: University of Western Australia Press, 1969).

George Willis Cooke, *A Guide-book to the Poetic and Dramatic Works of Robert Browning* (Boston and New York: Houghton Mifflin—Riverside Press, 1891).

Norton B. Crowell, *A Reader's Guide to Robert Browning* (Albuquerque, New Mexico: University of New Mexico Press, 1972).

William De Vane, *A Browning Handbook* (New York: Appleton-Century-Crofts, 1955).

Philip Drew, ed., *Robert Browning: A Collection of Critical Essays* (Boston: Houghton-Mifflin, 1966).

Philip Drew, *The Poetry of Browning: A Critical Introduction* (London: Methuen, 1970).

W. H. Griffin and H. C. Minchen, *The Life of Robert Browning* (London: Methuen, 1938).

Park Honan, *Browning's Characters: A Study in Poetic Technique* (New Haven: Yale University Press, 1961).

Roma A. King, Jr., *The Bow and the Lyre: The Art of Robert Browning* (Ann Arbor: University of Michigan Press, 1957).

Robert Langbaum, *The Poetry of Experience: The Dramatic Monologue in Modern Literary Tradition* (New York: Random House, 1957).

Boyd Litzinger and K. L. Knickerbocker, eds., *The Browning Critics* (Lexington: University of Kentucky Press, 1965).

Betty Miller, *Robert Browning: A Portrait* (New York: Scribner, 1953).

J. Hillis Miller, *The Disappearance of God: Five Nineteenth Century Writers* (Cambridge, Mass.: Harvard University Press, 1963). Chapter III on Browning.

William O. Raymond, *The Infinite Moment and Other Essays in Robert Browning,* 2nd ed. (Toronto: University of Toronto Press, 1965).

Maisie Ward, *Robert Browning and His World.* I. The Private Face, 1812-1861. II. Two Robert Brownings? 1861-1889. (New York: Holt, Rinehart and Winston, 1967-1969).

Many unsystematic but penetrating comments on Browning are found scattered through the works of Ezra Pound: *Personae* (New York: New Directions, 1949), *The Letters of Ezra Pound* (New York: Harcourt, 1950), and *The Literary Essays of Ezra Pound* (New York: New Directions, 1954), as well as in the *Cantos.*

Emily Dickinson

Her Life

To her neighbors in Amherst, Massachusetts, Emily Dickinson was first of all the daughter of a distinguished local citizen. An eighth generation New Englander, Edward Dickinson was a prosperous lawyer, with an office squarely in the middle of Amherst; he served a term in Congress and was an active community leader, as well as treasurer of Amherst College. Kindliness and austerity were mingled in his personality. Emily saw in him something godlike, and the Freudians have noted that all her subsequent infatuations involved men older than herself. Mrs. Dickinson, who seems to have made relatively little impression on Emily, is remembered as a dutiful and submissive wife. Three children were born to them—Emily (1830), William Austin, and Lavinia; the latter was later to play a key role in making the poems available for publication.

Emily's formal education included seven years of on-and-off attendance at Amherst Academy, plus a year at Mount Holyoke Female Seminary, the ancestor of the modern college. She showed interest and ability in English and science, and had her problems with mathematics. Her classmates remembered her as lively and witty. Just when she began to write poetry seriously is hard to say. We know that at the age of twenty-one she wrote her famous letter to a minor author and literary critic, Colonel T. W. Higginson, beseeching, "Are you too deeply occupied to say if my verse is alive?" Higginson, though troubled by her unconventional poetic technique, gave her encouragement and later helped to publicize her poetry when it was published after her death.

From about her mid-twenties she became more and more a recluse, cloistered in the family house, and eventually ceasing altogether to venture out. Friends came to see her, or received little gifts accompanied by notes often written in verse. Her village reputation as an eccentric grew and flourished.

The deepening seclusion was marked by an all-out commitment to poetry and a fantastic productivity. After her death in 1886 her poems were gradually published in installments as new caches were discovered—written on backs of bills, envelopes, scraps of paper, and stuffed into bureau drawers and sewing baskets. When the definitive edition was finally published in 1955, the three heavily annotated volumes included 1775 poems, although many are rough drafts or fragments.

Emily's decades as a recluse have given rise to endless speculation among relatives and neighbors in Amherst as well as among literary historians. Almost every year a new lover is "discovered" and is offered as the explanation of her seclusion. There is not space here to go into the controversies, often based on highly circumstantial evidence. The fact seems to be that she had a warm and generous heart, and at various times was deeply devoted to a number of men. It is quite possible that most of them had only the faintest idea of her intense feeling. One appears to have been a law student working for her father —Benjamin Franklin Newton. She became acquainted with him while a student at the Seminary. He praised her poetry and introduced her to the newest thought, such as Unitarianism, which thus far had not penetrated deeply into the Amherst area. He left town after two years and died of tuberculosis.

At the age of twenty-three she met the Reverend Charles Wadsworth, a famous preacher and pastor of a Presbyterian church in Philadelphia. Happily married, he was beyond her reach and hopes, but she turned to him for spiritual counsel and they corresponded off and on. It has been argued that many of her more agonized love poems spring from this hopeless love.

Much later she seems to have fallen deeply in love with Judge Lord of Amherst, a man considerably her elder. There may have been others. But it is at least highly questionable whether these unconsummated attachments are the explanation of her hermit ways. Her desire for seclusion seems to have grown quite gradually, and it coincides with her deepening commitment to peotry. Always in rather frail health, and with an awareness of her surroundings so intense that it could exhaust her, she may have found normal social life too draining, and have decided that she must concentrate on the thing that came to mean most to her, the poetry.

When she died of Bright's disease in 1886, her poems were in various stages of composition. Some were in final or semifinal form, written out neatly and sewed into little booklets. Others were in rough draft, often with many alternative readings indicated for particular words. Her first editors—Colonel Higginson and Mrs. Mabel Loomis Todd (wife of an Amherst professor) often had to decide which readings to choose; horrified by her eccentric spelling and punctuation they normalized these.

At the time of Dickinson's death about half a dozen of her poems had been published—one in an anthology, the others in newspapers. She herself made almost no attempt to find a publisher. The first selection of her poetry came out in book form four years after her death and created a considerable stir, enlivened by controversy over her peculiarities of craftsmanship. Since then her reputation has had up's and down's but is now firmly established. The recluse of Amherst is quite certainly the best woman poet the United has produced, and very likely the best woman poet who has ever written in English. Regardless of sex, she ranks with the major poets of the 19th century and may easily outlive all but a handful.

The Poet and Her Poetry

Emily Dickinson lived in a period when the old New England mindset was being profoundly modified by new thought. The first English settlers who came to Massachusetts viewed God as the invisible ruler; human institutions and laws were designed to express the will of the ultimate King of Kings. The theology was Calvinism, the strand of Protestantism that most strongly emphasizes the omnipotence and inscrutability of God. This religion was not one of easy emotionalism and blind faith. It was highly intellectual, formulated by an impressive sequence of thinkers. Those shaped by it had a profound reverence for education. Along with this went a sense of local responsibility that made the small New England villages a civic marvel to visiting foreigners.

The way of life produced by Calvinism had its grim aspects, but these should not be overemphasized. The fruits of the religion were often a sober joy. Nothing in Calvinism prevented Emily's father from feeding birds during an April snowstorm (hiding himself as he scattered the seed so they would not be embarrassed at receiving charity). He also once rang the church bells to summon the village to see the beauty of the aurora borealis. And Calvinism was compatible with gay sleigh rides, practical jokes, and verbal wit.

The Deism of the 18th century began the dilution of Calvinism, and the Unitarian movement within Congregationalism (ultimately it split away as a separate denomination) eroded the strict doctrines. Boston became a center of the new thought; Harvard capitulated. And Emerson, a generation older than Emily, was to find even Unitarianism too confining.

It was not so in Amherst. This village, which never reached a population of 5000 during Emily's time, was in the backwater of western Massachusetts. Old beliefs lingered on with scarcely diminished vigor. In the church that Emily attended, the traditional hymns of Issac Watts were sung Sunday after Sunday, and the preaching was uncompromising Calvinism. This was not to last forever, of course. Visiting lecturers brought samples of the new thought. Emerson was being read with varying degrees of disapproval. Only a few decades in the future lay the Gilded Age (the period of Emily's final years) when a religious way of life would be supplanted by the crude quest for profit.

Allen Tate has well summarized the transition:[1]

> [Puritan theocracy] gave final, definite meaning to life, the life of pious and impious, of learned and vulgar alike. . . . it gave an heroic proportion and a tragic mode to the experience of the individual. . . .
>
> But by 1850 the great fortunes had been made (in the rum, slave, and milling industries), and New England became a museum. The whatnots groaned under the load of knickknacks, the fine china dogs and cats, the

[1] "Emily Dickinson," from *Essays of Four Decades* (Chicago: Swallow Press)

> pieces of Oriental jade, the chips off the leaning tower of Pisa. . . . The Gilded Age had already begun. Where the old order, formidable as it was, had held all this personal experience, this eclectic excitement, in a comprehensible whole, the new order tended to flatten it out in a common experience that was not quite in common; it exalted more and more the personal and the unique in the interior sense. Where the old-fashioned puritans got together on a rigid doctrine and could thus be individualists in manners, the nineteenth-century New Englander, lacking a genuine religious center, began to be a social conformist. . . . A great idea was breaking up, and society was moving toward external uniformity, which is usually the measure of the spiritual sterility inside.

Emily Dickinson, as a poet, is a child of both periods. She certainly specialized in "the personal and the unique in the interior sense." At the same time, she had the eternal verities (now increasingly under attack) of the Calvinistic religion as a framework within which her sensibility could operate. If more often than not she plays the role of rebel or impish questioner, she at least has something to question and rebel against.

Emily Dickinson's life span covers the crucial period when the inevitable conflict of the Civil War was drawing nearer, and it includes the full heyday of the robber baron period after that war. During her lifetime the United States, at least the northern portion, was transformed from a world of farms and small towns to an increasingly urbanized and industrialized world. Except for noticing the railroad that her father helped to route through Amherst—and delighting in it as a small child might—she hardly indicates any awareness of these transforming events.

One does not read Emily Dickinson for tidings of important historical events, but for news of the soul—the poet's and by extension that of the reader. Few poets have more accurately and subtly mapped the states of consciousness that mortals experience particularly in the face of elemental emotions such as love, loss, fear, and the thought of death. She traveled widely, but within her mind and heart.

Coupled with this inward observation was a fantastically observing eye turned outward, searching the garden in which she lovingly tended vegetables and flowers, and roaming in imagination if not in fact through the natural world beyond it. Her startlingly vivid ways of describing, say, a snake or a bird, often make the reader feel he has really looked at the object for the first time. But though her poetry is full of nature, this is rarely nature for its own sake. It is nature in relation to the perceiving and experiencing heart and mind, often nature as a storehouse of symbols depicting the drama within the solitary individual.

How did Emily Dickinson learn her craft? She received some advice from Colonel Higginson, who at first tried to steer her toward a more conventional type of poetry and encountered her quiet but absolutely firm resistance. She was also taught by church services, by books, and most of all by herself.

Any reader who is familiar with Protestant hymns inherited from the 17th and 18th century will recognize their strong influence in Emily Dickinson's poetry. Her stanza forms are often precisely those of well-knows hymns. It may be that her fondness for imperfect rhymes owes a debt to the hymnal, where *home* can be made to rhyme with *come*, and *God* with *road*. In any case, the hymnal provided her with a basic education in prosody, and her poems often illustrate that astoundingly new wine can be poured into very old bottles.

Two other important instructors were Shakespeare, whom she often quotes or paraphrases, and the King James Bible, which she knew in considerable detail.

Evidence for her other reading is incomplete, although it is clear that she was devoted to Keats, and had read many though not all of the other major 18th and 19th century poets. There is no evidence of acquaintance with Blake (with whom she is often compared), Coleridge, or Shelley. Nor do we know whether she ever got around to reading her great American contemporary, Whitman. The one mention is a letter (1862) to Colonel Higginson: "You speak of Mr. Whitman. I never read his book but was told that it was disgraceful."

But all these matters are the minutiae of scholarship. Emily Dickinson cannot be explained as the product of her period and its changing worldview, nor is her poetry a mere product of her reading. Every major poet is unique. Emily Dickinson bears a flavor of her time and place, and shows some influence of other poets, but at core she is herself and only herself.

A word first about the appearance of the poems. The early editors of Emily Dickinson normalized her eccentric punctuation (or sometimes lack of it) and her spelling, and frequently replaced regionalisms with standard English. In their bolder moments they straightened out her rhythms and rhymes and even rewrote whole lines. For this reason, the text of the poems here (based on the definitive edition, Thomas H. Johnson, ed., *The Poems of Emily Dickinson*) may often differ from the one you are familiar with. Professor Johnson has followed the actual manuscripts, with all their personal idiosyncracies. Where Emily Dickinson herself has indicated several possible word choices, he has, of course, been obliged to single out the reading that he considers most effective.

The first poem is rarely quoted, and perhaps is not one of her major achievements. But it illustrates certain qualities of her poetry:

It is an Honorable Thought

It is an honorable Thought
And makes One lift One's Hat
As One met sudden Gentlefolk
Upon a daily Street

That We've immortal Place
Though Pyramids decay
And Kingdoms, like the Orchard
Flit Russetly away

Like John Donne, Emily Dickinson juxtaposes violently dissimilar images. Here the first stanza seems to reflect smalltown New England life in the mid-19th century, with its curious combination of democracy and social rank. As the daughter of "Squire" Dickinson, she was concious of these subtleties without being obsessed by them. Here one has a picture of a "daily street"—in which all at once "sudden Gentlefolk" appear. A contrast is set up between "sudden" and "daily". A little moment of revelation is suggested; something out of the ordinary has occured. To "lift One's Hat" is to acknowledge the special meaning of the encounter.

The little vignette of the encounter with "sudden Gentlefolk" is a comparison; the poem is not *about* the Gentlefolk. Rather, it is concerned with an intimation of immortality in the midst of daily life. This is what the first line, "It is an honorable Thought," refers to. That line, and the next one, "And makes One lift One's Hat," suggest the reaction of respect, almost of awe, that the intuition of immortality evokes.

The first stanza, therefore, is a tone-setter. It prepares the way for the second stanza with its air of wonder as the speaker contemplates the eternity, the "immortal Place" of the individual as contrasted with the transcience of man's creations—Pyramids and Kingdoms.

Thus far we have evaded the word, "Russetly." But it makes all the difference. To "flit away" is a colorless way of saying something. To "flit Russetly away" suddenly links the disappearance of kingdoms with everyday experiences, such as the autumnal leaves on apple trees turning russet and drifting from the branches. "Kingdoms, like the Orchard/Flit Russetly away" suggests that the Kingdoms have had their day and are now dying a natural death. This contrasts with the brave assertion about human destiny—"We've immortal Place."

The use of the adverbial suffix, *-ly*, to create the word "Russetly" is an unusual thing, though of course poets tend to be more daring in their treatment of grammar than most prose writers are. The thought could have been more conventionally expressed (if one disregards distortions in the meter) by saying "And Kingdoms, like the Russet Orchard / Flit away." But now the word Russet takes on a static quality. The reader gets the picture of an orchard that is permanently russet, and that is suddenly seen no more. The way Dickinson phrases the picture is dynamic. Things happen "Russetly."

The apt choice of the word can be illustrated in another way. Suppose the last two lines were changed to read, "And Kingdoms, like the Orchard / Flit Brownly away." All at once a tone of mystery and magic disappears. *Brownly* seems a very flat word compared with "Russetly. Partly this is because russet is a less common word. It may also be because russet has a number of secondary meanings which enrich the primary sense. Among other things, russet can mean: homespun cloth of this color, a kind of leather, and a particular kind of winter apple. These submerged meanings operate on the reader's awareness.

This poem well illustrates how feeble any paraphrase of a good poem is likely to be. The bare philosophic meanings could be reduced to "It is amazing to think that though man's works decay, he himself is immortal." But that is not even the ghost of the poem. The poem is immortality experienced in terms of tipping one's hat and watching pyramids decay and Kingdoms vanishing like russet apple leaves in an early November wind.

The next poem is one written as a message to Dickinson's nephew, Edward Dickinson, then a student at Amherst College.

The Bible is an antique Volume—

The Bible is an antique Volume—
Written by faded Men
At the suggestion of Holy Spectres—
Subjects—Bethlehem—

Eden—the ancient Homestead—
Satan—the Brigadier—
Judas—the Great Defaulter—
David—the Troubadour—
Sin—a distinguished Precipice
Others must resist—
Boys that "believe" are very lonesome—
Other Boys are "lost"—
Had but the Tale a warbling Teller—
All the Boys would come—
Orpheus' Sermon captivated—
It did not condemn—

The poem illustrates a lover's quarrel with the strong Calvinistic tradition in which Dickinson was reared. Although her poetry rarely or never hints at atheistic denials, she frequently calls God to account and demands explanations, much as a child might question his parent's motives and deeds. When she wrote of the Bible it was with considerable familiarity, since it permeated both church and family life. Alone of her family, she failed to take the solemn step of joining the church (a much more demanding commitment than today), feeling perhaps that her controversy with the divine scheme of things disqualified her—or perhaps simply unwilling to bind herself to a fixed set of beliefs. All the same, religion remains one of the constant themes of her poetry.

The poem seems written to express a fellow felling with a young man who perhaps found the Bible difficult going. The poet identifies with him by the choice of language. The Bible, it appears, is an *antique* book, suggesting both a treasured heirloom and something out of date, old-fashioned, perhaps in bad repair. It was written by *faded* men—which emphasizes how long ago they lived. It was composed "At the suggestion of Holy Spectres"—a takeoff on the conventional phrase, "the inspiration of the Holy Spirit." *Spirit* and *spectre* can both suggest a ghost, but only *spirit* can also mean the Holy Ghost, whereas *spectre*, when applied to a ghost arising from the dead, suggests something horrible. By changing *spirit* to *spectre*, the idea of the inspiration of the Bible has been laughingly rephrased.

Much of the language is designed to humanize the Bible. Eden is described not as paradise but as "the ancient Homestead," as though it were a house and farm. Satan is not a fallen angel but a Brigadier—a military officer. Perhaps this rank was chosen to suggest brigand. Judas, who betrayed Christ, is the Great Defaulter. The word can mean transgressor, though this usage is obsolete. More commonly it means a person who fails to account for money he holds in trust. Its flavor is thus financial and legal. David is praised as the Troubadour—a word suggesting the wandering musicians of the Middle Ages who serenaded ladies in their castles. Is there a wry reference here to David's extensive love life?

Continuing with the poem—

1. Comment on the tone and message of these four lines: "Sin—a distinguished Precipice/ Others must resist—/ Boys that 'believe' are very lonesome —/ Other Boys are 'lost'—"

2. What is the exact effect of "warbling"? What sort of person is a "warbling Teller"?

3. In one of the manuscripts, Emily Dickinson lists more than a dozen possible alternatives to "warbling" (Johnson, III, p. 1067). Some of them are: typic, hearty, bonnie, tropic, friendly, mellow. Go through this list and see if you find one that you prefer to "warbling." If so, why? If you prefer "warbling," show why, *in the context of this particular* poem, it is preferable.

4. Explain the function of the reference to Orpheus, and how it brings the poem to conclusion.

The above poem is worth a second look if you are interested in the effects that can be achieved by various kinds of half rhyme. A whole series of modulations occurs. Dickinson begins with assonance—*Men / Bethlehem*. Then she rhymes *Brigadier / Troubadour*. The two consonants of the final syllabe, *d* and *r*, rhyme, but the vowels do not. This goes by the technical name of consonance. Next come the rhymes *resist / lost*, and example of "slant rhyme." (The vowels are different, but the consonants that follow are the same.)

Why all these subtle varieties of partial rhyme? One reason is surely the fact that English, as compared with French or Italian, is a poor language for rhyming. But in the case of Dickinson, these seems to have been a conscious desire to modulate between various sorts of partial rhyme, thereby achieving subtler effects than would be gained by strict adherence to perfect rhyme. In any case, she was one of the pioneers in extending the variety of rhyme by redefining the term, and her example has been followed by many subsequent poets.

The next poem is one frequently anthologized, as a marvelously fresh and accurate bit of observation:

A narrow Fellow in the Grass

A narrow Fellow in the Grass
Occasionally rides—
You may have met Him—did you not
His notice sudden is—

The Grass divides as with a Comb—
A spotted shaft is seen—
And then it closes at your feet
And opens further on—
He likes a Boggy Acre

A Floor too cool for Corn—
Yet when a Boy, and Barefoot—
I more than once at Noon
Have passed, I thought, a Whip lash
Unbraiding in the Sun
When stooping to secure it
It wrinkled, and was gone—

Several of Nature's People
I know, and they know me—
I feel for them a transport
Of cordiality—

But never met this Fellow
Attended, or alone
Without a tighter breathing
And Zero at the Bone—

Does the snake "stand for" anything? Certainly not anything that can easily be named. It is a mistake to assume that because natural things are sometimes used as symbols in poetry, they are always uses symbolically. Sometimes a poet wants to present a fact of nature in all its concreteness. Emily Dickinson's snake exists in his absolute identity as snake, unlike Blake's serpent (see page 55) which serves as a complex religious symbol.

To understand how the snake is depicted in his absolute essence, notice the phrases used to describe him:

narrow Fellow
rides
sudden
The Grass divides as with a Comb
spotted shaft
Whip lash / Unbraiding in the Sun
wrinkled

This is not an anthropomorphic snake. No effort has been made to establish similarities between him and mankind. He is slender, quick of movement, spotted in color, able to wind and unwind, capable of moving through grass and marking his presence by lightly pressing down the blades of grass.

The snake is not depicted as dangerous or evil, he is simply different. Different not merely from human beings but from animals and birds. The sense of the utterly alien envelopes him as human eyes observe him. That vision leads to the final stanza:

But never met this Fellow
Attended, or alone

Without a tighter breathing
And Zero at the Bone—

It is not that the snake has poison fangs, or that it is the wicked snake who tempted Eve into eating the mortal fruit. This snake is more like the strange creatures that science fiction writers describe on other planets: it lives its own life according to its own nature, a complete alien; there is no way (or need) to build a bridge of understanding and communication with it. This sense of the utterly different inspires "a tighter breathing" and "Zero at the Bone."

1. Is the next to last stanza on the same level of intensity as the rest of the poem? Is it essential for the total meaning and mood of the poem? Discuss.

2. Take the phrase "Zero at the Bone" and see whether you can make a paraphrase, not using the words "Zero" and "Bone." Does "Zero" have one precise meaning here?

3. Study the way the poem moves from very attenuated rhyme to strict rhyme at the end. What effect does this have on your responses to the poem?

A humming bird provides the subject for two of Dickinson's poems. The first was written around 1862, when she was in her early thirties; the second was written seventeen years later. They provide an interesting example of how a poet may attempt one subject, and then come back to it much later, making a completely fresh start.

Within my Garden, rides a Bird

Within my Garden, rides a Bird
Upon a single Wheel—
Whose spokes a dizzy Music make
As' twere a travelling Mill—

He never stops, but slackens
Above the Ripest Rose—
Partakes without alighting
And praises as he goes,

Till every spice is tasted—
And then his Fairy Gig
Reels in remoter atmospheres—
And I rejoin my Dog,

And He and I, perplex us
If positive, 'twere we—
Or bore the Garden in the Brain
This Curiosity—

But He, the best Logician,
Refers my clumsy eye—
To just vibrating Blossoms!
An Exquisite Reply!

A Route of Evanescence

A Route of Evanescence
With a revolving Wheel—
A Resonance of Emerald—
A Rush of Cochineal—
And every Blossom on the Bush
Adjusts it's tumbled Head—
The mail from Tunis, probably,
An easy Morning's Ride—

1. Which do you consider the more successful poem? Give specific reasons for your answer. This will involve pointing out strengths and weaknesses in the poems, perhaps specific lines or phrases.

2. Rebecca Patterson argues[2] that the humming bird functions as an erotic symbol in the second poem, though probably not in the first. She builds her case by analogy with the bee, which she asserts is sometimes "embarrassingly phallic" in Dickinson's poetry. She cites various passages, such as "Did the Harebell loose her girdle / To the lover Bee" and a poem describing the aggressive visit of a bee to a rose, ending, "Their Moment consummated—/ Remained for him—to flee—." Do you agree that the humming bird is an erotic symbol in the second poem?

Emily Dickinson specialized almost as much as John Donne in the nuances of death, but whereas his framework is always firmly theological, she is more concerned with the psychological aspects of the process of dying—as well as with the unanswered question of life beyond death. One of her most famous poems on the subject is:

Because I could not stop for Death—

Because I could not stop for Death—
He kindly stopped for me—
The Carriage held but just Ourselves—
And Immortality.

[2] "Emily Dickinson's Hummingbird," *The Educational Leader,* XXII (July, 1958).

We slowly drove—He knew no haste
And I had put away
My labor and my leisure too,
For His Civility—

We passed the School, where Children strove
At Recess—in the Ring—
We passed the Fields of Gazing Grain—
We passed the Setting Sun—

Or rather—He passed Us—
The Dews drew quivering and chill—
For only Gossamer, my Gown—
My Tippet—only Tulle—

We paused before a House that seemed
A Swelling of the Ground—
The Roof was scarcely visible—
The Cornice—in the Ground—

Since then—'tis Centuries—and yet
Feels shorter than the Day
I first surmised the Horses Heads
Were toward Eternity—

Here, as in so many of her poems, the imagery is drawn from small and somewhat prim and proper 19th-century Amherst. The same air of decorum prevails as in "It is an Honorable Thought." Death is a gentlemen, courteously inviting a lady to ride in his carriage. As Thomas H. Johnson puts it,[3]

> . . . Emily Dickinson envisions Death as a person she knew and trusted, or believed that she could trust. He might be any Amherst gentlemen. . . . The carriage holds but the two of them, yet the ride, as she states with quiet emphasis, is a last ride together. Clearly there has been no deception on his part. They drive in a leisurely manner, and she feels completely at ease. Since she understands it to be a last ride, she of course expects it be be unhurried. Indeed, his graciousness in taking time to stop for her at that point and on that day in her life when she was so busy she could not possibly have taken time to stop for him, is a mark of special politeness.

1. Courtesy and good manners play a big part in Emily Dickinson's poetry. Single out the words and phrases that emphasize them in this poem. Does this emphasis on well-bred manners weaken in any way the impact of the poem?

2. Make out two additional lists of words and phrases: those that empha-

[3] *Emily Dickinson: An Interpretive Biography* (Cambridge, Mass.: The Belknap Press of Harvard University, 1955), 222-23.

size nature and daily human activities; those that suggest hearse and grave. Discuss as specifically as possible the way the interweaving of the three sets of images creates the particular tone of the poem.

If the last poem seems to postulate some kind of continued awareness beyond death, the next one centers on the brute process of dying, as consciousness fades away.

I heard a Fly buzz—When I died—

I heard a Fly buzz—when I died—
The Stillness in the Room
Was like the Stillness in the Air—
Between the Heaves of Storm—

The Eyes around—had wrung them dry—
And Breaths were gathering firm
For that last Onset—when the King
Be witnessed—in the Room—

I willed my Keepsakes—Signed away
What portion of me be
Assignable—and then it was
There interposed a Fly—

With Blue—uncertain stumbling Buzz—
Between the light—and me—
And then the Windows failed—and then
I could not see to see—

As many commentators have pointed out, this poem presents the classical tableau of a Victorian deathbed scene. Friends and relatives have gathered around for the final moment, which presumably is in a home, amid familiar surroundings. There has been weeping and sighs. The spectators are perhaps awaiting the last words, which were often an affirmation of religious belief and sure faith in heaven.

Into this scene of sad decorum obtrudes what must be the most debated fly in all of literary history. Witness the controversy between Gerhard Friedrich and John Ciardi:[4]

> In an atmosphere of outward quiet and inner calm, the dying person collectedly proceeds to bequeath his or her worldly possessions, and

[4] Gerhard Friedrich, "Dickinson's 'I Heard a Fly Buzz When I Died,'" *The Explicator,* XIII (April 1955), Item 35. John Ciardi, "Dickinson's 'I Heard a Fly Buzz When I Died,'" *The Explicator,* XIV (January 1956), Item 22.

while engaged in this activity of "willing," finds his attention withdrawn by a fly's buzzing. The fly is introduced in intimate connection with "my keepsakes" and "what portion of me be assignable"; it follows—and is the culmination of—the dying person's preoccupation with cherished material things no longer of use to the departing owner. In the face of death, and even more of a possible spiritual life beyond death, one's concern with a few earthly belongings is but a triviality, and indeed a distraction from a momentous Issue. . . . Even so small a . . . creature is sufficient to separate the dying person from "the light," i.e. to blur the vision, to short-circuit mental concentration, so that spiritual awareness is lost.

—GERHARD FRIEDRICH

Mr. Friedrich's argument is coherent and respectable, but I feel it tends to make Emily more purely mystical than I sense her to be. I understand that fly to be the last kiss of the world, the last buzz from life. Certainly Emily's tremendous attachment to the physical world, and her especial delight both in minute creatures for their own sake, and in minute actions for the sake of dramatic implications that can be loaded into them, hardly needs to be documented. . . .

I find myself better persuaded, therefore, to think of the fly not as a distraction taking Emily's thoughts from glory and blocking the divine light . . . , but as a last dear sound from the world as the light of consciousness sank from her, i.e. "the windows failed." And so I take the last line to mean simply: "And then there was no more of me, and nothing to see with."

—JOHN CIARDI

How does one resolve this controversy? The familiar device of seeking some paradox by which both interpretations are valid, as aspects of a larger meaning, is worth trying, but this reader, for one, has not been able to pull it off. There seems a headon conflict between the two interpretations.

At least three approaches are possible, in descending order of importance: (1) Test each interpretation against the whole poem. See whether every line, indeed every phrase, is compatible with the interpretation you are testing. Be concerned with tone and mood as well as the literal meaning of the words. Does one interpretation seem more completely consistent with the *poem as a whole*? (2) Do any other poems by Dickinson provide clues as to which interpretation is the more likely? (3) Does anything you know about her background and the events of her life throw any light on the controversy?

1. Try the approaches suggested above. Which of the interpretations seems most plausible to you? If neither does, develop your own—but make certain it will fit the *entire* poem, not just parts.

2. Comment on the following words and phrases. Indicate what particular emphasis or nuance each contributes to the poem:

Heaves of Storm
Breaths were gathering firm
Onset
Assignable
I could not see to see

3. This poem and the last one both make use of familiar imagery—a carriage ride, a deathbed scene. Both deal with death. How would you characterize the *difference* in the total effect of the two poems?

4. Find a hymn tune that fits this poem and try singing it.

We now consider two additional short poems, more briefly.

I taste a liquor never brewed—

I taste a liquor never brewed—
From Tankards scooped in Pearl—
Not all the Frankfort Berries
Yield such an Alcohol!

Inebriate of Air—am I—
And Debauchee of Dew—
Reeling—thro endless summer days—
From inns of Molten Blue—

When "Landlords" turn the drunken Bee
Out of the Foxglove's door—
When Butterflies—renounce their "drams"—
I shall but drink the more!

Till Seraphs swing their snowy Hats—
And Saints—to windows run—
To see the little Tippler
From Manzanilla come!

The Johnson edition points out that the mysterious Manzanillo is a city on the southern coast of Cuba, associated by Emily Dickinson with the export of rum.

1. Sometimes a poem is one "sustained metaphor." Such seems the case here. Exhilaration and exultation are pictured in terms of intoxication. Discuss the poem as a sustained metaphor, showing how the descriptive phrases and actions all contribute.

2. Some of the language seems extravagant—for example, "Tankards

scooped in Pearl." List other examples. How do these instances of apparent overstatement affect the poem?

There's a certain Slant of light,

There's a certain Slant of light,
Winter Afternoons—
That oppresses, like the Heft
Of Cathedral Tunes—

Heavenly Hurt, it gives us—
We can find no scar,
But internal difference,
Where the Meanings, are—

None may teach it—Any—
'Tis the Seal Despair—
An imperial affliction
Sent us of the Air—

When it comes, the Landscape listens—
Shadows—hold their breath—
When it goes, 'tis like the Distance
On the look of Death—

Austin Warren says of this poem:[5]

> "There's a certain slant of light" is a poem ostensibly about winter afternoons with their "Heavenly Hurt" and their "Seal Despair"; when that winter light goes, "tis like the Distance / On the look of Death." In this poem "Death" is a metaphor for winter light and at the same time winter light is a metaphor for death: one inclines to say, preponderantly the latter.

1. Do you agree with Warren's last statement? What clues does the poem give you, one way or the other?

2. Why do you think the poet chose these particular words?— Heft (instead of *weight*), imperial, look (instead of *face*).

And finally a group of love poems. Possibly most or all of them were inspired by her hopeless passion for the Reverend Charles Wadsworth. She met him at the age of twenty-three, in 1854. In 1861 he accepted a call to San Francisco and this seems to have marked the crisis of her life. For the next few years she had her period of maximum poetic productivity, including a vast number of love poems with an astounding range of moods from despair to exaltation.

[5] "Emily Dickinson," *The Sewanee Review* (Autumn 1957).

The poems that follow constitute a little anthology of the moods of love. If Dickinson had been more set on publication, she might have put these and other poems together in a coherent sequence, like Dante's *La Vita Nuova.* As it is, each stands alone, but all are unified by her experience and sensibility.

The Soul selects her own Society—

The Soul selects her own Society—
Then—shuts the Door—
To her divine Majority—
Present no more—

Unmoved—she notes the Chariots—pausing—
At her low Gate—
Unmoved—an Emperor be kneeling
Upon her Mat—

I've known her—from an ample nation—
Choose One—
Then—close the Valves of her attention—
Like Stone—

Wild Nights—Wild Nights! [6]

Wild Nights—Wild Nights!
Were I with thee
Wild Nights should be
Our luxury!

Futile—the Winds—
To a Heart in port—
Done with the Compass—
Done with the Chart!

Rowing in Eden—
Ah, the Sea!
Might I but moor—Tonight—
In Thee!

[6] This poem troubled Colonel Higginson, who wrote to Mrs. Todd, the joint editor of the first collection of Dickinson's poetry: "One poem only I dread a little to print—that wonderful 'Wild Nights,'—lest the malignant read into it more than that virgin recluse ever dreamed of putting there. Has Miss Lavinia any shrinking about it? You will understand & pardon my solicitude. Yet what a loss to omit it! Indeed it is not to be omitted."—Quoted in Millicent Todd Bingham, *Ancestors' Brocades* (New York: Harper, 1945), p. 127.

The Way I read a Letter's—this—

The Way I read a Letter's—this—
'Tis first—I lock the Door—
And push it with my fingers—next—
For transport it be sure—

And then I go the furthest off
To counteract a knock—
Then draw my little Letter forth
And slowly pick the lock—

Then—glancing narrow, at the Wall—
And narrow at the floor
For firm Conviction of a Mouse
Not exorcised before—

Peruse how infinite I am
To no one that You—know—
And sigh for lack of Heaven—but not
The Heaven God bestow—

I got so I could hear his name—

I got so I could hear his name—
Without—Tremendous gain—
That Stop-sensation—on my Soul—
And Thunder—in the Room—

I got so I could walk across
That Angle in the floor,
Where he turned so, and I turned—how—
And all our Sinew tore—

I got so I could stir the Box—
In which his letters grew
Without that forcing, in my breath—
As Staples—driven through—

Could dimly recollect a Grace—
I think, they call it "God"—
Renowned to ease Extremity—
When Formula, had failed—

And shape my Hands—
Petition's way,
Tho' ignorant of a word
That Ordination—utters—

My Business, with the Cloud,
If any Power behind it, be,
Not subject to Despair—
It care, in some remoter way,
For so minute affair
As Misery—
Itself, too great, for interrupting—more—

My Life had stood—a Loaded Gun—

My Life had stood—a Loaded Gun—
In Corners—till a Day
The Owner passed—identified—
And carried Me away—

And now We roam in Sovreign Woods—
And now We hunt the Doe—
And every time I speak for Him—
The Mountains straight reply—

And do I smile, such cordial light
Upon the Valley glow—
It is as a Vesuvian face
Had let it's pleasure through—

And when at Night—Our good Day done—
I guard My Master's Head—
'Tis better than the Eider-Duck's
Deep Pillow—to have shared—

To foe of His—I'm deadly foe—
None stir the second time—
On whom I lay a Yellow Eye—
Or an emphatic Thumb—

Though I than He—may longer live
He longer must—than I—
For I have but the power to kill,—
Without—the power to die—

After great pain, a formal feeling comes—

After great pain, a formal feeling comes—
The Nerves sit ceremonious, like Tombs—
The stiff Heart questions was it He, that bore,
And Yesterday, or Centuries before?

The Feet, mechanical, go round—
Of Ground, or Air, or Ought—
A Wooden way
Regardless grown,
A Quartz contentment, like a stone—

This is the Hour of Lead—
Remembered, if outlived,
As Freezing persons, recollect the Snow—
First—Chill—then Stupor—then the letting go—

There came a Day at Summer's full,

There came a Day at Summer's full,
Entirely for me—
I thought that such were for the Saints,
Where Resurrections—be—

The Sun, as common, went abroad,
The flowers, accustomed, blew,
As if no soul the solstice passed
That maketh all things new—

The time was scarce profaned, by speech—
The symbol of a word
Was needless, as at Sacrament,
The Wardrobe—of our Lord—

Each was to each The Sealed Church,
Permitted to commune this—time—
Lest we too awkward show
At Supper of the Lamb.

The Hours slid fast—as Hours will,
Clutched tight, by greedy hands—
So faces on two Decks, look back,
Bound to opposing lands—

And so when all the time had leaked,
Without external sound
Each bound the Other's Crucifix—
We gave no other Bond—

Sufficient troth, that we shall rise—
Deposed—at length, the Grave—
To that new Marriage,
Justified—through Calvaries of Love—

SELECTIVE BIBLIOGRAPHY

The edition of Dickinson's poetry used in this text is Thomas H. Johnson, ed., *The Poems of Emily Dickinson,* 3 vol. (Cambridge, Mass.: Belknap Press of Harvard University Press). This edition is based on a careful study of the original manuscripts and faithfully reproduces the peculiarities of the poet's spelling and punctuation.

Caesar R. Blake and Carlton F. Welles, *The Recognition of Emily Dickinson: Selected Criticism Since 1890* (Ann Arbor: University of Michigan Press, 1964).

Charles Roberts Anderson, *Emily Dickinson's Poetry: Stairway of Surprise* (New York: Holt, Rinehart and Winston, 1960).

John Cody, *After Great Pain: The Inner Life of Emily Dickinson* (Cambridge, Mass.: Belknap Press of Harvard University, 1971).

Denis Donoghue, *Emily Dickinson* (Minneapolis: University of Minnesota Press, 1969).

Albert J. Gelpi, *Emily Dickinson: The Mind of the Poet* (Cambridge, Mass.: Harvard University Press, 1965).

Thomas Johnson, *Emily Dickinson: An Interpretative Biography* (Cambridge, Mass.: Belknap Press of Harvard University Press, 1955).

Ruth Miller, *The Poetry of Emily Dickinson* (Middletown, Conn.: Wesleyan University Press, 1968).

Richard B. Sewall, ed., *Emily Dickinson: A Collection of Critical Essays* (Englewood Cliffs, N. J.: Prentice-Hall, 1963)———, *The Life of Emily Dickinson* (New York: Farrar, Straus & Giroux, 1974).

George Whicher, *This Was a Poet* (New York: Scribner, 1938).

W. B. Yeats

His Life

William Butler Yeats, born 1865 in Ireland, was a minor 19th century poet and a major 20th-century poet. By the time of his death in 1939, he was widely recognized as the greatest English language poet of his times.

Yeats, unlike many poets, never burned out. In his last years he had a tremendous burst of creativity and wrote fresh and moving poems as his physical energy waned. Most of his finest poems were written in middle or old age. Meanwhile, throughout his life, he was constantly reexamining his earlier work and often drastically rewriting individual poems.

Yeats is a complex person to deal with, although the influences that shaped him are fairly clear, as are his major interests. First, his father, John Butler Yeats—an artist—was a major influence. So was the countryside around Sligo where his mother's people lived. In addition, Yeats was much influenced by the folk tales of the peasants in that area. How much the region meant to him is dramatized by his decision to be buried in the small yard of Drumcliff Church where once his great-grandfather was rector.

Another major influence on Yeats was the political situation of Ireland and his own heritage, which was Anglo-Irish. Ireland had long been under English domination. In the latter part of the 19th and the early part of the 20th century there was a mounting struggle for home rule. These were the days of the rise and fall of the great Irish leader, Parnell. The struggle grew in intensity around the time of World War I and culminated in the Easter rising of 1916, celebrated by Yeats in one of his most memorable poems. Only in 1921 was the Irish goal achieved, when the Irish Republic was recognized by England. Even then and to this day the six northern counties, commonly called Ulster, chose to remain under the British flag. During this whole period of conflict and frequent violence, Yeats was not so much involved in the revolutionary struggle and outright warfare as he was in the attempt to create a national literature, especially in the theater, which would help to shape the national ideals and recreate the "Romantic Ireland" that he believed to have existed in the past.

If you have read James Joyce's *Portrait of the Artist,* you know that the hero, Stephen Dedalus, felt there were nets flung about any aspiring Irish artist—nets of family, church, and state—and that the two latter were foreign. Ireland, as Stephen saw it, was a country dominated by a foreign church (Rome) and a foreign government (England). Stephen went so far as to feel that even English was not his native language, since Gaelic was the original language of Ireland. Yeats did not feel these nets to the same degree. Perhaps he did not feel them at all. His family was Anglo-Irish and he was brought up in the Anglican Church. English was the language his ancestors had always spoken. His family's English ties were so close that they often spent part of the year in London. Yeats himself attended British as well as Irish schools. But like many of the Anglo-Irish, who provided so much of Ireland's cultural and political leadership, Yeats was psychologically Irish rather than English. However, because of the relatively free lives lived by Anglo-Irish of his social level, he did not have Joyce's sense of suffocation, and was able to live and work in Ireland, while Joyce fled to the continent to escape the "nets."

The years of Yeats' youth and early manhood were turbulent ones for him, due both to exterior events and to the crises that affected his interior life. He had a mind that inherited his father's skepticism but he also had a deep need for some kind of overall answer to the chaos of the world. Since he found no answer in organized religion, he sought an answer in all sorts of unconventional ways. Even as a young man he was convinced, in spite of his skeptical streak, that there were spirits and a world beyond this visible one, and that this second world affected and impinged on the mundane world. He struggled to see through the veil that kept them apart.

This interest in exploring the world beyond the visible world attracted him early in life to William Blake, and led him to edit an edition of that visionary poet. Toward the end of his life he went to Majorca with Swami Shri Purohit to work on a translation of the Upanishads. Along the way he experimented with magic, primarily as taught by the Theosophical Society. A few years later he joined the Hermetic Order of the Golden Dawn, a secret society whole initiates were supposed gradually to master the secrets of that world beyond the veil.

Thus his quest for esoteric knowledge began early and continued to the end of his life. Yeats himself states it this way:[1]

> I was unlike others of my generation in one thing only. I am very religious, and deprived by Huxley and Tyndall, whom I detested, of the simple-minded religion of my childhood, I had made a new religion, almost an infallible church of poetic tradition, of a fardel of stories, and of personages, and of emotions, inseparable from their first expression, passed on from generation to generation by poets and painters with some help from philosophers and theologians. I wished for a world, where I could discover this tradition perpetually, and not in pictures and poems only, but in tiles round the chimney-piece and in the hangings that kept out the draft. I had even created a dogma: "Because these imaginary people are created out of the deepest instinct of man, to be his measure and his norm, whatever I can imagine those mouths speaking may be the nearest I can go to truth." When I listened they seemed always to speak of one thing only: they, their loves, every incident of their lives, were steeped in the supernatural.

In addition to the influence of Irish legends, the current political situation, and the cults that intrigued him, Yeats experienced other profound influences

[1] *The Autobiography of William Butler Yeats* (New York: Collier Books, 1924, 1965), p. 77.

on his life. One was Maud Gonne, whom he met in 1889. Her image haunted him until his own marriage in 1917. She was his Helen of Troy, called by some the most beautiful woman in Ireland. She had an incendiary nature which added to her appeal. Yeats fell hopelessly and completely in love with her—her presence moves through his poetry, and he wrote *The Countess Cathleen* for her to act in. Together they explored some of the mysteries of the secret societies. She, however, was more politically oriented than Yeats; reports have it that on occasion she even carried a bomb in her handbag. At any rate, she consistently refused to marry him. It was a devastating blow to him when suddenly in 1903 she married Captain John McBride, whom Yeats in his poem on the Easter uprising later termed "a drunken, vainglorious lout." Even though the marriage was a failure, and Maud left her husband within a few years, she refused to get a divorce. Then, when McBride was executed by the British for his role in the Easter rebellion, she would not consider marriage to Yeats, who by now was 52 years old. Only after this ultimate refusal did Yeats finally marry—and find to his delight that his wife possessed the gift of automatic writing. A whole new world opened up, revealed, he believed, by the spirits who guided his wife's hand. The material obtained in this way found publication in *A Vision* (1925).

Meanwhile Yeats was writing and publishing poems and plays. He had been named the Director of the Abbey Theatre in 1906 along with Lady Gregory; had lectured widely in Great Britain and the United States; in 1923 he was awarded the Nobel Prize for literature. His marriage, if not to a Helen of Troy, brought him stability and personal happiness. He even founded a family with the birth of a daughter in 1919 and a son in 1921. During the twenties he served for a time in the Irish Senate.

There is another important influence on Yeats that goes back to the turn of the century. This is Lady Augusta Gregory, then a widow in her forties and herself a writer. She had great rapport with the peasants in the Gort area and on her great estate of Coole, and collected their folk tales. It was she who provided Yeats with a place where he could pull himself together when tortured by his unrequited love for Maud Gonne, and who shared with him the peasant legends and in general offered him the calm and security he badly needed. He spend many of his summers on her estate; his initials, along with those of many other poets, can still be seen on the great beech tree in the garden. Eventually, in 1919, Yeats bought an old tower, Thoor Ballylee, situated a few miles from Coole, and moved his family into it.

It was contact with Lady Gregory that gave him insight into the aristocratic values that were disappearing as the great houses were broken up or burned down in civil turmoil. To the end of his life he celebrated the values that Lady Gregory stood for. He was more sympathetic to the extremes—the aristocrat and the peasant—than to intermediates. In the last few years of his life, after the death of Lady Gregory in 1932, he found similar satisfaction in the friendship of the Englishwoman, Lady Dorothy Wellesley. (Eventually, the stately house at Coole was torn down and the state now owns the property. The great beeches that line the entrance road are still there, but otherwise, except for the autograph tree, "all is changed, changed utterly.")

In the 1930's, because of his skepticism of the leveling process and scorn of the middle classes, Yeats flirted with the fringe of semi-fascist movements, such as the Green Shirts, for whom he wrote marching songs. His commitment to any systematic philosophy of fascism seems very unlikely, and he never became deeply involved, as compared, say, with Ezra Pound in Italy. But his marked lack of sympathy for left-wing movements and his aristocratic airs were enough to earn him the suspicion of many young poets, such as Auden, who were more revolutionary in belief.

It is obvious that Yeats was a quester. Throughout his life, in his researches into secret societies, automatic writing, and his human relations, he was seeking "unity of Being." When he published *A Vision* in 1925 (revised in 1937), he felt he had at last found the answer. This book needs to be read as a whole to understand Yeats' mature system of thought. There is not space to go deeply into it now, but reference will be made to certain aspects of the system, when these are relevant to particular poems.

Yeats died in France in 1939, but it was not until 1948—due to the war—that his body was brought back to Ireland and buried in Drumcliff churchyard under the shadow of Ben Bulben. His epitaph was written by himself—three lines from "Under Ben Bulben."

Cast a cold eye
On life, on death.
Horseman, pass by!

The Poet and His Poetry

It is important to know something about the ideas that shaped Yeats' poetry. The early poems, say until 1900, are largely concerned with legendary Ireland and with the occult. Two attitudes compete. In the first, there is the longing to abandon completely the daily world and become a permanent inhabitant of the land of Faerie. In the occult poems, there is more a striving to unite the worlds of "the oatmeal chest" and the reality that lies beyond.

Yeats was aware of the dichotomy in his nature, and in a letter to Katherine Tyman in 1888 he told her he had noticed things about his poetry that he had not been aware of before, that it was:[2]

> . . . almost all a flight into fairyland from the real world. . . . The Chorus to the "Stolen Child" sums it up—that it is not the poetry of insight and knowledge but of longing and complaint—the cry of the heart against necessity. I hope some day to alter that and write poetry of insight and knowledge.

In the period from 1900 on, the mundane world figures much more in Yeats' poetry. Though he rarely used his poetry for strictly political purposes, he was not immune to the upheaval around him. We see his response to the leveling process which he abhorred in poems like "To a House Shaken by the Rent Agitation." There are poems which refer to specific events, such as "Easter 1916." His elegy to an Ireland even he could not resurrect is contained in "September 1913." Although World War I seems to have touched him very little, his elegy to Robert Gregory and his "An Irish Airman Foresees His Death" show his awareness of the conflict. But it is in poems like "The Second Coming," "Meditations in Time of Civil War," and "Nineteen Hundred and Nineteen" that we feel Yeats' conviction that a cycle of history is ending and another is about to begin. In these poems there is sorrow for the loss of lovely things, the disappearance of innocence and ceremony.

There is another aspect of Yeats that we have not mentioned at all—one that became increasingly important to him—his theory of the mask.

In his *Autobiography* Yeats remarks:[3]

> There is a relation between discipline and the theatrical sense. If we cannot imagine ourselves as different from what we are and assume that second self, we cannot impose a discipline upon ourselves, though we may accept one from others. Active virtue as distinguished from the passive acceptance of a current code is therefore theatrical, consciously dramatic, the wearing of a mask. It is the condition of arduous full life.

[2] Allan Wade, ed., *Letters* (New York: Macmillan Company, 1954), p. 63.
[3] Pp. 317-18.

> One constantly notices in very active natures a tendency to pose, or if the pose has become a second self a preoccupation with the effect they are producing. One notices this in Plutarch's *Lives*, and every now and then in some modern who has tried to live by classical ideas, in Oscar Wilde, for instance, and less obviously in men like Walt Whitman. Wordsworth is often flat and heavy, partly because his moral sense has no theatrical element, it is an obedience to a discipline which he has not created.

The role of the Mask as Yeats saw it is well summarized by John Unterecker:[4]

> His problem therefore, was to discover a technique by which the personal could somehow be objectified, be given the appearance of impersonal "truth" and yet retain the emotive force of privately felt belief. A partial solution was the theory of the Mask which, perhaps compounded from popular psychology on one hand and occult material on the other, was used by Yeats to make public his secret selves.
>
> We are all familiar enough with the false faces we wear in the ordinary business of life, the unreal and different persons we present to parents, teachers, employers, lovers, and tax collectors. Most of us, little concerned with truth, present still another false face to ourselves, "the real me," and live and die happy in our deception. The writer interested in reality, however, must make a more difficult decision: he much choose one as genuinely real or, if he is like Yeats, find ultimate reality not in any one of them but in their interaction.
>
> "Reality," for Yeats, is neither to be found in that buried self which directs and orders a man's life or in its Mask, the anti-self, but in the product born of their struggle: Extroverts, Yeats felt, must flee their Masks. Introverts—painters, writers, musicians; all creative men—must recognize their own proper Masks, ideal opposites, and in trying to become those nearly impossible other selves create the dramatic tensions from which art arises.
>
> The doctrine of the Mask erects, therefore, on the artist's personality a kind of private mythology in which the individual struggles to become that which is most unlike himself: the introvert artist puts on an extrovert Mask; the subjective man assumes the Mask of the man of action. And because mythology and history, reducing men to types, mere images, simpler figures than flesh and blood men, does offer us patterns, we can, if we will, choose our Mask from those stored up by the past. A modern

[4] *A Reader's Guide to William Butler Yeats* (New York: Farrar, Straus & Giroux, copyright © 1959 By John Unterecker), pp. 16-17. Essay reprinted in Unterecker, ed., *Yeats: A Collection of Critical Essays* (Englewood Cliffs, N.J.: Prentice-Hall, 1963), p. 30.

introvert's Mask—say Yeats'—might in many ways resemble one of the great stone faces of myth—say Cuchulain's face, a hero striding out of the remote legendary Irish past, a man of action, great fighter and great lover.

We see the idea of the mask dramatized in such poems as "Ego Dominus Tuus," "The Mask," and later in his life in the Crazy Janes poems where the poet affects a female persona.

Of course, there are many poems where the mask does not enter, though even his love poems to Maud Gonne are less naked and subjective than are Keats' to Fanny Brawne. By mythologizing Maud, and turning her into another Helen, Yeats manages to keep a certain objectivity.

In one aspect of his poetry, however, Yeats never wears a mask. That is when he expresses his hatred of growing old and his anger at the dissolution of his physical body, as in "Sailing to Byzantium" where he says "An aged man is but a paltry thing" In 1934 he even underwent a rejuvenation operation in hopes of staving off inevitable decay. It is interesting that though the operation did not stay his physical deterioration, it seemed to result in a remarkable burst of creativity and the writing of several of his greatest poems.

From his very earliest days, Yeats sought a system of symbols to make sense of reality and to undergird his poems. In many of his youthful poems one finds the rose, which was symbolically important in the Order of the Golden Dawn. In fact, a book of poems he published in 1893 bore that title. But the symbols were not pulled together into what was to him a coherent whole until after his marriage and the revelations provided by his wife's automatic writing. In 1925 he published the first version of *A Vision*, a prose book in which he tried to explain his philosophic system—"the unity of being"—which he felt he had attained through the "instructors" who guided his wife in her automatic writing. Though the book is at times a maze for the reader, certain elements in it make sense and help to explain many of Yeats' otherwise esoteric poems. We need to be concerned with several important ideas he presents but the book is much too involved to attempt more than a superficial summary here.[5]

Yeats considered history to be a cyclical process, not a steady progression toward some ultimate goal. In his system the great wheel revolves every 2000 years, bringing the end of one cycle and the start of another. Each cycle begins with the interaction of a god and a bird. For instance, the era of Greek civilization began when Zeus in the guise of a swan raped Leda. The beginning of the Christian era stemmed from the Dove (or the Holy Ghost) and the impregnation of the Virgin Mary. The year 2000 will see the end of the Christian era and the start of another, as yet unknown, era. If we enderstand this cyclical process, poems like "Leda and the Swan," "The Mother of God,"

[5] The most convenient summary is provided by A. G. Stock, *W. B. Yeats: His Poetry and Thought* (Cambridge, England: University Press, 1961).

and "The Second Coming" are more meaningful. Yeats also believed in what he called the *anima mundi,* which seems to be much like Jung's theory of the collective unconscious. In other words, everything is stored in the great world memory and can, especially by the artist, be called up through the use of symbols. So we have history as a cyclical process, we have the *anima mundi,* and we also have a belief in reincarnation. According to this doctrine, each human life goes through a cycle from birth to death and is reincarnated in another birth. The moon is the force that seems to govern this process. During the course of a month, the moon, in revolving around the earth, goes through 28 phases. Phase one is the dark phase or complete objectivity. Phase 15 is the full moon or complete subjectivity. The other 26 phases are varying mixtures of subjectivity and objectivity. These 28 phases apply not only to human life but to social phases as well.

Yeats, in *A Vision,* is fascinated with the interactions of opposites (the gyres) —the idea that one historical phase unwinds what the previous phase has wound. To him, thesis and anthithesis are eternal processes, going on simultaneously.

Certainly the system provided Yeats, as he stated, with "metaphors for poetry." Whatever else the system may mean to us, it meant a great deal to Yeats. In a letter to Edward Dulac[6] he says: "I do not know what my book will be to others—nothing perhaps. To me it means a last act of defence against the chaos of the world, and I hope for ten years to write out of my renewed security."

One more preliminary consideration—Yeats's concept of Byzantium. His interest in Medieval Byzantium began very early in his life. He was haunted by the thought of a historical time and place where real unity was possible. In his famous evaluation of the Byzantine period he says in *A Vision:*[7]

> I think that in early Byzantium, maybe never before or since in recorded history, religious, aesthetic and practical life were one, that architect and artificers—though not, it may be, poets, for language had been the instrument of controversy and must have grown abstract—spoke to the multitude and the few alike. The painter, the mosaic worker, the worker in gold and silver, the illuminator of sacred books, were almost impersonal, almost perhaps without the consciousness of individual design, absorbed in their subject-matter and that the vision of a whole people.

[6] Quoted in Stock, p. 151.

[7] Pp. 279-80.

Poems

Now let us consider the poems themselves. To illustrate Yeats' earlier period, when the world of faerie beckoned so persuasively, "The Stolen Child" (1889) will serve as a good example.

The Stolen Child

Where dips the rocky highland
Of Sleuth Wood in the lake,
There lies a leafy island
Where flapping herons wake
The drowsy water-rats;
There we've hid our faery vats,
Full of berries
And of reddest stolen cherries.
Come away, O human child!
To the waters and the wild
With a faery, hand in hand,
For the world's more full of weeping than you can understand.

Where the wave of moonlight glosses
The dim grey sands with light,
Far off by furthest Rosses
We foot it all the night,
Weaving olden dances,
Mingling hands and mingling glances
Till the moon has taken flight;
To and fro we leap
And chase the frothy bubbles,
While the world is full of troubles
And is anxious in its sleep.
Come away, O human child!
To the waters and the wild
With a faery, hand in hand,
For the world's more full of weeping than you can understand.

Where the wandering water gushes
From the hills above Glen-Car,
In pools among the rushes
That scarce could bathe a star,
We seek for slumbering trout
And whispering in their ears
Give them unquiet dreams;
Leaning softly out
From ferns that drop their tears

Over the young streams.
Come away, O human child!
To the waters and the wild
With a faery, hand in hand,
For the world's more full of weeping than you can understand.

Away with us he's going,
The solemn-eyed:
He'll hear no more the lowing
Of the calves on the warm hillside
Or the kettle on the hob
Sing peace into his breast,
Or see the brown mice bob
Round and round the oatmeal-chest.
For he comes, the human child,
To the waters and the wild
With a faery, hand in hand,
From a world more full of weeping than he can understand.

The poem speaks to the reader like a lullabye from half-forgotten memories. There is something otherworldly about its music, and its repeated refrain beats at the mind and spirit, weaving a spell. The pictures the poem paints, the regular rhythm—everything pulls the reader's thoughts and yearnings toward a kind of Eden where the sorrows of this world no longer prevail. "*For the world's more full of weeping that you can understand*" speaks to anyone beyond the first years of childhood.

The poem requires no intricate technical analysis, but it is interesting to observe that in creating a sense of fairyland, Yeats makes use of familiar scenes near Sligo–Sleuth Wood, Rosses, Glen-Car lake. He was, in fact, building on legends of the local countrymen who believed the area to be frequented by fairies and to have an entrance (at Rosses) into fairyland proper.

As we read the poem, we move through a landscape haunted by the supernatural, and seem to be present as the fairies move carefree among stolen cherries and slumbering trout, while wooing the boy to leave the dreary, daily world.

By stanza four, the boy has been won over. He will go, "solemn–eyed," to fairyland. Suddenly the setting changes. The world is still "more full of weeping than he can understand," but it is also a place of warm, human memories —"the lowing / Of the calves on the warm hillside," "the kettle on the hob"; a world where he once saw "the brown mice bob/ Round and round the oatmeal-chest." Implicit in the poem is the price a human pays when he leaves the human world. There is a price if he stays, a price if he leaves.

"The Stolen Child" is a lyrical, uncomplicated poem, full of the tension between this world and the land of heart's desire; the poem recognizes the meaningfulness of each world. To reject fairyland is a loss, but to forsake the daily world for the land of heart's desire is also a loss. The two worlds here are severed beyond joining; one must choose.

At the end of the poem, the child has chosen—though with backward glances. The *For* of the last lines has changed—it is now *From*—from a world of weeping, but a world that also has brown mice who like oatmeal.

Yeat's sense of language and its musical properties is very evident in the poem. For example, in the third stanza there is a great deal of alliteration, and the sounds chosen, *s* and *w*, have a quiet, rustling quality, fitting the quiet tone of the poem (scarce, star, seek, slumbering, etc.; wandering, water, whispering).

The form of the poem is a marvel of variety-within-unity. Note, first, the number of lines in each stanza—12,15, 14, 12. The length of the stanza expands in the middle part of the poem, then contracts back to the original length, 12 lines. It is as though the poem has come full circle. Perhaps this reversion to the length of the first stanza also echoes the theme of the poem. In the first stanza, the daily world is wholly to be avoided. In the last stanza, the appeal of that daily, sorrowful world is for the first time recognized. Thus, by having the same length for the first and last stanzas, a kind of "equal time" is perhaps given to the two visions of the world.

1. Each middle section (between the first four and last four lines) has a different rhyme scheme. Do you think this is just for variety, or can you think of other reasons for it?

2. In general, each stanza divides (by its rhyme scheme) into a beginning, middle, and end. But in stanza two, one of the rhymes for the beginning section (light/night) carries on into the middle section (flight). Why do you think Yeats did this?

3. As you think about poems by other authors, can you remember any where the principle of "variety-within-unity" was reflected in the rhyme scheme?

The next poem reflects a pensive evening and a quiet conversation.

Adams's Curse

We sat together at one summer's end,
That beautiful mild woman, your close friend,
And you and I, and talked of poetry.
I said: 'A line will take us hours maybe;
Yet if it does not seem a moment's thought,
Our stitching and unstitching has been naught.
Better go down upon your marrow-bones
And scrub a kitchen pavement, or break stones
Like an old pauper, in all kinds of weather;

For to articulate sweet sounds together
Is to work harder than all these, and yet
Be thought an idler by the noisy set
Of bankers, schoolmasters, and clergymen
The martyrs call the world.'

                    And thereupon
That beautiful mild woman for whose sake
There's many a one shall find out all heartache
On finding that her voice is sweet and low
Replied: 'To be born woman is know—
Although they do not talk of it at school—
That we must labour to be beautiful.'

I said: 'It's certain there is no fine thing
Since Adam's fall but needs much labouring.
There have been lovers who thought love should be
So much compounded of high courtesy
That they would sigh and quote with learned looks
Precedents out of beautiful old books;
Yet now it seems an idle trade enough.'

We sat grown quiet at the name of love;
We saw the last embers of daylight die,
And in the trembling blue-green of the sky
A moon, worn as if it had been a shell
Washed by time's waters as they rose and fell
About the stars and broke in days and years.

I had a thought for no one's but your ears:
That you were beautiful, and that I strove
To love you in the old high way of love;
That it had all seemed happy, and yet we'd grown
As weary-hearted as that hollow moon.

This poem bears the mark of Yeat's love for Maud Gonne. It is addressed to her, reflecting a visit to her and her sister. The poem also shows Yeats' attempt to use common, conversational language, and to get away from poetic clichés and sentimentality. For the most part he succeeds, though an occasional "literary" word like *naught* creeps in.

Sometimes a title is just a convenient label, but in this case not. It reverberates. In the Christian tradition, Adam was expelled from Eden for his disobedience. He not only lost his primal innocence, but was sentenced to earn his living by the sweat of his brow. Work began, as a curse imposed by God. With exile from Eden also came the ravages of time and the fact of mortality.

The curse imposed on Adam is reflected in the poem. It is colored by an awareness of time's remorseless steps, of change, of inevitable death. The necessity of work is also central in the poem: a woman working to be beautiful, love demanding great efforts of the spirit, the poet laboring long and hard to make his poetry sound as though it had just been dashed off. All these require hard work. And all but the poetry succumb to mortality. Thus "Adam's Curse" is a testament to the immortality of art, the production of which seems to the average person nothing but idleness.

The poem first introduces the three characters—Yeats, Maud Gonne, and Maud's sister, Kathleen. They are talking about poetry. Yeats is explaining how a line of poetry can require endless labor even though it appears effortless. Then the "beautiful mild woman" (Kathleen) replies that a woman's beauty also demands effort. Implied is the idea that it, too, appears natural, and that all that goes into it is hidden from the world.

The poet, in the following stanza, speaks again and says that love, also requires labor, and many lovers have sought for examples and precedents in the past. Then the three fall silent, conscious of the passage of time. In the final stanza the poem narrows down to the poet and his love "for no one's but your ears." He has tried to love rightly, but the "old high way of love" somehow works no longer. Time has had its effect; love will die as surely as the beauty of a woman fades, no matter how much labor goes into either. At the end, the poet's thoughts are "weary-hearted" and the final image is the "hollow moon."

The proportions of the poem are interesting. The first two stanzas deal with writing poetry and the infinite labor required. Then one stanza (number 3) is devoted to the hard work that goes into keeping beautiful. The poem is now at about its halfway point. The remaining three stanzas concentrate on love, the labor of it, and the failure. Thus the reference to beauty and the strenuous labor of maintaining it is a kind of transition stanza, leading naturally enough away from talk of poetry and toward talk of love.

The lines are basically iambic pentameter, though with a good many variations to give a sense of freedom and colloquial rhythms. The lines are grouped in rhyming pairs, the "heroic couplet" beloved of 18th-century poets. This is a form often used in essaylike poems, where a smooth flow of thought is essential. It is here handled so as to be inconspicuous, rather like the beat of a distant, half-heard drum. Notice how often there is *no* pause at the end of a first line of a couplet; the first line slides unobtrusively into the second. Sometimes a couplet is broken between stanzas; for example, *enough* ending stanza four and *love* ending the first line of stanza five. In all these ways, the blatant quality of rhyme is played down and the easy, colloquial flow of the poem is accentuated. But at the same time, the rhyme, half submerged, gives a beat and discipline.

The poem has the tone of the end of things. The conversation is taking place "at one summer's end," and the time is sunset, moving toward twilight and moonlight. The moon is "hollow." The word is significant. Does it suggest the passing of a love that is also hollow? And even, by implication, does it suggest that the writing of poetry is equally hollow? At the end of the poem, words —the tools of the poet—have failed—"We sat grown quiet at the name of love." Time and mortality quietly infiltrate the scene. The reader is made aware of the ephemeral quality of human love and human beauty, the ravages of time, the days and years which inevitably bring changes. Though the poem makes no explicit statement, the reader asks himself—is it the same with works of art? Does time have the power to destroy them also? Or can the works of man's imagination (unlike human beauty and love) endure to defy time?

1. In what ways is this a more realistic poem than "The Stolen Child?"

2. Show specifically how Yeats' use of language has changed since he wrote "The Stolen Child."

3. This poem grew out of an actual conversation. What does this poem show about the relation between life and art?

4. Show in detail the uses Yeats made of the moon for his poetic purposes.

Now we consider a poem that carries a certain ambiguity in the language itself.

The Dolls

A DOLL in the doll-maker's house
Looks at the cradle and bawls:
'That is an insult to us.'
But the oldest of all the dolls,
Who had seen, being kept for show,
Generations of his sort,
Out-screams the whole shelf: 'Although
There's not a man can report
Evil of this place,
The man and the woman bring
Hither, to our disgrace,
A noisy and filthy thing.'
Hearing him groan and stretch
The doll-maker's wife is aware
Her husband has heard the wretch,
And crouched by the arm of his chair,
She murmurs into his ear,
Head upon shoulder leant:
'My dear, my dear, O dear,
It was an accident.'

Yeats has linked this poem to "The Magi" in some of his comments; you might want to read the latter at this point (p. 150) and see whether it throws any light on "The Dolls."

First, the rhythm. If you read the poem aloud, you find that it has a very conversational tone. Its rhythm is not produced by traditional metrical feet such as the iambic but by the simple device of having three strong stresses in each line and a varying number of unstressed syllables:

> A doll in the doll-maker's house
>
> Looks at the cradle and bawls:
>
> This is an insult to us.'
>
> But the oldest of all the dolls,
>
> Who had seen, being kept for show,

The poem is written in a continuous flow, without any formal division into stanzas, but the rhyme scheme is that of a succession of quatrains—abab, cdcd, etc. Thus the rhyming creates four-line units that exist in a kind of counterpoint with the smooth, undivided movement of the entire poem.

The poem has humor, or perhaps satire is a better word. The dolls in their indignation are mock-heroic figures, passionately discussing questions that poets and philosophers love to debate. Yeats, in fact, is still exploring the same question as in the preceding poem—the relationship between the real and the ideal; between the perfection of art and its very artificiality (the dolls) contrasted with noisy, filthy reality, that world "so full of weeping" (the baby). The dolls are insulted by the advent of the baby, a "noisy and filthy thing"; it has spoiled their esthetic paradise. They "scream" about the disgrace the baby brings into their ordered existence.

Then comes the line, "Hearing him groan and stretch," and the pronoun *him* is conveniently ambiguous. To whom does it refer? The baby, the doll, the husband? And who is the wretch—the doll or the baby? And is the *accident* the birth of the baby or the outburst of the doll? *O dear* is ambiguous also—is it a kind of exclamation, or is it addressed to the husband? This section of the poem illustrates how a poet can achieve complicated implications by capitalizing on the looseness and vagueness of language. A language in which everything had to be expressed with absolute, univocal precision would be fatal to the art of poetry, but fortunately such languages do not exist.

Certainly in "The Dolls" the world of the dolls and the world of the babies are far apart; they share space but no assumptions in common. They are as separate as the land of the fairies and the oatmeal chest in "The Stolen Child."

The question arises—will it help to take into account everything we know about Yeats and his system of thought? Perhaps there are certain recurrent themes running through his poetry, and we can discern several of them here. One has already been mentioned—the opposing claims of "art" and "life."

Yeat's insistence on coupling "The Dolls" with "The Magi" suggests that another theme is present—the idea of the cycles of history. The advent of the baby perhaps brings a new era into the doll-maker's home. With a new era comes the destruction of accustomed order and tranquility. Life will never again be the same for the dolls. When you read "The Second Coming," (page 152) you may want to refer back to "The Dolls" and see if you can find similarities of theme.

1. Compare the mood of this poem with that of "Adam's Curse." Show how the choice of words helps to control the moods of the two poems.

2. Can you explain why Yeats used an iambic rhythm for "Adam's Curse," but not for "The Dolls?"

Now two of Yeats' poems, both written much later. In the persona of "Crazy Janes," Yeats—who in old age felt bursts of sexual passion—is arguing for the union of soul and body, and asserting that love is not possible without such union. Here he pulls the world of spirit and the world of reality together and fuses them, as Blake did, in sexual union.

Crazy Jane is celebrated in a whole series of poems. Below is one of them.

Crazy Jane Talks with the Bishop

I MET the Bishop on the road
And much said he and I.
'Those breasts are flat and fallen now,
Those veins must soon be dry;
Live in a heavenly mansion,
Not in some foul sty.'

'Fair and foul are near of kin,
And fair needs foul,' I cried.
'My friends are gone, but that's a truth
Nor grave nor bed denied,
Learned in bodily lowliness
And in the heart's pride.

'A woman can be proud and stiff
When on love intent;
But Love has pitched his mansion in
The place of excrement;
For nothing can be sole or whole
That has not been rent.'

The poem is direct and stark. Crazy Janes meets the bishop who has previously—in another poem of the series—reproved her for her wanton ways. He now sententiously reminds her that she is old and should turn her thoughts to heaven. He characterizes her life as "a foul sty." But Jane has a higher wisdom. By experience she has learned the relationship between body and spirit—that "Fair and foul are near of kin." In the final stanza come the magnificent lines, "But Love (note the capital letter) has pitched his mansion in / The place of excrement." There is both a literal and metaphorical connotation here. Then finally come the lines: "For nothing can be sole or whole / That has not been rent."

Whether Yeats was consciously aware of it or not, the words *sole* and *whole* lend themselves to punning and consequently enlarge and reinforce the two previous lines—"But Love has pitched his mansion in / The place of excrement."

The choice of words in this poem is particularly interesting:

1. *Mansion* is used twice, in two very different contexts. Why in both places? And why this word rather than *house* or *home*?

2. In the last stanza, the phrase "pitches his mansion" is rather odd, since usually tents rather than houses are "pitched." Why do you think Yeats used it?

3. Read "The Circus Animals' Desertion" (page 147) and compare it with the present poem. Note especially the lines: "I must lie down where all the ladders start, / In the foul rag-and-bone shop of the heart."

In the final decade of his life, plagued by ill health, Yeats was yet able to bring together the two sides of his nature and somehow fuse what once had been so sundered. To see the final fusion, consider this poem:

Long-Legged Fly

That civilisation may not sink,
Its great battle lost,
Quiet the dog, tether the pony
To a distant post;
Our master Caesar is in the tent
Where the maps are spread,
His eyes fixed upon nothing,
A hand under his head.
Like a long-legged fly upon the stream
His mind moves upon silence.

That the topless towers be burnt
And men recall that face,
Move most gently if move you must
In this lonely place.

She thinks, part woman, three parts a child,
That nobody looks; her feet
Practise a tinker shuffle
Picked up on a street.
Like a long-legged fly upon the stream
Her mind moves upon silence.

That girls at puberty may find
The first Adam in their thought,
Shut the door of the Pope's chapel,
Keep those children out.
There on that scaffolding reclines
Michael Angelo.
With no more sound than the mice make
His hand moves to and fro.
Like a long-legged fly upon the stream
His mind moves upon silence.

This is a poem which calls to mind "Adam's Curse," but here the three characters with their three activities are presented as sources of strength and creativity for the world—rather than conveying a sense of the loss of love and beauty to the ravages of time. The haunting refrain pulls the poem together into a vibrant quietude.

There are only three stanzas. The first celebrates the warrior-statesman, Caesar; the second, Helen of Troy with all her beauty and what she meant in the world of Homer; and finally, the artist, Michelangelo, painting the ceiling of the Sistine Chapel. Each exists in silence, like a long-legged fly upon the stream. Each also shaped and reshaped the world. Perhaps the position of Michelangelo in the place of emphasis, the final stanza, suggests that the artist had the greatest effect of all.

Helen and Caesar seem almost lost in reverie while Michelangelo's hand moves purposely on. And in the section on Michelangelo there are also sexual overtones:

> The girls at puberty may find
> The first Adam in their thought,

Michelangelo, lying on his back facing the ceiling of the Sistine Chapel, was painting the Creation. Here is certainly a reference to Yeats' belief that sex was part of creativity—as he said, "The marriage bed is the symbol of the solved antimony."

The poem is not only pulled together by the refrain but by other repetitions. The first line of each stanza begins with *That* and the third line of each stanza contains a command—"Quiet the dog, tether the pony," "Move most gently," "Shut the door." As we look at each character, Caesar's hand is under his head, Helen's feet are practising a "tinker shuffle," and Michelangelo's hand "moves to and fro," like the hand of God at the moment of creation.

1. The poem deals with three very active persons. How does it create the sense of stillness?

2. What is accomplished by the refrain? (If it were omitted, what would be changed?)

3. Compare the mood of this poem with that of "Adam's Curse," and show how the differing moods are created.

Now for a couple of poems with a few discussion questions:

The Circus Animals' Desertion

I

I sought a theme and sought for it in vain,
I sought it daily for six weeks or so.
Maybe at last, being but a broken man,
I must be satisfied with my heart, although
Winter and summer till old age began
My circus animals were all on show,
Those stilted boys, that burnished chariot,
Lion and woman and the Lord knows what.

II

What can I but enumerate old themes?
First that sea-rider Oisin led by the nose
Through three enchanted islands, allegorical dreams,
Vain gaiety, vain battle, vain repose,
Themes of the embittered heart, or so it seems,
That might adorn old songs or courtly shows;
But what cared I that set him on to ride,
I, starved for the bosom of his faery bride?

And then a counter-truth filled out its play,
The Countess Cathleen was the name I gave it;
She, pity-crazed, had given her soul away,
But masterful Heaven had intervened to save it.
I thought my dear must her own soul destroy,
So did fanaticism and hate enslave it,
And this brought forth a dream and soon enough
This dream itself had all my thought and love.

And when the Fool and Blind Man stole the bread
Cuchulain fought the ungovernable sea;
Heart-mysteries there, and yet when all is said
It was the dream itself enchanted me:

Character isolated by a deed
To engross the present and dominate memory.
Players and painted stage took all my love,
And not those things that they were emblems of.

III

Those masterful images because complete
Grew in pure mind, but out of what began?
A mound of refuse or the sweepings of a street,
Old kettles, old bottles, and a broken can,
Old irons, old bones, old rags, that raving slut
Who keeps the till. Now that my ladder's gone,
I must lie down where all the ladders start,
In the foul rag-and-bone shop of the heart.

1. In general, what is the poet talking about in this poem?
2. What does "Lion and woman" refer to?
3. To whom does the second stanza refer?
4. Do the three final lines throw any light on the creative process as Yeats experienced it?

The Wild Swans at Coole

The trees are in their autumn beauty,
The woodland paths are dry,
Under the October twilight the water
Mirrors a still sky;
Upon the brimming water among the stones
Are nine-and-fifty swans.

The nineteenth autumn has come upon me
Since I first made my count;
I saw, before I had well finished,
All suddenly mount
And scatter wheeling in great broken rings
Upon their clamorous wings.

I have looked upon those brilliant creatures,
And now my heart is sore.
All's changed since I, hearing at twilight,
The first time on this shore,
The bell-beat of their wings above my head,
Trod with a lighter tread.

Unwearied still, lover by lover,
They paddle in the cold
Companionable streams or climb the air;
Their hearts have not grown old;
Passion or conquest, wander where they will,
Attend upon them still.

But now they drift on the still water,
Mysterious, beautiful;
Among what rushes will they build;
By what lake's edge or pool
Delight men's eyes when I awake some day
To find they have flown away?

1. What emotion does this poem express?
2. What characteristics of the swans are conveyed by the poem?
3. What is the effect of giving the exact number of the swans?
4. Does some kind of change of attitude or feeling occur in the course of the poem? If so, describe it.
5. The stanzas rhyme *ababcc.* Why do you think Yeats chose this form?

Finally, we include a few Yeats poems to read on your own.

The Lake Isle of Innisfree

I will arise and go now, and go to Innisfree,
And a small cabin build there, of clay and wattles made:
Nine bean-rows will I have there, a hive for the honeybee,
And live alone in the bee-loud glade.

And I shall have some peace there, for peace comes dropping slow,
Dropping from the veils of the morning to where the cricket sings;
There midnight's all a glimmer, and noon a purple glow,
And evening full of the linnet's wings.

I will arise and go now, for always night and day
I hear lake water lapping with low sounds by the shore;
While I stand on the roadway, or on the pavements grey,
I hear it in the deep heart's core.

No Second Troy

Why should I blame her that she filled my days
With misery, or that she would of late
Have taught to ignorant men most violent ways,
Or hurled the little streets upon the great,

Had they but courage equal to desire?
What could have made her peaceful with a mind
That nobleness made simple as a fire,
With beauty like a tightened bow, a kind
That is not natural in an age like this,
Being high and solitary and most stern?
Why, what could she have done, being what she is?
Was there another Troy for her to burn?

The Magi

Now as at all times I can see in the mind's eye,
In their stiff, painted clothes, the pale unsatisfied ones
Appear and disappear in the blue depth of the sky
With all their ancient faces like rain-beaten stones,
And all their helms of silver hovering side by side,
And all their eyes still fixed, hoping to find once more,
Being by Calvary's turbulence unsatisfied,
The uncontrollable mystery on the bestial floor.

Easter 1916

I have met them at close of day
Coming with vivid faces
From counter or desk among grey
Eighteenth-century houses.
I have passed with a nod of the head
Or polite meaningless words,
Or have lingered awhile and said
Polite meaningless words,
And thought before I had done
Of a mocking tale or a gibe
To please a companion
Around the fire at the club,
Being certain that they and I
But lived where motley is worn:
All changed, changed utterly:
A terrible beauty is born.

That woman's days were spent
In ignorant good-will,
Her nights in argument
Until her voice grew shrill.
What voice more sweet than hers
When, young and beautiful,

She rode to harriers?
This man had kept a school
And rode our wingèd horse;
This other his helper and friend
Was coming into his force;
He might have won fame in the end,
So sensitive his nature seemed,
So daring and sweet his thought.
This other man I had dreamed
A drunken, vainglorious lout.
He had done most bitter wrong
To some who are near my heart,
Yet I number him in the song;
He, too, has resigned his part
In the casual comedy;
He, too, has been changed in his turn,
Transformed utterly:
A terrible beauty is born.

Hearts with one purpose alone
Through summer and winter seem
Enchanted to a stone
To trouble the living stream.
The horse that comes from the road,
The rider, the birds that range
From cloud to tumbling cloud,
Minute by minute they change;
A shadow of cloud on the stream
Changes minute by minute;
A horse-hoof slides on the brim.
And a horse plashes within it;
The long-legged moor-hens dive,
And hens to moor-cocks call;
Minute by minute they live:
The stone's in the midst of all.

Too long a sacrifice
Can make a stone of the heart.
O when may it suffice?
That is Heaven's part, our part
To murmur name upon name,
As a mother names her child
When sleep at last has come
On limbs that had run wild.
What is it but nightfall?
No, no, not night but death;
Was it needless death after all?
For England may keep faith
For all that is done and said.

We know their dream; enough
To know they dreamed and are dead;
And what if excess of love
Bewildered them till they died?
I write it out in a verse—
MacDonagh and MacBride
And Connolly and Pearse
Now and in time to be,
Wherever green is worn,
Are changed, changed utterly:
A terrible beauty is born.

The Second Coming

Turning and turning in the widening gyre
The falcon cannot hear the falconer;
Things fall apart; the centre cannot hold;
Mere anarchy is loosed upon the world,
The blood-dimmed tide is loosed, and everywhere
The ceremony of innocence is drowned;
The best lack all conviction, while the worst
Are full of passionate intensity.

Surely some revelation is at hand;
Surely the Second Coming is at hand.
The Second Coming! Hardly are those words out
When a vast image out of *Spiritus Mundi*
Troubles my sight: somewhere in sands of the desert
A shape with lion body and the head of a man,
A gaze blank and pitiless as the sun,
Is moving its slow thighs, while all about it
Reel shadows of the indignant desert birds.
The darkness drops again; but now I know
That twenty centuries of stony sleep
Were vexed to nightmare by a rocking cradle,
And what rough beast, its hour come round at last,
Slouches towards Bethlehem to be born?

Sailing to Byzantium

I

That is no country for old men. The young
In one another's arms, birds in the trees
—Those dying generations—at their song,
The salmon-falls, the mackerel-crowded seas,
Fish, flesh, or fowl, commend all summer long
Whatever is begotten, born, and dies.
Caught in that sensual music all neglect
Monuments of unageing intellect.

II

An aged man is but a paltry thing,
A tattered coat upon a stick, unless
Soul clap its hands and sing, and louder sing
For every tatter in its mortal dress,
Nor is there singing school but studying
Monuments of its own magnificence;
And therefore I have sailed the seas and come
To the holy city of Byzantium.

III

O sages standing in God's holy fire
As in the gold mosaic of a wall,
Come from the holy fire, perne in a gyre,
And be the singing-masters of my soul.
Consume my heart away; sick with desire
And fastened to a dying animal
It knows not what it is; and gather me
Into the artifice of eternity.

IV

Once out of nature I shall never take
My bodily form from any natural thing,
But such a form as Grecian goldsmiths make
Of hammered gold and gold enamelling
To keep a drowsy Emperor awake;
Or set upon a golden bough to sing
To lords and ladies of Byzantium
Of what is past, or passing, or to come.

SELECTIVE BIBLIOGRAPHY

The edition of Yeats' poetry used in this text is *The Collected Poems of W.B. Yeats* (New York: Macmillan, 1958).

Harold Bloom, *Yeats* (New York: Oxford University Press, 1970).

Denis Donoghue, *William Butler Yeats* (New York: Viking, 1971).

Denis Donoghue and J.P. Mulryne, eds., *An Honored Guest,* (London: Edward Arnold, 1965).

Richard Ellmann, *Yeats, The Man and the Masks* (New York: Dutton Paperback, 1948).

Richard Ellmann, *The Identity of Yeats* (New York: Oxford University Press, 1964).

T.R. Henn, *The Lonely Tower* (New York: Barnes and Noble; London: Methuen, 1965).

Daniel Hoffman, *Barbarous Knowledge, Myth in the Poetry of Yeats, Graves and Muir* (New York: Oxford University Press, 1967).

Norman Jeffares, *A Commentary on the Collected Poems of W.B. Yeats* (Stanford: Stanford University Press, 1968).

Vivienne Koch, *W. B. Yeats, the Tragic Phase: A Study of the Last Poems* (Baltimore: John Hopkins University Press, 1951).

Jon Stallworthy, *Between the Lines: Yeats' Poetry in the Making* (Oxford: Clarendon Press, 1963).

A. G. Stock, *W. B. Yeats, His Poetry and Thought* (Cambridge, England: Cambridge University Press, 1964).

John Unterecker, *A Reader's Guide to William Butler Yeats* (New York: Octagon, 1971).

John Unterecker, ed., *Yeats: A Collection of Critical Essays* (Englewood Cliffs, N.J.: Prentice-Hall, 1963).

William Butler Yeats, *The Autobiography* (New York: Collier, 1971).

Letters on Poetry from W.B. Yeats to Dorothy Wellesley (Oxford Paperbacks, 1964).

For a student who wants to probe more deeply we suggest also W. B. Yeats, *A Vision* (New York: Macmillan, 1956).

Robert Frost

His Life

The paradoxes in Robert Frost's life began early. Although he was eventually acclaimed as the archetypal New England poet, his mother, Isabelle Moodie, was born near Edinburgh, Scotland. His father, William Prescott Frost, was so alienated from his New England background that he took his bride to San Francisco (where he worked as a journalist) and named his first child Robert Lee Frost (1874), in honor of the Confederacy's foremost general.

Young Robert was only eleven when his father died of tuberculosis. Mrs. Frost, with Robert and his sister, traveled east to fulfill her husband's paradoxical deathbed desire to be buried in his ancestral New England. She remained in the area, where she had relatives, and supported herself and the two children by school teaching.

Until the age of twelve, Robert Frost had never read an entire book on his own initiative. He impressed his neighbors as lazy and aimless. His four years in the Lawrence (Mass.) high school marked an intellectual turning point. He did well in his courses and tied for valedictorian honors with Elinor White. They fell in love and had a stormy courtship, intensified by Frost's extreme fits of jealousy. At one stage, when their relationship was going badly, he destroyed his copy of a booklet of poems he had printed for her to celebrate the first poem he sold to a newspaper, and ran away to the Dismal Swamp in Virginia. Eventually, three years after graduation from high school, the two were married. In the interim, Frost had attended Dartmouth for part of a semester, worked as a gate-tender, taught school, and had a stint of newspaper reporting.

Two years after his marriage he entered Harvard as a special student, but dropped out two years later. Meanwhile, children came in rapid succession, and the financial prospects of the family seemed dim. Finally, his paternal grandfather willed him a fairly substantial annuity, and gave him a small farm at Derry, New Hampshire, on condition that he would stay there for ten years. Frost proved better at celebrating the life of a small farmer than being one, and within a few years was teaching school again. Meanwhile, he published a few poems here and there, but his name remained almost totally unknown to the reading public.

In late 1911 he sold the Derry farm and the next year sailed with his family to England. There he became acquainted with many of the most significant young British poets, and formed a strong friendship with one of them, Edward Thomas, later killed in World War I. Of more practical importance was the American Poet, Ezra Pound, who vigorously promoted Frost's poetry. Two books, *A Boy's Will* and *North of Boston,* were published in England during Frost's time there. When he and his family returned to the United States in early 1915 the second book had already come out in an American edition, and the poet found himself something of a celebrity, a reputation that steadily increased with his successive books and frequent poetry readings.

The pattern of his mature life began to take shape. Primarily, he wrote and published poetry, and received increasing honors—including scores of honorary degrees and four Pulitzers. Frequently, for a short period of time or for several years, he served as a poet-in-residence; his association with Amherst was particularly long-lived. He was in great demand to read his own poetry, and gradually developed an individual style of presentation—the poems slowly read in a strong New England accent, with salty commentaries between poems in which the poet paid his tart respects to the human scene and to his poetic or political enemies. He became an American institution. Congress twice hailed him on his birthday, he read a poem at President Kennedy's inauguration, and Kennedy sent him on a goodwill mission to Russia which climaxed when Khrushchev visited him at his sickbed and the two had an extended conversation on international relations. He long outlived his wife, wrote and published poetry almost to the end, and died in 1963 at the age of 88.

The Poet and His Poetry

A favorite word with Robert Frost was "contraries," and his life was full of them. The "mask" he wore for his public readings was that of the shrewd, tough-minded, but stable cracker-barrel philosopher. Inwardly he was an extremely unstable person, subject to suicidal and murderous impulses, close to paranoia, keeping a loaded revolver always close at hand. He must have been a difficult husband and father, yet his letters reveal that one of his most frequent activities was sending substantial checks to his grown-up children when they were in difficulties. He was so jealous of rival poets that in conversations 40 years after his rise to fame he was still compulsively belittling Edgar Lee Masters, who at one time was frequently mentioned with Frost as a "new poet" of equal stature. But another favorite word of Frost's was "magnanimity," and he was one of the small group of influential literary people who secured the release of a formidable poetic competitor, Ezra Pound, from St. Elizabeth's Hospital in Washington.

His personal ife was shot through with afflictions and griefs. Of his six children, two died in infancy, one of childbed fever, one committed suicide, and another went insane. His relationship with his wife, while probably a deep one, was also tormented, with his rages matched against her long silences. Only gradually, with the publication of his letters and the Thompson biography has the full extent of his psychological turmoil become generally known. The "mask" he wore in public was perhaps as much to protect himself from full knowledge of his own dark depths as to give the public what it wanted. At any rate, he was not a simple man, and his poetry is far less simple—and often much darker—than it appears on the surface.

Frost would never pin himself down to one final philosophic position. At times he pictures the universe as bleakly as Thomas Hardy, at other times he suggests the possibility of ultimate meaning—like the "something" working contrary to entropy in "West-Running Brook"—but will not give it a name. An Old Testament understanding of God pervades his thinking and feeling, but he has nothing to do with conventional religion, and is perfectly ready like Job to argue with God. There is in his poetry a sense of lurking perils; man's toehold on earth and sanity itself are fragile and not to be counted on. All the same, some of the most powerful poems affirm man's survival despite the dark and frightening universe he inhabits.

He was the supreme individualist. A pioneer college dropout, he encouraged his best students to do likewise. He was equally contemptuous of conformist religion and standardized agnosticism. He satirized materialistic money-grubbing, but attacked with great venom the social planning and do-good-ism of Franklin Roosevelt's New Deal program. He always seemed a minority of one, and visibly enjoyed the role. What he believed in with most constancy was himself and his talent, although there were long stretches of time when he doubted both. He also respected the archaic, small-scale way of life of northern New England, but he did not romanticize it.

A reader of Frost should not be deceived by his apparently conventional poetic technique. His modernity was not in the forms but what he did with them. For example, his blank verse can echo the actual rhythms of informal conversation in a way that not much previous poetry had done as sensitively. He was basically as "modern" a poet as Eliot or Pound, but his "mask" long deceived the public, the literary critics, and perhaps at times himself.

Frost is often thought of as a "nature poet." The term needs qualification. He uses nature and its moods for symbols of the human condition, and he frequently sets his human dramas within the framework of nature. But there is little in his poetry to suggest an identity between man and nature. He is fundamentally a humanist poet in the sense that his concern is man and individual men and women.

He had a very strong sense of history—America's first of all, but the human story in general. Unlike other poets who see the world as changing for better or worse, Frost saw it as essentially what it has always been. "The time was neither wrong nor right," he says in "Acquainted with the Night."

In his life and in his poetry Frost was a man of "contraries." He dramatizes the tension of light and dark, past and present, man and nature. He does not settle for easy answers; the tensions and questions remain.

Most of Frost's memorable poems were written in early adulthood and middle age. But to the end he occasionally wrote poems of surprising beauty and power, mingled with cute or crochety versifications. A selection of his best work would make a volume of several hundred pages. By any set of standards, he is one of four or five contestants for the honor of being the greatest poet America has yet produced.

First, a short and seemingly simple poem. The general picture it paints can be taken in on the first reading.

Design

I found a dimpled spider, fat and white,
On a white heal-all, holding up a moth
Like a white piece of rigid satin cloth—
Assorted characters of death and blight
Mixed ready to begin the morning right,
Like the ingredients of a witches' broth—
A snow-drop spider, a flower like a froth,
And dead wings carried like a paper kite.

What had that flower to do with being white,
The wayside blue and innocent heal-all?
What brought the kindred spider to that height,
Then steered the white moth thither in the night?
What but design of darkness to appall?—
If design govern in a thing so small.

Before asking yourself whether a poem is on several levels, it is a good idea to experience the most obvious level fully. Here is a picture dominated by the color white. The word *white* by itself suggests purity and splendor. But *white* is a two-sided word. You can also speak of someone's turning "white with fear."

In Frost's poem, the connotations of *white* are sinister. The very word *spider* evokes impressions of a creature not generally admired for its beauty, and the combination of *fat* and *white* in the first line suggests a repulsive creature indecently gorged with its prey. If Frost had refered in line 3 to merely a white piece of satin cloth, a pleasing picture would have been created, but by adding *rigid* a tone suggesting lifelessness and death is added. The beautiful phrase in line 7, "a flower like a froth," cannot undo the associations which have already been established. Innocent beauty is engulfed in something gruesome. Line 8, with its "dead wings carried like a paper kite," drives home the deadly implications of whiteness in the poem. The actively alive character is the obscenely fat, white, and dimpled spider (the word *dimpled* gets twisted from its pleasant meaning) and the white wings of the moth, normally a thing of grace and beauty, are dead and stiff.

This does not quite exhaust the implications of white. When the poem refers to "a white heal-all," the word *white* is not superfluous. The heal-all, a low plant also called selfheal and used in folk medicine, usually has purple or blue blossoms. A white variant occasionally occurs, as in this instance, completing the corruption of that color. The name of the plant also seems to have an ironic touch—the flower has not healed anything for the moth. Another example of irony is the description of the "snowdrop spider." The snowdrop is an early blossoming plant with a single, delicate white flower.

Some poets would be content to let the philosophical meaning of the poem emerge from a series of pictures, such as those just discussed. Frost typically takes a double-pronged approach. He suggests meaning by creating pictures, and then spells it out more explicitly. The middle lines of the first stanza comment on the picture that has been created—"Assorted characters of death and blight / Mixed ready to begin the morning right, / Like the ingredients of a witches' broth—". Any lingering idea that this is a poem about the innocent charm of nature is abruptly negated. It is not mere death that is pictured here, but something evil, like the activities of the three witches in *Macbeth.*

By the end of the first stanza the goodness and beauty of nature have been revealed as a comfortable illusion. In the final stanza the poem moves into a series of agonized questions like those Job asked the Lord. Has some will or force brought about the coincidence of the spider and the moth? Who, what?

At this point, the poem seems to reach a climax of evil forebodings in line 13—"What but design of darkness to appall?" It is the old and agonizing question when goodness and beauty are overshelmed by evil and ugliness. Is it possible that the universe is not merely a physical *darkness* but a moral darkness? Does some evil intelligence have the final word—in human life and in the life of nature?

And yet, the poem does not end at this point. It has one further and more frightening possibility to suggest—"If design govern in a thing so small." An evil universe would still be one with order and design. Events would not be random. They would represent the will of the universe. But suppose there is no order, no design. Suppose everything is random. Shakespeare writing *Macbeth* or a dimpled spider and moth coming to the same flower in the dead of night—both are the results of sheer accident, blind chance. Therefore; no meaning to anything, not even to the words *good* and *evil.*

The question is left unanswered. The fall-back position is that there is a *design of darkness* to appall. The one untenable position, in terms of this particular poem, is that which finds an easy and cheerful meaning in all the operations of the universe.

At this point the poem, "Design," is in danger of turning into a philosophic treatise. In particular, we may lose sight of several things that make it a poem, not a formal essay.

For instance, there are odd and often humorous combinations of words. One expects to see a dimpled child, but not a dimpled spider. The phrase, "Assorted characters of death and blight" suggest loungers in a bar or police court.

"Mixed ready to begin the morning right" has an ironic ring—begin the morning right from whose viewpoint? The spider's? The first stanza thus has a deliberately mixed tone, jolly and grisly at the same time. It is serious but not solemn as it introduces the final stanza in which both the humorous and bizarre details fade away and the plain questions are addressed to existence.

The use of the rhyme words is worth noticing. *Right* is pronounced the same as *rite,* and almost inevitably the reader takes line 5 as a pun—"begin the morning rite."[1] This imparts the flavor of an obscene ceremony, a kind of Black Mass mocking the wholesome aspects of nature. Another word with complex implications is *appall* in line 13. Its modern meaning is "to fill with dismay or horror," but the word retains something of the flavor it had in Old French, when it meant "to turn pale." Thus *appall* reinforces the earlier references to *fat and white, white heal-all,* etc.

By this time you may feel there has been enough talk *about* the poem. This reaction is a wholesome one. In reading a poem, you start out with your own spontaneous reaction to it. Then you examine the poem in more detail, trying to see "how it works" and whether there are levels of meaning and feeling that escaped your first reading. This stage is the one that literary critics concentrate on. But there is a further stage when you return to the poem and read it in as relaxed a way as you did the first time. If stage two has worked, you will discover your first reaction to the poem still alive in all its spontaneity, but now enriched by any understandings the deeper study has given you. The goal is to respond spontaneously, but more deeply and richly.

1. If all you knew about Frost was that he wrote this poem, what impression would you have of his personality? Refer to specific parts of the poem.
2. Why do you think Frost chose the heal-all as the flower in the poem?
3. Why do you think he used the verb *brought* to refer to the spider and *steered* for the moth?
4. Compare the theme of this poem with that of Blake's "The Tyger."

Another poem in which "whiteness" plays a controlling part is this one:

The Onset

Always the same, when on a fated night
At last the gathered snow lets down as white
As may be in dark woods, and with a song
It shall not make again all winter long
Of hissing on the yet uncovered ground,

[1] For an interesting discussion, see Reuben A. Brower, *The Poetry of Robert Frost* (New York: Oxford University Press, 1963), pp. 102-08.

I almost stumble looking up and round,
As one who overtaken by the end
Gives up his errand, and lets death descend
Upon him where he is, with nothing done
To evil, no important triumph won,
More than if life had never been begun.

Yet all the precedent is on my side:
I know that winter death has never tried
The earth but it has failed: the snow may heap
In long storms an undrifted four feet deep
As measured against maple, birch, and oak,
It cannot check the peeper's silver croak;
And I shall see the snow all go downhill
In water of a slender April rill
That flashes tail through last year's withered brake
And dead weeds, like a disappearing snake.
Nothing will be left white but here a birch,
And there a clump of houses with a church.

The poem begins with *a fated night* when the masses of snow descend, signaling the start of the long New England winter. The poem ends with the disappearance of snow, when the only white things left are the birch, alive after the long winter, and the clump of *houses with a church* which also have outlasted the white snow.

If this poem is compared with "Design," you can see that the word, *white,* does not have one fixed and standardized connotation. In "Design," the multiple associations of *white* are the contrast between purity and innocence on one hand, and evil and death on the other. In "The Onset" *white* first suggests the power of nature, oblivious of man's existence and desires. Then, by a reversal of associations, the word becomes "humanized" at the end, recalling not the blind power of winter storms, but man's activities and achievements—houses, a church. Winters come and go, snow falls and finally melts, but man's imprint on the earth—a clump of houses with a church—remains.

So much for the general theme of the poem, which represents the poet in one of his more affirming moods. But to leave it at that is to turn the poem into a dry prose paraphrase. The reader is not a distant observer of a yearly process; he is caught up in it, so that in imagination he experiences the yearly cycle of death and renewal.

The tone that dominates the first stanza is inevitability. "Always the same" points to the annual nature of the event. It may come earlier or later, but it always comes, "on a fated night." The snow that has been biding its time descends in the "dark woods." Whiteness and darkness now combine to give a double picture of death, with all bright colors banished. The sense of the finality of winter is heightened by the lines, "with a song / It shall not make again all winter long / Of hissing on the yet uncovered ground." The lingering warmth of the earth is being dissipated by the falling snow, and the world is left to the white, cold death of winter.

The feeling of a find of paralysis in nature and man is developed in the following lines:

> I almost stumble looking up and round,
> As one who overtaken by the end
> Gives up his errand, and lets death descend
> Upon him where he is . . .

Each reader will have a different mental picture here. Some may think of pioneer days and a person caught by a sudden blizzard between two widely separated houses. To others it may recall tragedies of arctic exploration. In the poem, however, the ground is "yet uncovered"; the enveloping death has merely given its first signals. The imagination of the speaker translates the warning into a fact of the immediate future. A failure of will is implied, the inability to struggle against odds that will soon be hopeless. All memory of past life seems empty and unreal—"More than if life had never been begun."

One technical feature of the poem is significant at this point. For the most part, the poem is written in rhymed couplets, but at the end of the first section the rhyme is repeated three times—done, won, begun. The extra rhyme in a passage of rhyming couplets is a device often used by poets to accentuate the sense of finality. If Frost had stopped with *no important triumph won,* the section would have seemed complete. But by adding "More than if life had never been begun" he intensified the negative conclusion.

The second stanza, in contrast with the first, is based on the demonstrated certainty that winter does not last forever—"Yet all the precedent is on my side: / I know that winter death has never tried / The earth but it has failed . . . " The disappearance of snow in the spring is summarized in two pictures. One is that of the peeper (tree frog) with his sounds both beautiful and unesthetic—but suggesting vibrant life awaking from a long sleep—a "silver croak." The peeper is a kind of natural pioneer, symbolizing nature as it rises to new life from the long embrace by snow. The other picture is—

> And I shall see the snow all go downhill
> In water of a slender April rill
> That flashes tail through last year's withered brake
> And dead weeds, like a disappearing snake.

The poem has come almost full circle. At the onset of winter, there was "hissing on the yet uncovered ground." In retrospect, this hissing points toward the final melting of the snow, when it disappears in snake-like rills through the dead vegetation of last year. Perhaps it is not too fanciful to imagine that winter came putting an evil charm of silence and sleep over the earth, as though a cosmic serpent had cast a paralyzing spell, and now the spell has been undone as the peeper practices his silver croak and the masses of snow change into life-giving water disappearing with the sinuous movements of a snake through "the withered brake" of last year. Whiteness has been routed, by some force within nature itself. All that is left white is friendly to life—the birch tree, a clump of houses, a church.

This is a simpler, more direct poem than "Design." It has a clear-cut philosophic stance that the poet dramatizes—in this one poem at least. The two poems, however, both inquire into the nature of reality—is it random or meaningful? Good, evil, or neutral? Focused on life or death? Some questions that may suggest further dimensions are offered below.

1. "Design" is a sonnet. "The Onset" is written in rhymed couplets. Do you think the choice was arbitrary on the part of the poet? Or does the rhyme scheme of each poem have something to do with the effect the poet is trying to create?

2. If the tone of "Design" is "jolly-grisly," how would you describe the tone of "The Onset"? Is the tone maintained throughout, or does the poet contradict it at places?

3. Discuss the ways in which Frost creates a tension between an affirmative and a negative view in this poem.

4. Frost's use of adjectives is often interesting. Why do you think he chose these particular ones?—fated (line 1), gathered (2), dark (3), important (10), slender (19), disappearing (21).

5. A symbol is often capable of more than one significance in the context of different poems. Compare Frost's use of snake imagery in "The Onset" with Blake's in "I Saw a Chapel All of Gold" (page 55).

6. One rather odd phrase in "The Onset" is "with nothing done to evil." What does this phrase accomplish?

Sometimes Frost built an entire short poem on one image. An example:

Moon Compasses

I stole forth dimly in the dripping pause
Between two downpours to see what there was.
And a masked moon had spread down compass rays
To a cone mountain in the midnight haze,

As if the final estimate were hers;
And as it measured in her calipers,
The mountain stood exalted in its place.
So love will take between the hands a face . . .

Before looking at the way the imagery functions here, something should be said about the sound effects. Frost is not a poet who uses rhyme for the sake of using rhyme, nor is he intoxicated by the sheer music that a poem can create. The meaning of a poem is always paramount with him, and particular sound effects are integrated with the meaning, contributing to it and intensifying its impact. For this reason, there seems at first something odd about the unusual amount of alliteration in such a short poem. Is the poet simply trying to create a rich texture by using alliteration scattered throughout the poem, or is something more involved?

The sounds that alliterate are *d, m,* and *c:*

dimly	masked	compass
dripping	moon	cone
downpours	mountain	calipers
	measured	
	mountain	

The alliteration of the sound of *m* runs through most of the poem. *M* is a soft, humming sound that can be prolonged indefinitely. It seems to provide a kind of acoustical background to the poem, a quiet and gentle music.

Of more interest is the way the three alliterating sounds fall into groups that strengthen the meaning of the poem. The words alliterating on *d*—dimly, dripping, downpours—all serve to set the physical scene in which the poem takes place. The words alliterating on *m* emphasize the relation between the moon and the mountain. And the words alliterating on *c* all relate to the process of measuring or caressing.

Now looking at the poem as a whole—notice first how a quiet, subdued tone is established at the beginning. To "steal forth" suggests a quiet, almost clandestine walk. "Dimly" emphasizes the subdued tone. "Between two downpours" has a quality of lull, of momentary stillness. The very vagueness of "to see what there was" fits the quiet, tentative mood so far established.

With the third line the basic imagery is introduced. "Compass rays" from the moon are touching a "cone mountain." *Cone* is a term from geometry, as is also *compass* in its several meanings. A compass is first of all an instrument for indicating directions; the needle points north and the other directions are fixed in their relation to the north. The lines on a circular compass start at the center and radiate outward in all directions. The moon, then, is like the fixed point at the center of a compass, and its rays reach out to the mountain, which is described as a cone, as though the whole scene were an illustration in a geometry textbook.

But *compass* has an additional meaning which seems to be dominant as the poem goes on. This second kind of compass consists of two legs that can be brought closer together or farther apart. It can be used for drawing circles of varying size, and it is also used (like *calipers,* mentioned later in the poem) to measure diameters.

There is always the risk of overinterpreting a poem, but in "Moon Compasses" there does seem a progression in the way the compass image is used. At its first appearance it suggests the type of compass used for telling directions. The rays are coming from the moon as if it were the center of the compass. Then the meaning of compass shifts toward the type that is used like calipers to measure diameters. Such a compass measures by grasping the object between its two moveable legs. The moon is taking the measure of the mountain, and the mountain gleams in the rays of the measuring moon.

Looked at one way, the moon is dominating the mountain, even imprisoning it between the legs of the calipers. But it is a domination that glorifies, because it is not really domination at all, but the embrace of a lover. The transition to the human meaning of the poem comes in "The mountain stood exalted in its place." In the last line, the analogy is summarized: "So love will take between the hands a face . . . "

What began as a brief nature description (lines 1 and 2) has moved into a complex symbolism involving moon and mountain and their relation; all this as a symbol of love. The plain, human meaning is given in the last line. But that line by itself is empty; it is full only because the reader experiences it as the climax and affirmation of what has been said in terms of geometrical procedures. From nature, to geometry, to human relationship—this is the movement of the poem. The reader is left with a sense of love as precise as geometry, as radiant as rays from the moon, as mysterious as a hazy night, as torrential as downpours of rain.

In thinking about the following questions, try to keep the poem as a whole in mind. You are concerned with how particular phrases or lines operate in the framework of the complete poem.

1. In the phrase "masked moon" do you think *masked* serves any purpose beyond simple description?

2. Suppose the fifth line ("As if the final estimate were hers") were omitted. Disregard the violence this would do to the rhyme scheme. Would the effect of the poem be altered in any way? If so, how?

3. Look up *exalt* in a good dictionary. How many different shades of meaning do you think it has in line 7?

4. Reread Donne, "A Valediction: Forbidding Mourning" (page 27). Discuss similarities and differences in the way he and Frost have used compasses as a symbol.

Many of Frost's best-known poems, particularly psychological narratives like "The Death of the Hired Man" and "Home Burial," are written in blank verse—unrhymed iambic pentameter. This verse line came into existence in English poetry shortly before the time of Shakespeare, and has had a long and vigorous history.

Iambic rhythm is close to the natural rhythm of English speech. If you say, "I went to town to buy some shoes" you are speaking in iambic rhythm. Many quite ordinary sentences, when the speaker has no poetic intentions, come out as iambic. If you took the above sentence and changed it to "I went to town to buy a pair of shoes" it would be blank verse—unrhymed iambic pentameter:

Ĭ wént tŏ tówn tŏ búy ă páir ŏf shóes

Iambic rhythm is the least artificial of the meters commonly used in English poetry, because it is closest to normal speech. When used with a certain regularity in a poem, it sounds like a kind of heightened speech instead of something clearly distinct from prose conversation. For this reason it is especially useful in plays and in poems where a conversational quality is desired.

It is easy to understand why iambic rhythm has attracted poets as diverse as Shakespeare and Frost, but why did they settle on the five-foot line? Here one can only speculate. Perhaps the reason is that a line of poetry tends to have a slight pause somewhere in it even if the punctuation doesn't indicate this. For example, "I went to town to buy some shoes" has a slight break in the thought, after *town.* "I went to town (pause) to buy some shoes." Each half consists of two iambic feet. In the longer version, the sentence breaks into one unit of two feet and one of three feet—"I went to town (pause) to buy a pair of shoes." A poem written in lines of four or six iambic feet might become monotonous and singsongy because the pause would usually come squarely in the middle. A five-foot line avoids that. If there is a pause, one half of the line will be longer than the other. Perhaps it is this very asymmetry that poets find more interesting than the simpler patterns of meter and pauses dictated by an iambic line with an even number of feet.

The poets who have used blank verse most skillfully have not been content with a metronome regularity of rhythm. Iambic pentameter is the norm, but they constantly introduce variations, partly for variety, and partly to echo the speech patterns of the human voice as it responds to various emotions.

Here are a couple of examples from Frost's poems. In each case, the actual way the line would be stressed in conversation is indicated above the line, and the theoretical iambic rhythm is given beneath. First, a line from "Moon Compasses" to illustrate absolutely regular iambic pentameter:

Sŏ lóve wĭll táke bĕtwéen thĕ hánds ă fáce . . .
˘ ´ ˘ ´ ˘ ´ ˘ ´ ˘ ´

The actual rhythm (above the line) and the theoretical rhythm (below the line) correspond exactly. This is an instance of strict iambic rhythm.

According to the conventions of metrics, the line could be modified by adding an unstressed syllable at the end. Thus, if one changed the line to "So love will take between the hands a kitten," the line would still be considered regular.

But regularity is almost as much the exception as the rule in Frost. He constantly diverges from the strict norm, comes back to it, diverges again. Take two lines from "The Death of the Hired Man":

> Something you somehow haven't to deserve.

> At his age for the little he can do?

Read each of these lines aloud. First read it naturally, then read it as though it were strict iambic rhythm. You will quickly discover how artificial the latter sounds. The first line has only three iambic feet if read naturally (second, third, fifth). The first foot is the opposite of iambic—trochaic. The fourth foot consists of two unstressed syllables, technically called a *pyrrhic* foot. As for the second line, much depends on whether your natural reading stresses *his* and *he.* Here the *his* is treated as stressed, *he* as unstressed. This way of reading the lines gives only two strict iambic feet—the third and fifth.

It is important to remember that, in the hands of a good poet, these variations from iambic rhythm (or from any other meter) are usually a mark of skill, not ignorance. The poet is creating a far more subtle and life like rhythm than he would achieve by a monotonous adherence to the strict rhythm.

The next poem is a good example of the subtle changes that can be rung on the basic blank verse line.

West-Running Brook

"Fred, where is north?"
"North? North is there, my love.
The brook runs west."
"West-Running Brook then call it."
(West-Running Brook men call it to this day.)
"What does it think it's doing running west
When all the other country brooks flow east
To reach the ocean? It must be the brook
Can trust itself to go by contraries
The way I can with you—and you with me—
Because we're—we're—I don't know what we are.
What are we?"
Young or new?"
"We must be something.
We've said we two. Let's change that to we three.

As you and I are married to each other,
We'll both be married to the brook. We'll build
Our bridge across it, and the bridge shall be
Our arm thrown over it asleep beside it.
Look, look, it's waving to us with a wave
To let us know it hears me."
"Why, my dear,
That wave's been standing off this jut of shore—"
(The black stream, catching on a sunken rock,
Flung backward on itself in one white wave,
And the white water rode the black forever,
Not gaining but not losing, like a bird
White feathers from the struggle of whose breast
Flecked the dark stream and flecked the darker pool
Below the point, and were at last driven wrinkled
In a white scarf against the far-shore alders.)
"That wave's been standing off this jut of shore
Ever since rivers, I was going to say,
Were made in heaven. It wasn't waved to us.

"It wasn't, yet it was. If not to you,
It was to me—in an annunciation."

"Oh, if you take it off to lady-land,
As't were the country of the Amazons
We men must see you to the confines of
And leave you there, ourselves forbid to enter—
It is your brook! I have no more to say."

"Yes, you have, too. Go on. You thought of something."

"Speaking of contraries, see how the brook
In that white wave runs counter to itself.
It is from that in water we were from
Long, long before we were from any creature.
Here we, in our impatience of the steps,
Get back to the beginning of beginnings,
The stream of everything that runs away.
Some say existence like a Pirouot
And Pirouette, forever in one place,
Stands still and dances, but it runs away;
It seriously, sadly, runs away
To fill the abyss's void with emptiness.
It flows beside us in this water brook,
But it flows over us. It flows between us
To separate us for a panic moment.
It flows between us, over us, and *with* us.
And it is time, strength, tone, light, life, and love—
And even substance lapsing unsubstantial;
The universal cataract of death

That spends to nothingness—and unresisted,
Save by some strange resistance in itself,
Not just a swerving, but a throwing back,
As if regret were in it and were sacred.
It has this throwing backward on itself
So that the fall of most of it is always
Raising a little, sending up a little.
Our life runs down in sending up the clock.
The brook runs down in sending up our life.
The sun runs down in sending up the brook.
And there is something sending up the sun.
It is this backward motion toward the source,
Against the stream, that most we see ourselves in,
The tribute of the current to the source.
It is from this in nature we are from.
It is most us."
"Today will be the day
You said so."
"No, today will be the day
You said the brook was called West-Running Brook."

"Today will be the day of what we both said."

This is a dramatic dialogue, but with a third voice—a commentator functioning like the chorus in a Greek play. The two characters in the drama are a man and woman, married, apparently young and wandering together like an Adam and Eve intent on giving names to their discoveries.

The personalities of the two are sharply etched. The wife sees everything as personal. She imagines the brook as going "by contraries / The way I can with you," and describes it as "waving to us with a wave / To let us know it hears me." The brook becomes an "annunciation" to her, evoking memories of the time when the angel Gabriel came to Mary to prophesy the birth of Jesus. And the wife has the final word, still personal, when she sums up the discovery of the brook: " 'Today will be the day of what we both said.' "

Fred, her husband, is scientific and philosophic. He gives a naturalistic explanation of why the white wave goes counter to the direction of the brook, and his response to his wife's talk of annunciation is in words reflecting traditional male views of women:

"Oh, if you take it off to lady-land,
As't were the country of the Amazons
We men must see you to the confines of
And leave you there, ourselves forbid to enter—"

Shortly afterward he launches into a long philosophic monologue in which the flowing brook and its contrary white wave become symbols of the way the universe operates.

The poem on the simplest level is a narrative about a husband and wife who discover a brook, name it, and talk about it. It is also two characterizations, with the brook serving to bring out the traits of the two and facets of their relation. But beyond this, it is one of the poems in which Frost most fully dramatizes a way of looking at reality and man's place in it. The warning given earlier would apply here—one should not assume that a finished and final philosophic system is presented in "West Running Brook." Frost's philosophic poems always maintain an "as if" or "possibly" quality.

Frost frequently uses a kind of natural symbolism. Thus he can be distinguished from Yeats, for example, who wrote a book to explain his private system of symbols, and freely scatters such private symbols as *gyres* (see page 136) through his poems. Frost inclined more toward using public symbols. A road forking in two directions is a public symbol, suggesting the necessity of choice, and so Frost uses it in "The Road Not Taken." A stream is another natural symbol. The pre-Socratic philosopher, Heraclitus, used it as a symbol of the endless processes of nature. It has been often used to suggest the idea of continuity within constant change, and it is a natural symbol of the course of life, headed always downhill toward the final ocean.

First of all, the brook perversely runs west even though the other neighborhood streams dutifully run east, toward the sea. Presumably somewhere along the way the brook will turn east, but for the moment it is defying the normal course of events.

A still more significant fact is that the brook, as the result of a hidden rock, perpetually generates a wave that runs counter to the direction of the current. The commentator describes this at length; it seems the symbolic center of the poem. The sunken rock remains invisible; one knows it is there only by the results. The stream is black, but the contrary wave is white, and the white wave rides the black water; brightness is lifted higher than darkness, brightness rising above the level of a stream that steadily loses altitude as it meanders toward the ultimate sea. The husband meditates:

> "Speaking of contraries, see how the brook
> In that white waves runs counter to itself.
> It is from that in water we were from
> Long, long before we were from any creature."

The flow of the brook downhill toward the eventual and inevitable sea suggests individual and collective death. The modern imagination, influenced by science, is haunted by a vision of a universe that ultimately "runs down" into a condition of total entropy. The brook, by itself, is a natural symbol of this process, with two differences: One, though the individual drops of water in the brook inevitably reach the finality of the ocean, the brook continues to flow. As a process it goes on indefinitely. This would suggest that though lives end, life continues. The second difference is that this particular brook wilfully goes in the wrong direction and simultaneously sends up a wave of a different color, going in a direction opposite to its current.

The husband recognizes the brook as a symbol of time and death, but he sees in the backward-flung wave a power at work contrary to universal entropy:

The universal cataract of death
That spends to nothingness—and unresisted,
Save by some strange resistance in itself,
Not just a swerving, but a throwing back,
As if regret were in it and were sacred.
It has this throwing backward on itself
So that the fall of most of it is always
Raising a little, sending up a little.

He then talks of "sending up." Entropy is not simple exhaustion and annihilation, but somehow imparts new energy to other things—"Our life runs down in sending up the clock."—"The brook runs down in sending up our life." He adds, "And there is something sending up the sun."

At this point, the husband seems to be suggesting some ultimate source of power and life, from which everything else derives its ability to run counter to the ceaseless movement toward silence and death. And man is somehow of one nature with this source:

It is this backward motion toward the source,
Against the stream, that most we see ourselves in,
The tribute of the current to the source.
It is from this in nature we are from.
It is most us.

It is vital to note that the poet does not imprison himself in a dogmatic philosophic position. The force that is "sending up the sun" is not named as God or given any scientific title. It is simply and vaguely *something.* But what the elaborated symbolism of the brook does suggest is that the very nature of the universe has built into it a drive going counter to death and entropy. Man, with his restlessness and Faustian longing to transcend the limitations of his creaturely condition, is responding to the nature of the source, the *something,* from which he came.

At this point the poem is in danger of becoming an abstract philosophic meditation. The human context is restored as the husband finishes his little oral treatise. The wife, noncommital about his theories, values them because he was the one who advanced them: "Today will be the day / You said so." Her husband turns the tribute around to her: " 'No, today will be the day / You said the brook was called West Running Brook.' " And the wife combines their dedications: " 'Today will be the day of what we both said.' " The human meaning of the stroll and conversation, regardless of whether any great truth has been revealed, has been restored and affirmed by the closing words.

1. In one of his early letters, Frost says:[2]

> . . . I alone of English writers have consciously set myself to make music out of what I may call the sound of sense. Now it is possible to have sense without the sound of sense (as in much prose that is supposed to pass muster but makes very dull reading) and the sound of sense without sense (as in Alice in Wonderland which makes anything but dull reading). The best place to get the abstract sound of sense is from voices behind a door that cuts off the words. Ask yourself how these sentences would sound without the words in which they are embodied:
>
> You mean to tell me you can't read?
> I said no such thing.
> Well read then.
> You're not my teacher.
>
> . . . Verse in which there is nothing but the beat of the metre furnished by the accents of the pollysyllabic words we call doggerel. Verse is not that. Neither is it the sound of sense alone. It is a resultant from those two.

Perhaps Frost makes himself out too unique, since Shakespeare likewise superimposed the "sound of sense" (actual speech rhythms) upon "the beat of the metre." But Frost achieved unusual success in maintaining a basic meter while giving the impression of completely spontaneous conversation. Find a section of several lines in which he did this, and scan it—indicate above the line the actual way the syllables would be stressed, and below the lines the theoretical beat of the iambic rhythm.

2. Must this poem, "The Onset" and "Design" be taken as representing three different moods of the poet, or is there any way the angles of vision can be reconciled?

3. Does the voice of the "commentator" add anything to the effect of the poem? What would be gained or lost if he were omitted, and any of his essential lines shifted to the man or woman?

4. Two pairs of words dominate the closing part of the poem: "runs down" and "sending up." Is there any implication in the poem that this stroll and discovery of the brook are a part of the double process?

[2] Thompson, *Selected Letters,* pp. 80-1.

5. Of the Frost poems we have read, one was a sonnet, two were in rhymed couplets, and one was in blank verse. Can you speculate as to why he chose the particular form in each case?

In recent decades many detailed studies of individual poems have been made by a variety of literary critics and poets. Familiarity with some of these essays is one of the best ways to discover how to approach a poem, any poem. Below is one of Frost's most famous short lyrics, and excerpts from a long essay by the poet and critic, John Ciardi.

First read the poem carefully and respond to it in your own way. Jot down your impressions of what the poem is saying and doing. Then read Ciardi's essay, and decide for yourself, on the basis of the poem before you, to what extent you agree with him, and to what extent you hold to another interpretation. You may also find it interesting to return to some of the Frost poems that you have already read and see whether the Ciardi essay suggests additional approaches to them.

Stopping by Woods on a Snowy Evening

Whose woods these are I think I know.
His house is in the village, though;
He will not see me stopping here
To watch his woods fill up with snow.

My little horse must think it queer
To stop without a farmhouse near
Between the woods and frozen lake
The darkest evening of the year.

He gives his harness bells a shake
To ask if there is some mistake.
The only other sound's the sweep
Of easy wind and downy flake.

The woods are lovely, dark, and deep,
But I have promises to keep,
And miles to go before I sleep,
And miles to go before I sleep.

Below are excerpts from Ciardi's essay:[3]

Even the TV audience can see that this poem begins as a seemingly-simple narration of a seemingly-simple incident but ends by suggesting

[3] "Robert Frost: The Way to the Poem," *Saturday Review*, XL (April 12, 1958), pp. 13-15, 65.

meanings far beyond anything specifically referred to in the narrative. And even readers with only the most casual interest in poetry might be made to note the additional fact that, though the poem suggests those larger meanings, it is very careful never to abandon its pretense to being simple narration. There is duplicity at work. The poet pretends to be talking about one thing, and all the while he is talking about many others. . . .

In scene one, which coincides with stanza one, a man—a New England man—is driving his sleigh somewhere at night. It is snowing, and as the man passes a dark patch of woods he stops to watch the snow descend into the darkness. We know, moreover, that the man is familiar with these parts (he knows who owns the woods and where the owner lives), and we know that no one has seen him stop. As scene one forms itself in the theatre of the mind's-eye, therefore, it serves to establish some as yet unspecified relation between the man and the woods. . . .

The errand, I will venture a bit brashly for lack of space, is left generalized in order the more aptly to suggest *any* errand in life and, therefore, life itself. The owner is there because he is one of the forces of the poem. Let it do to say that the force he represents is the village of mankind (that village at the edge of winter) from which the poet finds himself separated (has separated himself?) in his moment by the woods (and to which, he recalls finally, he has promises to keep). . . . Scene one, therefore, establishes not only a relation between the man and the woods, but the fact that the man's relation begins with his separation (though momentarily) from mankind. . . .

In scene two (stanzas two and three) a *foil* is introduced. In fiction and drama, a foil is a character who "plays against" a more important character. By presenting a different point of view or an opposed set of motives, the foil moves the more important character to react in ways that might not have found expression without such opposition. The more important character is thus more fully revealed—to the reader and to himself.The foil here is the horse.

The horse forces the question. Why did the man stop? Until it occurs to him that his "little horse must think it queer," he had not asked himself for reasons. . . .

In stanza two the question arises only as a feeling within the man. In stanza three, however (still scene two), the horse acts. He gives his harness bells a shake."What's wrong?" he seems to say. "What are we waiting for?"

By now, obviously, the horse—without losing its identity as horse—has also become a symbol. A symbol is something that stands for something else. Whatever that something else may be, it certainly begins as that order of life that does not understand why a man stops in the wintry middle of nowhere to watch the snow come down. (Can one fail to sense by now that the dark and the snowfall symbolize a death-wish, however momentary, *i.e.*, that hunger for final rest and surrender that a man may feel, but not a beast?'

So by the end of scene two the performance has given dramatic force to three elements that work upon the man. There is his relation to the world of the owner. There is his relation to the brute world of the horse. And there is that third presence of the unownable world, the movement of the all-engulfing snow across all the orders of life, the man's, the owner's, and the horse's—with the difference that the man knows of that second dark-within-the-dark of which the horse cannot, and the owner will not, know. . . .

But scene three (stanza four) produces a fourth force. This fourth force can be given many names. It is certainly better, in fact, to give it many names than to attempt to limit it to one. It is social obligation, or personal commitment, or duty, or just the realization that a man cannot indulge a mood forever. All of these and more. But, finally, he has a simple decision to make. He may go into the woods and let the darkness and the snow swallow him from the world of beast and man. Or he must move on. And unless he is going to stop here forever, it is time to remember that he has a long way to go and that he had best be getting there. (So there is something to be said for the horse, too.)

Then and only then, his question driven more and more deeply into himself by these cross-forces, does the man venture a comment on what attracted him: "The woods are lovely, dark and deep." His mood lingers over the thought of that lovely dark-and-deep (as do the very syllables in which he phrases the thought), but the final decision is to put off the mood and move on. He has his man's way to go and his man's obligations to tend to before he can yield. He has miles to go before his sleep. He repeats that thought and the performance ends.

But why the repetition? The first time Frost says "And miles to go before I sleep," there can be little doubt that the primary meaning is: "I have a long way to go before I get to bed tonight." The second time he says it, however, "miles to go" and "sleep" are suddenly transformed into symbols. What are those "something-elses" the symbols stand for? Hundreds of people have tried to ask Mr. Frost that question and he has always turned it away. He has turned it away *because he cannot answer it.* He could answer some part of it. But some part is not enough.

For a symbol is like a rock dropped into a pool: it sends out ripples in all directions, and the ripples are in motion. Who can say where the last ripple disappears? One may have a sense that he knows the approximate center point of the ripples, the point at which the stone struck the water.Yet even then he has trouble marking it surely. How does one make a mark on water? Oh very well—the center point of that second "miles to go" is probably approximately in the neighborhood of being close to meaning, perhaps, "the road of life"; and the second "before I sleep" is maybe that close to meaning "before I take my final rest," the rest in darkness that seemed so temptingly dark-and-deep for the moment of the mood. But the ripples continue to move and the light to change on the water, and the longer one watches the more changes he sees. Such shifting-and-being-at-the-same-instant is of the very sparkle and life of poetry. One experiences it as one experiences life, for everytime he looks at an experience he sees something new, and he sees it change as he watches it. And that sense of continuity in fluidity is one of the primary kinds of knowledge, one of man's basic ways of knowing, and one that only the arts can teach, poetry foremost among them.[4]

In the next two poems, you are mostly on your own, to decide what approaches will give you the deepest understanding.

The Oven Bird

There is a singer everyone has heard,
Loud, a mid-summer and a mid-wood bird,
Who makes the solid tree trunks sound again.
He says that leaves are old and that for flowers
Mid-summer is to spring as one to ten.
He says the early petal-fall is past,
When pear and cherry bloom went down in showers
On sunny days a moment overcast;
And comes that other fall we name the fall.
He says the highway dust is over all.
The bird would cease and be as other birds
But that he knows in singing not to sing.
The question that he frames in all but words
Is what to make of a diminished thing.

1. Compare this poem with "The Onset," which also deals with changes of season. Make two lists—the visual images used in the two poems. Can you explain how the images control the moods of the two poems?

2. Jot down the rhyme scheme. The poem has fourteen lines—like a sonnet—but the rhyme scheme does not correspond to any standard sonnet type. Is there any way in which the pattern of rhyming reinforces the movement of thought in the poem?

[4] The essay concludes with an interesting discussion of the intricate poetic form, and how Frost came to write the poem. The entire essay is available in Robert A. Greenberg and James G. Hepburn, eds., *Robert Frost: An Introduction* (New York: Holt, Rinehart, and Winston, 1961).

3. How would you interpret the lines, "The bird would cease and be as other birds / But that he knows in singing not to sing."?

4. Does the last line throw light on any of Frost's other poems?

After Apple-Picking

My long two-pointed ladder's sticking through a tree
Toward heaven still,
And there's a barrel that I didn't fill
Beside it, and there may be two or three
Apples I didn't pick upon some bough.
But I am done with apple-picking now.
Essence of winter sleep is on the night,
The scent of apples: I am drowsing off.
I cannot rub the strangeness from my sight
I got from looking through a pane of glass
I skimmed this morning from the drinking trough
And held against the world of hoary grass.
It melted, and I let it fall and break.
But I was well
Upon my way to sleep before it fell,
And I could tell
What form my dreaming was about to take.
Magnified apples appear and disappear,
Stem end and blossom end,
And every fleck of russet showing clear.
My instep arch not only keeps the ache,
It keeps the pressure of a ladder-round.
I feel the ladder sway as the boughs bend.
And I keep hearing from the cellar bin
The rumbling sound
Of load on load of apples coming in.
For I have had too much
Of apple-picking: I am overtired
Of the great harvest I myself desired.
There were ten thousand thousand fruit to touch,
Cherish in hand, lift down, and not let fall.
For all
That struck the earth,
No matter if not bruised or spiked with stubble,
Went surely to the cider-apple heap
As of no worth.
One can see what will trouble
This sleep of mine, whatever sleep it is.
Where he not gone,

The woodchuck could say whether it's like his
Long sleep, as I describe its coming on,
Or just some human sleep.

1. Can you find lines or phrases suggesting that this is more than a poem about picking apples?

2. Make a list of words and phrases that prepare you for the emphasis on sleep at the end of the poem.

3. Does the poem lead you to think that the apple picking is leading to hibernation or "just some human sleep" or something else?

Finally, a few additional Frost poems. As you read them, and recall the other Frost poems you have read, ask yourself whether you agree with the controversial remark of the literary critic, Lionel Trilling, when he spoke at a dinner honoring Frost on his 85th birthday—"I think of Robert Frost as a terrifying poet." Is the statement justified? Does it need to be balanced by other statements?

An Old Man's Winter Night

All out-of-doors looked darkly in at him
Through the thin frost, almost in separate stars,
That gathers on the pane in empty rooms.
What kept his eyes from giving back the gaze
Was the lamp tilted near them in his hand.
What kept him from remembering what it was
That brought him to that creaking room was age.
He stood with barrels round him—at a loss.
And having scared the cellar under him
In clomping here, he scared it once again
In clomping off—and scared the outer night,
Which has its sounds, familiar, like the roar
Of trees and crack of branches, common things,
But nothing so like beating on a box.
A light he was to no one but himself
Where now he sat, concerned with he knew what,
A quiet light, and then not even that.
He consigned to the moon—such as she was,
So late-arising—to the broken moon,
As better than the sun in any case
For such a charge, his snow upon the roof,
His icicles along the wall to keep;
And slept. The log that shifted with a jolt
Once in the stove, distrubed him and he shifted,

And eased his heavy breathing, but still slept.
One aged man—one man—can't keep a house,
A farm, a countryside, or if he can,
It's thus he does it of a winter night.

"Out, Out—"

The buzz saw snarled and rattled in the yard
And made dust and dropped stove-length sticks of wood,
Sweet-scented stuff when the breeze drew across it.
And from there those that lifted eyes could count
Five mountain ranges one behind the other
Under the sunset far into Vermont.
And the saw snarled and rattled, snarled and rattled,
As it ran light, or had to bear a load.
And nothing happened: day was all but done.
Call it a day, I wish they might have said
To please the boy by giving him the half hour
That a boy counts so much when saved from work.
His sister stood beside them in her apron
To tell them "Supper." At the word, the saw,
As if to prove saws knew what supper meant,
Leaped out at the boy's hand, or seemed to leap—
He must have given the hand. However it was,
Neither refused the meeting. But the hand!
The boy's first outcry was a rueful laugh,
As he swung toward them holding up the hand,
Half in appeal, but half as if to keep
The life from spilling. Then the boy saw all—
Since he was old enough to know, big boy
Doing a man's work, though a child at heart—
He saw all spoiled. "Don't let him cut my hand off—
The doctor, when he comes. Don't let him, sister!"
So. But the hand was gone already.
The doctor put him in the dark of ether.
He lay and puffed his lips out with his breath.
And then—the watcher at his pulse took fright.
No one believed. They listened at his heart.
Little—less—nothing!—and that ended it.
No more to build on there. And they, since they
Were not the one dead, turned to their affairs.

Desert Places

Snow falling and night falling fast, oh, fast
In a field I looked into going past,
And the ground almost covered smooth in snow,
But a few weeds and stubble showing last.

The woods around it have it—it is theirs.
All animals are smothered in their lairs.
I am too absent-spirited to count;
The loneliness includes me unawares.

And lonely as it is, that loneliness
Will be more lonely ere it will be less—
A blanker whiteness of benighted snow
With no expression, nothing to express.

They cannot scare me with their empty spaces
Between stars—on stars where no human race is.
I have it in me so much nearer home
To scare myself with my own desert places.

A Record Stride

In a Vermont bedroom closet
With a door of two broad boards
And for back wall a crumbling old chimney
(And that's what their toes are towards),

I have a pair of shoes standing,
Old rivals of sagging leather,
Who once kept surpassing each other,
But now live even together.

They listen for me in the bedroom
To ask me a thing or two
About who is too old to go walking,
With too much stress on the who.

I wet one last year at Montauk
For a hat I had to save.
The other I wet at the Cliff House
In an extra-vagant wave.

Two entirely different grandchildren
Got me into my double adventure.
But when they grow up and can read this
I hope they won't take it for censure.

I touch my tongue to the shoes now,
And unless my sense is at fault,
On one I can taste Atlantic,
On the other Pacific, salt.

One foot in each great ocean
Is a record stride or stretch.
The authentic shoes it was made in
I should sell for what they would fetch.

But instead I proudly devote them
To my museum and muse;
So the thick-skins needn't act thin-skinned
About being past-active shoes.

And I ask all to try to forgive me
For being as overelated
As if I had measured the country
And got the United States stated.

Neither Out Far Nor In Deep

The people along the sand
All turn and look one way.
They turn their back on the land.
They look at the sea all day.

As long as it takes to pass
A ship keeps raising its hull;
The wetter ground like glass
Reflects a standing gull.

The land may vary more;
But wherever the truth may be—
The water comes ashore,
And the people look at the sea.

They cannot look out far.
They cannot look in deep.
But when was that ever a bar
To any watch they keep?

Directive

Back out of all this now too much for us,
Back in a time made simple by the loss
Of detail, burned, dissolved, and broken off
Like graveyard marble sculpture in the weather,

There is a house that is no more a house
Upon a farm that is no more a farm
And in a town that is no more a town.
The road there, if you'll let a guide direct you
Who only has at heart your getting lost,
May seem as if it should have been a quarry—
Great monolithic knees the former town
Long since gave up pretense of keeping covered.
And there's a story in a book about it:
Besides the wear of iron wagon wheels
The ledges show lines ruled southeast-northwest,
The chisel work of an enormous Glacier
That braced his feet against the Arctic Pole.
You must not mind a certain coolness from him
Still said to haunt this side of Panther Mountain.
Nor need you mind the serial ordeal
Of being watched from forty cellar holes
As if by eye pairs out of forty firkins.
As for the woods' excitement over you
That sends light rustle rushes to their leaves,
Charge that to upstart inexperience.
Where were they all not twenty years ago?
They think too much of having shaded out
A few old pecker-fretted apple trees.
Make yourself up a cheering song of how
Someone's road home from work this once was,
Who may be just ahead of you on foot
Or creaking with a buggy load of grain.
The height of the adventure is the height
Of country where two village cultures faded
Into each other. Both of them are lost.
And if you're lost enough to find yourself
By now, pull in your ladder road behind you
And put a sign up CLOSED to all but me.
Then make yourself at home. The only field
Now left's no bigger than a harness gall.
First there's the children's house of make-believe,
Some shattered dishes underneath a pine,
The playthings in the playhouse of the children.
Weep for what little things could make them glad.
Then for the house that is no more a house,
But only a belilaced cellar hole,
Now slowly closing like a dent in dough.
This was no playhouse but a house in earnest.
Your destination and your destiny's
A brook that was the water of the house,
Cold as a spring as yet so near its source,
Too lofty and original to rage.

(We know the valley streams that when aroused
Will leave their tatters hung on barb and thorn.)
I have kept hidden in the instep arch
Of an old cedar at the waterside
A broken drinking goblet like the Grail
Under a spell so the wrong ones can't find it,
So can't get saved, as Saint Mark says they mustn't.
(I stole the goblet from the children's playhouse.)
Here are your waters and your watering place.
Drink and be whole again beyond confusion.

For Once, Then, Something

Others taunt me with having knelt at well-curbs
Always wrong to the light, so never seeing
Deeper down in the well than where the water
Gives me back in a shining surface picture
Me myself in the summer heaven, godlike,
Looking out of a wreath of fern and cloud puffs.
Once, when trying with chin against a well-curb,
I discerned, as I thought, beyond the picture,
Through the picture, a something white, uncertain,
Something more of the depths—and then I lost it.
Water came to rebuke the too clear water.
One drop fell from a fern, and lo, a ripple
Shook whatever it was lay there at bottom,
Blurred it, blotted it out. What was that whiteness?
Truth? A pebble of quartz? For once, then, something.

Fire and Ice

Some say the world will end in fire,
Some say in ice.
From what I've tasted of desire
I hold with those who favor fire.
But if it had to perish twice,
I think I know enough of hate
To say that for destruction ice
Is also great
And would suffice.

SELECTIVE BIBLIOGRAPHY

The edition of Frost's poetry used in this text is Edward Connery Lathem, ed., *The Poetry of Robert Frost* (New York: Holt, 1969)

Reuben Brower, *The Poetry of Robert Frost: Constellations of Intention* (New York: Oxford University Press, 1963).

John Ciardi, *How Does a Poem Mean?* (Cambridge, Mass.: Riverside Press, 1959). The essay on "Stopping by Woods on a Snowy Evening," pp. 670-77.

Reginald Cook, *Robert Frost: A Living Voice* (Amherst, Massachusetts: The University of Massachusetts Press, 1974).

James M. Cox, ed., *Robert Frost: A Collection of Critical Essays* (Englewood Cliffs, N.J.: Prentice-Hall, 1962).

Jean Gould, *Robert Frost: The Aim Was Song* (New York: Dodd, Mead. 1964).

Edward Connery Lathem, ed., *Interviews with Robert Frost* (New York: Holt, Rinehart & Winston, 1966).

Marshall Louis Mertins, *Robert Frost, Life and Talks-Walking* (Norman, Okla.: University of Oklahoma Press, 1965).

Elizabeth Sergeant, *Robert Frost: The Trial by Existence* (New York: Holt, Rinehart & Winston, 1960).

Lawrance Thompson, *Fire and Ice: The Art and Thought of Robert Frost* (New York: Russell & Russell, 1961).

———, *Robert Frost: The Early Years, 1874-1915* (New York: Holt, Rinehart & Winston, 1966).

———, *Robert Frost: The Years of Triumph, 1915-1938* (New York: Holt, Rinehart & Winston, 1970).

———, ed., *Selected Letters of Robert Frost* (New York: Holt, Rinehart & Winston, 1964).

William Carlos Williams

His Life

How William Carlos Williams achieved what he did is cause for wonder. He was a successful doctor who practiced his profession for more than 40 years; at the same time his literary output was prodigious. According to one of his editors,[1] he wrote a "total of 49 books in every literary form we know and in forms we still have trouble classifying. He wrote some 600 poems, 4 full-length plays, an opera libretto, 52 short stories, 4 novels, a book of essays and criticism, his autobiography, a biography of his mother, an American history, a book of letters." This same editor goes on to say, "He was the instrument of change. Without him one cannot account for contemporary American poetry."

What sort of man was he—this poet and physician who balanced two demanding careers, each apparently enriching the other? The bare facts of his life may give some clue, but his poetry provides a richer answer. He was born in Rutherford, New Jersey, in 1883; he practiced medicine there; he died there in 1963; he knew that part of New Jersey with a passionate intensity. Although he traveled widely, as Thoreau did not, he could have echoed Thoreau—"I have traveled much in Rutherford." The sense of the local is basic to his poetry.

Williams' father was of English descent. His mother, born in Puerto Rico, had a mixture of Spanish, Jewish, and English blood. She came of an artistic family, and had at one time studied art in Paris. Rutherford must have posed adjustment problems for her.

The poet himself insisted he might as easily have turned to painting as writing, and certainly his poems show great visual awareness. It was during his medical studies at the University of Pennsylvania that he came into contract with Ezra Pound and began writing poetry. He achieved his M.D. degree in 1906 and during 1909 to 1910 worked in pediatrics in Leipzig. This was not his first foreign experience. In his boyhood he had gone to school in Switzerland for several years.

When the Leipzig year was over, he came home to set up practice in Rutherford and to marry Florence Herman, the "Flossie" who figures in so many of his poems. For a long time most of his work appeared in little underground magazines or was privately printed. But he knew many of the Imagist poets as well as painters of the time—men like Charles Demuth and Man Ray. All these people were trying to break through in their art to a fresh angle of vision, a more honest and direct confrontation with their material. It was a time of ferment, and Williams was exhilarated by all the creativity. Early

[1] William Carlos Williams, *Imaginations.* Introduction by Webster Schott (New York: New Directions, 1970), p. IX.

he discovered certain things about his own aims and they served him the rest of his life. For instance, he says in *I Wanted to Write a Poem:*[2]

> It is typical of me to want my first book of poems to be called simply *Poems.* And also typical that the first poem is called "Innocence" and the second "Simplicity." I appear to be stating my case right from the beginning. The first line in the first poem reads, "Innocence can never perish." I really believed that then and I really believe it now. It is something intrinsic in a man. And I still care about simplicity. I have been outspoken all my life, but honestly outspoken. I try to say it straight, whatever is to be said.

Many of his compatriots in the arts were fleeing America, Pound and Eliot among them. Williams early knew that path was not for him. As his and Pound's paths further diverged, he began to question what men like these were doing and how valid their efforts were. He knew that he had to remain where his roots were—that he had to probe "the local"—and only through an understanding of his own and his region's history would he be able to discover the authentic language to embody it. This all came to a culmination in his long five-book epic, *Paterson,* which took several decades to write.

Slowly his reputation grew. He found a sympathetic and reputable publisher in New Directions. He continued to practice medicine until 1951 when a stroke compelled his retirement. During the 40 years of his medical career he had written whenever a moment offered itself—between patients, late at night, driving his car. Obviously his contact with human life as a doctor fed his poetry. After he was forced into retirement by illness (his son, Bill, took over the practice) the writing still went on. In the opinion of many readers, the last collection, *Pictures from Brueghel,* has a depth, a mastery, and a loveliness that even surpasses his earlier work. Like Yeats in old age he had a tremendous burst of creative activity.

Though Williams had a "Keats phase," he was more strongly influenced by Walt Whitman and Emily Dickinson. In fact, he says of the latter:[3] "Emily was my patron saint. She was also an American, seeking to divide the line in some respectable way." He was also intrigued because the maiden name of his English grandmother was Emily Dickinson. As for Williams' own influence, his impact is evident in many contemporary poets such as Charles Olson, Denise Levertov, and Allen Ginsberg.

The judgment of time will determine Williams' ultimate place in American literature, but it seems secure. Certainly, parts of *Paterson* and his love poem to his wife, "Asphodel, that Greeny Flower," are in the front rank of American poetry.

[2] William Carlos Williams, *I Wanted to Write a Poem.* Ed. Edith Heal (Boston: Beacon Press, 1958), p. 9.

[3] *Writers at Work,* 3rd series, *Paris Review Interviews,* ed. George Plimpton (New York: Viking, 1968), p. 12.

The Poet and His Poetry

Williams was impressed by T. S. Eliot's ability—though Eliot's path was not the one he chose to take. But the publication of *The Waste Land* in 1922 and the subsequent furore over it deeply disturbed him. Even before *The Waste Land,* Williams had this to say when Eliot's *Prufrock* appeared:[4]

> I had a violent feeling that Eliot had betrayed what I believed in. He was looking backward; I was looking forward. He was a conformist with wit, learning which I did not possess. He knew French, Latin, Arabic, God knows what. I was interested in that. But I felt he had rejected America and I refused to be rejected and so my reaction was violent. I realized the responsibility I must accept. I knew he would influence all subsequent American poets and take them out of my sphere. I had envisioned a new form of poetic composition, a form for the future. It was a shock to me that he was so tremendously successful; my contemporaries flocked to him—away from what I wanted. It forced me to be successful.

After *The Waste Land* was published, Williams likened it to the explosion of an atomic bomb which shattered his world. He goes on to say,[5]

> Our work staggered to a halt for a moment under the blast of Eliot's genius which gave the poem back to the academics. . . . Critically Eliot returned us to the classroom just at the moment when I felt that we were on the point of an escape to matters much closer to the essence of a new art form itself—rooted in the locality which should give it fruit. . . . If with his skill he could have been kept here to be employed by our slowly shaping drive, what strides might we not have taken! . . . By his walking out on us we were stopped for a moment, cold. It was a bad moment.

These comments are revealing in that they show certain of Williams' concerns at the start of his career. He would not turn his back on America—but rather find his source in the local. True, in *Paterson* he portrays men and women cut off from their roots and unable to find their way—just as Eliot does in *The Waste Land.* But *Paterson* has some answers—characters who have found the redeeming language. In Book Five, written a number of years after the first four were conceived, Williams shows that man's imagination embodied in his art is a redemptive force.

In fact, all of Williams' work is centered in a belief in the power of the imagination. He shares this exalting of the imagination with poets like Blake, Shelley, and Wallace Stevens. And language provides the means for speaking and revealing the imagination. But in Williams' view, our words were British

[4] Williams, *I Wanted to Write a Poem,* p. 30.

[5] *The Autobiography of William Carlos Williams* (New York: Random House, 1951), pp. 146, 174.

words trying to do American work. The American imagination had to create a new language to express the American experience. He attempted in *In the American Grain,* a prose book, to express his imaginative understanding of the forces that shaped the American continent.

Many of these ideas infuse *Paterson.* For instance, Williams abhorred the Puritans and their influence on our history. As he saw it, they viewed the wilderness and the Indian only as objects to use and exploit. Love had no place, and they had no imagination to lift and redeem their lives.

In his drive to break free from the old and create a new language, Williams was struggling to find some metrical principle that would go beyond free verse of the Whitman kind. Very early he had decided rhyme was not for him, because it got in his way.[6] "These two decisions, not to rhyme and to begin lines with lower case letters, were made very early. The decisions lasted all the rest of my life." He continues, "The rhythmic unit decided the form of my poetry. When I came to the end of a rhythmic unit (not necessarily a sentence) I ended the line. . . . I didn't go in for long lines because of my nervous nature. I couldn't."

This experimentation with the rhythmic line eventually led to the discovery of what Williams called the "variable foot," which he felt was the principle he had been searching for since he began to write. It is difficult to be entirely certain just how to describe this, because it seems to depend so completely on the reader's ear and sense of rhythm. These do not always correspond to the way Williams hears the line. So, again, it is better to let Williams describe it in his own words. It was a section in *Paterson* Two that apparently brought things to a focus. Of this section he says:[7]

> Several years afterward in looking over the thing I realized I had hit upon a device (that is the practical focus of a device) which I could not name when I wrote it. My dissatisfaction with free verse came to a head in that I always wanted a verse that was ordered, so it came to me that the concept of the foot itself would have to be altered in our new relativistic world. . . . The foot not being fixed is only to be described as variable. If the foot itself is variable, it allows order in so-called free verse. Thus the verse becomes not free at all but just simply variable, as all things in life properly are. From the time I hit on this I knew what I was going to have to do.

And again, in a *Paris Review* interview,[8] he was asked this question: "What do you think you yourself have left of special value to the new poets?" Williams' answer was:

[6] Williams, *I Wanted to Write a Poem,* p. 15.

[7] *I Wanted to Write a Poem,* p. 82.

[8] *Writers at Work,* p. 29.

> The variable foot—the division of the line according to a new method that would be satisfactory to an American. It's all right if you are not intent on being national. But an American is forced to try to give the intonation. Either it is important or it is not important. It must have occurred to an American that the question of the line *was* important. The American idiom has much to offer us that the English language has never heard of.

In his obsession with discovering a new line or measure for his poetry, Williams rejected conventional English meters and felt that the first objective of American poets should be the invention of their own prosody. English prosody, as he saw it, reflected English history and conditions. American poets must throw it out and evolve a prosody reflecting their own heritage.

One more observation about Williams' variable foot. Usually Williams' verse has very short lines, and they are frequently arranged in threes; but the breaks in the triad are dictated by the qualities of each individual line, so that the lines vary in length. As we move into the poetry, especially that written after 1950, this may all become clearer. But Williams' concerns should certainly be clear by now—the American experience, the power of the imagination through words to embody that experience, a rejection of the traditional and academic, his belief in the concrete and specific—"no ideas but in things." There is always the struggle to find the honest and redeeming language, and the exploration of the variable foot as a way of catching the intonations of American speech.

Before we end this section, just a brief comment on Williams' chief themes, especially as they are expressed in *Paterson.*

The germ of *Paterson* (1926) appeared very early. There is a poem by that title in his early *Collected Poems* with the repeated line, "Say it, no ideas but in things." A somewhat later poem, "Paterson: the Falls," points toward the local as the center of his imagination.

As Williams first conceived *Paterson,* it was to be a poem in four books—a long poem, perhaps best described as an epic, in which, as Book One appeared in 1946, the author's note stated:[9]

> This is the first part of a long poem in four parts—that a man in himself is a city, beginning, seeking, achieving and concluding his life in ways which the various aspects of a city may embody—if imaginatively conceived—any city, all the details of which may be made to voice his most intimate convictions. Part One introduces the elemental character of the place. The second Part will comprise the modern replicas. Three will seek a language to make them vocal, and Four, the river below the falls will be reminiscent of episodes—all that any one man may achieve in a lifetime.

[9] *I Wanted to Write a Poem,* p. 71.

As it actually turned out, Book Four hardly fits the original description, and as Williams continued to brood and meditate he saw the poem itself as a process, like life, open ended, and in 1958 he added Book Five and was contemplating and had made notes for Book Six at the time of his death in 1963.

Williams explains in various notes why he chose Paterson, New Jersey, as his archetypal city. It had an important colonial history, but even more, it had a river and a falls. As he says,[10] "I took the river as it followed its course down to the sea; all I had to do was follow it and I had a poem. . . . Finally I let form take care of itself; the colloquial language set the pace."

Paterson, as one looks at it—all 284 pages in the New Directions paperback—seems a pastiche. Prose passages break into the poetry; there are old newspaper accounts of the region, letters quoted verbatim, a rich cast of characters, occasional fragments from other poems, advertisements, etc. From this welter of material it is sometimes hard to pluck out "the radiant gist." But several themes are reiterated again and again. Certainly *Paterson* depicts the modern consciousness in all its chaos and lack of unity—against a backdrop of the river and falls. One sees the divorce of modern life from the living language. The imagination is blocked, men and women unable to communicate and love, leading to divorce. To Williams, part of the blockage is due to the Puritan mentality with its cruelty and exploitation. Against this mentality the poem presents instances of genuine love and devotion—the man and his dog, the evangelist in the Park, Madame Curie, Père Sebastian Rasles.

As the river flows toward the sea the pollution increases and so does the corruption of the characters depicted. The language is lost. The past can offer nothing and the final stanzas of Book Four insist that "the sea is not our home." Home is inland, back to the continent of America, the local, the falls and the river. There language must be found. Finally, in Book Five, Paterson has returned to the old scenes and discovers that what endures is love, imagination, and art. Louis Martz has a succinct comment in his essay on *Paterson* Five:[11]

> So the new Book V suggests that we might regard *Paterson* as a kind of tapestry woven out of memories and observations, composed by one man's imagination, but written in part by his friends, his patients, and all the milling populace of Paterson, past and present. . . .
>
> The whole, as Williams insists, is a "fiction" ("pay attention") but it is at the same time a personal testament to the poet's vehement belief "that there is a source in America for everything we think or do."

[10] *I Wanted to Write a Poem,* p. 73.

[11] Louis L. Martz, "The Unicorn in Paterson: William Carlos Williams," *Thought,* Vol. XXXV, No. 135 (Winter, 1960) p. 543.

Pervading all Williams' poetry is the faith in the redeeming power of imagination

> It is the imagination
> which cannot be fathomed.
> It is through this hole
> we escape

Imagination has the last laugh at death itself—

> Through this hole
> at the bottom of the cavern
> of death, the imagination
> escapes intact.[12]

[12] *Paterson* (New York: New Directions, 1963), p. 247 (Book V).

On reading William's poems one is startled by how much nature imagery weaves through them. Although an urban poet, Williams knew a great deal about trees and plants and flowers. For instance, Part III of "Promenade" is typical. Williams and his small son have been for a walk before breakfast.

from *Promenade*

Oh, then a wreath! Let's
refresh something they
used to write well of.

Two fern plumes. Strip them
to the mid-rib along one side.
Bind the tips with a grass stem.
Bend and interwist the stalks
at the back. So!
Ah! now we are crowned!
Now we are a poet!
Quickly!
A bunch of little flowers
for Flossie—the little ones
only:

a red clover, one
blue heal-all, a sprig of
bone-set, one primrose,
a head of Indian tobacco, this
magenta speck and this
little lavender!

Home now, my mind!—
Sonny's arms are icy, I tell you—
and have breakfast!

This simple poem with its blunt commands (strip, bind, bend) moves at a breathless pace. The stroll, the catalogue of flowers, Sonny's icy arms, the thought of breakfast—what familiar human experience is summarized here. But the poem says far more. The father is crowned with a fern wreath, evoking memories of the Olympic games in ancient Greece. With his son as witness, he is acclaimed a victor. And they do not return home empty-handed; there are the little flowers they take back as an offering to the wife-mother. The warmth and understanding of these shared relationships is perceived against the setting of early morning chill and threatening rain.

A poem could hardly be simpler or more direct. It is written in common speech without the adornment of rhyme. The rythm is easy and flexible. The language seems to tumble out in the short, nervous lines that Williams perfected.

1. Why does the poet say "now we are crowned!" instead of using "I"? (line 9)

2. Comment on how these lines help control the feeling of the poem: (a) "something they / used to write of well." (b) "the little ones / only:" (c) "Home now, my mind!—"

3. What is the function of line 11, which consists of the single word, "Quickly!"?

Or consider the poem, "The Birdsong," one of his later ones:

The Birdsong

Disturb the balance, broken bird
the distress of the song
cuts through an ample silence
sweeping the trees.

It is the trouble
of the brook that makes it loud,
the current broke to give
out a burbling

breaks the arched stillness,
ripples the tall grass
gone to heady seed, bows the heads
of goldenrod

that bear a vulgar happiness,
the bay-berry,
briars—
break also your happiness for me.

This, too, is a poem expressed very simply. It has a stripped down quality. There is no rhyme, and the metrical pattern is easy and loose. It does, however, make heavy use of alliteration for its effects, with the repeated *b*'s and *s*'s throughout the poem.

The key works are *broken* and *break.* The birdsong and the brook both break the silence. Autumn is approaching. It is the time when grass is going to seed and the goldenrod is blooming.

What is happening? Are the man and woman together in a woods or field?

Why *broken bird*? What can one make of the last two lines—"briars—/break also your happiness for me."?

The poem is more intricate both structurally and thematically than appears on the surface. There was a balance till the bird's song appears on the surface. There was a balance till the bird's song broke it—till the current of the brook, also, broke the stillness. The grass and goldenrod perhaps represent the balance that is broken by the wind, the vulgar happiness that is disturbed by the birdsong and the brook.

Are we justified in carrying all this further and finding in it Williams' preoccupation with language—the right language which can express and embody the truths of the imaginations? And is this tied in with the bird in distress and the balance broken by the current, the happiness of the human relationship broken by briars—so that language that can make it whole again?

This is all speculative. But it does illustrate some of the thickets of complexity that can surround what appears to be a very simple poem. It illustrates how such a poem can tease and challenge the imagination.

1. Note again how many words began with *b* and *s*. What effect does this have on the "feel" of the poem?

2. Why do you think the poet used these phrases?

(a) "the distress of the song" (b) "an ample silence"
(c) "the arched stillness" (d) "gone to heavy seed"
(e) "your happiness for me"

Now a very short poem that reverberates beyond its literal meaning—

Complete Destruction

It was an icy day,
We buried the cat,
then took her box
and set match to it

in the back yard.
Those fleas that escaped
earth and fire
died by the cold.

Certainly, there is not ambiguity here. The cat is buried, the box burned, and the fleas that escaped the burial and the fire are frozen to death. The language is stark. Most of the words are only one syllable. The poem consists of two short sentences, flatly declarative. It is hard to imagine a poem that, at first glance seems more stripped of complexity and adornment.

Yet again, this is a poem within which one can find multiple possibilities.

Is William talking about anything more than a commonplace occurrence? One remembers perhaps how Donne used the image of a flea (page 5), and perhaps Frost's poem "Fire and Ice," (page 186) sends a shiver of recognition down one's spine. One can hardly escape the question of how far Williams meant to carry the symbolic implications of the poem. And it is called "Complete Destruction." Is this a poem, as Frost's was, about the destruction of our human world—by either fire or ice?

This poem was written before the atomic bomb and the ecological crisis—and some will read later history into it. Is there anything wrong in this? One of the glories of poetry is that a valid poem can be read and reinterpreted by succeeding generations; its meaning unfolds with time, perhaps with implications that the poet himself was not consciously aware of. "Complete Destruction" was written long before Hiroshima; it is still fresh and powerful in the changed world of today.

Now for a longer poem, and one that says much more than its plain title promises:

Burning the Christmas Greens

Their time past, pulled down
cracked and flung to the fire
—go up in a roar

All recognition lost, burnt clean
clean in the flame, the green
dispersed, a living red,
flame red, red as blood wakes
on the ash—

and ebbs to a steady burning
the rekindled bed become
a landscape of flame

At the winter's midnight
we went to the trees, the coarse
holly, the balsam and
the hemlock for their green

At the thick of the dark
the momemt of the cold's
deepest plunge we brought branches
cut from the green trees

to fill our need, and over
doorways, about paper Christmas
bells covered with tinfoil
and fastened by red ribbons
we stuck the green prongs

in the windows hung
woven wreaths and above pictures
the living green. On the

mantle we build a green forest
and among those hemlock
sprays put a herd of small
white deer as if they

were walking there. All this!
and it seemed gentle and good
to us. Their time past,
relief! The room bare. We

stuffed the dead grate
with them upon the half burnt out
log's smoldering eye, opening
red and closing under them

and we stood there looking down.
Green is a solace
a promise of peace, a fort
against the cold (though we

did not say so) a challenge
above the snow's
hard shell. Green (we might
have said) that, where

small birds hide and dodge
and lift their plaintive
rallying cries, blocks for them
and knocks down

the unseeing bullets of
the storm. Green spruce boughs
pulled down by a weight of
snow—Transformed!

Violence leaped and appeared.
Recreant! roared to life
as the flame rose through and
our eyes recoiled from it.

In the jagged flames green
to red, instant and alive. Green!
those sure abutments . . . Gone!
lost to mind
and quick in the contracting

tunnel of the grate
appeared a world! Black
mountains, black and red—as

yet uncolored—and ash white,
an infant landscape of shimmering
ash and flame and we, in
that instant, lost,

breathless to be witnesses,
as if we stood
ourselves refreshed among
the shining fauna of that fire.

It should now be evident that Williams fulfills his own belief—"No ideas but in things." His poems are rooted in the concrete—trees, flowers, people, common objects, Paterson. So it is with "Burning the Christmas Greens." Again a simple, homey experience—decorating the house for Christmas with the greens and when the season is past, disposing of them in the fireplace. The language, as always, is direct and full of action.

The first three stanzas give us a glimpse of the greens as they are consumed by the fire. The next six stanzas are a flashback to the gathering of the greens and the decorating of the house. The following four stanzas are almost a meditation about the greens, the color green, and the trees offering a shelter for birds against the storms of winter, their color transformed to white by the snow. The final five stanzas bring us back to the fire again—the greens now glowing red and then ash white, the transformation that occurs both in the greens and the man who is watching them burn. If one has read *Paterson*, inevitably the passage in Part II about the bottle mauled by the fire springs to mind. Is Williams suggesting much the same idea as in "Burning the Christmas Greens?" Here is the section from *Paterson*:

An old bottle, mauled by the fire
gets a new glaze, the glass warped
to a new distinction, reclaiming the
undefined. . . .

. . . . .

. . . . The glass
splotched with concentric rainbows
of cold fire that the fire has bequeathed
there as it cools, its flame
defied—the flame that wrapped the glass
deflowered, reflowered there by
the flame: a second flame, surpassing
heat

Certainly we have in both poems the idea of a transforming energy that is both destructive and creative. The old is destroyed but something new is created. The flames in "Burning the Christmas Greens" release another kind of beauty that stirs and energizes the imagination of the man who is watching the process —just as the bottle takes on a new glaze and a new shape as it is consigned to the flames.

The Christmas greens lose all their former shape and color, but they become "a landscape of flame." The poem is built on contrasts—green and red, winter's midnight, the dark against the light and heat of fire, the quiet and peace of the house decorated for Christmas and the roar of the flames as the greens are burnt. There is a meditation about how the greens shelter the birds and are white with snow—and then the holocaust which completely transforms them into the outlines of a miniature world. Their gleam lights the imagination of the poet.

It is as though nothing is ever lost. The greens are gone, but a new world is created—black and white, with "shining fauna." As part of the new world, the most important part, there is the poem that has been born.

Note how Williams plays on various words and sounds, though as usual there is no repetitive rhythm and no rhyme except by chance. Consider these lines:

> All recognition lost, burnt clean
> clean in the flame, the green
> dispersed, a living red,
> flame red, red as blood wakes
> on the ash—

The words *clean*, *flame*, and *red* are repeated and the *s* sound is picked up in *lost*, *dispersed*, and *wakes*. *Clean* and *green* do rhyme, all the more sharply because of the general lack of rhyme. Later in the final stanzas the imagery of *flame* and *ash white* is repeated, while the lovely center part of the poem deals with *green branches*, *green prongs*, *the living green*, the *green forest*.

"Green is a solace / a promise of peace," the poem says, the alliteration of the *p*'s giving a soothing, almost lullabye-like quality. The ash white is not just a realistic description of the effects of fire, but it later echoed by the herd of small white deer that decorate the mantle among the hemlock sprays. It is also linked in imagination to the snow that transforms the green in the winter woods. Red is used once in this section to describe the Christmas ribbons. So the three colors—green, red, and white—weave through the whole poem, transforming and being transformed in the pictures they paint. The poem deals, it is true, with a specific event that anyone disposing of Christmas decorations has observed. Also it dramatizes the whole idea of tension in the world between creativity and destruction, and what the human imagination can embody from the process.

Many of Williams' most moving poems are too long for reprinting in their entirety. But it would be a shameful thing to skip, altogether, such a profoundly beautiful love poem as "Asphodel, That Greeny Flower." It was written by the poet in old age to his beloved Flossie, and is full of comments about the warmth of their years together. It is a poem celebrating the triumph of their relationship over all obstacles to communication; love, like the asphodel, survives hell itself. On the human level, the man must see his wife for what she is in essence, not the aging body that a camera would record. She in turn, by the power of forgiveness, can contribute to the renewal and reaffirmation of love. This also requires an imaginative effort. Thus, in the poem, Williams unites his faith in both the power of love and the power of the imagination.

The asphodel of the title is a small flower with grayish leaves. In Greek mythology, it was thought to grow thickly in Hades, and it was often planted in cemeteries; Persephone was crowned with asphodels. Thus it is associated with death and the shadowy life beyond the grave.

At the beginning of the poem, Williams talks about the asphodel and its association with the other world. Then he moves to the relation between himself and his wife, and sketches its intricacies with loving accuracy, while flower references weave in and out of the poem. Finally, the poem ends with a "Coda", the concluding part of which is given below:

Only the imagination is real!
I have declared it
time without end.
If a man die
it is because death
has first
possessed his imagination.
But if he refuse death—
no greater evil
can befall him
unless it be the death of love
meet him
in full career.
Then indeed
for him
the light has gone out.
But love and the imagination
are of a piece,
swift as the light
to avoid destruction.
So we come to watch time's flight
as we might watch
summer lighting
or fireflies, secure,
by grace of the imagination,

safe in its care.
          For if
                    the light itself
has escaped,
          the whole edifice opposed to it
                    goes down.
Light, the imagination
          and love,
                    in our age,
by natural law,
          which we worship,
                    maintain
all of a piece
          their dominance.
So let us love
          confident as is the light
                    in its struggle with darkness
that there is as much to say
          and more
                    for the one side
and that not the darker
          which John Donne
                    for instance
among many men
          presents to us.
                    In the controversy
touching the younger
          and the older Tolstoi,
                    Villon, St. Anthony, Kung,
Rimbaud, Buddha
          and Abraham Lincoln
                    the palm goes
always to the light;
          Who most shall advance the light—
                    call it what you may!
The light
          for all time shall outspeed
                    the thunder crack.
Medieval pageantry
          is human and we enjoy
                    the rumor of it
as in our world we enjoy
          the reading of Chaucer,
                    likewise
a priest's raiment
          (or that of a savage chieftain).
                    It is all

a celebration of the light.
All the pomp and ceremony
of weddings,
"Sweet Thames, run softly
till I end
my song,"—
are of an equal sort.
For our wedding, too,
the light was wakened
and shone. The light!
the light stood before us
waiting!
I thought the world
stood still.
At the altar
so intent was I
before my vows,
so moved by your presence
a girl so pale
and ready to faint
that I pitied
and wanted to protect you.
As I think of it now,
after a lifetime,
it is as if
a sweet-scented flower
were poised
and for me did open.
Asphodel
has no odor
save to the imagination
but it too
celebrates the light.
It is late
but an odor
as from our wedding
has revived for me
and begun again to penetrate
into all crevices
of my world.

1. What is this poem saying about imagination life, and love?

2. Discuss the imagery of light as used in this poem.

3. What effect is created by the reintroduction of the asphodel at the end?

4. Study the rhythm in these three-line stanzas. Can you discern any guiding principle?

The next poem is inspired by one of the most famous of all paintings:

Landscape with the Fall of Icarus

According to Brueghel
when Icarus fell
it was spring

a farmer was ploughing
his field
the whole pageantry

of the year was
awake tingling
near

the edge of the sea
concerned
with itself

sweating in the sun
that melted
the wings' wax

unsignificantly
off the coast
there was

a splash quite unnoticed
this was
Icarus drowning

1. Look at the selection of details—spring, ploughing, and the like. Why do you think Williams selected these particular details from the painting?

2. What does each of these phrases contribute to the poem?—(a) According to Brueghel, (b) tingling / near, (c) the edge of the sea / concerned with itself, (d) quite unnoticed, (e) this was / Icarus drowning.

3. Read Auden's "Musée des Beaux Arts" (page 262) What similarities and differences of effect between the two poems do you find?

4. Williams used his usual three-line form of "variable feet." What is Auden's rhythm? His rhyme scheme? How does the more intricate formal structure of Auden's poem affect the "feel" of his poem as compared with Williams' poem?

And now here are a few poems to read on your own.

The Wind Increases

The harried
earth is swept
The trees
the tulip's bright
tips
sidle and
toss—

Loose your love
to flow

Blow!

Good Christ what is
a poet—if any
exists?

a man
whose words will
bite
their way
home—being actual

having the form
of motion

At each twigtip

new

upon the tortured
body of thought
gripping
the ground

a way
to the last leaftip

Dedication for a Plot of Ground

This plot of ground
facing the waters of this inlet
is dedicated to the living presence of
Emily Dickinson Wellcome
who was born in England, married,
lost her husband and with
her five year old son

sailed for New York in a two-master,
was driven to the Azores;
ran adrift on Fire Island shoal,
met her second husband
in a Brooklyn boarding house,
went with him to Puerto Rico
bore three more children, lost
her second husband, lived hard
for eight years in St. Thomas,
Puerto Rico, San Domingo, followed
the oldest son to New York,
lost her daughter, lost her "baby",
seized the two boys of
the oldest son by the second marriage
mothered them—they being
motherless—fought for them
against the other grandmother
and the aunts, brought them here
summer after summer, defended
herself here against thieves,
storms, sun, fire,
against flies, against girls
that came smelling about, against
drought, against weeds, storm-tides,
neighbors, weasels that stole her chickens,
against the weakness of her own hands,
against the growing strength of
the boys, against wind, against
the stones, against trespassers,
against rents, against her own mind.

She grubbed this earth with her own hands,
domineered over this grass plot,
blackguarded her oldest son
into buying it, lived here fifteen years,
attained a final loneliness and—

If you can bring nothing to this place
but your carcass, keep out.

The Poor

By constantly tormenting them
with reminders of the lice in
their children's hair, the
School Physician first
brought their hatred down on him.

But by this familiarity
they grew used to him, and so,
at last,
look him for their friend and adviser.

The Thinker

My wife's new pink slippers
have gay pom-poms.
There is not a spot or a stain
on their satin toes or their sides.
All night they lie together
under her bed's edge.
Shivering I catch sight of them
and smile, in the morning.
Later I watch them
descending the stair,
hurrying through the doors
and round the table,
moving stiffly
with a shake of their gay pom-poms!
And I talk to them
in my secret mind
out of pure happiness.

The Red Wheelbarrow

so much depends
upon

a red wheel
barrow

glazed with rain
water

beside the white
chickens.

Io Baccho!

God created alcohol
and it wasn't privately for the Russians
God created alcohol
and it wasn't for Dr. Goldsmith

It was for Mrs. Reiter
who is bored with having children
though she loves them.
God created alcohol to release
and engulf us. Shall I
say it is the only evidence of God
in this environment?

Mrs. R. doesn't drink
but drink and I told the angel,
God created alcohol!
—if it weren't for that I'd say
there wasn't Any—
thinking of Mrs. R. who is
one eighth American Indian
and what with the pain in her guts
stands like an Indian
"If I had the strength"
Why should I bother to tell you?

God created alcohol
Shall I swoon like Mr. Keats?
and not from looking
at a Grecian urn. God created alcohol
to allay us

Rogation Sunday

O let the seeds be planted
and the worry and unrest be invited!
Let that which is to come
of the weather and our own weakness
be accepted!

Let work mate with fertility
the man and the soil join to produce
a world, a world of blade and blossom!
We believe! We believe
in the wonder of continuous revival,
the ritual of the farm.

This is our world and this
is our message to the world and to each other:
Let the seed be planted, the man
and the soil be ploughed equally
by the joy in the planting—

that the grass, the grasses that bear
the seeds: oat, rye and corn
and other yield
speak their message of revival and thrive
by our labor this Maytime.

Coda:

Who shall reap the harvest?
To whom shall the praise be given?
No man—but all men together in love
and devotion. There is no other harvest
and no other praise!
O let the seeds be planted and the rain
and the sun and the moon add their wonder.

The Stolen Peonies

What I got out of women
was difficult
to assess Flossie

not you
you lived with me
many years you remember

that year
we had the magnificent
stand of peonies

how happy we were
with them
but one night

they were stolen
we shared the
loss together thinking

of nothing else for
a whole day
nothing could have

brought us closer
we had been
married ten years

From *The Desert Music*

How shall we get said what must be said?

Only the poem.

Only the counted poem, to an exact measure:
to imitate, not to copy nature, not
to copy nature

NOT, prostrate, to copy nature
but a dance! to dance
two and two with him—
sequestered there asleep,
right end up!

A music
supersedes his composure, hallooing to us
across a great distance . .

wakens the dance
who blows upon his benumbed fingers!

Only the poem
only the made poem, to get said what must
be said, not to copy nature, sticks
in our throats .

From *Paterson*

The descent beckons
as the ascent beckoned
Memory is a kind
of accomplishment
a sort of renewal
even
an initiation, since the spaces it opens are new
places
inhabited by hordes
heretofore unrealized,
of new kinds—
since their movements
are towards new objectives
(even though formerly they were abandoned)

No defeat is made up entirely of defeat—since
the world it opens is always a place
formerly
unsuspected. A

world lost,
a world unsuspected
beckons to new places
and no whiteness (lost) is so white as the memory
of whiteness .

With evening, love wakens
though its shadows
which are alive by reason
of the sun shining—
grow sleepy now and drop away
from desire .

Love without shadows stirs now
beginning to waken
as night
advances.

The descent
made up of despairs
and without accomplishment
realizes a new awakening :
which is a reversal
of despair.
For what we cannot accomplish, what
is denied to love,
what we have lost in the anticipation—
a descent follows,
endless and indestructible .

SELECTIVE BIBLIOGRAPHY

Most of the poems included in this chapter were taken from three books by Williams: *The Collected Earlier Poems of William Carlos Williams* (New York: New Directions, 1938, 1951), *The Collected Later Poems of William Carlos Williams* (New York: New Directions, 1944, 1963), and *Pictures from Brueghel and Other Poems* (New York: New Directions, 1949, 1962).

Since the student of this book presumably has not read *Paterson*, we have not included in the bibliography any critical studies dealing exclusively with that epic.

James E. Breslin, *William Carlos Williams: An American Artist* (New York: Oxford University Press, 1970).

John Malcolm Brinnin, *William Carlos Williams* (Minneapolis: University of Minnesota Press, 1963).

James Guimond, *The Art of William Carlos Williams* (Urbana: University of Illinois Press, 1968).

Vivienne Koch, *William Carlos Williams* (New York: New Directions, 1950).

Joseph Hillis Miller, *William Carlos Williams: A Collection of Critical Essays* (Englewood Cliffs, N.J.: Prentice-Hall, 1966).

Paul Sherman, *The Music of Survival* (Urban: University of Illinois Press, 1968).

Linda Wagner, *The Poems of William Carlos Williams: A Critical Study* (Middletown, Conn.: Wesleyan University Press, 1964).

Mike Weaver, *William Carlos Williams: The American Background* (Cambridge University Press, 1971).

William Carlos Williams, *In the American Grain* (New York: New Directions, 1956).

———in *Writers at Work,* 3rd series, *Paris Review Interviews,* ed. George Plimpton (New York: Viking, 1968). Prose.

———, *The Autobiography of William Carlos Williams* (New York: Random House, 1951).

———, *I Wanted to Write a Poem* (Boston: Beacon Press, 1968).

Wallace Stevens

His Life

In contrast to the other poets we have discussed, Wallace Stevens' biography seems stark. His thinking took no sudden change of direction, nor did events of the outside world shape the subject matter of his poetry, as much as was true for example, of W. H. Auden.

Stevens was born in Pennslyvania in October, 1879, into a family with Dutch and German roots. His youth, from his letters and biographical accounts, contained no agonizing rebellion nor alienation. Since his family valued things of the intellect, he entered Harvard as a special student in 1897 and left in 1900 without a degree to go into law school in New York, and in 1904 he was admitted to the New York State Bar.

In 1909 he married Elsie Kachel, having courted her since 1906, and he remained married to her until his death. He worked in various law firms and in 1916 joined the legal staff of the Hartford Accident and Indemnity Co., where he spent for the rest of his working life, becoming a vice-president in 1934. Elderly insurance executives still remember him as outstanding in that profession. By nature he was a conservative and considered himself a Taft Republican. His home life appears uneventful; one child, a daughter, Holly, was born in 1924. Stevens traveled extensively in his early days with the insurance company, but almost entirely within the continental United States. For relaxation he spent some weeks in Florida each year, especially around Key West, but as he grew older he stayed more and more in Hartford.

His poetry has numerous references to Europe and Asia but he never travelled abroad, although certainly he was affluent enough to do so. Outwardly he led a quiet, safe, "waspish" life. Yet what a rich store of mental images his poetry reveals: Here is a member of the "Establishment" whose writing is full of force and color, whose vocabulary is incredibly rich, and whose imagination works with full power. In fact, a belief in the power of the imagination to operate on reality and reveal the essence of existence is a cornerstone of his thinking and his work.

At first glance his life seems to be completely schizophrenic. He devoted himself wholeheartedly to his business career and most of his business associates were unaware of his passion for poetry. Although some of his poems were published in *Poetry* magazine as early as 1914, it was not until 1923, when he was 44 years old, that his first book, *Harmonium,* appeared.

Stevens' poetic reputation grew very slowly, for he is not an easy poet to comprehend, and his language is certainly complex. Moreover, many of his early critics felt he had great facility with words but that his work was too precious, too involved with "art for art's sake." It is true that Stevens almost never deals directly with social, economic, or political themes, and the 1930s were a time when economics and politics engaged a great many writers. But that does not mean that he was unaware of the great changes going on around him; many of his poems of that period are a search for some abiding order and a belief that art itself is a way of ordering chaos.

Gradually as he worked on, his reputation grew until in 1950 he was awarded the Bollinger prize for the *Auroras of Autumn*, and in 1954, in recognition of his 75th birthday, his *Collected Poems* appeared, and received the Pulitzer prize as well as the National Book Award for 1955, the year of his death. It is difficult to know whether Stevens' business contacts fed his poetry in the same way that Williams' medical practice enriched his. Williams seems more of one piece in his life and work than does Stevens, who appears to have consciously kept the two areas of his life firmly separated. Stevens was an austere man. Rarely does open emotion or personal experience appear as such in his work, although the comment has been made that "The Comedian as the Letter C" has elements of autobiography. There is no doubt that he had a fine mind and the ability to deal with complex ideas with grace and subtlety.

From what philosophic premise did he begin and where did he end? In the next section we deal briefly with three or four of the basic concepts with which he was concerned throughout his poetic career, and we will comment on his baroque style which, as he aged, "combed itself out" into simpler language.

The Poet and His Poetry

The complexity of Stevens' language spills over into any attempt to systematize his thinking, but a few generalizations will help. In some ways, Stevens is easier reading than many poets. First, the ideas he deals with are not nearly as esoteric or difficult as those we encounter in Yeats or Blake. Stevens never erected a system like Yeats' in *A Vision,* nor did he develop a mythology such as Blake imagined in his prophetic books. In fact, Stevens recognized change as the one constant in human life and was aware that nothing can be secure or fixed. A system to stop the flux would have contradicted his basic premise.

Stevens wrote variations on three major themes, and his thinking about these themes grew richer as he grew older. It is the way he expressed himself, his infinite variety of language rather than any radical change in thought, that impresses one. Certainly his rhetoric did change, and although his language is always rich and varied, it is much lusher in the early poems than in the later ones.

One thing is consistent—his ability to create intriguing titles:

The Paltry Nude Starts on a Spring Voyage
The Emperor of Ice Cream
Hymn from a Watermelon Patch
Ghosts as Cocoons
The Owl in the Sarcophagus
Angels surrounded by Paysans

A Necessary Angel is helpful in understanding some of Stevens' ideas, for it is a series of esssays written over a span of years that dealt primarily with the function of the poet and the relationship between imagination and reality. His *Letters* are also helpful, especially when he is commenting on specific poems. But in the end, no gloss, no prose paraphrase can take the place of the poems themselves with all their rich variety of language and verse form.

One is immediately struck, if he reads very much of Stevens, with the way nature operates in his poems, especially how the various seasons are used. There is constant reference to clouds and wind, sun and moon, and "this perishing earth." Two colors, green and blue, seem also to predominate. Particularly in "The Man with the Blue Guitar" blue stands for the imagination, green for "things as they are." When the moon appears in the poetry, it also represents the imagination, and the sun stands for reality. Stevens uses the sequence of the seasons to illustrate the constant change in human lives, though with no idea of a great cyclical sweep of history such as Yeats proposed. But the seasons, autumn and winter particularly, do have archetypal nuances, and they, together with summer, are much more important than spring, the season that moves most poets.

In an era of politicalization, from the early thirties on, Stevens steadfastly refused to be a political poet. It was not that he was apolitical, but his mind was the sort that saw the flux and upheaval in more universal than immediate terms. In *A Necessary Angel* he states forthrightly:[1]

> Then I am interested in the role of the poet and this is paramount. In this area of my subject I might be expected to speak of the social, that is to say sociological or political obligation of the poet. He has none . . . I do not think that a poet owes any more as a social obligation than he owes as a moral obligation, and if there is anything concerning poetry about which people agree it is that the role of the poet is not to be found in morals . . . I think that his function is to make his imagination theirs and that he fulfills himself only as he sees his imagination become the light in the minds of others.

In trying to summarize Stevens' chief concerns, we can, as Hi Simon did in his fine essay on "The Genre of Wallace Stevens,"[2] indicate three major themes. Simon's essay, however, was written in 1945 and therefore does not take into account the final ten years of Stevens' work. But it is obvious that the theme he explored all his life was the relationship between imagination and reality. "The Man with the Blue Guitar" is a prime example of his thinking on this theme. Though Stevens never ceased to probe the bond between the two, it appears that the emphasis on reality increased as he aged.

In a second major concern, Stevens considered change and process to be the underlying principle of human existence, and he also saw the bond between the subjective aspects of life and the object as constantly shifting. This resulted in part from the fact that he was unable to find meaning in any organized theology, as did Eliot and Donne, and his poetry is full of the death of old myths and old traditions. To Stevens, paradise is on this earth, if anywhere, and this earth and this life are all we have; "Death is the mother of beauty"; all is change. These thoughts echo throughout his poetry. For him the old gods are dead. At the same time he is aware that we must believe in some fiction or myth. We must turn to ourselves, and by a marriage of imagination and things as they are—including evil—we break through to whatever meaning we can find. Stevens seems more concerned with the process than with any final answer, because he is convinced there can never be a final answer.

Long before the term became a household word it seems that Stevens' thinking had many links to French existentialism. "Sunday Morning" among the early poems illustrates this. And in a letter to Hi Simons written in 1940 he said:[3]

[1] Wallace Stevens, *Tne Necessary Angel* (New York: Vintage Books, 1942, 1951), pp. 27-29.

[2] In Marie Borroff, ed., *Wallace Stevens: A Collection of Critical Essays* (Englewood Cliffs, N.J.: Prentice-Hall, Inc., 1963), pp. 43-53. (originally published in *The Sewanee Review,* LIII, No. 4 (Autumn 1945).

[3] Holly Stevens, ed., *Letters of Wallace Stevens* (New York: Alfred A. Knopf, 1970), p. 369.

> The idea of God is a thing of the imagination. We no longer think that God was, but was imagined. The idea of pure poetry, essential imagination, as the highest objective of the poet, appears to be, at least potentially, as great as the idea of God, and for that matter greater, if the idea of God is only one of the things of the imagination.

Later on, in the same year he wrote to Henry Church:[4]

> The major poetic idea in the world is and always has been the idea of God. One of the visible movements of the modern imagination is the movement away from the idea of God. The poetry that created the idea of God will either adapt it to our different intelligence, or create a substitute for it, or make it unnecessary.

Hence, reality must be faced. The supreme fiction must be found by the power of the imagination, which imposes an order on "things as they are" and thus reveals some ultimate though temporary reality neither "things as they are" or the mind acting on them, but a fusion of the two. It is supremely the poet who can accomplish this feat, so "the theory of poetry" becomes "the theory of life."

To sum up, the relationship between imagination and reality, the constant change and flux inherent in life, the changing relationship between human consciousness and the objective world, and the poet's central role in all this —these are Stevens' major themes expressed in memorable poetry which covers a span of more than 40 years.

His poetry shows tremendous variety in structure, style, and use of language, though the subject matter is more limited. Back in 1932, R. P. Blackmur said:[5]

> "The most striking if not the most important thing about Mr. Stevens' verse is its vocabulary . . . The important thing about Mr. Stevens' vocabulary is not the apparent oddity of certain words, but the uses to which he puts those words with others. It is the way that Mr. Stevens combines kinds of words, unusual in a single context, to reveal the substance he had in mind, which is of real interest to the reader.

For instance, note in "The Emperor of Ice Cream," a poem we will discuss in the next section, how language is used.

> Call the roller of big cigars
> The muscular one, and bid him whip
> In kitchen cups concupiscent curds.

[4] Stevens, *Letters,* p. 378.

[5] *Language as Gesture* (New York: Harcourt, Brace and Co., 1952), p. 221. Reprinted in Ashley Brown and Robert S. Haller, eds., *The Achievement of Wallace Stevens* (Philadelphia: New York: J. B. Lippincott Company, 1962).

Or take these lines from "Le Monocle de Mon Oncle" to describe the process of aging:

> Our bloom is gone. We are the fruit thereof.
> Two golden gourds distended on our vines,
> In the autumn weather, splashed with frost,
> Distended by hale fatness, turned grotesque,
> We hang like warty squashes, streaked and rayed.

Note the conjunction of "hale fatness" and the "golden gourds" with the word "distended". Note also the contrast between distended golden gourds and "warty squashes." There are images here in profusion, and they all join to serve the poet's attempt to give an objective description of growing old. It is interesting here to contrast this poem with Eliot's "Prufrock" (p. 349).

Notice also as you read Stevens' poetry the range of his poetics. He is at home in rhyme, in regular meter, in blank verse, in free verse, couplets, long lines, short lines, triplets—almost any form seems to fit his talent. He is not as facile as Auden, but he is the master of almost any form he chooses to use, and his talent found particular satisfaction in the long poem where he had a chance to ring changes on his thoughts and let his imagination go more fully. Though he wrote some fine short poems, it is the long ones that seem most representative—poems like "Sunday Morning," "Notes Toward a Supreme Fiction," "The Man with the Blue Guitar," "An Ordinary Evening in New Haven," and "The Comedian as the Letter C." The latter has been characterized as Stevens' *Portrait of the Artist* and one critic called it his *Ulysses.*

Perhaps most of this will fall into place as we examine some of the poems. Because of space limitations, relatively little can be done here with the longer poems, but the reader who learns to read the short ones perceptively is prepared to explore those of greater length, should his interest in Stevens lead him to the library.

One apology. Copyright limitations prevented our including as much of Stevens' poetry as we wished. We hope this deficiency will motivate the reader to seek out other poems on his own.

Poems

We begin with a short poem written fairly early in Stevens' career—"The Emperor of Ice Cream." In 1933 he said this about it:[6]

> I think I should select from my poems as my favorite, The Emperor of Ice Cream. This wears a deliberately commonplace costume, and yet seems to me to contain something of the essential gaudiness of poetry; this is the reason I like it.

And many years later in 1945 in another letter he wrote.[7]

> The ice cream poem is a good example of a poem that has its own singularity . . . the words "concupiscent curds" have no genealogy; they are merely expressive: at least I hope they are expressive. They express the concupiscence of life, but, by contrast with the things in relation to them in the poem, they express or accentuate life's destitution, and it is this that gives them something more than a cheap lustre.

The Emperor of Ice-Cream

Call the roller of big cigars,
The muscular one, and bid him whip
In kitchen cups concupiscent curds.
Let the wenches dawdle in such dress
As they are used to wear, and let the boys
Bring flowers in last month's newspapers.
Let be be finale of seem.
The only emperor is the emperor of ice-cream

Take from the dresser of deal,
Lacking the three glass knobs, that sheet
On which she embroidered fantails once
And spread it so as to cover her face.
If her horny feet protrude, they come
To show how cold she is, and dumb.
Let the lamp affix its beam.
The only emperor is the emperor of ice-cream.

How do you respond to the poem? What do you think it is all about? Does the structure give any clue? There are two stanzas of eight lines, each with an identical final line. The rhythm has considerable variation, and the poem is one of action with the imperative of *call, take,* and three uses of *let.* There is rhyme,

[6] *Letters,* p. 500.
[7] *Letters,* p. 500.

but it only occurs as true rhyme in the final two lines of each stanza and in come / dumb. But the poem is held together by alliteration—"call, kitchen, cups, concupiscent, curds, cover, come, cold, dawdle, dress, deal dresser, dumb," etc. There are several words that you may need to look up. What exactly is the meaning of "concupiscent" and "deal"? What is the relation between the first stanza and the second? Why the title? Blackmur's discussion of it in *Language as Gesture* is provocative:[8]

> The poem might be called Directions for a Funeral, with Two Epitaphs. We have a corpse laid out in the bedroom and we have people in the kitchen. The corpse is dead; then let the boys bring flowers in last month's (who would use today's?) newspapers. The corpse is dead; but let the wenches wear their everyday clothes—or is it the clothes they are used to wear at funerals? The conjunction of a muscular man whipping desirable desserts in the kitchen and the corpse protruding horny feet, gains its effect because of its oddity—not of fact, but of expression: the light frivolous words and rapid meters. Once made the conjunction is irretrievable and in its own measure exact. Two ideas or images about death—the living and the dead—have been associated, and are now permanently fused. If the mind is a rag-bag pull out two rags and sew them together. If the materials were contradictory, the very contradiction, made permanent, becomes a kind of unison. By associating ambiguities found in nature in a poem we reach a kind of clarity, a kind of transfiguration even, whereby we learn *what* the ambiguity was.
>
> The point is, that the oddity of association would not have its effect without the couplets which conclude each stanza with the pungency of good epitaphs. Without the couplets, the association would sink from wit to low humor or simple description. What, then, do the couplets mean? Either, or both, of two things. In the more obvious sense, "Let be be finale of seem," in the first stanza, means, take whatever seems to be, as really being; and in the second stanza, "Let the lamp affix its beam," means let it be plain that this woman is dead, that these things, impossibly ambiguous as they may be, are as they are. In this case, "The only emperor is the emperor of ice-cream," implies in both stanzas that the only power worth heeding is the power of the moment, of what is passing, of the flux.
>
> The less obvious sense of the couplets is more difficult to set down because, in all its difference, it rises out of the first sense, and while contradicting and supplanting, yet guarantees it. The connotation is, perhaps, that ice-cream and what it represents is the only power *heeded,* not the only power there is to heed. The irony recoils on itself: what

[8] *Language as Gesture*, pp. 228-229.

seems *shall* finally be; the lamp *shall* affix its beam. The only emperor is the emperor of ice-cream. The king is dead; long live the king.

The virtue of the poem is that it discusses and settles these matters without mentioning them. The wit of the couplets does the work.

1. Do Blackmur's comments take into account Stevens' coment of 1945? Do the comments clarify or muddy the watters?

2. Is there any way you can reconcile Blackmur's comments and Stevens' statement?

3. Are you satisfied that the phrase "Emperor of Ice-Cream" means that the only power worth heeding is the power of the moment?

The Pleasures of Merely Circulating

The garden flew round with the angel,
The angel flew round with the clouds,
And the clouds flew round and the clouds flew round
And the clouds flew round with the clouds.

Is there any secret in skulls,
The cattle skulls in the woods?
Do the drummers in black hoods
Rumble anything out of their drums?

Mrs. Anderson's Swedish baby
Might well have been German or Spanish,
Yet that things go round and again go round
Has rather a classical sound.

The "Pleasures of Merely Ciculating" is another of Stevens' memorable short poems in which the word repetition itself suggests the circularity of existence. Look at the first stanza—in those four lines *angel* appears twice, *clouds* is repeated five times, and the words *flew around* occur four times. Hence, a whirling pattern is immediately established. Then look at the title, "The Pleasures of merely Circulating." How does that word *merely* condition your response to the poem? Would it have been different if Stevens had omitted it?

The second stanza, again of four lines, strikes a more somber tone and consists of two ominous questions. Here Stevens depends for his effects not on rhyme, but on the end words of each line, each one syllable. Some of the ominous feeling comes from the drummers in *black* hoods.

The final stanza is lighter in tone, and the *round* of the first stanza is repeated, as though coming full circle. But there is a change—*flew* is replaced by the more prosaic *go*.

This poem does not have Stevens' usual intricacy of language. It speaks directly and hauntingly. What does the third stanza suggest in answer to the questions of the second stanza? Stevens rather reluctantly commented on this poem in a letter to Hi Simons[9] in 1940. "The spectacle of order is so vast that it resembles disorder, it resembles the fortuitous. Swedish babies are as likely as not to have been something else. But for all the apparent fortuitousness of things, they hold together. Here again the explanation destroys the poem." This is the way life is, a vast process sweeping to no predestined end, death and chance play their part, and the very title itself, in spite of stanza two, lends a light touch to the poem. The process itself is what matters.

1. Compare and contrast this poem with Yeats' "Second Coming" (p.000) Does the idea of "circulating" correspond to Yeats' cyclical view of history? Or are their concepts of time and change fundamentally different?

2. Images of "going round" occur in the first and last stanzas, but not in the middle one. Why?

Evening Without Angels

the great interests of man: air and
light, the joy of having a body, the
voluptuousness of looking.
MARIO ROSSI

Why seraphim like lutanists arranged
Above the trees? And why the poet as
Eternal *chef d'orchestre*?

Air is air,
Its vacancy glitters round us everywhere.
Its sounds are not angelic syllables
But our unfashioned spirits realized
More sharply in more furious selves.

And light
That fosters seraphim and is to them
Coiffeur of haloes, fecund jeweller—
Was the sun concoct for angels or for men?
Sad men made angels of the sun, and of
The moon they made their own attendant ghosts,
Which led them back to angels, after death.

[9] Letters, p. 348.

Let this be clear that we are men of sun
And men of day and never of pointed night,
Men that repeat antiquest sounds of air
In an accord of repetitions. Yet,
If we repeat, it is because the wind
Encircling us, speaks always with our speech.

Light, too, encrusts us making visible
The motions of the mind and giving form
To moodiest nothings, as, desire for day
Accomplished in the immensely flashing East,
Desire for rest, in that descending sea
Of dark, which in its very darkening
Is rest and silence spreading into sleep.

. . . Evening, when the measure skips a beat
And then another, one by one, and all
To a seething minor swiftly modulate.
Bare night is best. Bare earth is best. Bare, bare,
Except for our own houses, huddled low
Beneath the arches and their spangled air,
Beneath the rhapsodies of fire and fire,
Where the voice that is in us makes a true response,
Where the voice that is great within us rises up,
As we stand gazing at the rounded moon.

"Evening Without Angels" is typical of Stevens' rhetoric in the way it clearly expresses his belief that "man is the intelligence of his soul," and that earth is all we have, and that whatever meaning there is comes from "the voice that is in us." He communicates all this in images of air and light, the physical universe.

The focus of the poem begins with the lofty word *seraphim* and in the last stanza narrows down to "bare earth," our houses "huddled low" where "the voice that is great within us rises up." Alan Perlis[10] concludes that the poem's "implication is that the moon is rounded by our rounded mouths, which form a melody." This poem is perhaps a stronger "hymn to man" than many of Stevens' poems, yet man is central in them all. But observe the language he uses here which sheds so much radiance on the poem.

And light
That fosters seraphim and is to them
Coiffeur of haloes, fecund jeweller—

[10] *Wallace Stevens: A World of Transforming Shapes* (Lewisburg, Pa.: Bucknell University Press, 1975), p. 57.

Note the juxtaposition of "fecund" and "jeweller" or the delightful phrase "Coiffeur of haloes." When Stevens is talking about air he says "its vacancy glitters round us everywhere." Have you ever thought of vacancy as glittering? But light fades and we come to the beautiful final stanza "To a seething minor swiftly modulate" And, then, "Bare night is best. Bare earth is best. Bare, bare."

1. What does the title suggest to you? Does it set the tone of the poem?

2. If someone asked you to summarize the theme of the poem, what would you say?

3. What is lost when a summary or paraphrase is studied in place of the poem itself? (Use this poem to illustrate.)

Now to get the flavor of Stevens more completely, let us look at two excerpts from his longer poems, especially since he seemed to need that mode to best work out his ideas—and Stevens' poetry is certainly much more intellectual than emotional or dramatic. "Sunday Morning" is one of Stevens' earlier poems where a woman is musing about the world around her and her longing for "some imperishable bliss" which shall remain when her transient encounter with earth is ended. Her meditations gradually lead her to understand that "death is the mother of beauty," that earth is paradise enough and here, if anywhere, our hearts can be at home. And thus she comes to accept death as part of the process, and we see her response to this "perishing earth" in Stanza IV.

from *Sunday Morning*

She says, "I am content when wakened birds,
Before they fly, test the reality
Of misty fields, by their sweet questionings;
But when the birds are gone, and their warm fields
Return no more, where, then, is paradise?"
There is not any haunt of prophecy,
Nor any old chimera of the grave,
Neither the golden underground, nor isle
Melodious, where spirits gat them home,
Nor visionary south, nor cloudy palm
Remote on heaven's hill, that has endured
As April's green endures; or will endure
Like her remembrance of awakened birds,
Or her desire for June and evening, tipped
By the consummation of the swallow's wings.

The poem is divided into eight stanzas of fifteen lines each. Although the rhythm varies it is predominantly iambic, and as the stanza quoted illustrates, there is no true rhyme in the poem. What do you think holds it together poetically? Is it the tone? The words? The rhythm? In a letter to L. W. Payne, Jr., in 1928, Stevens made this comment on "Sunday Morning":[11]

> "This is not essentially a woman's meditation on religion and the meaning of life. It is anybody's meditation . . . The poem is simply an expression of paganism, although, of course, I did not think that I was expressing paganism when I wrote it."

1. Can you compare this excerpt with one of Browning's poems? What difference in attitude toward life and its fulfillment do you find?

2. What does this poem say about the nature of paradise?

"The Man with the Blue Guitar," written some years later, questions from many angles the relationship between the imagination and "things as they are." Observe how different the form is from "Sunday Morning." This poem has 33 stanzas, written entirely in couplet form. Iambic tetrameter is evident in the early stanzas and the movement goes from an insistent beat, almost sing-song in spots, to a quieter, less obtrusive rhythm. The man with the guitar is, of course, the poet, and when the book was first published Stevens had this to say on the dust jacket:[12]

> This group deals with the incessant conjunctions between things as they are and things imagined. Although the blue guitar is a symbol of the imagination, it is used most often simply as a reference to the individuality of the poet, meaning by the poet any man of imagination.

As late as 1953 Stevens again elaborated on "The Man with the Blue Guitar":[13]

> The general intention of the *Blue Guitar* was to say a few ahings that I felt impelled to say 1. about reality: 2. about the imagination: 3. their inter-relations: and 4. my attitude toward each of these things. This is the general scope of the poem, which is confined to the area of poetry and makes no pretense of going beyond that area.

Let us see how he expresses this poetically, taking only one section of the poem.

[11] Letters, p. 250.
[12] A. Walton Litz, *Introspective Voyager: The Poetic Development of Wallace Stevens* (New York: Oxford University Press, 1972), p. 232.
[13] *Letters*, p. 788.

from *The Man with the Blue Guitar*

XXV

He held the world upon his nose
And this-a-way he gave a fling.

His robes and symbols, ai-yi-yi—
And that-a-way he twirled the thing.

Sombre as fir-trees, liquid cats
Moved in the grass without a sound.

They did not know the grass went round.
The cats had cats and the grass turned gray

And the world had worlds, ai, this-a-way:
The grass turned green and the grass turned gray.

And the nose is eternal, that-a-way.
Things as they were, things as they are,

Things as they will be by and by . . .
A fat thumb beats out ai-yi-yi.

Notice the rhyme, the rhythm, the movement, the word repetition—the thumb beating out "ai-yi-yi". Why does he describe the thumb as fat? Who is holding the world upon his nose and what kind of image does this suggest —is it humorous? Are the cats symbolic?

Fortunately, Stevens did a kind of explanation of the poem for Hi Simons and in his comment on this section he lets us know what he was attempting:[14]

> The man of imagination juggles the world on the tip of his nose, but the world does not realize that it moves as an imagination directs. People go about their accustomed jobs, unconscious of what is occurring. And the imagination is eternal. The figure (he) with his robes, the cats, the being and begetting are merely paraphernalia used to produce an effect of comedy. The poet is a comedian. Liquid cats = cats that move as smoothly as if liquid. They are solemn black blobs on the mind's eye, sombre as fir trees. When the imagination is moving rapidly, it identifies things only approximately, and to stop to define them would be to stop altogether. No doubt these sombre cats are merely sombre people going about their jobs. Anyhow, one is trying to do a poem which may be organized out of whatever material one can snatch up. The fat thumb, etc, = stupid people at the spectacle of life, which they enjoy but do not understand.

[14] *Letters*, p. 361.

1. Does this explanation enhance or diminish your response to the poem?

2. Study the language of Section XXV. Is it appropriate to the serious thought being expressed?

The following short poem does unusual things with a common object.

The Snow Man

One must have a mind of winter
To regard the frost and boughs
Of the pine-trees crusted with snow;

And have been cold a long time
To behold the junipers shagged with ice,
The spruces rough in the distant glitter

Of the January sun; and not to think
Of any misery in the sound of the wind,
In the sound of a few leaves,

Which is the sound of the land
Full of the same wind
That is blowing in the same bare place

For the listener, who listens in the snow,
And, nothing himself, beholds
Nothing that is not there and the nothing that is.

1. Compare this poem with Frost's "Stopping by Woods on a Snowy Evening." (page 176).

2. Comment on what Stevens said about the poem:[15] "I shall explain The Snow Man as an example of the necessity of identifying oneself with reality in order to understand and enjoy it."

The next poem is a relatively late one. "To An Old Philosopher in Rome," written about the old age of Santayana, a famous philosopher, and published just about the time that Santayana died.

[15] *Letters*, p. 464

To an Old Philosopher in Rome

On the threshold of heaven, the figures in the street
Become the figures of heaven, the majestic movement
Of men growing small in the distances of space,
Singing, with smaller and still smaller sound,
Unintelligible absolution and an end—

The threshold, Rome, and that more merciful Rome
Beyond, the two alike in the make of the mind.
It is as if in a human dignity
Two parallels become one, a perspective, of which
Men are part both in the inch and in the mile.

How easily the blown banners change to wings . . .
Things dark on the horizons of perception,
Become accompaniments of fortune, but
Of the fortune of the spirit, beyond the eye,
Not of its sphere, and yet not far beyond,

The human end in the spirit's greatest reach,
The extreme of the known in the presence of the extreme
Of the unknown. The newsboys' muttering
Becomes another murmuring; the smell
Of medicine, a fragrantness not to be spoiled . . .

The bed, the books, the chair, the moving nuns,
The candle as it evades the sight, these are
The sources of happiness in the shape of Rome,
A shape within the ancient circles of shapes,
And these beneath the shadow of a shape

In a confusion on bed and books, a portent
On the chair, a moving transparence on the nuns,
A light on the candle tearing against the wick
To join a hovering excellence, to escape
From fire and be part only of that of which

Fire is the symbol: the celestial possible.
Speak to your pillow as if it was yourself.
Be orator but with an accurate tongue
And without eloquence, O, half asleep,
Of the pity that is the memorial of this room,

So that we feel, in this illumined large,
The veritable small, so that each of us
Beholds himself in you, and hears his voice
In yours, master and commiserable man,
Intent on your particles of nether-do,

Your dozing in the depths of wakefulness,
In the warmth of your bed, at the edge of your chair, alive
Yet living in two worlds, impenitent
As to one, and, as to one, most penitent,
Impatient for the grandeur that you need

In so much misery; and yet finding it
Only in misery, the afflatus of ruin,
Profound poetry of the poor and of the dead,
As in the last drop of the deepest blood,
As it falls from the heart and lies there to be seen,

Even as the blood of an empire, it might be,
For a citizen of heaven though still of Rome.
It is poverty's speech that seeks us out the most.
It is older than the oldest speech of Rome.
This is the tragic accent of the scene.

And you—it is you that speak it, without speech,
The loftiest syllables among loftiest things,
The one invulnerable man among
Crude captains, the naked majesty, if you like,
Of bird-nest arches and of rain-stained-vaults.

The sounds drift in. The buildings are remembered.
The life of the city never lets go, nor do you
Ever want it to. It is part of the life in your room.
Its domes are the architecture of your bed.
The bells keep on repeating solemn names

In choruses and choirs of choruses,
Unwilling that mercy should be a mystery
Of silence, that any solitude of sense
Should give you more than their peculiar chords
And reverberations clinging to whisper still.

It is a kind of total grandeur at the end,
With every visible thing enlarged and yet
No more than a bed, a chair and moving nuns,
The immensest theatre, the pillared porch,
The book and candle in your ambered room,

Total grandeur of a total edifice,
Chosen by an inquisitor of structures
For himself. He stops upon this threshold,
As if the design of all his words takes form
And frame from thinking and is realized.

It might help to know that Santayana was a well-known writer and philosopher who spent the last years of his life in a convent in Rome being cared for by the sisters, though much of his active life was spent in this country and at one time he taught at Harvard.

1. What is the form of the poem? Free verse, Blank verse?

2. Why does Stevens speak of two Romes? What is "that more merciful Rome?" Does this poem say something about the relationship between fiction and fact?

3. What about the images of everyday life—the newsboys, the bed, the books, the chair, the nun, the candle? How is the light of the candle used?

4. Does the poem seem unified? Does the old philosopher become a symbol? What is the relationship between the philosopher and his thoughts on Rome and its buildings?

5. Do you agree with Frank Doggett's comment on this poem?[16]

> This exquisite poem finally achieves a synthesis of the imagery of the buildings of Rome and the thought of the philosopher until the imagery of the city as an edifice becomes a metaphor for the philosophic structure of the philosopher—a structure of thought to be left as a building or city may be left, standing there for other inhabitants.

A few more poems to read on your own:

Anecdote of the Jar

I placed a jar in Tennessee,
And round it was, upon a hill.
It made the slovenly wilderness
Surround that hill.

The wilderness rose up to it,
And sprawled around, no longer wild.
The jar was round upon the ground
And tall and of a port in air,

It took dominion everywhere.
The jar was gray and bare.
It did not give of bird or bush,
Like nothing else in Tennessee.

[16] *Stevens' Poetry of Thought* (Baltimore: the Johns Hopkins Press, 1966). p. 124.

Peter Quince at the Clavier

I

Just as my fingers on these keys
Make music, so the selfsame sounds
On my spirit make a music, too.

Music is feeling, then, not sound;
And thus it is that what I feel,
Here in this room, desiring you,

Thinking of your blue-shadowed silk,
Is music. It is like the strain
Waked in the elders by Susanna.

Of a green evening, clear and warm,
She bathed in her still garden, while
The red-eyed elders watching, felt

The basses of their beings throb
In witching chords, and their thin blood
Pulse pizzicati of Hosanna.

II

In the green water, clear and warm,
Susanna lay.
She searched
The touch of springs,
And found
Concealed imaginings.
She sighed,
For so much melody.

Upon the bank, she stood
In the cool
Of spent emotions.
She felt, among the leaves,
The dew
Of old devotions.

She walked upon the grass,
Still quavering.
The winds were like her maids,
On timid feet,
Fetching her woven scarves,
Yet wavering.

A breath upon her hand
Muted the night.
She turned—
A cymbal crashed,
And roaring horns.

III

Soon, with a noise like tambourines,
Came her attendant Byzantines

They wondered why Susanna cried
Against the elders by her side;

And as they whispered, the refrain
Was like a willow swept by rain.

Anon, their lamps' uplifted flame
Revealed Susanna and her shame.

And then, the simpering Byzantines
Fled, with a noise like tambourines.

IV

Beauty is momentary in the mind—
The fitful tracing of a portal;
But in the flesh it is immortal.
The body dies; the body's beauty lives.
So evenings die, in their green going,
A wave, interminably flowing.
So gardens die, their meek breath scenting
The cowl of winter, done repenting.
So maidens die, to the auroral
Celebration of a maiden's choral.
Susanna's music touched the bawdy strings
Of those white elders; but, escaping,
Left only Death's ironic scraping.
Now, in its immortality, it plays
On the clear viol of her memory,
And makes a constant sacrament of praise.

The Idea of Order at Key West

She sang beyond the genius of the sea.
The water never formed to mind or voice,
Like a body wholly body, fluttering
Its empty sleeves; and yet its mimic motion
Made constant cry, caused constantly a cry,
That was not ours although we understood,
Inhuman, of the veritable ocean.

The sea was not a mask. No more was she.
The song and water were not medleyed sound
Even if what she sang was what she heard,
Since what she sang was uttered word by word.
It may be that in all her phrases stirred
The grinding water and the gasping wind;
But it was she and not the sea we heard.

For she was the maker of the song she sang.
The ever-hooded, tragic-gestured sea
Was merely a place by which she walked to sing.
Whose spirit is this? we said, because we knew
It was the spirit that we sought and knew
That we should ask this often as she sang.

If it was only the dark voice of the sea
That rose, or even colored by many waves;
If it was only the outer voice of sky
And cloud, of the sunken coral water-walled,
However clear, it would have been deep air,
The heaving speech of air, a summer sound
Repeated in a summer without end
And sound alone. But it was more than that,
More even than her voice, and ours, among
The meaningless plungings of water and the wind,
Theatrical distances, bronze shadows heaped
On high horizons, mountainous atmospheres
Of sky and sea.
                         It was her voice that made
The sky acutest at its vanishing.
She measured to the hour its solitude.
She was the single artificer of the world
In which she sang. And when she sang, the sea,
Whatever self it had, became the self
That was her song, for she was the maker. Then we,
As we beheld her striding there alone,
Knew that there never was a world for her
Except the one she sang and, singing, made.

Ramon Fernandez, tell me, if you know,
Why, when the singing ended and we turned
Toward the town, tell why, the glassy lights,
The lights in the fishing boats at anchor there,
As the night descended, tilting in the air,
Mastered the night and portioned out the sea,
Fixing emblazoned zones and fiery poles,
Arranging, deepening, enchanting night.

Oh! Blessed rage for order, pale Ramon,
The maker's rage to order words of the sea,
Words of the fragrant portals, dimly-starred,
And of ourselves and of our origins,
In ghostlier demarcations, keener sounds.

Angel Surrounded by Paysans

One of the countrymen:

There is
A welcome at the door to which no one comes?

The angel:

I am the angel of reality,
Seen for a moment standing in the door.

I have neither ashen wing nor wear of ore
And live without a tepid aureole,

Or stars that follow me, not to attend,
But, of my being and its knowing, part.

I am one of you and being one of you
Is being and knowing what I am and know.

Yet I am necessary angel of earth,
Since, in my sight, you see the earth again,

Cleared of its stiff and stubborn, man-locked set,
And, in my hearing, you hear its tragic drone

Rise liquidly in liquid lingerings,
Like watery words awash; like meanings said

By repetitions of half-meanings. Am I not,
Myself, only half of a figure of a sort,

A figure half seen, or seen for a moment, a man
Of the mind, an apparition apparelled in

Apparels of such lightest look that a turn
Of my shoulder and quickly, too quickly, I am gone?

SELECTIVE BIBLIOGRAPHY

The edition of Stevens' poetry used in this book is *The Collected Poems of Wallace Stevens* (New York: Alfred A. Knopf, 1971).

Lucy Beckett, *Wallace Stevens* (New York and London: Cambridge University Press, 1974).

Michel Benamore, *Wallace Stevens and the Symbolist Imagination* (Princeton, N.J.: Princeton University Press, 1972).

Richard Blessing, *Wallace Stevens' Whole Harmonium* (Syracuse: Syracuse University Press, 1970).

Marie Borroff, ed., *Wallace Stevens: A Collection of Critical Essays* (Englewood Cliffs, N.J.: Prentice-Hall, 1963).

Ashley Brown and Robert Holler, eds., *The Achievement of Wallace Stevens* (Philadelphia and New York: J. B. Lippincott, 1962).

Robert Buttel, *Wallace Stevens: The Making of Harmonium* (Princeton, N.J.: Princeton University Press, 1967).

Frank Doggett, *Stevens' Poetry of Thought* (Baltimore: Johns Hopkins Paperback, 1966).

Walton Litz, *Introspective Voyager: The Poetic Development of Wallace Stevens* (New York: Oxford University Press, 1972).

Frank Kermode, *Wallace Stevens*. Evergreen Pilot books (New York: Grove Press,1961).

Samuel French Morse, *Wallace Stevens: Life as Poetry* (New York: Pegasus, 1970).

Robert Pack, *Wallace Stevens: An Approach to His Poetry and Thought* (New York: Gordeau Press, 1968).

Roy Harvey Pearce and J. Hillis Miller, eds., *The Act of the Mind: Essays on the Poetry of Wallace Stevens* (Baltimore: Johns Hopkins Press, 1965).

Alan Perlis, *Wallace Stevens: A World of Transforming Shapes* (Lewisburg, Pa.: Bucknell University Press, 1975).

Herbert J. Stern, *Wallace Stevens: Art of Uncertainty* (Ann Arbor: University of Michigan Press, 1966).

Wallace Stevens, *The Necessary Angel: Essays on Reality and the Imagination* (New York: Vintage, 1951).

Holly Stevens, ed., *Letters of Wallace Stevens* (New York: Alfred A. Knopf, 1970).

Helen Vendler, *On Extended Wings: Wallace Stevens' Longer Poems* (Cambridge, Mass.: Harvard Paperback).

W. H. Auden

His Life

W. H. Auden was born 1907 in York; the family moved shortly thereafter to Birmingham, in the heart of industrial England. His father was a well-known physician with wide scientific interests; his mother had been a nurse. Farther back in the family line were numerous Anglican priests.

Up to the age of sixteen, Wystan Hugh Auden was planning a career as a mining engineer. But once his interest in poetry was aroused—by the chance remark of a friend, as he tells the story—he set about mastering the craft and soon emerged as the most discussed new British poet of the 1930s, with the possible exception of his utterly different contemporary, Dylan Thomas. But Auden's scientific and technological interests were not abandoned; something of the scientist's or engineer's eye for exact observation characterizes his poetry.

During his time at Oxford (1925-1928) he published his first book, *Poems,* on a private press owned by his poet-friend, Stephen Spender. A revised edition by a regular publisher was to establish Auden's reputation in 1930. Meanwhile, at Oxford he became by force of personality and wide if unsystematic reading, the center of a small literary circle, including Christopher Isherwood and Stephen Spender.

After his university years, Auden taught at a school in Scotland, meanwhile writing and publishing profusely. A trip with Isherwood to Iceland resulted in a joint work, *Letters from Iceland* (1937); their trip to China—at the time of the Sino-Japanese War—led to another joint book, *Journey to a War* (1939). The same year Auden moved to the United States and eventually became a U. S. citizen. During his time in America he taught intermittently at a number of universities and colleges. His nearest approach to a permanent home was New York City. At one time he frequently stayed on the Italian island of Ischia; later, he purchased a house in Austria for part-time use, and celebrated his new second home in *About the House* (1965). In 1972 he accepted an invitation from his old school, Christ College, Oxford, to become permanent poet-in-residence. The next year he suddenly died while on a visit to Austria.

In addition to being one of the most prolific modern poets, Auden composed libretti for operas, edited anthologies, translated foreign poetry, and wrote a great deal of literary criticism, much of which is collected in *The Dyer's Hand* (1962).

Auden and the other poets of his generation came along in the shadow of the established giants—Eliot, Pound, Yeats. It was a time when the Great Depression was throwing the Western world into chaos and threatening its stability; fascism in both its Italian and German varieties was also on the march. The threat of war constantly grew. There was a preoccupation with political and social issues; many of the most gifted young writers ranged from outright Communists to Marxist fellow-travelers. In this literary atmosphere,

Auden's early poetry was commonly taken as Marxist and revolutionary, though—as we shall learn—it was perhaps less so than it appeared at the time; Freud looms larger than Marx, although Marx is not entirely lacking.

When Auden had his "conversion" to poetry in his teens, he began reading a wide variety of poets and was soon influenced by an odd assortment—de la Mare, W. H. Davies, A.E. (George W. Russell), and most of all Thomas Hardy. Other influences in his early period were Edward Thomas, and, of course, T. S. Eliot. These influences were assimilated so early that even Auden's first published poems show relatively little trace of them.

From the beginning, Auden's thought was strongly colored by psychological theories. Freud, of course, plays a major role, but lesser known figures are at least as important. Two are the American "healer," Homer Lane, and his disciple, John Layard. They taught that physical illness is a warning signal from the soul, an indication that the individual has been false to his own nature, by permitting the uptight but plausible Devil to cage the liberating God within. Another nonconformist psychologist who fascinated Auden was Georg Groddeck, with his belief that disease is the result of some cosmic spirit evolving toward self-awareness. These interests of Auden began early; at Oxford he was the amateur and self-appointed analyst to his friends.

The so-called Marxist period in Auden's poetry corresponds roughly to the 1930s, but during all that time the psychological strand was the stronger. Then comes his return to Christianity around 1940 (and to credal Anglo-Catholicism at that) which so horrified many of his admirers. His understanding of Christianity was deeply colored by Kierkegaard's Christain existentialism with its insistence on the significance of the absurd and the radical quality of the leap of faith. Another strong influence was Reinhold Niebuhr, who emphasizes man as a "fallen" creature but yet capable of accepting Grace in the midst of a fallen society whose complete redemption is harder to conceive. Niebuhr also wrote much on political and social matters and the religious insights that can provide practical guidance. This aspect of his thought figured large in Auden's poetry.

All in all, the continuities in Auden's intellectual and poetic development are more important than any talk of "periods." The psychological stance, colored first by Marxism and later subsumed by Christianity, remained a constant, while the particulars of his poetic style went through many evolutions and mutations.

The Poet and His Poetry

As a young man, Auden looked like a character from a Scandinavian saga — and, in fact, some of his remote ancestors came from Iceland. He was long, lanky, with almost colorless hair, and he displayed a supreme indifference to matters of dress and style. With increasing years his face became very lined so that his sharp eyes peered forth from a tangled maze of wrinkles.

In personality he lacked the public solemnity of T. S. Eliot, and indeed he often gave the impression of the playful buffoon, as he had appeared to his Oxford friends. He had a special gift for needling the pompous. When at the University of Michigan an education student asked him, during a forum on teaching, what he would do if a pupil said, "I won't do this assignment." Auden replied in a flatly emphatic voice, "I would whip that child." When in the midst of standardized acedemic liberals he had a way of referring to candles as "Nigger lights," and remarking casually that in his childhood home, tradesmen and Baptists entered through the back door. His own liberal credentials were meanwhile impeccable. Long before the courts moved, he was refusing to lecture before segregated audiences, and his vision of the human condition, expressed throughout his work, is a generous and all-embracing one.

Less picturesque than his fondness for needling the smug were the frequent instances of quiet compassion. When Erica Mann (daughter of Thomas Mann) was in danger of being returned to Germany where the Nazis were waiting, Auden married her to give her British nationality. (The marriage having served its humane purpose, they were later divorced. Auden, a homosexual, never remarried.) When he was teaching at the University of Michigan he became an unappointed counselor and father figure to many students who would arrive disconsolate and drunken at his apartment and somehow end up with a place to sleep it off, and breakfast prepared by the poet next morning.

Something of the impish schoolboy lurked in the grown man. Profoundly serious in his major poetry, he had the light touch, often seeming to stand off and mock the serious poet at work. It is as though an internal dialogue between poet and kibitzer were being carried on. He rarely aimed at an elevated "high seriousness" style. In his use of language he is closer to an Alexander Pope—or a Gilbert and Sullivan operetta—than to a Milton.

A playful fascination with language itself was with Auden from the start. In an epigrammatic statement that does not entirely explain his own poetry, he once asked an imaginary questioner[1]

> "Why do you want to write poetry?" If the young man answers, "I have important things I want to say," then he is not a poet. If he answers, "I like hanging around words listening to what they say," then maybe he is going to be a poet.

[1] Charles D. Abbott, ed., *Poets at Work* (New York: Harcourt, 1948), p. 171.

He was fascinated by the forms of poetry. Insisting that he felt like a carpenter 90 percent of the time when writing a poem, he experimented with almost every form from classical qualitative meters to Old English alliterative verse, plus the sonnet, sestina, and countless forms he invented himself.

His poetry stands at the opposite end of the spectrum from a Whitman or a Ginsberg. There is no emphasis on spontaneous composition, "organic form," or naturalness of language. Rather, Auden stresses the fact that a poem is an artifact, a thing deliberately made, and that[2]

> A poem is a rite; hence its formal and ritualistic character. Its use of language is deliberately and ostentatiously different from talk. Even when it employs the diction and rhythms of conversation, it employs them as a deliberate informality, presupposing the norm with which they are intended to contrast.

Explicit philosophic, psychiatric, and theological language is common in Auden's early poetry; he is preeminently a poet of ideas. In his later work, the ideas are often less explicitly presented, but rather are implied. Increasingly, since about 1950, as Justin Replogle points out in *Auden's Poetry,* Auden was revealed as a comic poet—but not comic in the sense of laughing at someone sliding on a banana peel. He wrote with the ultimate serentiy of one who found the divine revealed everywhere, in the midst of man's fallen estate and the general absurdity of all human affairs. Toward the end, the observant eye was as keen and unsentimental as ever. It could see a thousand things wrong, but it saw also the overarching rightness of all things.

The charge of obscurity has often been hurled against Auden. Much of his early poetry (sparsely represented in this book) is almost opaque because of his perverse use of a private mythology that he and his school frinds created. Other kinds of obscurity arise from his immensely wide reading and the references he casually introduces; at times the topical references may require footnotes. But his work as a whole is probably easier going than Eliot or the later Yeats, and many of the poems are perfectly lucid—at least on the primary level—in the first reading.

One final word about Auden. Poets vary greatly in the amount of attention they give to current history. One could read the collected works of a Theodore Roethke and be scarcely aware of fascism, World War II, the cold war, or race problems. To read Auden is to be plunged into history from the time of the Great Depression to the early 1970s. Almost every important historical event, or social or cultural development, is commented on somewhere in his verse. This may make much of his work difficult for future centuries.But this alone should not banish him to the specialists. Although the absolute merit of Auden's poems varies greatly, as he himself recognized in his successive win-

[2] W. H. Auden, *The Dyer's Hand* (New York: Random House, 1962), p. 58

nowings for new editions, there is a large and solid core of poetry that may very well earn for him the position of the major English-language poet in the generation immediately after Yeats, Pound, Eliot, and Frost. Another apology. With Auden, as with Stevens we are obliged to give a somewhat niggardly representation of his work, again because of copyright restrictions.

Poems

First, a short poem from Auden's early work:

O Where Are You Going?

'O where are you going?' said reader to rider,
'That valley is fatal when furnaces burn,
Yonder's the midden whose odours will madden,
That gap is the grave where the tall return.'

'O do you imagine,' said fearer to farer,
'That dusk will delay on your path to the pass,
Your diligent looking discover the lacking
Your footsteps feel from granite to grass?'

'O what was that bird,' said horror to hearer,
'Did you see that shape in the twisted trees?
Behind you swiftly the figure comes softly,
The spot on your skin is a shocking disease.'

'Out of this house'—said rider to reader,
'Yours never will'—said farer to fearer,
'They're looking for you'—said hearer to horror,
As he left them there, as he left them there.

Before we consider the thought and mood of this poem, the form is worth examining. It is the sort of poem as far removed from free verse as possible; the deliberate artifice of the poet is evident in every detail.

The rhythm is mainly anapestic, with a few variations. This rhythm, consisting of two unstressed syllables followed by a stressed one (◡◡/), is rarely used in serious poetry. It seems more suitable for light verse. But then used, it can impart an impetuous quality. The poem seems to plunge ahead, as though on a run-away horse. Try reading the first stanza aloud and see if you unconsciously speed up as you go along.

The one place where the rhythm sharply changes is in the last line.

Ăs hĕ léft thĕm thĕre, ăs hĕ léft thĕm thĕre.

Here, there are only two heavily stressed syllables, as compared with the four in the other lines. The poem comes to a stop with a jolting thump, as though to suggest that something decisive has happened.

The rhyming is odd. The even lines of the first three stanzas rhyme conventionally enough (burn/return, pass/grass, trees/disease) but the odd lines use a sort of half rhyme (reader/rider, midden/madden, etc.) which, in fact, is not traditional rhyme at all. It consists of keeping all the sounds the same except for the stressed vowels—the technical name is *double consonance.* (Plain consonance would be rhymes like mill/mull, hit/hate, etc.)

Why the use of this offbeat kind of rhyme in the odd lines? One reason may be simply that all the exact rhymes in English have been worked to death. It is hard for a poet to restore to the rhymes, love/dove, the freshness they must have had when some inspired poet first hit upon them. If a poet wishes to rhyme *lover,* he has only these unpromising possibilities: cover, discover, glover, plover, recover, rediscover, shover, and uncover. No wonder that many modern poets have experimented with various unconventional types of rhyme, to get out of the well-worn tracks.

Or perhaps Auden was having some fun, making a technical experiment. Always aware of the craftsmanship of poetry, Auden deliberately experimented in many directions. It is conceivable that the poem started as a technical experiment.

It doesn't matter. It is best to abandon this attempt to guess the author's motives, and simply concentrate on the poem itself. What effect is created by the use of double consonance? In thinking about this, note that each pair of consonating words automatically involves alliteration (*r*eader/*r*ider, etc.) and that a great deal of extra alliteration is worked into the poem (fatal . . . furnaces, gap . . . grave, etc).

Each reader will have his own response to these devices. Perhaps they engender a sense of obsessive hysteria. It is as though certain emotions keep pounding at your brain; terrors dance about. You are caught in a whirling cage of threatening words and mental pictures. It is a poem that reads as though sanity were on its utmost border, ready to collapse into hysteria.

Certainly the images of the poem seem to come from a world of experience, half fairy tale (the grimmer sort) and half schizophrenia. There is an ominous valley with blazing furnaces, a midden (refuse heap or dunghill) whose stench threatens mind as well as nose. A sinister bird appears amid twisted trees; skin is blotched by signs of a shocking disease.

A generalized sense of terror is created, like a child's nightmare. Paralysis of the will, perhaps outright madness, seem the approaching consequences. But all this is only the mood of the poem. The poem is also a capsule drama, dramatizing two different attitudes toward danger and the possibility of action. The two forces can be listed:

Group 1	*Group 2*
reader	rider
fearer	farer
horror	hearer

Look first at Group 2. *Rider* is a word rich in associations. It can suggest the military hero, the man on horseback; a knight going forth on a quest; a fairy-tale prince journeying into the wilderness to wake the sleeping beauty. In any case, it implies movement and decisive action. The word *farer* is a half-obsolete synonym for traveler. But *traveler* suggests someone jetting to Europe, or Willi Loman of *Death of a Salesman* trying to cover his New England territory. By contrast, *farer* evokes perhaps a pilgrim, at least someone engaged in a quest. *Hearer* has fewer nuances, but does suggest that the quest hero—if that is what we have—is surrounded by fearful voices beating against his ears, trying to unnerve him.

The voices are characterized as reader, fearer, and horror. *Reader* suggests a withdrawn and futile intellectualism. *Reader* in fact is a *fearer,* seeking security by staying in one place and concentrating on the private world of books. *Horror* perhaps has implication of madness in it.

What is the poem as a whole saying? It seems to present two choices: action and inaction. The poet's verdict is in favor of action: *rider* exhorts *reader,* "Out of this house." But what kind of action? The poem dates from the early years of the Great Depression when the twin threats of fascism and war were inescapable. Very likely Auden's first readers, eager to find revolutionary appeals in every poem, took this poem as a call to arms: raise the flag of revolution, renounce the corrupt older society, and create the new. And, indeed, such thoughts may have been in Auden's mind as he wrote the four stanzas. But take the poem out of its historical context and look at it by itself on the printed page. What remains, unmistakably, is some kind of a summons to courage and action: political perhaps but not necessarily so. One could interpret the poem in purely psychological terms as a recognition of the need to face the circling horrors of the soul but not be frozen into inaction by them; the poem could be an appeal to abandon introspection, disregard anxieties, and move forward to whatever goals the *rider* may have.

Now consider a few questions:

1. What is the force of "where the tall return?"
2. What is the particular effect created by the word *shocking* in line 12?
3. Discuss the mental pictures the poet presents, and how they contribute to a nightmare feeling.

Another poem from Auden's early period shows the same psychological preoccupations, but with the political dimensions more clearly spelled out.

Consider

Consider this and in our time
As the hawk sees it or the helmeted airman:
The clouds rift suddenly—look there
At cigarette-end smouldering on a border
At the first garden party of the year.

Pass on, admire the view of the massif
Through plate-glass windows of the Sport Hotel;
Join there the insufficient units
Dangerous, easy, in furs, in uniform
And constellated at reserved tables
Supplied with feelings by an efficient band
Relayed elsewhere to farmers and their dogs
Sitting in kitchens in the stormy fens.

Long ago, supreme Antagonist,
More powerful than the great northern whale
Ancient and sorry at life's limiting defect,
In Cornwall, Mendip, or the Pennine moor
Your comments on the highborn mining-captains,
Found they no answer, made them wish to die
—Lie since in barrows out of harm.
You talk to your admirers every day
By silted harbours, derelict works,
In strangled orchards, and the silent comb
Where dogs have worried or a bird was shot.
Order the ill that they attack at once:
Visit the ports and, interrupting
The leisurely conversation in the bar
Within a stone's throw of the sunlit water,
Beckon your chosen out. Summon
Those handsome and diseased youngsters, those women
Your solitary agents in the country parishes;
And mobilize the powerful forces latent
In soils that make the farmer brutal
In the infected sinus, and the eyes of stoats.
Then ready, start your rumour, soft
But horrifying in its capacity to disgust
Which, spreading magnified, shall come to be
A polar peril, a prodigious alarm,
Scattering the people, as torn-up paper
Rags and utensils in a sudden gust,
Seized with immeasurable neurotic dread.

Seekers after happiness, all who follow
The convolutions of your simple wish,
It is later than you think; nearer that day
Far other than that distant afternoon
Amid rustle of frocks and stamping feet
They gave the prizes to the ruined boys.
You cannot be away, then, no
Not though you pack to leave within an hour,
Escaping humming down arterial roads:
The date was yours; the prey to fugues,

Irregular breathing and alternate ascendancies
After some haunted migratory years
To disintegrate on an instant in the explosion of mania
Or lapse for ever into a classic fatigue.

At first glance this poem is very different from "O Where Are You Going?" The latter is written in a form as intricate as a Chinese puzzle. "Consider" is plainer in its technique. There is no dallying with rhyme, and the rhythm approaches prose; at most there is a tendency to have four heavy stresses to a line, as in Old English verse, but the general flow is rough and irregular. The first poem used imagery suggesting a nightmare or surrealist painting; "Consider" seems more straightforward and factually descriptive. It is, however, more opaque and difficult to explicate than "O Where."

The beginning states the point of view—"As the hawk sees it or the helmeted airman." The early Auden, in reaction against romantic subjectivism, argued that a poet should write with clinical detachment. He is the scientist looking through a microscope and describing what he observes; he is the aviator studying the features of the landscape from a great height. The beginning of the poem serves notice that the poet is speaking from an impersonal height, making a diagnosis of the distant human condition.

The language has a curious formality, almost a touch of pedantry about it —"admire the view of the massif," "Join there the insufficient units," "constellated at reserved tables." The speaker might be describing the movements of atoms or galaxies, instead of those of human beings.

The first section is clear enough in the picture it soberly paints. We are watching the idle rich in one of their pleasure spots. The line, "Supplied with feelings by an efficient band," suggests an inner emptiness that must be filled by professional entertainments. The whole effect of the section is reminiscent of the opening part of Eliot's *Waste Land,* where the neurotic speaker says: "In the mountains, there you feel free. / I read, much of the night, and go south in the winter."

The music of the band is apparently being broadcast—"Relayed elsewhere to farmers and their dogs / Sitting in kitchens in the stormy fens." This is the one passing reference in the first section to the masses of humanity.

The second section involves an initial question: Who or what is the antagonist?" This has been commonly taken to mean death, but John Fuller suggests a more interesting possibility:[3]

> Critics take the "supreme Antagonist" to be death, but the tautology implicit in death making the highborn mining–captains "wish to die" seems clumsy. Both the Old English *Bestiary* and *Paradise Lost* (I, 200) compare the whale with Satan, as, I believe, Auden is doing. In Auden's

[3] *A Reader's Guide to W. H. Auden* (New York: Farrar, Straus & Giroux, 1970), p. 47.

> glossary of Christian and psychological terms (BM Notebook, fol. 44) Satan is seen as the Censor, responsible for repressing man's natural instincts and bringing about that selfconsciousness which separates him from the rest of the animal kingdom. It is this division in men and society, keeping them from their real desires, that Auden is anatomizing in the poem. The Antagonist's admirers, the ill, are in ascendancy and are themselves responsible for the malaise, the "immeasurable neurotic dread," which conditions them.

The reference might also suggest Moby Dick, bringing destruction to Captain Ahab, who was already far on the road to self-destruction through his own suicidal impulses.

The second section with its formal language and disjointed grammar makes difficult reading, but a sense of evil and psychological illness pervades it. The Antagonist seems to be egging the ill on to a final disaster: "Order the ill that they attack at one: . . . Beckon your chosen out. Summon / Those handsome and diseased youngsters, those women / Your solitary agents in the country parishes; . . . "

Could "those women" be a reference to the country mansions that Yeats so much extolled in his poetry? Here the reference is followed quickly by a grotesque allusion to stoats—a weasel with brown fur in summer, turning white in winter (ermine). Is it stretching things too far to see in the mention of the stoat a symbol of he crude background of riches? The judge or woman wearing ermine is adorned with the fur of the common stoat. In any case, the world observed from a hawk's-eye viewpoint is one in which the very soils are sick—they "make the farmer brutal / in the infected sinus. . . . " The section goes on to a cataclysmic vision of destruction, "Scattering the people, as torn-up paper / Rags and utensils in a sudden gust." The reason for catastrophe is stated in the last line of the section: "Seized with immeasurable neurotic dread."

The poem up to this point has been a blend of psychological analysis and social criticism, the latter often implied rather than explicitly stated. It now moves in the last section to a precise conclusion, rather like a doctor detailing his diagnosis to a patient with an incurable ailment. The gravity of the situation is not denied—"I is later than you think." This phrase, often carved on sundials, has a solemn tone of *momento mori* about it. The future will not be like the distant past when the social order seemed in good condition (though rotten inside)—"that distant afternoon / Amid rustle of frocks and stamping feet / They gave the prizes to the ruined boys." Does this mean that the school boys were already hopelessly neurotic in spite of their successes? Or had they been ruined (inhibited and repressed?) by the system? At any rate, the poem moves toward a deepening sense of doom. Flight is impossible. Disintegration is imminent.

The final lines illustrate one of the problems of poetry. To make a personal confession—when I first read them, I thought the symbolism was based on music (because of the phrase, "prey to fugues"), and I frantically tried to make sense of "Irregular breathing" and "alternate ascendancies." My difficulty was that I had not read William McDougall, *An Outline of Abnormal Psychology,* published in 1926, shortly before Auden wrote the poem. Auden evidently had read the book. As Fuller points out, the mysterious phrases at the end of the poem are technical terms used by McDougall: a fugue is "a form of amnesia involving compulsive travel"; alternate ascendancies are "cases of alternating personalities with reciprocal amnesia like fugues."

Knowledge of these technical terms sharpens one's grasp of the conclusion, though not really modifying it. The poem from beginning to end has the tone of a severely detached physician sizing up the extent of the mental disease and finding it past remedy. To the incurably ill he can offer only the alternatives of disintegration "in the explosion of mania" or permanent exhaustion.

Most readers do not find this poem as successful as "O Where?" The reasons require a look at one peculiarity of Auden's verse. Critics have noted that in Auden's work there seems to be both a Poet and a kibitzer or Antipoet. Auden himself was insistent that one should not romanticize poetry and expect too much of it. He found it difficult or unrewarding to maintain too lofty and bardic a stance when he wrote. At their best, the Poet and the kibitzer coexist within the same Auden, affirming and mocking the meaningfulness of poetry. But in this particular poem, a very early one, the kibitzer seems to have sneaked in through the back door and then have been welcomed with delight by Auden, who perhaps was growing tired of the high style so alien to most of his work. It may be "Consider" represents an early stage when Auden was just beginning to develop a particular style in which seriousness and mockery were later on to deepen and reinforce each other.

Something of this sort is what Justin Replogle suggests:[4]

> After plunging from lofty dignity to sinuses and stoats' eyes, the speaker next frightens the sick with the bogy of a destructive "rumour . . . horrifying in its capacity to disgust," a rumor likely to become for them "A Polar peril, a prodigious alarm." . . . The speaker, who began as a Poet, turned into an Antipoet. Can auden possibly have fallen unintentionally into such comic circumstances? I think the answer is yes—that is, at *first* the comedy was unintentional. Once it began, Auden purposely continued it. The first lapses seem clearly unplanned. And even at the end the poem struggles bravely to maintain some vestige of its formal idiom and Poetic persona, as though retention of both were part of the original plan. The disaster occurs, I think, because though Auden as Poet

[4] *Auden's Poetry* (Seattle and London: University of Oregon Press, 1969), pp. 107-08.

is forced to be solemn, elevated, and seriously concerned with large weighty matters such as the evolution of cultural collapse, he wears this mask somewhat awkwardly. . . .

If Replogle is right in his speculations, this poem represents one of the moments when a young poet is somewhat blindly striving to find his own individual voice, and has not fully discovered it yet. It will be worthwhile to keep this in mind, and in other poems look for ways in which the rivalry between Poet and Antipoet is resolved.

1. Make a list of particular words (such as *massif,* used instead of mountain) that impart a scientific, impersonal, precise tone to passages in which the "Poet" speaks. In each case, try to think of a simpler equivalent. Rewrite a passage of half a dozen lines, using the simpler words. What happens to the poem?

2. Do you think the rhythm of this poem is appropriate? Why or why not?

3. Notice the places where the specific details seem to imply childhood and youth. What does this emphasis suggest in the total meaning of the poem?

4. Assuming that the reader knows his McDougall, are the last five lines of the poem effective? You might wish to examine the effect they produce, coming right after the talk of prize day at a school and the impossibility of flight.

The next poem is an elegy, a traditional type of poetry—a lamentation for the death of someone. The dead man happens to be a major poet, and it comes as no surprise to find that the poem deals as much with the nature and role of art as with Yeats.

In Memory of W. B. Yeats

(d. Jan. 1939)

I

He disappeared in the dead of winter:
The brooks were frozen, the airports almost deserted,
And snow disfigured the public statues;
The mercury sank in the mouth of the dying day.
What instruments we have agree
The day of his death was a dark cold day.

Far from his illness
The wolves ran on through the evergreen forests,
The peasant river was untempted by the fashionable quays;
By mourning tongues
The death of the poet was kept from his poems.

But for him it was his last afternoon as himself,
An afternoon of nurses and rumours;
The provinces of his body revolted,
The squares of his mind were empty,
Silence invaded the suburbs,
The current of his feeling failed; he became his admirers.

Now he is scattered among a hundred cities
And wholly given over to unfamiliar affections,
To find his happiness in another kind of wood
And be punished under a foreign code of conscience.
The words of a dead man
Are modified in the guts of the living.

But in the importance and noise of to-morrow
When the brokers are roaring like beasts on the floor of the Bourse,
And the poor have the sufferings to which they are fairly accustomed,
And each in the cell of himself is almost convinced of his freedom,
A few thousand will think of this day
As one thinks of a day when one did something slightly unusual.
What instruments we have agree
The day of his death was a dark cold day.

II

You were silly like us; your gift survived it all:
The parish of rich women, physical decay,
Yourself. Mad Ireland hurt you into poetry.
Now Ireland has her madness and her weather still,
For poetry makes nothing happen: it survives
In the valley of its making where executives
Would never want to tamper, flows on south
From ranches of isolation and the busy griefs,
Raw towns that we believe and die in; it survives,
A way of happening, a mouth.

III

Earth, receive an honoured guest:
William Yeats is laid to rest.
Let the Irish vessel lie
Emptied of its poetry.

In the nightmare of the dark
All the dogs of Europe bark,
And the living nations wait,
Each sequestered in its hate;

Intellectual disgrace
Stares from every human face,
And the seas of pity lie
Locked and frozen in each eye.

Follow, poet, follow right
To the bottom of the night,
With your unconstraining voice
Still persuade us to rejoice;

With the farming of a verse
Make a vineyard of the curse,
Sing of human unsuccess
In a rapture of distress;

In the deserts of the heart
Let the healing fountain start,
In the prison of his days
Teach the free man how to praise.

This elegy is an exceedingly cold one. Almost nothing is said about Yeats the man. Apart from a description of the deathbed scene, written with a cosmic and clinical detachment, there is only the reference to "silly like us," probably referring to Yeat's preoccupation with the occult, and a glancing mention of the "parish of rich women," suggesting Yeats' love of old country mansions and their gracious life. For the rest, Yeats becomes a sort of cultural monument, a symbol of the great poet; the poem is far more about the role of the artist in society than about one particular poet.

The historical fact is that Yeats was under suspicion by the rising young British poets of the 1930s. Auden himself shared this feeling. It was impossible not to admire the greatness of Yeats' poetry, but the poet himself seemed theatrically romantic, addicted to useless passions like theosophy, and insufficiently sympathetic with modern, progressive thought in the realm of political and social action.Thus the life and achievement of Yeats posed for a poet of Auden's generation a number of baffling questions about the relation of art to life.

In rereading the poem, note how the versification becomes tighter as the poem progresses. Part I is in rather relaxed free verse. Part II consists mostly of lines with four strong stresses, a somewhat more more definite rhythm than in the first part. There is also a great deal of partial rhyme: all/still, decay/poetry, survives/executives/griefs, as well as an instance of outright rhyme (south-/mouth) to bring the section to a clean conclusion. From a technical viewpoint, section II is a transition. The poem is becoming tighter, moving toward the epigrammatic section III in which definite statements are made about the role of the arts. And in this final section the versification becomes very strict: each stanza consists of two rhymed couplets (exact rhymes, no approximations) and the rhythm is a precise /˘/˘/˘/.

The form alone would suggest that the poem is moving from the tentative to the definite. A rereading of the three sections confirms this initial impression.

The first stanza of section I sets the scene. Winter, cold day, dark, when Yeats died. There is a clinical impersonality in the concluding lines—"What instruments we have agree / The day of his death was a dark cold day."

The second stanza pictures nature continuing its usual processes, indifferent to the death of the poet. There is also the implication that the poetry, as distinct from the poet, remains alive and full of vitality. A separation between poet and poetry is implied in "The death of the poet was kept from his poems."

The third stanza is a highly elaborate description of the process of death, using figures of speech taken from revolutionary events. The fourth stanza reverts to the theme of the contrast between poet and poetry. With death, the poet as a physical being ceases to exist. What is left is the poetry, to be assimilated and interpreted by those who read it—"The words of a dead man / Are modified in the guts of the living."

The fifth stanza emphasizes that though this is a day like other days, there are a few people who will remember it as "slightly unusual," a flat way to describe the day on which a major poet died. The theme of inner freedom is briefly introduced—"And each in the cell of himself is almost convinced of his freedom." A tentative, understated tone pervades the stanza, and it concludes with a restatement of the objective fact—"The day of his death was a dark cold day."

Section II is addressed directly to Yeats. As pointed out earlier, one would get very little idea of the man Yeats (or what kind of poetry he wrote) from this section. He was silly, he was involved with rich women, he suffered physical decay, he was wounded into becoming a poet. In the objective, social world, nothing has been changed by his poetry. Poets are not the unacknowledged legislators of the world." . . . poetry makes nothing happen." It is "A way of happening, a mouth."

Section III is addressed first to the Earth, then to "poet," meaning not Yeats in particular but any poet. Yeats is quickly buried—"Earth, receive an honoured guest: / William Yeats is laid to rest." The poem moves on to picture the condition of Europe, threatened by fascism and nazism and on the brink of war. The poet had no way to destroy fascism or prevent war. Rather, he is summoned to use his unconstraining voice to inspire rejoicing; to make the curse under which mankind labors (exile from the Garden of Eden?) a blessing; to find even in failure a cause for celebration, to irrigate parched hearts; to reveal freedom-within–necessity; to sing praises.

So much for the paraphrasable content of the poem. But such a bald summary misses many of the subtleties of tone. Perhaps these questions will be of use:

1. The kibitzer or Antipoet seems to speak occasionally in this poem. For example., "When the brokers are roaring like beasts on the floor of the Bourse." List any other lines where the Antipoet speaks. How does his voice

contribute to the total impact of the poem? Does he clarify or intensify anything the poem is saying?

2. Can the statement, "Poetry makes nothing happen," be reconciled with the affirmations about the nature and role of poetry? Is Auden caught in a contradiction?

3. John Fuller points out in *A Reader's Guide to W. H. Auden* that Auden, in an article[5] entitled "The Public *v.* the late Mr. William Butler Yeats"—written about the same time as the poem—argued that "art is a product of history, not a cause . . . it does not reenter history as an effective agent." Do you agree with this? Can you think of any examples of poetry, ancient or modern, that has in even a slight degree affected the course of history?

4. Do you find stanza three of section I a suitable and effective way of describing a death?

5. Think about each of the lines below and discuss how they contribute to the tone of the poem:

> And snow disfigured the public statues;
>
> The peasant river was untempted by the fashionable quays;
>
> The current of his feeling failed; he became his admirers.
>
> Now Ireland has her madness and her weather still,
>
> In the prison of his days / Teach the free man how to praise.

6. Section III has the same "Twinkle, twinkle, little star" meter as Blake's first "Introduction" (page 41). Reread the latter. Does this coincidence imply anything about the relation of form and poetic effect?

The fullest poetic expression of Auden's Christianity is found in *For the Time Being: A Christmas Oratorio.* The poem, reflecting the period of World War II, pictures a world obsessed with anxieties and a collapse of self-confidence. A rational order has failed, and madness and ruins are everywhere. As the Narrator explains:

> If, on account of the political situation,
> There are quite a number of homes without roofs, and men
> Lying about in the countryside neither drunk nor asleep,
> And all sailings have been cancelled till further notice,
> If it's unwise now to say much in letters, and if,

[5] *Partisan Review,* VI (Spring 1939).

Under the subnormal temperatures prevailing,
The two sexes are at present the weak and the strong,

The anxiety is more than fear of war and social collapse. It is a sense of the Void, the absence of God, coupled with a fear that God, infinitely dangerous, might suddenly reveal Himself. The chorus, in a poem describing the condition of mankind, desperately acknowledges that "The Pilgrim Way has led to the Abyss" and concludes that

Nothing can save us that is possible:
We who must die demand a miracle.

For the Time Being, then, is the Christmas story—the coming of God in the form of a baby born in a stable—told as though it were contemporary. The three wise men sound like college professors weary with their researches; the shepherds make biting remarks about the educated and wealthy who yearn for the simple life but never practice it; King Herod, a tormented liberal and rationalist, calls out the army to slaughter the innocents so that superstition may not destroy the frail fabric of civilization.

Meanwhile, the divine incursion takes place at Bethlehem, and the Holy Family flees to Egypt to escape the army unleashed by Herod. The event of Christmas has come and gone. Life returns to some pretense of normality—the accustomed routines, anxieties, and miseries—with haunting memories of more than mortal possibilities.

The tone of *For the Time Being,* its combination of modern wit and underlying seriousness, is well illustrated by the Narrator's words to Joseph when the latter is worried about what the neighbors will think of him when they discover Mary's pregnancy.

Narrator

For the perpetual excuse
Of Adam for his fall—"My little Eve,
God bless her, did beguile me and I ate,"
For his insistence on a nurse,
All service, breast, and lap, for giving Fate
Feminine gender to make girls believe
That they can save him, you must now atone,
Joseph, in silence and alone;
While she who loves you makes you shake with fright,
Your love for her must tuck you up and kiss good night.

For likening Love to war, for all
The pay-off lines of limericks in which
The weak resentful bar-fly shows his sting,
For talking of their spiritual

Beauty to chorus-girls, for flattering
The features of old gorgons who are rich,
For the impudent grin and Irish charm
  That hides a cold will to do harm,
Today the roles are altered; you must be
The Weaker Sex whose passion is passivity.

  For those delicious memories
Cigars and sips of brandy can restore
To old dried boys, for gallantry that scrawls
  In idolatrous detail and size
A symbol of aggression on toilet walls,
For having reasoned—"Woman is naturally pure
Since she has no moustache," for having said,
  "No woman has a business head,"
You must learn now that masculinity,
To Nature, is a non-essential luxury.

  Lest, finding it impossible
To judge its object now or throatily
Forgive it as eternal God forgives,
  Lust, tempted by this miracle
To more ingenious evil, should contrive
A heathen fetish from Virginity
To soothe the spiritual petulance
  Of worn-out rakes and maiden aunts,
Forgetting nothing and believing all,
You must behave as if this were not strange at all.

  Without a change in look or word,
You both must act exactly as before;
Joseph and Mary shall be man and wife
  Just as if nothing had occurred.
There is one World of Nature and one Life;
Sin fractures the Vision, not the Fact; for
The Exceptional is always usual
  And the Usual exceptional.
To choose what is difficult all one's days
As if it were easy, that is faith. Joseph, praise.

1. What does this poem say about the sins of men against women?

2. What religious insight is contained in it?

3. Point out places where Auden uses everyday experiences to make a philosophic or religious point.

The next poem is written in a "middle style" that Auden increasingly used; one finds neither the high rhetoric of the "Poet" nor the antic mockery of the "Antipoet."

The Shield of Achilles

She looked over his shoulder
  For vines and olive trees,
Marble well-governed cities
  And ships upon untamed seas,
But there on the shining metal
  His hands had put instead
An artificial wilderness
  And a sky like lead.

A plain without a feature, bare and brown,
  No blade of grass, no sign of neighbourhood,
Nothing to eat and nowhere to sit down,
  Yet, congregated on its blankness, stood
  An unintelligible multitude,
A million eyes, a million boots in line,
Without expression, waiting for a sign.

Out of the air a voice without a face
  Proved by statistics that some cause was just
In tones as dry and level as the place:
  No one was cheered and nothing was discussed;
  Column by column in a cloud of dust
They marched away enduring a belief
Whose logic brought them, somewhere else, to grief.

She looked over his shoulder
  For ritual pieties,
White flower-garlanded heifers,
  Libation and sacrifice,
But there on the shining metal
  Where the altar should have been,
She saw by his flickering forge-light
  Quite another scene.

Barbed wire enclosed an arbitrary spot
  Where bored officials lounged (one cracked a joke)
And sentries sweated for the day was hot:
  A crowd of ordinary decent folk
  Watched from without and neither moved nor spoke
As three pale figures were led forth and bound
To three posts driven upright in the ground.

The mass and majesty of this world, all
  That carries weight and always weighs the same
Lay in the hands of others; they were small

And could not hope for help and no help came:
What their foes liked to do was done, their shame
Was all the worst could wish; they lost their pride
And died as men before their bodies died.

She looked over his shoulder
For athletes at their games,
Men and women in a dance
Moving their sweet limbs
Quick, quick, to music,
But there on the shining shield
His hands had set no dancing-floor
But a weed-choked field.

A ragged urchin, aimless and alone,
Loitered about that vacancy, a bird
Flew up to safety from his well-aimed stone:
That girls are raped, that two boys knife a third,
Were axioms to him, who'd never heard
Of any world where promises were kept,
Or one could weep because another wept.

The thin-lipped armourer,
Hephaestos hobbled away,
Thetis of the shining breasts
Cried out in dismay
At what the god had wrought
To please her son, the strong
Iron-hearted man-slaying Achilles
Who would not live long.

The background of the poem comes obviously from the *Iliad.* Thetis is the mother of Achilles, who eventually slays Hector, and in turn is killed by an arrow in the heel (his only vulnerable spot), shot by Paris.

Auden's poem is about the Trojan War, but the reader senses almost immediately that it is also about the postwar world of the cold war period, when memories of the militaristic regimes were still vivid, and totalitarianism—in both its fascist and Stalinist forms—lingered on in certain countries. Why the use of an ancient epic as framework for a poem commenting on the modern world? For one thing, the tale of the Trojan War provides a framework within which one can look at the modern world. The framework also permits a certain "distancing." The poet can stand off and look at contemporary events as though he were reading a description of them in Herodotus. He sees everything under the aspect of eternity, rather than as a welter of confused impressions. Finally, the traditional framework makes possible some ironical implications about the role of the artist, here represented by Hephaestos. The classical ideal of harmonious order, piety, and beauty cannot suffice for the contemporary artist, who is surrounded by quite a different kind of world and is compelled to deal with it in his work.

The contrast between the classical ideal and the modern reality is emphasized by the form of the poem. The stanzas depicting the first are written in shorter lines; those dealing with the latter are in rime royal, a seven-line stanza form (rhyming ababbcc) much employed by Chaucer, Shakespeare, and later poets, particularly for narrative poems. Structurally, then, the contrast between ideal and reality is made visible on the printed page.

It is also a contrast between "vines and olive trees," "well-governed cities," "White flower-garlanded heifers," "athletes at their games," "Men and women in a dance," on the one hand, and a voice, issuing perhaps from a loudspeaker (line 16), and dully invoking statistical evidence to justify war. Death itself has become meaningless, as in the scene (lines 34-44) where three men are tortured to death in an empty parody of the Crucifixion.

1. Why do you think Auden chose a short-line stanza form for describing the classical, humanistic ideal, and a long-lined form for the modern reality?

2. Study these lines and see why you think each is included:

> A million eyes, a million boots in line, / Without
> expression, waiting for a sign. (14-5)
>
> A crowd of ordinary decent folk / Watched from without
> and neither moved or spoke (34-5)
>
> All / That carried weight and always weighs
> the same (38-9)
>
> Men and women in a dance / Moving their sweet limbs /
> Quick, quick, to music, (47-9)
>
> the strong / Iron-hearted man-slaying Achilles /
> Who would not live long. (65-7)

The next poem, like the elegy on Yeats, has something to say about the relation of life to art. See whether you think it expresses the same thing:

Musée des Beaux Arts

About suffering they were never wrong,
The Old Masters: how well they understood
Its human position; how it takes place

While someone else is eating or opening a window or just walking dully along;
How, when the aged are reverently, passionately waiting
For the miraculous birth, there always must be
Children who did not specially want it to happen, skating
On a pond at the edge of the wood:
They never forgot
That even the dreadful martyrdom must run its course
Anyhow in a corner, some untidy spot
Where the dogs go on with their doggy life and the torturer's horse
Scratches its innocent behind on a tree.

In Brueghel's *Icarus,* for instance: how everything turns away
Quite leisurely from the disaster; the ploughman may
Have heard the splash, the forsaken cry,
But for him it was not an important failure; the sun shone
As it had to on the white legs disappearing into the green
Water; and the expensive delicate ship that must have seen
Something amazing, a boy falling out of the sky,
Had somewhere to get to and sailed calmly on.

As John Fisher points out, three Breughel paintings are involved here: *The Fall of Icarus, The Numbering at Bethlehem* (lines 5-7), and *The Massacre of the Innocents* (line 12).

1. Discuss this poem as one dealing with the relation between life and art.

2. Study the various kinds of rhyme and half-rhyme used in the poem. What effect is created?

3. Compare the poem with Williams' "Landscape with the Fall of Icaruc" (page 206). Are the two poems expressing the same theme? If so, how would you describe the difference in total effect? (If they are not expressing the same theme, what is the theme of the Williams' poem?)

And finally, a few additional Auden poems—from his earlier to later periods—for you to read on your own.

Schoolchildren

Here are all the captivities, the cells are as real,
but these are unlike the prisoners we know,
who are outraged or pining or wittily resigned
or just wish all away.

For these dissent so little, so nearly content
with the dumb play of dogs, with licking and rushing;
the bars of love are so strong, their conspiracies
weak like the vows of drunkards.

Indeed, their strangeness is difficult to watch:
the condemned see only the fallacious angels of a vision,
so little effort lies behind their smiling,
  the beast of vocation is afraid.

But watch them, set against our size and timing
their almost neuter, their slightly awkward perfection;
for the sex is there, the broken bootlace is broken:
  the professor's dream is not true.

Yet the tyranny is so easy. An improper word
scribbled upon a fountain, is that all the rebellion?
A storm of tears wept in a corner, are these
  the seeds of a new life?

Macao

A weed from Catholic Europe, it took root
Between some yellow mountains and a sea,
Its gay stone houses an exotic fruit,
A Portugal-cum-China oddity.

Rococo images of Saint and Saviour
Promise its gamblers fortunes when they die,
Churches alongside brothels testify
That faith can pardon natural behavior.

A town of such indulgence need not fear
Those mortal sins by which the strong are killed
And limbs and governments are torn to pieces:

Religious clocks will strike, the childish vices
Will safeguard the low virtues of the child,
And nothing serious can happen here.

An Island Cemetery

This graveyard with its umbrella pines
Is inferior in status to the vines
And, though new guests keep crowding in,
Must stay the size it's always been.

Where men are many, acres few,
The dead must be cultivated too,
Like seeds in any farmer's field
Are planted for the bones they yield.

It takes about eighteen months for one
To ripen into a skeleton,
To be washed, folded, packed in a small
Niche hollowed out of the cemetery wall.

Curiosity made me stop
While sextons were digging up a crop:
Bards have taken it too amiss
That Alexanders come to this.

Wherever our personalities go
(And, to tell the truth, we do not know),
The solid structures they leave behind
Are no discredit to our kind.

Mourners may miss, and they do, a face,
But at least they cannot detect a trace
Of those fish-like hungers, mammalian heats,
That kin our flesh to the coarser meats.

And who would be ashamed to own
To a patience that we share with stone,
This underlying thing in us
Which never at any time made a fuss?

Considering what our motives are,
We ought to thank our lucky star
That Love must ride to reach his ends
A mount which has no need of friends.

SELECTIVE BIBLIOGRAPHY

The Auden poems included in this book are taken from *Collected Shorter Poems 1927-1957* (New York: Random House, 1966) and *For the Time Being* (New York: Random House, 1944).

W. H. Auden, *The Dyer's Hand and Other Essays* (New York: Random House, 1962).

George W. Bohlke, *The Later Auden* (New Brunswick, N. J.: Rutgers University Press, 1970).

Joseph Warren Beach, *The Making of the Auden Canon* (Minneapolis: University of Minnesota Press, 1957).

John G. Blair, *The Poetic Art of W. H. Auden* (Princeton, N. J.: Princeton University Press, 1965).

Dennis Davidson, *W. H. Auden* (London: Evans Bros., 1970).

Frances Duchener, *The Case of the Helmeted Airman: A Study of W. H. Auden's Poetry* (Totowa, N.J.: Rowman & Littlefield, 1972).

John Fuller, *A Reader's Guide to W. H. Auden* (New York: Straus & Giroux, 1970).

Richard Hoggart, *Auden: An Introductory Essay* (London: Chatto & Windus, 1951).

Gerald Nelson, *Change of Heart: A Study of the Poetry of W. H. Auden* (Berkeley: University of California Press, 1969).

Justin Replogle, *Auden's Poetry* (Seattle: University of Washington Press, 1969).

Monroe Spears, *The Poetry of W. H. Auden: The Disenchanted Island* (New York: Oxford University Press, 1963).

Monroe Spears, ed., *Auden: A Collection of Critical Essays* (Englewood Cliffs., N.J.: Prentice-Hall, 1964).

Allen Ginsberg

His Life

Allen Ginsberg was born in 1926 in Paterson, New Jersey, the city celebrated by William Carlos Williams. His father, a high school teacher, was a lyric poet, publishing in a variety of periodicals. His mother's insanity was a daily fact of life, and is movingly described in his famous elegy for her, "Kaddish." Ginsberg himself, in early adulthood, was to spend eight months in the Psychiatric Institute at the Columbia-Presbyterian Medical Center, and to horrify various psychoanalysts by insisting that William Blake had spoken to him. Visionary and seemingly unstable, he none the less developed into a remarkably productive poet and one of the most effective leaders of literary, New Left, and "new consciousness" movements.

Along the way the young poet received encouragement from varied sources. One was his teacher, Miss Morgan, "a spinster lady of the old school," as Ginsberg describes her. He was seven at the time, and she powerfully stimulated his interest in books. Columbia University was a mixed blessing—it introduced him to the academically accepted poets, but was a blank in regard to the poets who most interested him, such as Pound, Williams, and Rimbaud.

At the age of 22, he had his breakthrough vision of William Blake. In an oddly frank description of the event,[1] he explained that he had been masturbating while reading "Ah, Sunflower!" and that during the post-orgasmic *triste* he suddenly heard a deep, grave voice speaking to him and knew beyond doubt that this was Blake. "It was like an 'Ancient of Days,' " Ginsberg recalls. He was flooded by a sense of cosmic relation and awareness—an experience echoed and amplified in much of his subsequent poetry.

Ginsberg was greatly befriended by William Carlos Williams, who wrote introductions to several of his early books. Meanwhile, there was a living to be earned, which the young poet managed with a variety of jobs, ranging from dishwashing to market research. The latter was eventually made obsolete by IBM equipment, whereupon he resolved to be a full-time poet and take his chances.

The literary-critical climate in the New York of the early 1950s was extremely suspicious of the kind of free verse poetics that Ginsberg was exploring, and he received little attention until he went to San Francisco where Lawrence Ferlinghetti published his long poem, "Howl." Charges of obscenity were brought against it and a famous trial followed, at which celebrated poets testified in defense of the poem. The verdict was acquittal. Meanwhile, the mass media had discovered the "Beats." Ginsberg, along with other writers such as Jack Kerouac, Philip Whalen, Mike McClure, Philip Lamantia, Gary Snyder, and Gregory Corso leaped into prominence as rebels against academic

[1] George Plimpton, ed., *Writers at Work: The Paris Review Interviews.* Third Series. (New York: Viking, 1967), pp. 300ff.

critical standards—and also against many aspects of American life in the cold war and Vietnam periods. Ginsberg himself insists that the group was less concerned with "protesting against" than with making a positive affirmation *for* "a gnostic, surrealist, imagist, ecological consciousness tinged with meditative Buddhism."

Recognition of the freshness and power of Ginsberg's poetry came slowly; the mass media mostly denounced him as "wild-eyed." The established literary critics also denounced or ignored him. In retrospect, however, clearly he and his fellow poets mark a watershed in the development of American poetry; to a large extent they have provided poetic models for younger poets coming along. Belated recognition was accorded him in 1974 when he shared the National Book Award in poetry with Adrienne Rich.

In recent years, Ginsberg has traveled widely, and has developed a growing interest in the Orient and its religious traditions. He has been in constant demand on college campuses. His participation in antiwar demonstrations and his outspoken advocacy of changes in the legal status of "obscene" artworks, drugs, and homosexuality have kept him in the public eye and have provoked the vigilant attention of the police. Less known to public and police is his private generosity; most of his income goes into a foundation to help needy writers and artists.

The Poet and His Poetry

Allen Ginsberg is important in at least three ways. First, he has produced some of the most interesting and moving poetry of recent years. It is true that he is uneven, and his inclination to compose spontaneously with little or no revision accentuates a kind of sincerity but results at times in awkward or inflated lines. Some of his long poems sag here and there; some of his short ones are ephemera. Yet when all this is said, he remains a highly impressive poet, creating at his best (and he is often at his best) a volume and variety of good poetry that few of his poetic generation can match. Readers who know his work only from "Howl" and a few other anthology pieces have no idea how subtly varied his poetry is, and what a ride range of subjects and moods he can handle.

Second, he is important in literary history as the most celebrated member of the generation of poets in the 1950s, who sharply diverged from the dominant poetic tendencies of the time, and who took much of American poetry off in a different direction.

Third, although this is not to be sharply distinguished from what was just said, he is important as one of the main creators and celebrants of the "new consciousness." The unabashed defense of homosexuality, psychedelic drugs, and four-letter words foreshadowed many tendencies of the late 1960s and 1970s. But more important is the angle of vision, the way of experiencing life and looking at everything, that gradually emerges as one reads Ginsberg's poetry. He represents, perhaps, post-Aristotelian man, impatient of an excessive reliance on cool "dualistic reason" and affect-less logic, looking for a different kind of "no-mind" reason and "heart logic," to be found as much in sex, Zen exercises, and moments of intuition as in the obsessive formal operations of brain or abstractly programmed computer.

To view Ginsberg in perspective, something more needs to be said about the American poetic scene of the 1940s, and early 1950s. Any generalization is too simple, but it is fair to say that the main tendencies reflected the more cerebral modern poets, such as T. S. Eliot, W. B. Yeats, and W. H. Auden. It was a poetry that was often highly opaque to a quick reading, filled with esoteric literary allusions. The poetic forms were frequently intricate and carefully wrought. Though poetry might deal with daily life, the individual poem primarily existed in the autonomous realm of esthetics. Most poets agreed with Auden that "poetry makes nothing happen." Nothing, that is, of a public sort, in the "real world."

In short, it was a highly intellectual kind of poetry and its main public was other poets and professional critics and scholars. It was more suitable for reading silently in solitude than for chanting, singing to music, or combining with dance in dim coffeehouses or mass rallies. There were, of course, the nonconformists, in places like Black Mountain College (North Carolina), New

York, San Francisco, and scattered in other localities. They represented an alternative approach—the lineage of Whitman, William Carlos Williams, and certain aspects of Pound—even that of Vachel Lindsay and Carl Sandburg. They tended toward free or "organic" verse, a concern for the common life, a conception of the poet as public bard rather than an esthetic recluse. They also shared in most cases a profound sense of unease and alienation as they examined many aspects of American life.

The "academics" and the "wild men," they have sometimes been called (not that every poet could be fitted into one of these categories). The significance of Ginsberg is that he was the major leader of the wild men and their most gifted poet, and that—from the time of the mid 1950s when "Howl" was charged with obscenity—the tendencies represented by Ginsberg and his fellow poets have steadily grown so that he now stands close to the mainstream of current American poetry, a position he no doubt finds awkward at times.

Ginsberg is often called a mystic, and he is one, in the sense that Blake also was a mystic. Or Whitman. Despite his intense interest in Far Eastern mysticism, Ginsberg has not adopted the life-denying stance sometimes associated with Oriental spirituality. He is very much like Whitman in his affirmation of the natural goodness of everything, most emphatically including the body. In the poem, "Footnote to Howl," he writes:

> The world is holy! The soul is holy! The skin is holy! The nose is holy!
> The tongue and cock and hand and asshole holy!
> Everything is holy! everybody's holy! everywhere is holy! every day is
> in eternity! Everyman's an angel!

Also, Ginsberg has long had an intense concern with America's problems —war, race, poverty, police brutality, alienation—and has often drawn his subject matter from these public concerns. Unlike the more academic poets, who frequently seem to be playing a serious word game but still a game, he insists that "there's no distinction, there should be no distinction between what we write down and what we really know to begin with . . . the hypocrisy of literature has been—you know like there's supposed to be formal literature, which is supposed to be different from . . . in subject, in diction, and even in organization, from our quotidian inspired lives."[2]

Ginsberg emphasizes sincerity and spontaneity as essentials of good poetry. To achieve greater spontaneity and to penetrate beneath the surface of consciousness, he has experimented with composing on the tape recorder and with using psychedelic drugs. The stress on spontaneity also throws light on the poet's antipathy for extensive revision, since the latter can involve a sort of coldblooded, analytic attitude toward words and lines originally set own in the nakedness of self-revelation. Revision, Ginsberg fears, can "lead to lies."

[2] Plimpton, pp. 288-89.

Ginsberg had at Columbia an education that most would consider excellent, though he recalls it as "academic" (in the bad sense) and far removed from daily reality. At any rate, it made him familiar with many poets, ancient and modern. Those that Columbia neglected, Ginsberg read on his own. He knows his John Donne and other older classics, but the poets he mentions as especially influential include an odd assortment: Pound, Basil Bunting, Shelley, Hart Crane, Blake, Christopher Smart, Poe, Sandburg, portions of the Bible, William Carlos Williams, and more recently "Dylan the Minstrel."

Ginsberg's early poetry shows the particularly strong influence of Williams, especially in the short-line stanzas that Williams perfected. And from Williams (who got it from Blake) he learned the phrase to describe his own anti-abstract poetic stance—"No ideas but in things."

A final word before looking at some of Ginsberg's poems in detail. It is quite possible that none of the poems will seem strange or startling to you. If so, that is evidence that the poetric revolution of the 1950s, led by Ginsberg as much as by any one person, was successful. It means that he and similar-minded poets have redefined, for the present moment at least (no redefinition is final) what the word Poetry can mean.

It is not an "art for art's sake" definition. Ginsberg views his writing in a wider perspective. In a letter he states:

> The motif behind most of my activity is articulation of present consciousness in hope that frank attention (in posters, music or say TV or mass peace rituals) will lead to breakthru and articulation in the right place at right time of some complete endless clear consciousness, limitless realization, in myself & in others. Poetry is a form of yogic meditation, so is any action, especially social (communal) actions. So is sitting alone by yourself.

As you read Ginsberg's poems, you might find it interesting to keep in mind a couple of quotations and determine to what extent you agree—and disagree —with them. The first is by Jane Kramer,[3] who insists on the radically American quality of Ginsberg's sensibility and poetry:

> It is impossible to imagine a Ginsberg in Morocco, and thinking about him here, I am beginning to understand how very much he belongs in and to the United States. Ginsberg is often called a mystic, but despite his exuberant plunges into Eastern disciplines and forms, Ginsberg's is that odd, optimistic, American brand of mysticism which he traces, quite rightly, back to Whitman, and which is rooted in humanism and in a romantic and visionary ideal of harmony among men.
>
> . . . Here in Morocco, at any rate, Ginsberg's exceptional tenderness

[3] Jane Kramer, *Allen Ginsberg in America* (New York: Vintage Books, 1970), p. xvii.

> toward his fellow beings would be considered quite mad by most self-respecting mystics or ecstatics who happened to encounter him. A Moroccan holy man plies his trade, which usually involves peddling the benefit of his blessedness to friends and neighbors, comfortably aloof from the moral traditions of his civilization, and, in fact, he is likely to regard questions of compassion and community and fellow-feeling as rather irrelevant to his pursuit of a lively ecstatic life.

The other quotation is from William Carlos Williams,[4] who finds in Ginsberg a sense of man's lostness and an alienation from literary traditions of the past:

> This young Jewish boy, already not so young any more, has recognized something that has escaped most of the modern age, he has found that man is lost in the world of his own head. And that the rhythms of the past have become like an old field long left unploughed and fallen into disuse. In fact they are excavating there for a new industrial plant.

One other thought, a speculative one. If Ginsberg represents the concept of the poet as a public figure, purifying and expressing the deepest consciousness of the people—in short, a bard—it may be that he is important not merely for his own poetry, significant as that is, but also as one who is changing the way people regard poets and poetry. Poetry, to the general public, has been a bookish thing, but more and more it is becoming oral. Probably ten college students will go to a poetry reading for one who will voluntarily buy and read a book of poetry. If poetry does, indeed, become primarily a spoken rather than a written art, the stage is set for it to play a role similar to that in ancient Greece or medieval Europe. The poet will be the one who gives the people the words wherewith to express their own deepest understanding and longing. He will be less a solitary searcher of his own soul, more a revealer of the collective soul. In this more public role, he may find himself forming alliances with the other public arts, such as music, drama, and dance. Poetry may evolve into a far more pervasive part of the general life than it has been, in the Western tradition, since the general spread of literacy.

The above is, frankly, speculative. But the difference between Ginsberg and the majority of the poets in this book may rest in part on a simple fact: they mostly wrote poems to be printed in books; he writes poems to be declaimed aloud to a visible and responding public of tangible men and women.

[4] Allen Ginsberg, *Empty Mirror.* With an Introduction by William Carlos Williams (New York: A Totem/Corinth Book, 1961), p. vi.

Poems

Some poets—perhaps Robert Frost is one—seem to develop a technique, a style, a voice early in their career, and spend a lifetime exploring and refining it. Others, like Yeats, experience sharp "mutations" along the way, forsaking their early manner and evolving a type of poetry so different that one might almost think a separate poet had composed it.

In the case of Ginsberg, there is a continuity of sensibility—the anguished awareness of everything that is wrong with the world combined with an intuitive or mystical faith that somehow holiness is everywhere. But Ginsberg's poetic technique underwent a sharp change. His earliest poems, as contained in *Empty Mirror,* are sometimes rhymed and often written in the short lines reminiscent of William Carlos Williams. Only in a few of the early poems does one find the long, Whitmanesque, cadenced lines characteristic of Ginsberg's later poetry. The tone, also, tends to be different. The early poems are often quiet, gently lyrical, whereas much of the later work has an oratorical vehemence, suggesting the bardic poetry of Whitman.

First, an early poem about nature, but pointing beyond mere factual description:

The Trembling of the Veil

Today out of the window
the trees seemed like live
organisms on the moon.

Each bough extended upward
covered at the north end
with leaves, like a green

hairy protuberance. I saw
the scarlet-and-pink shoot-tips
of budding leaves wave

delicately in the sunlight,
blown by the breeze,
all the arms of the trees
bending and straining downward

at once when the wind
pushed them.

Titles of poems are sometimes an afterthought on the part of the poet, serving as little more than a convenient label. In this case the title offers a clue to the deeper level of the poem. The reader is forewarned that this is not a simple poem describing nature, that it somehow involves an invitation or initiation into a mystery. A veil is a common symbol for something that conceals a secret. The title here may perhaps refer in part to a particularly famous veil that hid ultimate mysteries. In Matthew's account of the crucifixion of Jesus, it is stated that at the moment of death the veil in the Temple, which concealed sacred mysteries from profane eyes, was torn in two from top to bottom. The tearing of a veil is thus a symbol for some kind of revelation. The "trembling" of a veil suggests not a full revelation, but hovering on the edge of one.

The first stanza establishes several contrasts. The trees are growing on the earth, but it is as though they are sprouting from the cold, dead surface of the distant moon. The trees are intensely alive, more like animals than passive plants—thus a strong contrast is created between life and lifelessness. Perhaps there is a suggestion that the earth (the city?) where the trees are growing has the cold, sterile quality of the lunar surface. Or the moon reference may serve simply to suggest the remote, unknown, and mysterious. At any rate, there is the sense—created in the first stanza—of vehement life somehow triumphing over a discouraging setting.

The second and third stanzas increase the impression that the trees are alive as an animal is—"like a green / hairy protuberance," "shoot-tips / of budding leaves wave." The boughs extend upward, as though reaching for something. The real moon in the real sky? Heaven? Some ultimate revelation of meaning? They are covered *at the north end* with leaves—north is the fixed direction, and other directions are stated in relation to it. Again, it is as though the trees are a kind of pointer—toward something . . . toward whatever lies behind the "veil."

It is a two-way motion. "Each bough extended upward" and "all the arms of the trees / bending and straining downward" when the wind blows. If upward is thought of as movement toward some mystery and ultimate understanding, and downward suggests familiar earth, the trees are involved in both directions, perhaps implying, that any revelation is available on the earth in everyday life as much as in some hypothetical heaven.

In the final stanza the mention of the wind is evocative. The word for Spirit in the Old Testament is a Hebrew word which also means breath, and by an easy extension, *wind* is often used as a synonym for Spirit. There is the brief hint that Spirit (of God? of nature?) is rustling in the trees, moving their branches down to the earth where human beings dwell. The trees that at first seemed as far away as the moon are now approaching the human observer, propelled by the wind pushing against them.

One way of looking at the poem is simply to examine the contrasts in it:

Earth	Moon
Live things	Barrenness
Up	Down
Spirit	Nature

The poem as a whole seems to vindicate its title: it suggests a partial or anticipated revelation. The "Veil" has not been torn in two, but it is trembling, and the movement of the trees is earthward and the time of revelation seems drawing nearer.

Do you see what is wrong with this approach to the poem? Perhaps nothing wrong at all in the final conclusions; they seem to be justified by the poem, when it is studied line by line. But what we have done is leap too quickly from the title to a theory about the poem. We have concentrated on nuances of the idea of "revelation," and at times have treated the poem more as a philosophic treatise than as a poem.

We moved too quickly in looking for "the message of the poem." We should have lingered over the poem first, line by line, enjoying the full sensuous richness of the pictures it paints—"the trees seemed like live / organisms," "a green / hairy protuberance," "scarlet-and-pink shoot-tips," "wave / delicately in the sunlight," "bending and straining downward."

The imagination quickly sets to work, *seeing* the boughs and leaves in their movement, *feeling* the weight and movement of limbs, feeling the push of wind, even *smelling* the young leaf tips. These things are primary. Whether or not our explication of the poem has any validity, there is no doubt that nature is really being described in the poem, and that its full sensuous reality must be recognized and enjoyed before the reader goes on to look for a second level of meaning. And if that second level is found, it should have a smell of swaying trees still clinging to it.

The next, despite its startling title, is a quiet mood poem:

Marijuana Notation

How sick I am!
        that thought
always comes to me
        with horror.
Is it this strange
        for everybody?
But such fugitive feelings
have always been
        my métier.

Baudelaire—yet he had
great joyful moments
        staring into space,
looking into the
        middle distance,
contemplating his image
        in Eternity.

They were his moments
          of identity.
It is solitude that
produces these thoughts.

          It is December
almost, they are singing
          Christmas carols
in front of the department
stores down the block on
          Fourteenth Street.

Baudelaire, a major 19th-century French poet, often expresses an almost intolerable disgust with life, a kind of nausea of the spirit.

The form of this poem raises a question often asked. Are the line divisions in free verse arbitrary? In this case, why chop the poem up into lines that start at the left margin and other lines (usually shorter) that are indented?

The answer will depend on the poet and the particular poem. In a good poem, these decisions are not arbitrary. In much of Whitman, for instance, the line length corresponds to breath groups. This is also very often true with Ginsberg. But in "Marijuana Notation" the lines are so short that this explanation seems useless.

Here the short, indented lines seem to carry most of the impact, and the value of having them as separate lines is that the reader automatically pauses a bit in front of them, thus creating a moment of waiting and suspense before he comes to "that thought," "with horror," "for everybody?," and "my métier." Whether reading silently or aloud, the first stanza operates like this: "How sick I am! PAUSE that thought PAUSE always comes to me PAUSE with horror," etc. If it were not for the line divisions, the indented lines would follow too smoothly on the others and lose impact: "always comes to me with horror."

The indented lines seem to be the skeleton of the poem, carrying most of the meaning and emotional charge. Printed by themselves, they would still convey much of the poem:

that thought
with horror
for everybody?
my métier
staring into space,
middle distance,
in Eternity.
of identity
It is December
Christmas carols
Fourteenth Street.

1. Try rewriting the poem completely in short lines. So far as possible, do it by choosing certain of the lines above. Do not take any phrases from the longer lines unless this is absolutely necessary. Does your rewritten version have the same tone as the original? In what ways has the poem become a new poem? What purpose do the long lines serve?

Look up *métier* in the dictionary. (It is an English word, though borrowed from French.) Why is this word used instead of *trade* or *specialty*?

The next poem (represented by part I) is the one that made Ginsberg famous, thanks to the city fathers of San Francisco who tried unsuccessfully to pin charges of obscenity on it, him, and the publisher, Lawrence Ferlinghetti. The entire poem consists of three parts followed by "Footnote to Howl," in which almost every line begins with "holy," and the enumeration of holy objects ranges from the "world" and "tongue and cock," to "New York" and forgiveness."

from *Howl*

for
Carl Solomon

I

I saw the best minds of my generation destroyed by madness, starving
hysterical naked,
dragging themselves through the negro streets at dawn looking for an
angry fix,
angelheaded hipsters burning for the ancient heavenly connection to
the starry dynamo in the machinery of night,
who poverty and tatters and hollow-eyed and high sat up smoking in
the supernatural darkness of cold-water flats floating across the
tops of cities contemplating jazz,
who bared their brains to Heaven under the El and saw Mohammedan
angels staggering on tenement roofs illuminated,
who passed through universities with radiant cool eyes hallucinating
Arkansas and Blake-light tragedy among the scholars of war,
who were expelled from the academies for crazy & publishing obscene
odes on the windows of the skull,
who cowered in unshaven rooms in underwear, burning their money in
wastebaskets and listening to the Terror through the wall,
who got busted in their pubic beards returning through Laredo with a
belt of marijuana for New York,
who ate fire in paint hotels or drank turpentine in Paradise Alley, death,
or purgatoried their torsos night after night
with dreams, with drugs, with waking nightmares, alcohol and cock and
endless balls,

incomparable blind streets of shuddering cloud and lightning in the mind leaping toward poles of Canada & Paterson, illuminating all the motionless world of Time between,
Peyote solidities of halls, backyard green tree cemetery dawns, wine drunkenness over the rooftops, storefront boroughs of teahead joyride neon blinking traffic light, sun and moon and tree vibrations in the roaring winter dusks of Brooklyn, ashcan rantings and kind king light of mind,
who chained themselves to subways for the endless ride from Battery to holy Bronx on benzedrine until the noise of wheels and children brought them down shuddering mouth-wracked and battered bleak of brain all drained of brilliance in the drear light of Zoo,
who sank all night in submarine light of Bickford's floated out and sat through the stale beer afternoon in desolate Fugazzi's, listening to the crack of doom on the hydrogen jukebox,
who talked continuously seventy hours from park to pad to bar to Bellevue to museum to the Brooklyn Bridge,
a lost battalion of platonic conversationalists jumping down the stoops off fire escapes off windowsills off Empire State out of the moon,
yacketayakking screaming vomiting whispering facts and memories and anecdotes and eyeball kicks and shocks of hospitals and jails and wars,
whole intellects disgorged in total recall for seven days and nights with brilliant eyes, meat for the Synagogue cast on the pavement,
who vanished into nowhere Zen New Jersey leaving a trail of ambiguous picture postcards of Atlantic City Hall,
suffering Eastern sweats and Tangerian bone-grindings and migraines of China under junk-withdrawal in Newark's bleak furnished room,
who wandered around and around at midnight in the railroad yard wondering where to go, and went, leaving no broken hearts,
who lit cigarettes in boxcars boxcars boxcars racketing through snow toward lonesome farms in grandfather night,
who studied Plotinus Poe St. John of the Cross telepathy and bop kaballa because the cosmos instinctively vibrated at their feet in Kansas,
who loned it through the streets of Idaho seeking visionary indian angels who were visionary indian angels,
who thought they were only mad when Baltimore gleamed in supernatural ecstasy,
who jumped in limousines with the Chinaman of Oklahoma on the impulse of winter midnight streetlight smalltown rain,
who lounged hungry and lonesome through Houston seeking jazz or sex or soup, and followed the brilliant Spaniard to converse about America and Eternity, a hopeless task, and so took ship to Africa,

who disappeared into the volcanoes of Mexico leaving behind nothing but the shadow of dungarees and the lava and ash of poetry scattered in fireplace Chicago,
who reappeared on the West Coast investigating the F.B.I. in beards and shorts with big pacifist eyes sexy in their dark skin passing out incomprehensible leaflets,
who burned cigarette holes in their arms protesting the narcotic tobacco haze of Capitalism,
who distributed Supercommunist pamphlets in Union Square weeping and undressing while the sirens of Los Alamos wailed them down, and wailed down Wall, and the Staten Island ferry also wailed,
who broke down crying in white gymnasiums naked and trembling before the machinery of other skeletons,
who bit detectives in the neck and shrieked with delight in policecars for committing no crime but their own wild cooking pederasty and intoxication,
who howled on their knees in the subway and were dragged off the roof waving genitals and manuscripts,
who let themselves be fucked in the ass by saintly motorcyclists, and screamed with joy,
who blew and were blown by those human seraphim, the sailors, caresses of Atlantic and Caribbean love,
who balled in the morning and evenings in rosegardens and the grass of public parks and cemeteries scattering their semen freely to whomever come who may,
who hiccupped endlessly trying to giggle but wound up with a sob behind a partition in a Turkish Bath when the blonde & naked angel came to pierce them with a sword,
who lost their loveboys to the three old shrews of fate the one eyed shrew of the heterosexual dollar the one eyed shrew that winks out of the womb and the one eyed shrew that does nothing but sit on her ass and snip the intellectual golden threads of the craftsman's loom,
who copulated ecstatic and insatiate with a bottle of beer a sweetheart a package of cigarettes a candle and fell off the bed, and continued along the floor and down the hall and ended fainting on the wall with a vision of ultimate cunt and come eluding the last gyzym of consciousness,
who sweetened the snatches of a million girls trembling in the sunset, and were red eyed in the morning but prepared to sweeten the snatch of the sunrise, flashing buttocks under barns and naked in the lake,
who went out whoring through Colorado in myriad stolen night-cars, N.C., secret hero of these poems, cocksman and Adonis of Denver—joy to the memory of his innumerable lays of girls in empty lots & diner backyards, moviehouses' rickety rows, on

mountaintops in caves or with gaunt waitresses in familiar roadside lonely petticoat upliftings & especially secret gas-station solipisisms of johns, & hometown alleys too,
who faded out in vast sordid movies, were shifted in dreams, woke on a sudden Manhattan, and picked themselves up out of basements hungover with heartless Tokay and horrors of Third Avenue iron dreams & stumbled to unemployment offices,
who walked all night with their shoes full of blood on the snowbank docks waiting for a door in the East River to open to a room full of steamheat and opium,
who created great suicidal dramas on the apartment cliff-banks of the Hudson with the wartime blue floodlight of the moon & their heads shall be crowned with laurel in oblivion,
who ate the lamb stew of the imagination or digested the crab at the muddy bottom of the rivers of Bowery,
who wept at the romance of the streets with their pushcarts full of onions and bad music,
who sat in boxes breathing in the darkness under the bridge, and rose up to build harpsichords in their lofts,
who coughed on the sixth floor of Harlem crowned with flame under the tubercular sky surrounded by orange crates of theology,
who scribbled all night rocking and rolling over lofty incantations which in the yellow morning where stanzas of gibberish,
who cooked rotten animals lung heart feet tail borsht & tortillas dreaming of the pure vegetable kingdom,
who plunged themselves under meat trucks looking for an egg,
who threw their watches off the roof to cast their ballot for Eternity outside of Time, & alarm clocks fell on their heads every day for the next decade,
who cut their wrists three times successively unsuccessfully, gave up and were forced to open antique stores where they thought they were growing old and cried,
who were burned alive in their innocent flannel suits on Madison Avenue amid blasts of leaden verse & the tanked-up clatter of the iron regiments of fashion & the nitroglycerine shrieks of the fairies of advertising & the mustard gas of sinister intelligent editors, or were run down by the drunken taxicabs of Absolute Reality,
who jumped off the Brooklyn Bridge this actually happened and walked away unknown and forgotten into the ghostly daze of Chinatown soup alleyways & firetrucks, not even one free beer,
who sang out of their windows in despair, fell out of the subway window, jumped in the filthy Passaic, leaped on negroes, cried all over the street, danced on broken wineglasses barefoot smashed phonograph records of nostalgic European 1930's German jazz finished the whiskey and threw up groaning into the bloody toilet, moans in their ears and the blast of colossal steamwhistles,

who barreled down the highways of the past journeying to each other's hotrod-Golgotha jail-solitude watch or Birmingham jazz incarnation,
who drove crosscountry seventytwo hours to find out if I had a vision or you had a vision or he had a vision to find out Eternity,
who journeyed to Denver, who died in Denver, who came back to Denver & waited in vain, who watched over Denver & brooded & loned in Denver and finally went away to find out the Time, & now Denver is lonesome for her heroes,
who fell on their knees in hopeless cathedrals praying for each other's salvation and light and breasts, until the soul illuminated its hair for a second,
who crashed through their minds in jail waiting for impossible criminals with golden heads and the charm of reality in their hearts who sang sweet blues to Alcatraz,
who retired to Mexico to cultivate a habit, or Rocky Mount to tender Buddha or Tangiers to boys or Southern Pacific to the black locomotive or Harvard to Narcissus to Woodlawn to the daisychain or grave,
who demanded sanity trials accusing the radio of hypnotism & were left with their insanity & their hands & a hung jury,
who threw potato salad at CCNY lecturers on Dadaism and subsequently presented themselves on the granite steps of the madhouse with shaven heads and harlequin speech of suicide, demanding instantaneous lobotomy,
and who were given instead the concrete void of insulin metrasol electricity hydrotherapy psychotherapy occupational therapy pingpong & amnesia,
who in humorless protest overturned only one symbolic pingpong table, resting briefly in catatonia,
returning years later truly bald except for a wig of blood, and tears and fingers, to the visible madman doom of the wards of the madtowns of the East,
Pilgrim State's Rockland's and Greystone's foetid halls, bickering with the echoes of the soul, rocking and rolling in the midnight solitude-bench dolmen-realms of love, dream of life a nightmare, bodies turned to stone as heavy as the moon,
with mother finally ******, and the last fantastic book flung out of the tenement window, and the last door closed at 4 AM and the last telephone slammed at the wall in reply and the last furnished room emptied down to the last piece of mental furniture, a yellow paper rose twisted on a wire hanger in the closet, and even that imaginary, nothing but a hopeful little bit of hallucination—
ah, Carl, while you are not safe I am not safe, and now you're really in the total animal soup of time—
and who therefore ran through the icy streets obsessed with a sudden flash of the alchemy of the use of the ellipse the catalog the meter & the vibrating plane,

who dreamt and made incarnate gaps in Time & Space through images juxtaposed, and trapped the archangel of the soul between 2 visual images and joined the elemental verbs and set the noun and dash of consciousness together jumping with sensation of Pater Omnipotens Aeterna Deus
to recreate the syntax and measure of poor human prose and stand before you speechless and intelligent and shaking with shame, rejected yet confessing out the soul to conform to the rhythm of thought in his naked and endless head,
the madman bum and angel beat in Time, unknown, yet putting down here what might be left to say in time come after death,
and rose reincarnate in the ghostly clothes of jazz in the goldhorn shadow of the band and blew the suffering of America's naked mind for love into an eli eli lamma lamma sabacthani saxophone cry that shivered the cities down to the last radio
with the absolute heart of the poem of life butchered out of their own bodies good to eat a thousand years.

In part I, the longest section and the only one reproduced here, the emphasis on holiness is mostly implicit rather than stated in ringing biblical language. *It is implied by the agony of the descriptions.* The world of memory and experience through which Ginsberg leads the reader is one in which the holiness of all things is overlaid by madness, cruelty, desperation, but the intuition of an underlying holiness saves the poem from complete desperation.

Many of the allusions are presumably personal, and may carry extra meanings to the poet and his close friends. This need not trouble the ordinary reader. The general message and mood of the poem are clear enough. It is a cry of agony from one who sees the possibilities of creativity and love destroyed by an impersonal and unfeeling society. Although written in the mid 1950s, its feel foreshadows the student upheavals of the 1960s when a visceral reaction against cold, bureaucratic structures led to demonstrations, the Hippie movement, the rise of communes, and experiments with psychedelic drugs as a means of transcending the rigidities of the usual patterns of human interaction.

The theme is set in the first line—"I saw the best minds of my generation destroyed by madness, starving hysterical naked." There follows a long catalogue of the crazy things the "best minds" had done, each line usually introduced by *who,* so that practically the whole of part I refers back to the first line. The conducted tour of desperation and madness jumps back and forth across America, visiting asylums and jails and university campuses and jazz sessions. The tone is one of sustained hysteria, of heightened awareness and pain. The long lines seem written to be chanted or shouted. The poem accumulates force like a scream infinitely repeated with variations—but each time unmistakably a scream. This is poetry the exact opposite, say, of a Japanese Haiku or a sonnet. Everything is said, repeatedly said; the reader is bombarded with multiple invitations to the dark night of the soul.

The multitude of characters who rage in torment through the poem seem driven by a quest for which they hardly have words; they are tormented by the world as they experience it, and are haunted by a vision of love and holiness that the world does not permit. The agony of the quest is summarized in the last two lines of part I:

> and rose reincarnate in the ghostly clothes of jazz in the goldhorn shadow of the band and blew the suffering of America's naked mind for love into an eli eli lamma lamma sabacthani saxophone cry that shivered the cities down to the last radio
> with the absolute heart of the poem of life butchered out of their own bodies good to eat a thousand years.

The word *reincarnate* suggests the Greek and Oriental doctrine of reincarnation, and perhaps also glancingly refers to the incarnation of Christ and his resurrection. The biblical tone of the poem is strengthened by "eli eli lamma lamma sabacthani,"—My God, my God, why, why hast Thou forsaken me?", an echo of the beginning of Psalm 22 and also one of Christ's last utterances on the cross.

The poem as a whole is a dialogue between hope and despair, with despair the greater because daily reality denies the intuitively perceived ideal of another and more meaningful and loving style of life. If the poem were completely negative, the scream of anguish would be more muted. A tormented kind of affirmation ends part I, preparing the way for the endlessly repeated word, *Holy,* in the "Footnote."

Beauty amid sordidness and existing despite all that the world can do to destroy it—sudden gleams of meaning amid the horror of a nightmare—for example, lines 48-49:

> who wept at the romance of the streets with their pushcarts full of onions and bad music,
> who sat in boxes breathing in the darkness under the bridge, and rose up to build harpsichords in their lofts,

The mention of harpsichords interjects a touch of elegance, refined beauty. Replace it by steel drum or electric guitar and the effect is lost. A harpsichord kind of grace is struggling for existence and expression in the midst of the strident nightmare.

The picture of young men, alienated from the main American scene, and constantly on the go, looking for meaning, is contrasted with the America of the "establishment" (line 56):

> who were burned alive in their innocent flannel suits on Madison Avenue amid blasts of leaden verse & the tanked-up clatter of

> the iron regiments of fashion & the nitroglycerine shrieks of the fairies of advertising & the mustard gas of sinister intelligent editors, or were run down by the drunken taxicabs of Absolute Reality,

The intensely personal nature of the poem is illustrated by the above quotation. Ginsberg at one time earned his living from the Establishment by doing market research (flannel suits on Madison Avenue); at Columbia the English courses, he felt, concentrated on dully academic poets (leaden verse); he had difficulty getting a first book of poetry published (sinister intelligent editors).

"Howl" as a whole is a public poem as most of Yeats or Eliot is not. It requires no study or commentaries and no tracking down of learned references. The theme is so fully developed that if the reader is puzzled by an obscure personal reference here and there, he need not be troubled; the general thrust of the poem is made clear by a kind of poetic overkill, the same cataloguing technique that Whitman used. The best introduction to "Howl" is to read it aloud in a declamatory style, or to listen to Ginsberg's recording of the poem.

Thus far we have said nothing about the form. The obvious change that has taken place since the two early poems is that Ginsberg is now experimenting with long lines. The subdued, lyrical tone of the two early poems is also replaced by something much more rhetorical and strident. In the interview conducted by *The Paris Review,* Ginsberg. commented:[5]

> . . . I've never actually sat down and made a technical analysis of the rhythms that I write. . . . tending toward de DA de DA de de. . . . Tending toward dactylic, probably. . . . But it's more complicated than dactyl because dactyl is a three, three units, a foot consisting of three parts, whereas the actual rhythm is probably a rhythm which consists of five, six, or seven, like DA de de DA de de DA de de DA DA. Which is more toward the line of Greek dance rhythms—that's why they call them choriambic. . . . But it [analyzing his rhythms in terms of Greek metrics] doesn't do very much good, because I wasn't really working with a classical unit. I was working with my own neural impulse and writing impulses. See, the difference is between someone sitting down to write a poem in a definite preconceived metrical pattern and filling in that pattern, and someone working with his own physiological movements and *arriving* at it organically rather than synthetically. Nobody's got any objection to even iambic pentameter if it comes from a source deeper than the mind—that is to say, if it comes from the breathing and the belly and the lungs.

Good free verse is not just highly charged prose chopped up into lines. It

[5] Plimpton, pp. 282-283.

tends to be more rhythmic than prose, and often it makes use of other distinctively poetic devices. Alliteration to give an added intensity, for example. It weaves in and out of "Howl," as in the line 13, with its repeated *b*'s, *d*'s, and *t*'s:

> Peyote solidities of halls, backyard green tree cemetery dawns, wine drunkenness over the rooftops, storefront boroughs of teahead joyride neon blinking traffic light, sun and moon and tree vibrations in the roaring winter dusks of Brooklyn, ashcan rantings and kind king light of mind,

Another element of form figures prominently in "Howl," as Ginsberg himself has pointed out. The repetition of *who*:[6]

> . . . Part one uses repeated base who, as a sort of kithera BLANG, homeric (in my imagination) to mark off each statement, with rhythmic unit. So that's experiment with longer & shorter variations on a fixed base—the principle being, that each line has to be contained within the elastic of one breath—with suitable punctuatory expressions where the rhythm has built up enough so that I have to let off steam by building a longer climactic line in which there is a jazzy ride. All the ear I've ever developed goes into the balancing of those lines. The interesting moments when the rhythm is sufficiently powerful pushing ahead so I can ride out free and drop the key that holds it together. The method of keeping a long line still all poetic and not prosey is the concentration and compression of basically imageistic notations into surrealist or cubist phrasing, like hydrogen jukeboxes. . . . But I've tried to keep the language sufficiently dense in one way or another—use of primitive naive grammer (expelled for crazy), elimination of prosey articles & syntactical sawdust, juxtaposition of cubist style images, or hot rhythm.

1. Pick out some lines from "Howl" to illustrate the rhythmic patterns that Ginsberg discusses.

2. Do you agree that a rhythm should arise "organically" rather than being selected before the poet sets out to write? Why or why not?

3. Make a list of instances where Ginsberg has kept the language "dense" by use of *one* of the following devices: "primitive naive grammar," "elimination of prosey articles and syntactical sawdust," "juxtaposition of cubist style images."

4. Study the poem as a quest for holiness. Make a list of the ways in which that theme is implied, if not always explicitly stated, in part I.

[6] Kramer, p. 166.

5. "Howl," like most of Ginsberg's poetry, is designed for reading aloud. What are the artistic advantages and disadvantages of this kind of poetry as compared with poetry meant to be read silently to oneself?

The next poem is wistful and quiet, with a moment of revelation:

Cafe In Warsaw

These spectres resting on plastic stools
leather-gloved spectres flitting thru the coffeehouse one hour
spectre girls with scarred faces, black stockings thin eyebrows
spectre boys blond hair combed neat over the skull little chin beards
new specters talking intensely crowded together over black shiny tables late afternoon
the sad soprano of history chanting thru a hi-fidelity loudspeaker
—perspective walls & windows 18th century down New World Avenue to Sigmund III column'd
Sword upraised watching over Polish youth 3 centuries—
O Polish spectres what've you suffered since Chopin wept into his romantic piano
old buildings rubbled down, gaiety of all night parties under the air bombs,
first screams of the vanishing ghetto—Workmen step thru prewar pink-blue bedroom walls demolishing sunny ruins—
Now spectres gather to kiss hands, girls kiss lip to lip, red witchhair from Paris
& fine gold watches—to sit by the yellow wall with a large brown briefcase—
to smoke three cigarettes with thin black ties and nod heads over a new movie—
Spectres Christ and your bodies be with you for this hour while you're young
in postwar heaven stained with the sweat of Communism, your loves and your white smooth cheekskin soft in the glance of each other's eye.
O spectres how beautiful your calm shaven faces, your pale lipstick scarves, your delicate heels,
how beautiful you absent gaze, legs crossed alone at table with long eyelashes,
how beautiful your patient love together sitting reading the art journals—
how beautiful your entrance thru the velvet-curtained door, laughing into the overcrowded room,
how you wait in your hats, measure the faces, and turn and depart for an hour,

or meditate at the bar, waiting for the slow waitress to prepare red hot tea, minute by minute
standing still as hours ring in churchbells, as years pass and you will remain in Novy Swiat,
how beautiful you press your lips together, sigh forth smoke from your mouth, rub your hands
or lean together laughing to notice this wild haired madman who sits weeping among you a stranger.

This poem is very gentle as compared with "Howl" and many others. There is no hyperbole, no invocation of the cosmos, no cries of pain or ecstasy. It is a meditation in which the poet says things quietly and directly.

It is a poem of observation rather than participation; Ginsberg is the outsider, the "wild haired madman who sits weeping among you a stranger." The movement of the poem is toward affirmation. At the beginning everything is ghostly, emphasized by the repeated word, *spectre.* Colors are mostly black, suggesting a darkening of the human spirit, a kind of eclipse or quiet repression. The dark and ghostly quality of the scene is emphasized in the choice of words: black stockings, thin eyebrows, skull, black shiny tables, thin black ties. There is something meagre, subdued, repressed, half alive about the scene.

There follows a kind of historical resumé, suggesting the tragic history of Poland, a country always in danger of being dominated or annexed by its stronger neighbors. The phrase, "first screams of the vanishing ghetto," refers to the Ghetto uprising during World War II when, after a long and heroic resistance, the Jews of Warsaw were finally crushed by German military power. The "postwar heaven stained with the sweat of Communism" suggests the drab cold war years, under a Polish Communist régime and with the Soviet Union keeping a close watch. But after that reference (line 16), the tone of the poem changes. It is as though the observer continues to see the same scene, but suddenly discovers in the "spectres" a beauty that had previously eluded him—"how beautiful your calm shaven faces, your pale lipstick scarves. . . . "

It is a kind of epiphany, an experience not confined to poetry. Probably everyone has had it—watching something that seemed commonplace, dull, even repressive; then suddenly sensing a meaning and radiance to everything. Thus, very quietly and unobtrusely, a scene that begins with "These spectres resting on plastic stools" has been transformed to vibrant individuals who are beautiful in all their gestures and who "lean together laughing to notice this wild haired madman who sits weeping among you a stranger." The observer has first seen the cafe crowd through the spectacles of his own sorrows, and now suddenly realizes the meaning *to them* of their time in the cafe; he is more than ever a stranger, for he still weeps.

1. What poetic effect is created by the frequent use of "how" at the beginning of lines?

2. Suppose the final line ended with "or lean together laughing." How would the omission of the last half of the final line affect the impact of the poem?

Now, we include a few poems more briefly treated.

An Asphodel

O dear sweet rosy
        unattainable desire
. . . how sad, no way
        to change the mad
cultivated asphodel, the
        visible reality . . .

and skin's appalling
        petals—how inspired
to be so lying in the living
        room drunk naked
and dreaming, in the absence
        of electricity . . .
over and over eating the low root
        of the asphodel,
gray fate . . .

        rolling in generation
on the flowery couch
        as on a bank in Arden—
my only rose tonite's the treat
        of my own nudity.

1. Read the selection from William Carlos Williams' "Asphodel, That Greeny Flower" (page 203). Can you describe similarities and differences in the use each poet makes of the asphodel?

2. Pick out all the words having to do with flowers. Notice especially the mention of asphodel and the rose. Why these two in particular?

3. What do you make of "eating the low root / of the asphodel"?

Uptown

Yellow-lit Budweiser signs over oaken bars,
"I've seen everything"—the bartender handing me change of $10,
I stared at him amiably eyes thru an obvious Adamic beard—
with Montana musicians homeless in Manhattan, teen age
curly hair themselves—we sat at the antique booth & gossiped,

Madame Grady's literary salon a curious value in New York—
"If I had my way I'd cut off your hair and send you to Vietnam"—
"Bless you then" I replied to a hatted thin citizen hurrying to the bar-
room door
upon wet dark Amsterdam Avenue decades later—
"And if I couldn't do that I'd cut your throat" he snarled farewell,
and "Bless you sir" I added as he went to his fate in the rain, dapper
Irishman.

1. How is a sense of humor revealed in this poem?
2. Show how the poem builds to a climax.
3. Why do you think Ginsberg ends the poem with "dapper Irishman"?

Finally, a few poems to illustrate Ginsberg's variety.

Patna-Benares Express

Whatever it may be whoever it may be
The bloody man all singing all just
However he die
He rode on railroad cars
He woke at dawn, in the white light of a new universe
He couldn't do any different
He the skeleton with eyes
raised himself up from a wooden bench
felt different looking at the fields and palm trees
no money in the bank of dust
no nation but inexpressible grey clouds before sunrise
lost his identity cards in his wallet
in the bald rickshaw by the Maidan in dry Patna
Later stared hopeless waking from drunken sleep
dry mouthed in the RR Station
among sleeping shoeshine men in loincloth on the dirty concrete
Too many bodies thronging these cities now

Love Poem on Theme by Whitman

I'll go into the bedroom silently and lie down between the bridegroom
and the bride,
those bodies fallen from heaven stretched out waiting naked and restless,
arms resting over their eyes in the darkness,
bury my face in their shoulders and breasts, breathing their skin,
and stroke and kiss neck and mouth and make back be open and
known,

legs raised up crook'd to receive, cock in the darkness driven tormented and attacking
roused up from hole to itching head,
bodies locked shuddering naked, hot lips and buttocks screwed into each other
and eyes, eyes glinting and charming, widening into looks and abandon,
and moans of movement, voices, hands in air, hands between thighs,
hands in moisture on softened lips, throbbing contraction of bellies
till the white come flow in the swirling sheets,
and the bride cry for forgiveness, and the groom be covered with tears of passion and compassion,
and I rise up from the bed replenished with last intimate gestures and kisses of farewell—
all before the mind wakes, behind shades and closed doors in a darkened house
where the inhabitants roam unsatisfied in the night,
nude ghosts seeking each other out in the silence.

*The End**

I am I, old Father Fisheye that begat the ocean, the worm at my own ear, the serpent turning around a tree,
I sit in the mind of the oak and hide in the rose, I know if any wake up, none but my death,
come to me bodies, come to me prophecies, come all foreboding, come spirits and visions,
I receive all, I'll die of cancer, I enter the coffin forever, I close my eye, I disappear,
I fall on myself in winter snow, I roll in a great wheel through rain, I watch fuckers in convulsion,
car screech, furies groaning their basso music, memory fading in the brain, men imitating dogs,
I delight in a woman's belly, youth stretching his breasts and thighs to sex, the cock sprung inward
gassing its seed on the lips of Yin, the beasts dance in Siam, they sing opera in Moscow,
my boys yearn at dusk on stoops, I enter New York, I play my jazz on a Chicago Harpsichord,
Love that bore me I bear back to my Origin with no loss, I float over the vomiter

* According to a note appended by Ginsberg after the poem, "The End" records visions experienced after drinking Ayahuasca, an Amazon spiritual potion. "The message is: Widen the area of consciousness."

thrilled with my deathlessness, thrilled with this endlessness I dice and bury,
come Poet shut up eat my word, and taste my mouth in your ear.

Consulting I Ching Smoking Pot Listening to the Fugs Sing Blake

That which pushes upward
does not come back
He led me in his garden
tinkle of 20 year phonograph
Death is acommin in
and mocks my loss of liberty
One must see the Great Man
Fear not it brings blessing
No Harm
from the invisible world
Perseverance
Realms beyond
Stoned
in the deserted city
which lies below consciousness

I Am a Victim of Telephone

When I lay down to sleep dream the Wishing Well it rings
"Have you a new play for the brokendown theater?"
When I write in my notebook poem it rings
"Buster Keaton is under the brooklyn bridge on Frankfurt and Pearl . . . "
When I unsheath my skin extend my cock toward someone's thighs fat or thin, boy or girl
Tingaling—"Please get him out of jail . . . the police are crashing down"
When I lift the soupspoon to my lips, the phone on the floor begins purring
"Hello it's me—I'm in the park two broads from Iowa . . . nowhere to sleep last night . . . hit 'em in the mouth"
When I muse at smoke crawling over the roof outside my street window
purifying Eternity with my eye observation of grey vaporous columns in the sky
ring ring "Hello this is Esquire be a dear and finish your political commitment manifesto"
When I listen to radio presidents roaring on the convention floor
the phone also chimes in "Rush up to Harlem with us and see the riots"
Always the telephone linked to all the hearts of the world beating at once

crying my husbands gone my boyfriend's busted forever my poetry was rejected
won't you come over for money and please won't you write me a piece of bullshit
How are you dear can you come to Easthampton we're all here bathing in the ocean we're all so lonely
and I lay back on my pallet contemplating $50 phone bill, broke, drowsy, anxious, my heart fearful of the fingers dialing, the deaths, the singing of telephone bells
ringing at dawn ringing all afternoon ringing up midnight ringing now forever.

SELECTIVE BIBLIOGRAPHY

Most of the Ginsberg poems included in this book are taken from *Empty Mirror* (New York: Totem/Corinth Book, 1961), *Howl and Other Poems* (San Francisco: City Lights Books, 1956), *Kaddish and Other Poems 1958-1960* (San Francisco: City Lights Books, 1961), and *Planet News 1961-1967* (San Francisco: City Lights Books, 1968).

Allen Ginsberg, *Indian Journals March 1962-May 1963* (San Francisco: David Haselwood Books, 1970).

———, *Airplane Dreams: Compositions from Journals* (Toronto: Anansi, 1968).

Allen Ginsberg, *Allen Verbatim: Lectures on Poetry, Politics, Consciousness* (New York: McGraw-Hill, 1974).

Jane Kramer, *Allen Ginsberg in America* (New York: Random House, 1969).

Thomas F. Merrill, *Allen Ginsberg.* (New York: Twayne).

Writers at Work. 3rd series. Edited by George Plimpton (New York: Viking, 1968). Interview with Ginsberg.

Appendix
Ten Additional Poets

Andrew Marvell (1621-1678)

Son of an Anglican parson, Marvell graduated from Cambridge University in 1639. From 1642 to 1646 he seems to have been on the Continent, thus escaping the English civil war. He had Royalist leanings, but Cromwell's strength of character finally won him over, and from 1653 to 1957 he was tutor to Cromwell's ward. In 1657 he was appointed Latin Secretary and held that office until the Restoration. His poem on the death of Cromwell shows his admiration for the man. After the Restoration of the monarchy he protected Milton when the King's enemies were being brought to trial. In 1659 he was elected M. P. for Hull and was connected with the House of Commons for the rest of his life.

In reading Marvell's letters one finds a conscientious and meticulous public servant, but little of the private man is revealed. However, it is obvious that he was grounded in the Classics and, to some extent, he was influenced by Donne. His poetry at its best combines an urbane wit with a sensuous awareness. During his lifetime his poems were not published; after his death, his housekeeper, claiming to be his widow, published some of the manuscript poems. His social and political satires were not made public until 1687.

Young Love

I

Come little Infant, Love me now,
  While thine unsuspected years
Clear thine aged Fathers brow
  From cold Jealousie and Fears.

II

Pretty surely 'twere to see
  By young Love old Time beguil'd:
While our Sportings are as free
  As the Nurses with the Child.

III

Common Beauties stay fifteen;
  Such as yours should swifter move;
Whose fair Blossoms are too green
  Yet for Lust, but not for Love.

IV

Love as much the snowy Lamb
  Or the wanton Kid does prize,
As the lusty Bull or Ram,
  For his morning Sacrifice.

V

Now then love me: time may take
  Thee before thy time away:
Of this Need wee'l Virtue make,
  And learn Love before we may.

VI

So we win of doubtful Fate;
  And, if good she to us meant,
We that Good shall antedate,
  Or, if ill, that Ill prevent.

VII

Thus as Kingdomes, frustrating
  Other Titles to their Crown,
In the craddle crown their King,
  So all Forraign Claims to drown,

VIII

So, to make all Rivals vain,
  Now I crown thee with my Love;
Crown me with thy Love again,
  And we both shall Monarchs prove.

To his Coy Mistress

Had we but World enough, and Time
This coyness Lady were no crime.
We would sit down, and think which way
To walk, and pass our long Loves Day.
Thou by the *Indian Ganges* side
Shoulds't Rubies find: I by the Tide
Of *Humber* would complain. I would
Love you ten years before the Flood:
And you should if you please refuse
Till the Conversion of the *Jews.*
My vegetable Love should grow
Vaster then Empires, and more slow.
An hundred years should go to praise
Thine Eyes, and on thy Forehead Gaze.
Two hundred to adore each Breast:
But thirty thousand to the rest.
An Age at least to every part,
And the last Age should show your Heart.
For Lady you deserve this State;
Nor would I love at lower rate.
  But at my back I alwaies hear
Times winged Charriot hurrying near:

And yonder all before us lye
Desarts of vast Eternity.
Thy Beauty shall no more be found;
Nor, in thy marble Vault, shall sound
My ecchoing Song: then Worms shall try
That long preserv'd Virginity:
And your quaint Honour turn to dust;
And into ashes all my Lust.
The Grave's a fine and private place,
But none I think do there embrace.
  Now therefore, while the youthful hew
Sits on thy skin like morning dew,
And while thy willing Soul transpires
At every pore with instant Fires,
Now let us sport us while we may;
And now, like am'rous birds of prey,
Rather at once our Time devour,
Than languish in his slow-chapt pow'r.
Let us roll all our Strength, and all
Our sweetness, up into one Ball:
And tear our Pleasures with rough strife,
Thorough the Iron gates of Life.
Thus, though we cannot make our Sun
Stand still, yet we will make him run.

The unfortunate Lover

I

Alas, how pleasant are their dayes
With whom the Infant Love yet playes!
Sorted by pairs, they still are seen
By Fountains cool, and Shadows green.
But soon these Flames do lose their light,
Like Meteors of a Summers night:
Nor can they to that Region climb,
To make impression upon Time.

II

'Twas in a shipwrack, when the Seas
Rul'd, and the Winds did what they please,
That my poor Lover floting lay,
And, e're brought forth, was cast away:
Till at the last the master-Wave
Upon the Rock his Mother drave;
And there she split against the Stone,
In a *Cesarian Section.*

III

The Sea him lent these bitter Tears
Which at his Eyes he alwaies bears.
And from the Winds the Sighs he bore,
Which through his surging Breast do roar.
No Day he saw but that which breaks,
Through frighted Clouds in forked streaks.
While round the ratling Thunder hurl'd,
As at the Fun'ral of the World

IV

While Nature to his Birth presents
This masque of quarrelling Elements;
A num'rous fleet of Corm'rants black,
That sail'd insulting o're the Wrack,
Receiv'd into their cruel Care,
Th' unfortunate and abject Heir:
Guardians most fit to entertain
The Orphan of the *Hurricane.*

V

They fed him up with Hopes and Air,
Which soon digested to Despair.
And as one Corm'rant fed him, still
Another on his Heart did bill.
Thus while they famish him, and feast,
He both consumed, and increast:
And languished with doubtful Breath,
Th' *Amphibium* of Life and Death.

VI

And now, when angry Heaven wou'd
Behold a spectacle of Blood,
Fortune and He are call'd to play
At sharp before it all the day:
And Tyrant Love his brest does ply
With all his wing'd Artillery.
Whilst he, betwixt the Flames and Waves,
Like *Ajax,* the mad Tempest braves.

VII

See how he nak'd and fierce does stand,
Cuffing the Thunder with one hand;
While with the other he does lock
And grapple, with the stubborn Rock:
From which he with each Wave rebounds,
Torn into Flames, and ragg'd with Wounds.
And all he saies, a Lover drest
In his own Blood does relish best.

VIII

This is the only *Banneret*
That ever Love created yet:
Who though, by the Malignant Starrs,
Forced to live in Storms and Warrs:
Yet dying leaves a Perfume here,
And Musick within every Ear:
And he in Story only rules,
In a Field *Sable* a Lover *Gules.*

The Garden

I

How vainly men themselves amaze
To win the Palm, the Oke, or Bayes;
And their uncessant Labours see
Crown'd from some single Herb or Tree
Whose short and narrow verged Shade
Does prudently their Toyles upbraid;
While all Flow'rs and all Trees do close
To weave the Garlands of repose.

II

Fair quiet, have I found thee here,
And Innocence thy Sister dear!
Mistaken long, I sought you then
In busie Companies of Men.
Your sacred Plants, if here below,
Only among the Plants will grow.
Society is all but rude,
To this delicious Solitude.

III

No white nor red was ever seen
So am'rous as this lovely green.
Fond Lovers, cruel as their Flame,
Cut in these Trees their Mistress name.
Little, Alas, they know, or heed,
How far these Beauties Hers exceed!
Fair Trees! where s'eer your barkes I wound,
No Name shall but your own be found.

IV

When we have run our Passions heat,
Love hither makes his best retreat.
The *Gods,* that mortal Beauty chase,
Still in a Tree did end their race.

Apollo hunted *Daphne* so,
Only that She might Laurel grow.
And *Pan* did after *Syrinx* speed,
Not as a Nymph, but for a Reed.

V

What wond'rous Life in this I lead!
Ripe Apples drop about my head;
The Luscious Clusters of the Vine
Upon my Mouth do crush their Wine;
The Nectaren, and curious Peach,
Into my hands themselves do reach;
Stumbling on Melons, as I pass,
Insnar'd with Flow'rs, I fall on Grass.

VI

Mean while the Mind, from pleasure less,
Withdraws into its happiness:
The Mind, that Ocean where each kind
Does streight its own resemblance find;
Yet it creates, transcending these,
Far other Worlds, and other Seas;
Annihilating all that's made
To a green Thought in a green Shade.

VII

Here at the Fountains sliding foot,
Or at some Fruit-trees mossy root,
Casting the Bodies Vest aside,
My Soul into the boughs does glide:
There like a Bird it sits, and sings,
Then whets, and combs its silver Wings;
And, till prepar'd for longer flight,
Waves in its Plumes the various Light.

VIII

Such was that happy Garden-state,
While Man there walk'd without a Mate:
After a Place so pure, and sweet,
What other Help could yet be meet!
But 'twas beyond a Mortal's share
To wander solitary there:
Two Paradises 'twere in one
To live in Paradise alone.

IX

How well the skilful Gardner drew
Of flow'rs and herbes this Dial new;
Where from above the milder Sun
Does through a fragrant Zodiack run;

And, as it works, th' industrious Bee
Computes its time as well as we.
How could such sweet and wholsome Hours
Be reckon'd but with herbs and flow'rs!

An Epitaph upon ——

Enough: and leave the rest to Fame.
'Tis to commend her but to name.
Courtship, which living she declin'd,
When dead to offer were unkind.
Where never any could speak ill,
Who would officious Praises spill?
Nor can the truest Wit or Friend,
Without Detracting, her commend.
To say she liv'd a *Virgin* chast,
In this Age loose and all unlac't;
Nor was, when Vice is so allow'd,
Of *Virtue* or asham'd, or proud;
That her Soul was on *Heaven* so bent
No Minute but it came and went;
That ready her last Debt to pay
She summ'd her life up ev'ry day;
Modest as Morn; as Mid-day bright;
Gentle as Ev'ning; cool as Night;
'Tis true: but all so weakly said;
'Twere more Significant, *She's Dead.*

An Horatian *Ode upon* Cromwel's *Return From* Ireland.

The forward Youth that would appear
Must now forsake his *Muses* dear,
  Nor in the Shadows sing
  His Numbers languishing.
'Tis time to leave the Books in dust,
And oyl th' unused Armours rust:
  Removing from the Wall
  The Corslet of the Hall.
So restless *Cromwel* could not cease
In the inglorious Arts of Peace,
  But through adventrous War
  Urged his active Star.

And, like the three-fork'd Lightning, first
Breaking the Clouds where it was nurst,
  Did thorough his own Side
  His fiery way divide.
For 'tis all one to Courage high
The Emulous or Enemy;
  And with such to inclose
  Is more then to oppose.
Then burning through the Air he went,
And Pallaces and Temples rent:
  And *Caesars* head at last
  Did through his Laurels blast.
'Tis Madness to resist or blame
The force of angry Heavens flame:
  And, if we would speak true,
  Much to the Man is due.
Who, from his private Gardens, where
He liv'd reserved and austere,
  As if his highest plot
  To plant the Bergamot,
Could by industrious Valour climbe
To ruine the great Work of Time,
  And cast the Kingdome old
  Into another Mold.
Though Justice against Fate complain,
And plead the antient Rights in vain:
  But those do hold or break
  As Men are strong or weak.
Nature that hateth emptiness,
Allows of penetration less:
  And therefore must make room
  Where greater Spirits come.
What Field of all the Civil Wars,
Where his were not the deepest Scars?
  And *Hampton* shows what part
  He had of wiser Art.
Where, twining subtile fears with hope,
He wove a Net of such a scope,
  That *Charles* himself might chase
  To *Caresbrooks* narrow case.
That thence the *Royal Actor* born
The *Tragick Scaffold* might adorn:
  While round the armed Bands
  Did clap their bloody hands.
He nothing common did or mean
Upon that memorable Scene:
  But with his keener Eye
  The Axes edge did try:

Nor call'd the *Gods* with vulgar spight
To vindicate his helpless Right,
  But bow'd his comely Head,
  Down as upon a Bed.
This was that memorable Hour
Which first assur'd the forced Pow'r.
  So when they did design
  The *Capitols* first Line,
A bleeding Head where they begun,
Did fright the Architects to run;
  And yet in that the *State*
  Foresaw it's happy Fate.
And now the *Irish* are asham'd
To see themselves in one Year tam'd:
  So much one Man can do,
  That does both act and know.
They can affirm his Praises best,
And have, though overcome, confest
  How good he is, how just,
  And fit for highest Trust:
Nor yet grown stiffer with Command,
But still in the *Republick's* hand:
  How fit he is to sway
  That can so well obey.
He to the *Commons Feet* presents
A *Kingdome,* for his first years rents:
  And, what he may, forbears
  His Fame to make it theirs:
And has his Sword and Spoyls ungirt,
To lay them at the *Publick's* skirt.
  So when the Falcon high
  Falls heavy from the Sky,
She, having kill'd, no more does search,
But on the next green Bow to pearch;
  Where, when he first does lure,
  The Falckner has her sure.
What may not then our *Isle* presume
While Victory his Crest does plume!
  What may not others fear
  If thus he crown each Year!
A *Caesar* he ere long to *Gaul,*
To *Italy* an *Hannibal,*
  And to all States not free
  Shall *Clymacterick* be.
The *Pict* no shelter now shall find
Within his party-colour'd Mind;
  But from this Valour sad
  Shrink underneath the Plad:

Happy if in the tufted brake
The *English Hunter* him mistake;
  Nor lay his Hounds in near
  The *Caledonian* Deer.
But thou the Wars and Fortunes Son
March indefatigably on;
  And for the last effect
  Still keep thy Sword erect:
Besides the force it has to fright
The Spirits of the shady Night,
  The same *Arts* that did *gain*
  A *Pow'r* must it *maintain.*

On Mr. Milton's *Paradise lost*

When I beheld the Poet blind, yet bold,
In slender Book his vast Design unfold,
Messiah Crown'd, *Gods* Reconcil'd Decree,
Rebelling *Angels,* the Forbidden Tree,
Heav'n, Hell, Earth, Chaos, All; the Argument
Held me a while misdoubting his Intent,
That he would ruine (for I saw him strong)
The sacred Truths to Fable and old Song,
(So *Sampson* groap'd the Temples Posts in spight)
The World o'rewhelming to revenge his Sight.
  Yet as I read, soon growing less severe,
I lik'd his Project, the success did fear;
Through that wide Field how he his way should find
O're which lame Faith leads Understanding blind;
Lest he perplext the things he would explain,
And what was easie he should render vain.
  Or if a Work so infinite he spann'd,
Jealous I was that some less skilful hand
(Such as disquiet alwayes what is well,
And by ill imitating would excell)
Might hence presume the whole Creations day
To change in Scenes, and show it in a Play.
  Pardon me, *mighty Poet,* nor despise
My causeless, yet not impious, surmise.
But I am now convinc'd, and none will dare
Within thy Labours to pretend a Share.
Thou hast not miss'd one thought that could be fit,
And all that was improper dost omit:
So that no room is here for Writers left,
But to detect their Ignorance or Theft.
  That Majesty which through thy Work doth Reign

Draws the Devout, deterring the Profane.
And things divine thou treatst of in such state
As them preserves, and Thee inviolate.
At once delight and horrour on us seize,
Thous singst with so much gravity and ease;
And above humane flight dost soar aloft,
With Plume so strong, so equal, and so soft.
The *Bird* nam'd from that *Paradise* you sing
So never Flags, but alwaies keeps on Wing.
  Where couldst thou Words of such a compass find?
Whence furnish such a vast expense of Mind?
Just Heav'n Thee, like *Tiresias,* to requite,
Rewards with *Prophesie* thy loss of Sight.
  Well mightst thou scorn thy Readers to allure
With tinkling Rhime, of thy own Sense secure;
While the *Town-Bays* writes all the while and spells,
And like a Pack-Horse tires without his Bells.
Their Fancies like our bushy Points appear,
The Poets tag them; we for fashion wear.
I too transported by the *Mode* offend,
And while I meant to *Praise* thee, must Commend.
Thy verse created like thy *Theme* sublime,
In Number, Weight, and Measure, needs not *Rhime.*

Nostradamus's *Prophecy*

The blood of the Just London's firm Doome shall fix
And cover it in flames in sixty six;
Fireballs shall flye and but few see the traine
As farr as from Whitehall to Pudden lane
To burne the Cittye which againe shall rise
With high aspireing head towards those Skyes
Where Vengeance dwells, but there is one trick more
Tho the Walls stand to bring the City lower;
When Legislators shall their trust betray
Hir'd for their share to give the rest away
And those false Men the Soveraign People sent
Give Taxes to the King and Parliament.
When bare fac'd Villany shall not blush to cheat
And Checquer dores shall shut up Lombard street,
When Players shall use to act the parts of Queens
Within the Curtains and behind the Scenes,
When Sodomy is the Premier Ministers sport
And whoreing shall be the least sin att Court,
A Boy shall take his Sister for his Mate
And practise Incest between Seven and Eight,

And no Man knowes in whom to put his trust,
When even to rob the Checquer shall be Just,
When Declarations lye, when every Oath
Shall be in use at Court but faith and Troth,
When two good Kings shall be att Brantford knowne
And when att London their shall not be One,
When publike faith and Vowes and Payments stop,
Then London lately burnt shall be blowne up,
And Wooden shoes shall come to be the weare
When Cerberus shall be the Treasurer.
London shall then see, for it will come to pass,
A Greater Thief then Alexander was.
The Frogs shall then grow weary of their Crane
And pray to Jove to take him back againe.

Second Part.

When the Seal's given to a talking fool
Whom Wise men Laugh att and the Women Rule,
A Minister able only in his Tongue
To make starcht empty Speeches two hours long.
When an old Scotch Covenanter shall be
The Champion of the English Hierarchye,
When Bishops shall lay all Religion by
And strive by Law to 'stablish Tyrany,
When a lean Treasurer shall in one year
Make him self rich, his king and People bare,
When the Crowne's Heir shall English Men dispise
And think French onely Loyall, Irish wise,
Then wooden Shoos shall be the English weare
And Magna Carta shall no more appeare,
Then the English shall a Greater Tyrant Know
Then either Greek or Gallick Story shew,
Their Wives to his Lust expos'd, their Wealth to his spoyle
With groans to fill his Treasure they must toyle,
But like the Bellydes shall toyle in vaine
For that still fill'd runs out as fast againe;
Then They with envious Eyes shall Belgium See
And wish in vain Venetian Libertye.

John Keats (1795-1821)

Keats was born in London to a livery stable keeper and his wife. Denied the advantages of his wealthy contemporaries, Shelly and Byron, he knew in his short life additional burdens: the illness and death of his younger brother Tom, who died of tuberculosis, John Keats' struggle against the same disease, his passionate and aborted love for Fanny Brawne, and his discouragement because of the savage attacks made on his work by influential critics. In a desperate attempt to regain his health he went to Rome in 1820 in the company of a friend, Joseph Severn, and there he died early in 1821. At the end he was so sure he was a poetic failure that he asked Severn to engrave upon his tombstone only "Here Lies One Whose name Was Writ in Water."

Keats is best known for his sonnets and his great odes, although he wrote longer dramatic poems such as *Hyperion* and *Endymion* and many of his letters are masterpieces of expression. Much of what he believed can be summed up in his own words, "I am certain of nothing but the holiness of the heart's affections and the truth of imagination." Modern critics have extensively commented on his concept of "negative capability," by which a poet—Shakespeare was his prime example—is viewed as one capable of complete detachment, almost without a subjective personality, delighting equally in the creation of a Lear or an Iago.

To My Brothers

Small, busy flames play through the fresh laid coals,
  And their faint cracklings o'er our silence creep
  Like whispers of the household gods that keep
A gentle empire o'er fraternal souls.
And while, for rhymes, I search around the poles,
  Your eyes are fix'd, as in poetic sleep,
  Upon the lore so voluble and deep,
That aye at fall of night our care condoles.
This is your birth-day Tom, and I rejoice
  That thus it passes smoothly, quietly.
Many such eves of gently whisp'ring noise
  May we together pass, and calmly try
What are this world's true joys,—ere the great voice,
  From its fair face, shall bid our spirits fly.

"To One Who Has Been Long in City Pent"

To one who has been long in city pent,
  'Tis very sweet to look into the fair
  And open face of heaven,—to breathe a prayer
Full in the smile of the blue firmament.

Who is more happy, when, with heart's content,
  Fatigued he sinks into some pleasant lair
  Of wavy grass, and reads a debonair
And gentle tale of love and languishment?
Returning home at evening, with an ear
  Catching the notes of Philomel,—an eye
Watching the sailing cloudlet's bright career,
  He mourns that day so soon has glided by:
E'en like the passage of an angel's tear
  That falls through the clear ether silently.

On First Looking into Chapman's Homer

Much have I travell'd in the realms of gold,
  And many goodly states and kingdoms seen;
  Round many western islands have I been
Which bards in fealty to Apollo hold.
Oft of one wide expanse had I been told
  That deep-brow'd Homer ruled as his demesne;
  Yet did I never breathe its pure serene
Till I heard Chapman speak out loud and bold:
Then felt I like some watcher of the skies
  When a new planet swims into his ken;
Or like stout Cortez* when with eagle eyes
  He star'd at the Pacific—and all his men
Look'd at each other with a wild surmise—
  Silent, upon a peak in Darien.

On The Grasshopper and Cricket

The poetry of earth is never dead:
  When all the birds are faint with the hot sun,
  And hide in cooling trees, a voice will run
From hedge to hedge about the new-mown mead;
That is the Grasshopper's—he takes the lead
  In summer luxury,—he has never done
  With his delights; for when tired out with fun
He rests at ease beneath some pleasant weed.
The poetry of earth is ceasing never:
  On a lone winter evening, when the frost

* Keats' mistake. It should be Balboa.

Has wrought a silence, from the stove there shrills
The Cricket's song, in warmth increasing ever,
And seems to one in drowsiness half lost,
The Grasshopper's among some grassy hills.

from *Sleep and Poetry*

O for ten years, that I may overwhelm
Myself in poesy; so I may do the deed
That my own soul has to itself decreed.
Then will I pass the countries that I see
In long perspective, and continually
Tast their pure fountains. First the realm I'll pass
Of Flora, and old Pan: sleep in the grass,
Feed upon apples red, and strawberries,
And choose each pleasure that my fancy sees;
Catch the white-handed nymphs in shady places,
To woo sweet kisses from averted faces,—
Play with their fingers, touch their shoulders white
Into a pretty shrinking with a bite
As hard as lips can make it: till agreed,
A lovely tale of human life we'll read.
And one will teach a tame dove how it best
May fan the cool air gently o'er my rest;
Another, bending o'er her nimble tread,
Will set a green robe floating round her head,
And still will dance with ever varied ease,
Smiling upon the flowers and the trees:
Another will entice me on, and on
Through almond blossoms and rich cinnamon;
Till in the bosom of a leafy world
We rest in silence, like two gems upcurl'd
In the recesses of a pearly shell.

And can I ever bid these joys farewell?
Yes, I must pass them for a nobler life,
Where I may find the agonies, the strife
Of human hearts: for lo! I see afar,
O'ersailing the blue cragginess, a car
And steeds with streamy manes—the charioteer
Looks out upon the winds with glorious fear:
And now the numerous tramplings quiver lightly
Along a huge cloud's ridge; and now with sprightly
Wheel downward come they into fresher skies,
Tipt round with silver from the sun's bright eyes.
Still downward with capacious whirl they glide;
And now I see them on the green-hill's side

In breezy rest among the nodding stalks.
The charioteer with wond'rous gesture talks
To the trees and mountains; and there soon appear
Shapes of delight, of mystery, and fear,
Passing along before a dusky space
Made by some mighty oaks: as they would chase
Some ever-fleeting music on they sweep.
Lo! how they murmur, laugh, and smile, and weep:
Some with upholden hand and mouth severe;
Some with their faces muffled to the ear
Between their arms; some, clear in youthful bloom,
Go glad and smilingly athwart the gloom;
Some looking back, and some with upward gaze;
Yes, thousands in a thousand different ways
Flit onward—now a lovely wreath of girls
Dancing their sleek hair into tangled curls;
And now broad wings. Most awfully intent
The driver of those steeds is forward bent,
And seems to listen: O that I might know
All that he writes with such a hurrying glow.

The visions all are fled—the car is fled
Into the light of heaven, and in their stead
A sense of real things comes doubly strong,
And, like a muddy stream, would bear along
My soul to nothingness: but I will strive
Against all doubtings, and will keep alive
The thought of that same chariot, and the strange
Journey it went.

Ode to A Nightingale

I

My heart aches, and a drowsy numbness pains
  My sense, as though of hemlock I had drunk,
Or emptied some dull opiate to the drains
  One minute past, and Lethe-wards had sunk:
'Tis not through envy of thy happy lot,
  But being too happy in thine happiness,—
    That thou, light-wingèd Dryad of the trees,
      In some melodious plot
  Of beechen green, and shadows numberless,
    Singest of summer in full-throated ease.

II

O, for a draught of vintage! that hath been
  Cool'd a long age in the deep-delved earth,
Tasting of Flora and the country green,
  Dance, and Provençal song, and sunburnt mirth!
O for a beaker full of the warm South,
  Full of the true, the blushful Hippocrene,
    With beaded bubbles winking at the brim,
        And purple-stained mouth;
  That I might drink, and leave the world unseen,
    And with thee fade away into the forest dim:

III

Fade far away, dissolve, and quite forget
  What thou among the leaves hast never known,
The weariness, the fever, and the fret
  Here, where men sit and hear each other groan;
Where palsy shakes a few, sad, last gray hairs,
  Where youth grows pale, and spectre-thin, and dies;
    Where but to think is to be full of sorrow
        And leaden-eyed despairs,
    Where Beauty cannot keep her lustrous eyes,
      Or new Love pine at them beyond to-morrow.

IV

Away! away! for I will fly to thee,
  Not charioted by Bacchus and his pards,
But on the viewless wings of Poesy,
  Though the dull brain perplexes and retards:
Already with thee! tender is the night,
  And haply the Queen-Moon is on her throne,
    Cluster'd around by all her starry Fays;
        But here there is no light,
  Save what from heaven is with the breezes blown
    Through verdurous glooms and winding mossy ways.

V

I cannot see what flowers are at my feet,
  Now what soft incense hangs upon the boughs,
But, in embalmed darkness, guess each sweet
  Wherewith the seasonable month endows
The grass, the thicket, and the fruit-tree wild;
  White hawthorn, and the pastoral eglantine;
    Fast fading violets cover'd up in leaves;
        And mid-May's eldest child,
  The coming musk-rose, full of dewy wine,
    The murmurous haunt of flies on summer eves.

VI

Darkling I listen; and, for many a time
  I have been half in love with easeful Death,
Call'd him soft names in many a mused rhyme,
  To take into the air my quiet breath;
Now more than ever seems it rich to die,
  To cease upon the midnight with no pain,
    While thou art pouring forth thy soul abroad
      In such an ecstasy!
  Still wouldst thou sing, and I have ears in vain—
    To thy high requiem become a sod.

VII

Thou wast not born for death, immortal Bird!
  No hungry generations tread thee down;
The voice I hear this passing night was heard
  In ancient days by emperior and clown:
Perhaps the self-same song that found a path
  Through the sad heart of Ruth, when, sick for home,
    She stood in tears amid the alien corn;
      The same that oft-times hath
  Charm'd magic casements, opening on the foam
    Of perilous seas, in faery lands forlorn.

VIII

Forlorn! the very word is like a bell
  To toll me back from thee to my sole self!
Adieu! the fancy cannot cheat so well
  As she is fam'd to do, deceiving elf.
Adieu! adieu! thy plaintive anthem fades
  Past the near meadows, over the still stream,
    Up the hill-side; and now 'tis buried deep
      In the next valley-glades:
  Was it a vision, or a waking dream?
    Fled is that music:—Do I wake or sleep?

Ode on a Grecian Urn

I

Thou still unravish'd bride of quietness
Thou foster-child of a silence and slow time,
Sylvan historian, who canst thus express
A flowery tale more sweetly than our rhyme:
What leaf-fring'd legend haunts about thy shape
Of deities or mortals, or of both,
In Temple or the dales of Arcady?
What men or gods are these? What maidens loth?
What mad pursuit? What struggle to escape?
What pipes and timbrels? What wild ecstasy?

II

Heard melodies are sweet, but those unheard
Are sweeter; therefore, ye soft pipes, play on;
Not to the sensual ear, but, more endear'd,
Pipe to the spirit ditties of no tone:
Fair youth, beneath the trees, thou canst not leave
Thy song, nor ever can those trees be bare;
Bold Lover, never, bever canst thou kiss,
Though winning near the goal—yet, do not grieve;
She cannot fade, though thou hast not thy bliss,
For ever wilt thou love, and she be fair!

III

Ah, happy, happy boughs! that cannot shed
Your leaves, nor ever bid the Spring adieu;
And, happy melodist, unwearied,
For ever piping songs for ever new;
More happy love! more happy, happy love!
For ever warm and still to be enjoy'd,
For ever panting, and for ever young;
All breathing human passion far above,
That leaves a heart high-sorrowful and cloy'd
A burning forehead, and a parching tongue.

IV

Who are these coming to the sacrifice?
To what green altar, O mysterious priest,
Lead'st thou that heifer lowing at the skies,
And all her silken flanks with garlands drest?
What little town by river or sea shore,
Or mountain-built with peaceful citadel,
Is emptied of this folk, this pious morn?
And, little town, thy streets for evermore
Will silent be; and not a soul to tell
Why thou art desolate, can e'er return.

V

O Attic shape! Fair attitude! with brede
  Of marble men and maidens overwrought,
With forest branches and the trodden weed;
  Thou, silent form, dost tease us out of thought
As doth eternity: Cold Pastoral!
  When old age shall this generation waste,
    Thou shalt remain, in midst of other woe
Than ours, a friend to man, to whom thou say'st,
  'Beauty is truth, truth beauty,'—that is all
    Ye know on earth, and all ye need to know.

Lines on the Mermaid Tavern

Souls of Poets dead and gone,
What Elysium have ye known,
Happy field or mossy cavern,
Choicer than the Mermaid Tavern?
Have ye tippled drink more fine
Than mine host's Canary wine?
Or are fruits of Paradise
Sweeter than those dainty pies
Of venison? O generous food!
Drest as though bold Robin Hood
Would, with his maid Marian,
Sup and bowse from horn and can.

  I have heard that on a day
Mine host's sign-board flew away,
Nobody knew whither, till
An astrologer's old quill
To a sheepskin gave the story,
Said he saw you in your glory,
Underneath a new old sign
Sipping beverage divine,
And pledging with contented smack
The Mermaid in the Zodiac.
  Souls of Poets dead and gone,
What Elysium have ye known,
Happy field or mossy cavern,
Choicer than the Mermaid Tavern?

To Autumn

I

Season of mists and mellow fruitfulness,
  Close bosom-friend of the maturing sun;
Conspiring with him how to load and bless
  With fruit and vines that round the thatch-eves run;
To bend with apples and moss'd cottage-trees,
  And fill all fruit with ripeness to the core;
    To swell the gourd, and plump the hazel shells
  With a sweet kernel; to set budding more
And still more, later flowers for the bees,
Until they think warm days will never cease,
    For Summer has o'er-brimm'd their clammy cells.

II

Who hath not seen thee oft amid thy store?
  Sometimes whoever seeks abroad may find
Thee sitting careless on a granary floor,
  Thy hair soft-lifted by the winnowing wind;
Or on a half-reap'd furrow sound asleep,
  Drows'd with the fume of poppies, while thy hook
    Spares the next swath and all its twined flowers:
And sometimes like a gleaner thou dost keep
  Steady thy laden head across a brook;
  Or by a cyder-press, with patient look,
    Thou watchest the last oozings hours by hours.

III

Where are the songs of Spring? Ay, where are they?
  Think not of them, thou hast thy music too,—
While barred clouds bloom the soft-dying day,
  And touch the stubble-plains with rosy hue;
Then in a wailful choir the small gnats mourn
  Among the river sallows, borne aloft
    Or sinking as the light wind lives or dies;
And full-grown lambs loud bleat from hilly bourn;
  Hedge-crickets sing; and now with treble soft
  The red-breast whistles from a garden-croft;
    And gathering swallows twitter in the skies.

when I Have Fears That I May Cease to Be

When I have fears that I may cease to be
  Before my pen has glean'd my teeming brain,
Before high-piled books, in charactery,
  Hold like rich garners the full ripen'd grain;

When I behold, upon the night's starr'd face,
  Huge cloudy symbols of a high romance,
And think that I may never live to trace
  Their shadows, with the magic hand of chance;
And when I feel fair creature of an hour,
  That I shall never look upon thee more,
Never have relish in the faery power
  Of unreflecting love;—then on the shore
Of the wide world I stand alone, and think
Till love and fame to nothingness do sink.

On Fame

Fame, like a wayward Girl, will still be coy
  To those who woo her with too slavish knees,
But makes surrender to some thoughtless Boy,
  And dotes the more upon a heart at ease;
She is a Gipsey, will not speak to those
  Who have not learnt to be content without her;
A Jilt, whose ear was never whisper'd close,
  Who thinks they scandal her who talk about her;
A very Gipsey is she, Nilus-born,
  Sister-in-law to jealous Potiphar;
Ye love-sick Bards, repay her scorn for scorn,
  Ye Artists lovelorn, madmen that ye are!
Make your best bow to her and bid adieu,
Then, if she likes it, she will follow you.

Bright Star, Would I Were Steadfast as Thou Art

[*Written on a Blank Page in Shakespeare's Poems facing 'A Lover's Complaint'*]

Bright star, would I were stedfast as thou art—
  Not in lone splendour hung aloft the night
And watching, with eternal lids apart,
  Like nature's patient, sleepless Eremite,
The moving waters at their priestlike task
  Of pure ablution round earth's human shores,
Or gazing on the new soft-fallen mask
  Of snow upon the mountains and the moors—
No—yet still stedfast, still unchangeable,

Pillow'd upon my fair love's ripening breast,
To feel for ever its soft fall and swell,
Awake for ever in a sween unrest,
Still, still to hear her tender-taken breath,
And so live ever—or else swoon to death.

Old Meg

Old Meg she was a Gipsy,
And liv'd upon the Moors:
Her bed it was the brown heath turf,
And her house was out of doors.

Her apples were swart blackberries,
Her currants pods o' broom;
Her wine was dew of the wild white rose,
Her book a churchyard tomb.

Her Brothers were the craggy hills,
Her Sisters larchen trees—
Alone with her great family
She liv'd as she did please.

No breakfast had she many a morn,
No dinner many a noon,
And 'stead of supper she would stare
Full hard against the Moon.

But every morn of woodbine fresh
She made her garlanding,
And every night the dark glen Yew
She wove, and she would sing.

And with her fingers old and brown
She plaited Mats o' Rushes,
And gave them to the Cottagers
She met among the Bushes.

Old Meg was brave as Margaret Queen
And tall as Amazon:
And old red blanket cloak she wore;
A chip hat had she on.
God rest her aged bones somewhere—
She died full long agone!

The Poet

At morn, at noon, at Eve, and Middle Night
He passes forth into the charmed air,
With talisman to call up spirits rare
From plant, cave, rock, and fountain.—To his sight
The husk of natural objects opens quite
To the core; and every secret essence there
Reveals the elements of good and fair;
Making him see, where Learning hath no light.
Sometimes above the gross and palpable things
Of this diurnal sphere, his spirit flies
On awful wing; and with its destined skies
Holds premature and mystic communings;
Till such unearthly intercourses shed
A visible halo round his mortal head.

from *A Song About Myself*

From a Letter to Fanny Keats,
2 July 1818

I

There was a naughty Boy,
A naughty boy was he,
He would not stop at home,
He could not quiet be—
He took
In his Knapsack
A Book
Full of vowels
And a shirt
With some towels—
A slight cap
For night cap—
A hair brush,
Comb ditto,
New Stockings
For old ones
Would split O!
This Knapsack
Tight at's back

He rivetted close
And followed his nose
To the North,
To the North,
And follow'd his nose
To the North.

A.E. Housman (1859-1936)

Born near Bromsgrove, England, Housman grew up in a well-to-do family, though his father later lost most of his wealth. He was educated at Oxford, specializing in the Classics, but he failed the "Greats" examination and left without a degree. For a number of years he worked in a dull job as a civil servant in London, pursuing his interest in the Classics during his spare time. By 1892 he had enough of a reputation to be elected a professor at University College, London. Ultimately (1911) he was called to Cambridge as professor of Latin.

A sometimes abrasive literary critic, and an austere and lonely man, he published in 1896 a slim volume of poems called *A Shropshire Lad,* followed in 1922 by *Last Poems.* The year of his death *More Poems* appeared, selected by his brother Laurence. All lyrics, these poems reflected a man struggling "to keep the foreign laws of God and Man." They were nostalgic and for the most part presented a somber view of life. In reading them one needs to understand that Housman's life was largely shaped by an intense passion which he had for a fellow student, Moses Jackson, and by his agony at discovering his sexual aberration, and his struggle to cope with it in a Victorian society. He ceased writing poetry as he grew older. His reputation as a classical scholar was formidable, and he continued to teach until his death in 1936.

Loveliest of Trees, the Cherry Now

Loveliest of trees, the cherry now
Is hung with bloom along the bough,
And stands about the woodland ride
Wearing white for Eastertide.

Now, of my threescore years and ten,
Twenty will not come again,
And take from seventy springs a score,
It only leaves me fifty more.

And since to look at things in bloom
Fifty springs are little room,
About the woodlands I will go
To see the cherry hung with snow.

When I Was One-and-Twenty

When I was one-and-twenty
  I heard a wise man say,
'Give crowns and pounds and guineas
  But not your heart away;

Give pearls away and rubies
But keep your fancy free.'
But I was one-and-twenty,
No use to talk to me.

When I was one-and-twenty
I heard him say again,
'The heart out of the bosom
Was never given in vain;
'Tis paid with sighs a plenty
And sold for endless rue.'
And I am two-and-twenty,
And oh, 'tis true, 'tis true.

To An Athlete Dying Young

The time you won your town the race
We chaired you through the market-place;
Man and boy stood cheering by,
And home we brought you shoulder-high.

To-day, the road all runners come,
Shoulder-high we bring you home,
And set you at your threshold down,
Townsman of a stiller town.

Smart lad, to slip betimes away
From fields where glory does not stay
And early though the laurel grows
It withers quicker than the rose.

Eyes the shady night has shut
Cannot see the record cut,
And silence sounds no worse than cheers
After earth has stopped the ears:

Now you will not swell the rout
Of lads that wore their honours out,
Runners whom renown outran
And the name died before the man.

So set, before its echoes fade,
The fleet foot on the sill of shade,
And hold to the low lintel up
The still-defended challenge-cup.

And round that early-laurelled head
Will flock to gaze the strengthless dead
And find unwithered on its curls
The garland briefer than a girl's.

Bredon Hill

In summertime on Bredon
  The bells they sound so clear;
Round both the shires they ring them
  In steeples far and near,
  A happy noise to hear.

Here of a Sunday morning
  My love and I would lie,
And see the coloured counties,
  And hear the larks so high
  About us in the sky.

The bells would ring to call her
  In valleys miles away:
'Come all to church, good people;
  Good people, come and pray.'
  But here my love would stay.

And I would turn and answer
  Among the springing thyme,
'Oh, peal upon our wedding,
  And we will hear the chime,
  And come to church in time.'

But when the snows at Christmas
  On Bredon top were strown,
My love rose up so early
  And stole out unbeknown
  And went to church alone.

They tolled the one bell only,
  Groom there was none to see,
The mourners followed after,
  And so to church went she,
  And would not wait for me.

The bells they sound on Bredon,
  And still the steeples hum.
'Come all to church, good people,'—
  Oh, noisy bells, be dumb;
  I hear you, I will come.

White in the Moon the Long Road Lies

White in the moon the long road lies,
  The moon stands blank above;
White in the moon the long road lies
  That leads me from my love.

Still hangs the hedge without a gust,
  Still, still the shadows stay:
My feet upon the moonlit dust
  Pursue the ceaseless way.

The world is round, so travellers tell,
  And straight though reach the track,
Trudge on, trudge on, 'twill all be well,
  The way will guide one back.

But ere the circle homeward hies
  Far, far must it remove:
White in the moon the long road lies
  That leads me from my love.

The Immortal Part

When I meet the morning beam
Or lay me down at night to dream,
I hear my bones within me say,
'Another night, another day.

'When shall this slough of sense be cast,
This dust of thoughts be laid at last,
The man of flesh and soul be slain
And the man of bone remain?

'This tongue that talks, these lungs that shout,
These thews that hustle us about,
This brain that fills the skull with schemes,
And its humming hive of dreams,—

'These to-day are proud in power
And lord it in their little hour:
The immortal bones obey control
Of dying flesh and dying soul.

''Tis long till eve and morn are gone:
Slow the endless night comes on,
And late to fulness grows the birth

That shall last as long as earth.
'Wanderers eastward, wanderers west,
Know you why you cannot rest?
'Tis that every mother's son
Travails with a skeleton.

'Lie down in the bed of dust;
Bear the fruit that bear you must;
Bring the eternal seed to light,
And morn is all the same as night.

'Rest you so from trouble sore,
Fear the heat o' the sun no more,
Nor the snowing winter wild,
Now you labor not with child.

'Empty vessel, garment cast,
We that wore you long shall last.
—Another night, another day.'
So my bones within me say.

Therefore they shall do my will
To-day while I am master still,
And flesh and soul, now both are strong,
Shall hale the sullen slaves along,

Before this fire of sense decay,
This smoke of thought blow clean away,
And leave with ancient night alone
The stedfast and enduring bone.

As I Gird on for Fighting

As I gird on for fighting
  My sword upon my thigh,
I think on old ill fortunes
  Of better men than I.

Think I, the round world over,
  What golden lads are low
With hurts not mine to mourn for
  And shames I shall not know.

What evil luck soever
  For me remains in store,
'Tis sure much finer fellows
  Have fared much worse before.

So here are things to think on
  That ought to make me brave,
As I strap on for fighting
  My sword that will not save.

Grenadier

The Queen she sent to look for me,
  The sergeant he did say,
'Young man, a soldier will you be
  For thirteen pence a day?'

For thirteen pence a day did I
  Take off the things I wore,
And I have marched to where I lie,
  And I shall march no more.

My mouth is dry, my shirt is wet,
  My blood runs all away,
So now I shall not die in debt
  For thirteen pence a day.

To-morrow after new young men
  The sergeant he must see,
For things will all be over then
  Between the Queen and me.

And I shall have to bate my price,
  For in the grave, they say,
Is neither knowledge nor device
  Nor thirteen pence a day.

The Chestnut Casts His Flambeaux, and the Flowers

The chestnut casts his flambeaux, and the flowers
  Stream from the hawthorn on the wind away,
The doors clap to, the pane is blind with showers.
  Pass me the can, lad; there's an end of May.

There's one spoilt spring to scant our mortal lot,
  One season ruined of our little store.
May will be fine next year as like as not:
  Oh ay, but then we shall be twenty-four.

We for a certainty are not the first
  Have sat in taverns while the tempest hurled
Their hopeful plans to emptiness, and cursed
  Whatever brute and blackguard made the world.

It is in truth iniquity on high
  To cheat our sentenced souls of aught they crave,
And mar the merriment as you and I
  Fare on our long fool's-errand to the grave.

Iniquity it is; but pass the can.
  My lad, no pair of kings our mothers bore;
Our only portion is the estate of man:
  We want the moon, but we shall get no more.

If here to-day the cloud of thunder lours
  To-morrow it will hie on far behests;
The flesh will grieve on other bones than ours
  Soon, and the soul will mourn in other breasts.

The troubles of our proud and angry dust
  Are from eternity, and shall not fail.
Bear them we can, and if we can we must.
  Shoulder the sky, my lad, and drink your ale.

The Laws of God, the Laws of Man

  The laws of God, the laws of man,
He may keep that will and can;
Not I: let God and man decree
Laws for themselves and not for me;
And if my ways are not as theirs
Let them mind their own affairs.
Their deeds I judge and much condemn,
Yet when did I make laws for them?
Please yourselves, say I, and they
Need only look the other way.
But no, they will not; they must still
Wrest their neighbour to their will,
And make me dance as they desire
With jail and gallows and hell-fire.
And how am I to face the odds
Of man's bedevilment and God's?
I, a stranger and afraid
In a world I never made.
They will be master, right or wrong;
Though both are foolish, both are strong.

And since, my soul, we cannot fly
To Saturn nor to Mercury,
Keep we must, if keep we can,
These foreign laws of God and man.

The Fairies Break Their Dances

The fairies break their dances
  And leave the printed lawn,
And up from India glances
  The silver sail of dawn.

The candles burn their sockets,
  The blinds let through the day,
The young man feels his pockets
  And wonders what's to pay.

Now Dreary Dawns the Eastern Light

Now dreary dawns the eastern light,
  And fall of eve is drear,
And cold the poor man lies at night,
  And so goes out the year.

Little is the luck I've had,
  And oh, 'tis comfort small
To think that many another lad
  Has had no luck at all.

The First of May

The orchards half the way
  From home to Ludlow fair
Flowered on the first of May
  In Mays when I was there;
And seen from stile or turning
  The plume of smoke would show
Where fires were burning
  That went out long ago.

The plum broke forth in green,
  The pear stood high and snowed,
My friends and I between
  Would take the Ludlow road;

Dressed to the nines and drinking
  And light in heart and limb,
And each chap thinking
  The fair was held for him.

Between the trees in flower
  New friends at fairtime tread
The way where Ludlow tower
  Stands planted on the dead.
Our thoughts, a long while after,
  They think, our words they say;
Theirs now's the laughter,
  The fair, the first of May.

Ay, yonder lads are yet
  The fools that we were then;
For oh, the sons we get
  Are still the sons of men.
The sumless tale of sorrow
  Is all unrolled in vain:
May comes to-morrow
  And Ludlow fair again.

Easter Hymn

If in that Syrian garden, ages slain,
You sleep, and know not you are dead in vain,
Nor even in dreams behold how dark and bright
Ascends in smoke and fire by day and night
The hate you died to quench and could but fan,
Sleep well and see no morning, son of man.

But if, the grave rent and the stone rolled by,
At the right hand of majesty on high
You sit, and sitting so remember yet
Your tears, your agony and bloody sweat,
Your cross and passion and the life you gave,
Bow hither out of heaven and see and save.

Delight it Is in Youth and May

Delight it is in youth and May
  To see the morn arise,
And more delight to look all day
  A lover in the eyes.

Oh maiden, let your distaff be,
And pace the flowery meads with me,
  And I will tell you lies.

'Tis blithe to see the sunshine fail,
  And hear the land grow still,
And listen till the nightingale
  Is heard beneath the hill.
Oh follow me where she is flown
Into the leafy woods alone,
  And I will work you ill.

Parta Quies

Good-night; ensured release,
Imperishable peace,
    Have these for yours,
While sea abides, and land,
And earth's foundations stand,
    And heaven endures.

When earth's foundations flee,
Nor sky nor land nor sea
    At all is found,
Content you, let them burn:
It is not your concern;
    Sleep on, sleep sound.

Stephen Crane (1871-1900)

Born in New Jersey of a family whose roots went deep into Colonial America, Crane spent time at both Lafayette College and Syracuse University, but never received a degree. He gravitated to New York as a newspaper reporter and free-lance writer. Periods of intense poverty followed, and he acquired an undeserved reputation for depravity. Part of this was due to the material in his first novel, *Maggie: A Girl of the Streets,* and part to the rumors about the woman he "married."

Crane had never experienced war when he wrote *The Red Badge of Courage,* which established his reputation and prepared the way for him to become a war correspondent, first in Cuba and then in Greece. In 1896 his own experience with a shipwreck produced "The Open Boat," one of his best known short stories. He also wrote several volumes of gnomic poetry which baffled and sometimes infuriated his contemporaries.

His health wrecked by tuberculosis, Crane chose to live in England where he became a close friend of Joseph Conrad. Later he went to Germany, hoping to restore his health, and there he died at the age of twenty-nine. Although his life offered few periods of calm, his collected work, when eventually published, filled twelve volumes.

"In the Desert"

In the desert
I saw a creature, naked, bestial,
Who, squatting upon the ground,
Held his heart in his hands,
And ate of it.
I said: "Is it good, friend?"
"It is bitter—bitter," he answered;
"But I like it
Because it is bitter,
And because it is my heart."

"Once There Came a Man"

Once there came a man
Who said:
"Range me all men of the world in rows."
And instantly
There was terrific clamor among the people
Against being ranged in rows.
There was a loud quarrel, world-wide.
It endured for ages;
And blood was shed

By those who would not stand in rows,
And by those who pined to stand in rows.
Eventually, the man went to death, weeping.
And those who stayed in bloody scuffle
Knew not the great simplicity.

"A God in Wrath"

A god in wrath
Was beating a man;
He cuffed him loudly
With thunderous blows
That rang and rolled over the earth.
All people came running.
The man screamed and struggled,
And bit madly at the feet of the god.
The people cried:
"Ah, what a wicked man!"
And—
"Ah, what a redoubtable god!"

"I Saw a Man Pursuing the Horizon"

I saw a man pursuing the horizon;
Round and round they sped.
I was disturbed at this;
I accosted the man.
"It is futile," I said,
"You can never—"

"You lie," he cried,
And ran on.

"Behold, the Grave of a Wicked Man"

Behold, the grave of a wicked man,
And near it, a stern spirit.

There came a drooping maid with violets,
But the spirit grasped her arm.

"No flowers for him," he said.
The maid wept:
"Ah, I loved him."
But the spirit, grim and frowning:
"No flowers for him."

Now, this is it—
If the spirit was just,
Why did the maid weep?

"A Youth in Apparel That Glittered"

A youth in apparel that glittered
Went to walk in a grim forest.
There he met an assassin
Attired all in garb of old days;
He, scowling through the thickets,
And dagger poised quivering,
Rushed upon the youth.
"Sir," said this latter,
"I am enchanted, believe me,
To die, thus,
In this medieval fashion,
According to the best legends;
Ah, what joy!"
Then took he the wound, smiling,
And died, content.

"There Was One I Met upon the Road"

There was One I met upon the road
Who looked at me with kind eyes.
He said: "Show me of your wares."
And I did,
Holding forth one.
He said: "It is a sin."
Then I held forth another.
He said: "It is a sin."
Then I held forth another.
He said: "It is a sin."
And so to the end.
Always He said: "It is a sin."

At last, I cried out:
"But I have none other."
He looked at me
With kinder eyes.
"Poor soul," He said.

"The Ocean Said to Me Once"

The ocean said to me once:
"Look!
Yonder on the shore
Is a woman, weeping.
I have watched her.
Go you and tell her this,—
Her lover I have laid
In cool green hall.
There is wealth of golden sand
And pillars, coral-red;
Two white fish stand guard at his bier.

"Tell her this
And more,—
That the king of the seas
Weeps too, old, helpless man.
The bustling fates
Heap his hands with corpses
Until he stands like a child
With surplus of toys."

"I Stood Musing in a Black World"

I stood musing in a black world,
Not knowing where to direct my feet.
And I saw the quick stream of men
Pouring ceaselessly,
Filled with eager faces,
A torrent of desire.
I called to them:
"Where do you go? What do you see?"
A thousand voices called to me.
A thousand fingers pointed.
"Look! Look! There!"

I know not of it.
But, lo! in the far sky shone a radiance
Ineffable, divine,—

A vision painted upon a pall;
And sometimes it was,
And sometimes it was not.
I hesitated.
Then from the stream
Came roaring voices,
Impatient:
"Look! Look! There!"

So again I saw,
And leaped, unhesitant,
And struggled and fumed
With outspread clutching fingers.
The hard hills tore my flesh;
The ways bit my feet.
At last I looked again.
No radiance in the far sky,
Ineffable, divine,
No vision painted upon a pall;
And always my eyes ached for the light.
Then I cried in despair:
"I see nothing! Oh, where do I go?"
The torrent turned again its faces:
"Look! Look! There!"

And at the blindness of my spirit
They screamed:
"Fool! Fool! Fool!"

"God Lay Dead in Heaven"

God lay dead in Heaven;
Angels sang the hymn of the end;
Purple winds went moaning,
Their wings drip-dripping
With blood
That fell upon the earth.
It, groaning thing,
Turned black and sank.
Then from the far caverns
Of dead sins
Came monsters, livid with desire.
They fought,
Wrangled over the world,
A morsel.

But of all sadness this was sad,—
A woman's arms tried to shield
The head of a sleeping man
From the jaws of the final beast.

"I Explain the Silvered Passing of a Ship at Night"

I explain the silvered passing of a ship at night,
The sweep of each sad lost wave
The dwindling boom of the steel thing's striving
The little cry of a man to a man
A shadow falling across the greyer night
And the sinking of the small star.

Then the waste, the far waste of waters
And the soft lashing of black waves
For long and in loneliness.

Remember, thou, O ship of love
Thou leavest a far waste of waters
And the soft lashing of black waves
For long and in loneliness.

"I Have Heard the Sunset Song of The Birches"

"I have heard the sunset song of the birches
A white melody in the silence
I have seen a quarrel of the pines.
At nightfall
The little grasses have rushed by me
With the wind men.
These things have I lived," quoth the maniac,
"Possessing only eyes and ears.
But, you—
You don green spectacles before you look at roses."

"On the Desert"

On the desert
A silence from the moon's deepest valley.
Fire-rays fall athwart the robes
Of hooded men, squat and dumb.
Before them, a woman

Moves to the blowing of shrill whistles
And distant-thunder of drums
While slow things, sinuous, dull with terrible color
Sleepily fondle her body
Or more at her will, swishing stealthily over the sand.
The snakes whisper softly;
The whispering, whispering snakes
Dreaming and swaying and staring
But always whispering, softly whispering.
The wind streams from the lone reaches
Of Arabia, solemn with night,
And the wild fire makes shimmer of blood
Over the robes of the hooded men
Squat and dumb.
Bands of moving bronze, emerald, yellow
Circle the throat and the arms of her
And over the sands serpents move warily
Slow, menacing and submissive,
Swinging to the whistles and drums,
The whispering, whispering snakes,
Dreaming and swaying and staring
But always whispering, softly whispering.
The dignity of the accurséd;
The glory of slavery, despair, death
Is in the dance of the whispering snakes.

"A Newspaper Is a Collection of Half-Injustices"

A newspaper is a collection of half-injustices
Which, bawled by boys from mile to mile,
Spreads its curious opinion
To a million merciful and sneering men,
While families cuddle the joys of the fireside
When spurred by tale of dire lone agony.
A newspaper is a court
Where every one is kindly and unfairly tried
By a squalor of honest men.
A newspaper is a market
Where wisdom sells its freedom
And melons are crowned by the crowd.
A newspaper is a game
Where his error scores the player victory
While another's skill wins death.
A newspaper is a symbol;
It is fetless life's chronicle,

A collection of loud tales
Concentrating eternal stupidities,
That in remote ages lived unhaltered,
Roaming through a fenceless world.

"A Man Said to the Universe"

A man said to the universe:
"Sir, I exist!"
"However," replied the universe,
"The fact has not created in me
A sense of obligation."

"A Naked Woman and a Dead Dwarf"

A naked woman and a dead dwarf;
Wealth and indifference.
Poor dwarf!
Reigning with foolish kings
And dying mid bells and wine
Ending with a desperate comic palaver
While before thee and after thee
Endures the eternal clown—
—The eternal clown—
A naked woman.

"A God Came to a Man"

A god came to a man
And said to him thus:
"I have an apple
It is a glorious apple
Aye, I swear by my ancestors
Of the eternities before this eternity
It is an apple that is from
The inner thoughts of heaven's greatest.

"And this I will hang here
And then I will adjust thee here
Thus—you may reach it.
And you must stifle your nostrils

And control your hands
And your eyes
And sit for sixty years
But—leave be the apple."

The man answered in this wise:
"Oh, most interesting God
What folly is this?
Behold, thou hast moulded my desires
Even as thou hast moulded the apple.

"How, Then?"

"How, then?
Can I conquer my life
Which is thou?
My desires?
Look you, foolish god
If I thrust behind me
Sixty white years
I am a greater god than God
And, then, complacent splendor,
Thou wilt see that the golden angels
That sing pink hymns
Around thy throne-top
Will be lower than my feet."

"There Exists the Eternal Fact of Conflict"

There exists the eternal fact of conflict
And—next—a mere sense of locality.
Afterward we derive sustenance from the winds.
Afterward we grip upon this sense of locality.
Afterward, we become patriots.
The godly vice of patriotism makes us slaves,
And—let us surrender to this falsity
Let us be patriots

Then welcome us the practical men
Thrumming on a thousand drums
The practical men, God help us.
    They cry aloud to be led to war
    Ah—
    They have been poltroons on a thousand fields

And the sacked sad city of New York is their record
Furious to face the Spaniard, these people, and crawling worms
before their task
They name serfs and send charity in bulk to better men
They play at being free, these people of New York
Who are too well-dressed to protest against infamy

T. S. Eliot (1888-1965)

Eliot was born in St. Louis, Missouri, though his family had New England roots. After attending private secondary schools he went to Harvard where he graduated in 1909, and received a master's degree in 1910. He then studied in Europe but, caught by World War I, never completed his Ph.D. Finding England more to his taste than the United States, he settled there and in 1927 became a British citizen. For many years he was a bank clerk, but he joined the publishing firm of Faber and Faber in 1925 and was thereafter associated with them as an editor and adviser. His reputation as a poet advanced rapidly after publication of *The Waste Land* in 1922, and as he continued to publish not only poetry but criticism and drama (*Murder in the Cathedral, The Cocktail Party,* etc.), his list of awards and honorary degrees grew until in 1948 he was awarded the Nobel Prize in Literature.

In the 1920s Eliot became "an Anglo-Catholic in religion, a Classicist in literature and a royalist in politics." Though there has been a reaction against him in recent years, his influence cannot be ignored. Not only has his own work been influential, but his critical essays have led to a reevaluation of poets like John Donne and Andrew Marvell. In *The Waste Land* he saw accurately the ruin that was a legacy of World War I. He died in 1965, honored and celebrated, his last years made much happier by his second marriage, in 1957, to Valerie Gletcher.

The Love Song of J. Alfred Prufrock

S'io credessi che mia risposta fosse
a persona che mai tornasse al mondo,
questa fiamma staria senza più scosse.
Ma per ciò che giammai di questo fondo
non tornò vivo alcun, s'i'odo il vero,
senza tema d'infamia ti rispondo.

Let us go then, you and I,
When the evening is spread out against the sky
Like a patient etherised upon a table;
Let us go, through certain half-deserted streets,
The muttering retreats
Of restless nights in one-night cheap hotels
And sawdust restaurants with oyster-shells:
Streets that follow like a tedious argument
Of insidious intent
To lead you to an overwhelming question . . .
Oh, do not ask, 'What is it?'
Let us go and make our visit.

In the room the women come and go
Talking of Michelangelo.

The yellow fog that rubs its back upon the window-panes,
The yellow smoke that rubs its muzzle on the window-panes,
Licked its tongue into the corners of the evening,
Lingered upon the pools that stand in drains,
Let fall upon its back the soot that falls from chimneys,
Slipped by the terrace, made a sudden leap,
And seeing that it was a soft October night,
Curled once about the house, and fell asleep.

And indeed there will be time
For the yellow smoke that slides along the street
Rubbing its back upon the window-panes;
There will be time, there will be time
To prepare a face to meet the faces that you meet;
There will be time to murder and create,
And time for all the works and days of hands
That lift and drop a question on your plate;
Time for you and time for me,
And time yet for a hundred indecisions,
And for a hundred visions and revisions,
Before the taking of a toast and tea.

In the room the women come and go
Talking of Michelangelo.

And indeed there will be time
To wonder, 'Do I dare?' and, 'Do I dare?'
Time to turn back and descend the stair,
With a bald spot in the middle of my hair—
(They will say: 'How his hair is growing thin!')
My morning coat, my collar mounting firmly to the chin,
My necktie rich and modest, but asserted by a simple pin—
(They will say: 'But how his arms and legs are thin!')
Do I dare
Disturb the universe?
In a minute there is time
For decisions and revisions which a minute will reverse.

For I have known them all already, known them all—
Have known the evenings, mornings, afternoons,
I have measured out my life with coffee spoons;
I know the voices dying with a dying fall
Beneath the music from a farther room.
So how should I presume?

And I have known the eyes already, known them all—
The eyes that fix you in a formulated phrase,
And when I am formulated, sparwling on a pin,

When I am pinned and wriggling on the wall,
Then how should I begin
To spit out all the butt-ends of my days and ways?
  And how should I presume?

  And I have known the arms already, known them all—
Arms that are braceleted and white and bare
(But in the lamplight, downed with light brown hair!)
Is it perfume from a dress
That makes me so digress?
Arms that lie along a table, or wrap about a shawl.
  And should I then presume?
  And how should I begin?

. . . . .

Shall I say, I have gone at dusk through narrow streets
And watched the smoke that rises from the pipes
Of lonely men in shirt-sleeves, leaning out of windows? . . .

  I should have been a pair of ragged claws
Scuttling across the floors of silent seas.

. . . . .

And the afternoon, the evening, sleeps so peacefully!
Smoothed by long fingers,
Asleep . . . tired . . . or it malingers,
Stretched on the floor, here beside you and me.
Should I, after tea and cakes and ices,
Have the strength to force the moment to its crisis?
But though I have wept and fasted, wept and prayed,
Though I have seen my head (grown slightly bald) brought in upon a platter,
I am no prophet—and here's no great matter;
I have seen the moment of my greatness flicker,
And I have seen the eternal Footman hold my coat, and snicker,
And in short, I was afraid.

  And would it have been worth it, after all,
After the cups, the marmalade, the tea,
Among the porcelain, among some talk of you and me,
Would it have been worth while,
To have bitten off the matter with a smile,
To have squeezed the universe into a ball
To roll it towards some overwhelming question,
To say: 'I am Lazarus, come from the dead,
Come back to tell you all, I shall tell you all'—
If one, settling a pillow by her head,
  Should say: 'That is not what I meant at all.
  That is not it, at all.'

And would it have been worth it, after all,
Would it have been worth while,
After the sunsets and the dooryards and the sprinkled streets,
After the novels, after the teacups, after the skirts that trail along the floor—
And this, and so much more?—
It is impossible to say just what I mean!
But as if a magic lantern threw the nerves in patterns on a screen:
Would it have been worth while
If one, settling a pillow or throwing off a shawl,
And turning toward the window, should say:
'That is not it at all,
That is not what I meant, at all.'

. . . . .

No! I am not Prince Hamlet, nor was meant to be;
Am an attendant lord, one that will do
To swell a progress, start a scene or two,
Advise the prince; no doubt, an easy tool,
Deferential, glad to be of use,
Politic, cautious, and meticulous;
Full of high sentence, but a bit obtuse;
At times, indeed, almost ridiculous—
Almost, at times, the Fool.

I grow old . . . I grow old . . .
I shall wear the bottoms of my trousers rolled.

Shall I part my hair behind? Do I dare to eat a peach?
I shall wear white flannel trousers, and walk upon the beach.
I have heard the mermaids singing, each to each.

I do not think that they will sing to me.

I have seen them riding seaward on the waves
Combing the white hair of the waves blown back
When the wind blows the water white and black.

We have lingered in the chambers of the sea
By sea-girls wreathed with seaweed red and brown
Till human voices wake us, and we drown.

Morning at the Window

They are rattling breakfast plates in basement kitchens.
And along the trampled edges of the street
I am aware of the damp souls of housemaids
Sprouting despondently at area gates.

The brown waves of fog toss up to me
Twisted faces from the bottom of the street,
And tear from a passer-by with muddy skirts
An aimless smile that hovers in the air
And vanishes along the level of the roofs.

Sweeney Among the Nightingales

ὤμοι, πέπληγμαι καιρίαν πληγῆν ἔσω.

Apeneck Sweeney spreads his knees
Letting his arms hang down to laugh,
The zebra stripes along his jaw
Swelling to maculate giraffe.

The circles of the stormy moon
Slide westward toward the River Plate,
Death and the Raven drift above
And Sweeney guards the hornèd gate.

Gloomy Orion and the Dog
Are veiled; and hushed the shrunken seas;
The person in the Spanish cape
Tries to sit on Sweeney's knees

Slips and pulls the table cloth
Overturns a coffe-cup,
Reorganised upon the floor
She yawns and draws a stocking up;

The silent man in mocha brown
Sprawls at the windo-sill and gapes;
The waiter brings in oranges
Bananas figs and hothouse grapes;

The silent vertebrate in brown
Contracts and concentrates, withdraws;
Rachel *née* Rabinovitch
Tears at the grapes with murderous paws;

She and the lady in the cape
Are suspect, thought to be in league;
Therefore the man with heavy eyes
Declines the gambit, shows fatigue,

Leaves the room and reappears
Outside the window, leaning in,
Branches of wistaria
Circumscribe a golden grin;

The host with someone indistinct
Converses at the door apart,
The nightingales are singing near
The Convent of the Sacred Heart,

And sang within the bloody wood
When Agamemnon cried aloud
And let their liquid siftings fall
To stain the stiff dishonoured shroud.

The Hollow Men
1925

Mistah Kurtz—he dead.

The Hollow Men

A penny for the Old Guy

I

We are the hollow men
We are the stuffed men
Leaning together
Headpiece filled with straw. Alas!
Our dried voices, when
We whisper together
Are quiet and meaningless
As wind in dry grass
Or rats' feet over broken glass
In our dry cellar

Shape without form, shade without colour,
Paralysed force, gesture without motion;

Those who have crossed
With direct eyes, to death's other Kingdom
Remember us—if at all—not as lost
Violent souls, but only
As the hollow men
The stuffed men.

II

Eyes I dare not meet in dreams
In death's dream kingdom
These do not appear:
There, the eyes are
Sunlight on a broken column
There, is a tree swinging

And voices are
In the wind's singing
More distant and more solemn
Than a fading star.

Let me be no nearer
In death's dream kingdom
Let me also wear
Such deliberate disguises
Rat's coat, crowskin, crossed staves
In a field
Behaving as the wind behaves
No nearer—

Not that final meeting
In the twilight kingdom

III

This is the dead land
This is cactus land
Here the stone images
Are raised, here they receive
The supplication of a dead man's hand
Under the twinkle of a fading star.

Is it like this
In death's other kingdom
Waking alone
At the hour when we are
Trembling with tenderness
Lips that would kiss
Form prayers to broken stone.

IV

The eyes are not here
There are no eyes here
In this valley of dying stars
In this hollow valley
This broken jaw of our lost kingdoms

In this last of meeting places
We grope together
And avoid speech
Gathered on this beach of the tumid river

Sightless, unless
The eyes reappear
As the perpetual star

Multifoliate rose
Of death's twilight kingdom
The hope only
Of empty men.

V

Here we go round the prickly pear
Prickly pear prickly pear
Here we go round the prickly pear
At five o'clock in the morning.

Between the idea
And the reality
Between the motion
And the act
Falls the Shadow
For Thine is the Kingdom

Between the conception
And the creation
Between the emotion
And the response
Falls the Shadow
Life is very long

Between the desire
And the spasm
Between the potency
And the existence
Between the essence
And the descent
Falls the Shadow
For Thine is the Kingdom

For Thine is
Life is
For Thine is the

This is the way the world ends
This is the way the world ends
This is the way the world ends
Not with a bang but a whimper.

Journey of the Magi

'A cold coming we had of it,
Just the worst time of the year
For a journey, and such a long journey:
The ways deep and the weather sharp,

The very dead of winter.'
And the camels galled, sore-footed, refractory,
Lying down in the melting snow.
There were times we regretted
The summer palaces on slopes, the terraces,
And the silken girls bringing sherbet.
Then the camel men cursing and grumbling
And running away, and wanting their liquor and women,
And night-fires going out, and the lack of shelters,
And the cities hostile and the towns unfriendly
And the villages dirty and charging high prices:
A hard time we had of it.
At the end we preferred to travel all night,
Sleeping in snatches,
With the voices singing in our ears, saying
That this was all folly.

Then at dawn we came down to a temperate valley,
Wet, below the snow line, smelling of vegetation,
With a running stream and a water-mill beating the darkness,
And three trees on the low sky.
And an old white horse galloped away in the meadow.
Then we came to a tavern with vine-leaves over the lintel,
Six hands at an open door dicing for pieces of silver,
And feet kicking the empty wine-skiins.
But there was no information, and so we continued
And arrived at evening, not a moment too soon
Finding the place; it was (you may say) satisfactory.

All this was a long time ago, I remember,
And I would do it again, but set down
This set down
This: were we led all that way for
Birth or Death? There was a Birth, certainly,
We had evidence and no doubt. I had seen birth and death,
But had thought they were different; this Birth was
Hard and bitter agony for us, like Death, our death.
We returned to our places, these Kingdoms,
But no longer at ease here, in the old dispensation,
With an alien people clutching their gods.
I should be glad of another death.

E. E. Cummings (1894–1962)

He was born in Cambridge, Mass, and he grew up with great assets—a warm, loving family, economic security, and an environment full of creative and interesting people. He graduated from Harvard *magna cum laude* and went on to acquire a master's degree. In 1917 he sailed for France and joined the Ambulance Corps of the American Red Cross, only to be imprisoned by the French because they suspected him of disloyalty. When questioned he refused to say he hated Germans and would only repeat, "I like the French." His novel, *The Enormous Room,* recounts this episode. For a time after the war he lived in Paris, but returned to New York in 1924 to write and paint.

Cummings published many volumes of poetry in the ensuing years, all of them characterized by his syntactical experiments with language and reflecting his celebration of life and love. In *Six Non-Lectures,* delivered at Harvard in 1952 to 1953, he said, "I am someone who proudly and humbly affirms that love is the mystery of mysteries." He also went on to speak about "ecstasy and anguish, being and becoming, the immortality of the creative imagination and the indomitability of the human spirit." He accumulated many honors before his death in 1962, among them election to the American Academy of Poets in 1950 and the Bollingen prize in 1957. His third marriage in 1932 to photographer Marian Morehouse certainly contributed to his affirmation of love.

"In Just-"

in Just-
spring   when the world is mud-
luscious the little
lame balloonman

whistles   far   and wee

and eddieandbill come
running from marbles and
piracies and it's
spring

when the world is puddle-wonderful

the queer
old balloonman whistles
far   and   wee
and bettyandisbel come dancing

from hop-scotch and jump-rope and

it's
spring
and
     the

goat-footed

ballonMan whistles
far
and
wee

"The Cambridge ladies who live in furnished souls"

the Cambridge ladies who live in furnished souls
are unbeautiful and have comfortable minds
(also, with the church's protestant blessings
daughters, unscented shapeless spirited)
they believe in Christ and Longfellow, both dead,
are invariably interested in so many things—
at the present writing one still finds
delighted fingers knitting for the is it Poles?
perhaps. While permanent faces coyly bandy
scandal of Mrs. N and Professor D
. . . . the Cambridge ladies do not care, above
Cambridge if sometimes in its box of
sky lavender and cornerless, the
moon rattles like a fragment of angry candy

"it may not always be so; and i say"

it may not always be so; and i say
that if your lips, which i have loved, should touch
another's, and your dear strong fingers clutch
his heart, as mine in time not far away;
if on another's face your sweet hair lay
in such a silence as i know, or such
great writhing words as, uttering overmuch,
stand helplessly before the spirit at bay;

if this should be, i say if this should be—
you of my heart, send me a little word;
that i may go unto him, and take his hands,
saying, Accept all happiness from me.
Then shall i turn my face, and hear one bird
sing terribly afar in the lost lands.

"here is little Effie's head"

here is little Effie's head
whose brains are made of gingerbread
when the judgment day comes
God will find six crumbs

stooping by the coffinlid
waiting for something to rise
as the other somethings did—
you imagine His surprise

bellowing through the general noise
Where is Effie who was dead?
—to God in a tiny voice,
i am may the first crumb said

whereupon its fellow five
crumbs chuckled as if they were alive
and number two took up the song,
might i'm called and did no wrong

cried the third crumb, i am should
and this is my little sister could
with our big brother who is would
don't punish us for we were good;

and the last crumb with some shame
whispered unto God, my name
is must and with the others i've
been Effie who isn't alive

just imagine it I say
God amid a monstrous din
watch your step and follow me
stooping by Effie's little, in

(want a match or can you see?)
which the six subjunctive crumbs
twitch like mutilated thumbs:
picture His peering biggest whey

coloured face on which a frown
puzzles, but I know the way—
(nervously Whose eyes approve
the blessed while His ears are crammed

with the strenuous music of
the innumerable capering damned)
—staring wildly up and down
the here we are now judgment day

cross the threshold have no dread
lift the sheet back in this way.
here is little Effie's head
whose brains are made of gingerbread

"i like my body when it is with your"

i like my body when it is with your
body.   It is so quite new a thing.
Muscles better and nerves more.
i like your body.   i like what it does,
i like its hows.   i like to feel the spine
of your body and its bones, and the trembling
-firm-smooth ness and which i will
again and again and again
kiss,   i like kissing this and that of you,
i like, slowly stroking the, shocking fuzz
of your electric fur, and what-is-it comes
over parting flesh . . . . And eyes big love-crumbs,

and possibly i like the thrill

of under me you so quite new

"5"

5
derbies-with-men-in-them smoke Helmar
cigarettes   2
play backgammon, 3 watch

a has gold
teeth b pink
suspenders c
reads Atlantis

x and y play   b
cries "effendi" "Uh" "coffee"
"uh"   enter
paperboy, c

buys Bawstinamereekin, exit
paperboy   a finishes
Helmar   lights
another
        x and y

play, effendi approaches, sets
down coffee   withdraws
a and c discuss news in

turkish x and y play b spits
x and
y
play, b starts armenian record
                                                            pho
nographisrunn
ingd o w,   n   phonograph
                              stopS.

b swears in persian at phonograph
x wins   exeunt ax: by; c,
Goo dnightef fendi
. . . .

five men in derbies

"Jimmie's got a goil"

Jimmie's got a goil
                         goil
                              goil,
                                   Jimmie
's got a goil and
she coitnly can shimmie

when you see her shake
                                   shake
                                        shake,
                                                  when
you see her shake a
shimmie how you wish that you was Jimmie.

Oh for such a gurl
                         gurl
                              gurl,
                                   oh
for such a gurl to
be a fellow's twistandtwirl

talk about your Sal-
                    Sal-
                         Sal-,
                              talk
about your Salo
-mes but gimmie Jimmie's gal.

"come, gaze with me upon this dome"

come, gaze with me upon this dome
of many coloured glass, and see
his mother's pride, his father's joy,
unto whom duty whispers low

"thou must!" and who replies "I can!"
—yon clean upstanding well dressed boy
that with his peers full oft hath quaffed
the wine of life and found it sweet—

a tear within his stern blue eye,
upon his firm white lips a smile,
one thought alone: to do or die
for God for country and for Yale

above his blond determined head
the sacred flag of truth unfurled,
in the bright heyday of his youth
the upper class American

unsullied stands, before the world:
with manly heart and conscience free,
upon the front steps of her home
by the high minded pure young girl

much kissed, by loving relatives
well fed, and fully photographed
the son of man goes forth to war
with trumpets clap and syphilis

"the way to hump a cow is not"

the way to hump a cow is not
to get yourself a stool
but draw a line around the spot
and call it beautifool

to multiply because and why
dividing thens by nows
and adding and (i understand)
is hows to hump a cows

the way to hump a cow is not
to elevate your tool
but drop a penny in the slot
and bellow like a bool

to lay a wreath from ancient greath
on insulated brows
(while tossing boms at uncle toms)
is hows to hump a cows

the way to hump a cow is not
to push and then to pull
but practicing the art of swot
to preach the golden rull

to vote for me(all decent mem
and wonens will allows
which if they don't to hell with them)
is hows to hump a cows

"my father moved through dooms of love"

my father moved through dooms of love
through sames of am through haves of give,
singing each morning out of each night
my father moved through depths of height

this motionless forgetful where
turned at his glance to shining here;
that if(so timid air is firm)
under his eyes would stir and squirm

newly as from unburied which
floats the first who,his april touch
drove sleeping selves to swarm their fates
woke dreamers to their ghostly roots

and should some why completely weep
my father's fingers brought her sleep:
vainly no smallest voice might cry
for he could feel the mountains grow.

Lifting the valleys of the sea
my father moved through griefs of joy;
praising a forehead called the moon
singing desire into begin

joy was his song and joy so pure
a heart of star by him could steer
and pure so now and now so yes
the wrists of twilight would rejoice

keen as midsummer's keen beyond
conceiving mind of sun will stand,
so strictly(over utmost him
so hugely)stood my father's dream

his flesh was flesh his blood was blood:
no hungry man but wished him food;
no cripple wouldn't creep one mile
uphill to only see him smile.

Scorning the pomp of must and shall
my father moved through dooms of feel;
his anger was as right as rain
his pity was as green as grain

septembering arms of year extend
less humbly wealth to foe and friend
than he to foolish and to wise
offered immeasurable is

proudly and(by octobering flame
beckoned)as earth will downward climb,
so naked for immortal work
his shoulders marched against the dark

his sorrow was as true as bread:
no liar looked him in the head;
if every friend became his foe
he'd laugh and build a world with snow.

My father moved through theys of we,
singing each new leaf out of each tree
(and every child was sure that spring
danced when she heard my father sing)

then let men kill which cannot share,
let blood and flesh be mud and mire,
scheming imagine,passion willed,
freedom a drug that's bought and sold

giving to steal and cruel kind,
a heart to fear,to doubt a mind,
to differ a disease of same,
conform the pinnacle of am

though dull were all we taste as bright
bitter all utterly things sweet,
maggoty minus and dumb death
all we inherit,all bequeath

and nothing quite so least as truth
—i say though hate were why men breathe—
because my father lived his soul
love is the whole and more than all

"dying is fine)but Death"

dying is fine)but Death

?o
baby
i

wouldn't like

Death if Death
were
good:for

when(instead of stopping to think)you

begin to feel of it,dying
's miraculous
why?be

cause dying is

perfectly natural;perfectly
putting
it mildly lively(but

Death

is strictly
scientific
& artificial &

evil & legal)

we thank thee
god
almighty for dying
(forgive us,o life!the sin of Death

"When serpents bargain for the right to squirm"

When serpents bargain for the right to squirm
and the sun strikes to gain a living wage—
when thorns regard their roses with alarm
and rainbows are insured against old age

when every thrush may sing no new moon in
if all screech-owls have not okayed his voice
—and any wave signs on the dotted line
or else an ocean is compelled to close

when the oak begs permission of the birch
to make an acorn—valleys accuse their
mountains of having altitude—and march
denounces april as a saboteur

then we'll believe in that incredible
unanimal mankind(and not until)

"i thank You God for most this amazing"

i thank You God for most this amazing
day:for the leaping greenly spirits of trees
and a blue true dream of sky;and for everything
which is natural which is infinite which is yes

(i who have died am alive again today,
and this is the sun's birthday;this is the birth
day of life and of love and wings:and of the gay
great happening illimitably earth)

how should tasting touching hearing seeing
breathing any—lifted from the no
of all nothing—human merely being
doubt unimaginable You?

(now the ears of my ears awake and
now the eyes of my eyes are opened)

"l(a"

l(a
le
af
fa

ll

s)
one
l

iness

Dylan Thomas (1914–1953)

He was a flamboyant Welsh poet whose celebration of country life, love, and the complexities of the 20th century are verbally dazzling. At times he seemed carried away by the sheer music of language, and some of his poetry, particularly the sonnet sequence, "Altarwise by Owl-Light," is full of unusual imagery and references to a private mythology, which makes it difficult reading. As he grew older his language became less involved. Poems like "Fern Hill" or his birthday poems require no special understanding. Thomas never attended a university and was a somewhat indifferent student, though he read voraciously. In 1937 he married Caitlin Macnamara, a woman almost as colorful as he. They had a stormy life together—periods of great poverty, moments of intense joy, three children.

Thomas had a strong sense of the dramatic, and one of his loveliest creations is the poetic play, *Under Milk Wood*. This theatrical ability carried over into his poetry readings which were extremely successful, especially in the United States, where he earned a considerable amount of money, was lionized (largely by women to whom he was susceptible), and where he drank to excess. On his fourth American reading he literally destroyed himself with liquor, dying in New York City. His wife has written an account of their days together, *Leftover Life to Live*. Although he was not religious in the conventional sense, Thomas said that his poetry was written "In praise of God and for love of man."

I See the Boys of Summer

I

I see the boys of summer in their ruin
Lay the gold tithings barren,
Setting no store by harvest, freeze the soils;
There in their heat the winter floods
Of frozen loves they fetch their girls,
And drown the cargoed apples in their tides.

These boys of light are curdlers in their folly,
Sour the boiling honey;
The jacks of frost they finger in the hives;
There in the sun the frigid threads
Of doubt and dark they feed their nerves;
The signal moon is zero in their voids.

I see the summer children in their mothers
Split up the brawned womb's weathers,
Divide the night and day with fairy thumbs;
There in the deep with quartered shades
Of sun and moon they paint their dams
As sunlight paints the shelling of their heads.

I see that from these boys shall men of nothing
Stature by seedy shifting,
Or lame the air with leaping from its heats;
There from their hearts the dogdayed pulse
Of love and light bursts in their throats.
O see the pulse of summer in the ice.

II

But seasons must be challenged or they totter
Into a chiming quarter
Where, punctual as death, we ring the stars;
There, in his night, the black-tongued bells
The sleepy man of winter pulls,
Nor blows back moon-and-midnight as she blows.

We are the dark deniers, let us summon
Death from a summer woman,
A muscling life from lovers in their cramp,
From the fair dead who flush the sea
The bright-eyed worm on Davy's lamp,
And from the planted womb the man of straw.

We summer boys in this four-winded spinning,
Green of the seaweeds' iron,
Hold up the noisy sea and drop her birds,
Pick the world's ball of wave and froth
To choke the deserts with her tides,
And comb the county gardens for a wreath.

In spring we cross our foreheads with the holly,
Heigh ho the blood and berry,
And nail the merry squires to the trees;
Here love's damp muscle dries and dies,
Here break a kiss in no love's quarry.
O see the poles of promise in the boys.

III

I see you boys of summer in your ruin.
Man in his maggot's barren.
And boys are full and foreign in the pouch.
I am the man your father was.
We are the sons of flint and pitch.
O see the poles are kissing as they cross.

Especially When the October Wind

Especially when the October wind
With frosty fingers punishes my hair,
Caught by the crabbing sun I walk on fire
And cast a shadow crab upon the land,
By the sea's side, hearing the noise of birds,
Hearing the raven cough in winter sticks,
My busy heart who shudders as she talks
Sheds the syllabic blood and drains her words.

Shut, too, in a tower of words, I mark
On the horizon walking like the trees
The wordy shapes of women, and the rows
Of the star-gestured children in the park.
Some let me make you of the vowelled beeches,
Some of the oaken voices, from the roots
Of many a thorny shire tell you notes,
Some let me make you of the water's speeches.

Behind a pot of ferns the wagging clock
Tells me the hour's word, the neural meaning
Flies on the shafted disk, declaims the morning
And tells the windy weather in the cock.
Some let me make you of the meadow's signs;
The signal grass that tells me all I know
Breaks with the wormy winter through the eye.
Some let me tell you of the raven's sins.

Especially when the October wind
(Some let me make you of autumnal spells,
The spider-tongued, and the loud hill of Wales)
With fists of turnips punishes the land,
Some let me make you of the heartless words.
The heart is drained that, spelling in the scurry
Of chemic blood, warned of the coming fury.
By the sea's side hear the dark-vowelled birds.

Incarnate Devil

Incarnate devil in a talking snake,
The central plains of Asia in his garden,
In shaping-time the circle stung awake,
In shapes of sin forked out the bearded apple,
And God walked there who was a fiddling warden
And played down pardon from the heavens' hill.

When we were strangers to the guided seas,
A handmade moon half holy in a cloud,
The wisemen tell me that the garden gods
Twined good and evil on an eastern tree;
And when the moon rose windily it was
Black as the beast and paler than the cross.

We in our Eden knew the secret guardian
In sacred waters that no frost could harden,
And in the mighty mornings of the earth;
Hell in a horn of sulphur and the cloven myth,
All heaven in a midnight of the sun,
A serpent fiddled in the shaping-time.

And Death Shall Have No Dominion

And death shall have no dominion.
Dead men naked they shall be one
With the man in the wind and the west moon;
When their bones are picked clean and the clean bones gone,
They shall have stars at elbow and foot;
Though they go mad they shall be sane,
Though they sink through the sea they shall rise again;
Though lovers be lost love shall not;
And death shall have no dominion.

And death shall have no dominion.
Under the windings of the sea
They lying long shall not die windily;
Twisting on racks when sinews give way,
Strapped to a wheel, yet they shall not break;
Faith in their hands shall snap in two,
And the unicorn evils run them through;
Split all ends up they shan't crack;
And death shall have no dominion.

And death shall have no dominion.
No more may gulls cry at their ears
Or waves break loud on the seashores;
Where blew a flower may a flower no more
Lift its head to the blows of the rain;
Though they be mad and dead as nails,
Heads of the characters hammer through daisies;
Break in the sun till the sun breaks down,
And death shall have no dominion.

A Refusal To Mourn the Death, by Fire, of a Child in London

Never until the mankind making
Bird beast and flower
Fathering and all humbling darkness
Tells with silence the last light breaking
And the still hour
Is come of the sea tumbling in harness

And I must enter again the round
Zion of the water bead
And the synagogue of the ear of corn
Shall I let pray the shadow of a sound
Or sow my salt seed
In the least valley of sackcloth to mourn

The majesty and burning of the child's death.
I shall not murder
The mankind of her going with a grave truth
Nor blaspheme down the stations of the breath
With any further
Elegy of innocence and youth.

Deep with the first dead lies London's daughter,
Robed in the long friends,
The grains beyond age, the dark veins of her mother,
Secret by the unmourning water
Of the riding Thames.
After the first death, there is no other.

The Hunchback in the Park

The hunchback in the park
A solitary mister
Propped between trees and water
From the opening of the garden lock
That lets the trees and water enter
Until the Sunday sombre bell at dark

Eating bread from a newspaper
Drinking water from the chained cup
That the children filled with gravel
In the fountain basin where I sailed my ship
Slept at night in a dog kennel
But nobody chained him up.

Like the park birds he came early
Like the water he sat down
And Mister they called Hey mister
The truant boys from the town
Running when he had heard them clearly
On out of sound

Past lake and rockery
Laughing when he shook his paper
Hunchbacked in mockery
Through the loud zoo of the willow groves
Dodging the park keeper
With his stick that picked up leaves.

And the old dog sleeper
Alone between nurses and swans
While the boys among willows
Made the tigers jump out of their eyes
To roar on the rockery stones
And the groves were blue with sailors

Made all day until bell time
A woman figure without fault
Straight as a young elm
Straight and tall from his crooked bones
That she might stand in the night
After the locks and chains

All night in the unmade park
After the railings and shrubberies
The birds the grass the trees the lake
And the wild boys innocent as strawberries
Had followed the hunchback
To his kennel in the dark.

Do Not Go Gentle into that Good Night

Do not go gentle into that good night,
Old age should burn and rave at close of day;
Rage, rage against the dying of the light.

Though wise men at their end know dark is right,
Because their words had forked no lightning they
Do not go gentle into that good night.

Good men, the last wave by, crying how bright
Their frail deeds might have danced in a green bay,
Rage, rage against the dying of the light.

Wild men who caught and sang the sun in flight,
And learn, too late, they grieved it on its way,
Do not go gentle into that good night.

Grave men, near death, who see with blinding sight
Blind eyes could blaze like meteors and be gay,
Rage, rage against the dying of the light.

And you, my father, there on the sad height,
Curse, bless, me now with your fierce tears, I pray.
Do not go gentle into that good night.
Rage, rage against the dying of the light.

Fern Hill

Now as I was young and easy under the apple boughs
About the lilting house and happy as the grass was green,
  The night above the dingle starry,
    Time let me hail and climb
  Golden in the heydays of his eyes,
And honoured among wagons I was prince of the apple towns
And once below a time I lordly had the trees and leaves
    Trail with daisies and barley
  Down the rivers of the windfall light.

And as I was green and carefree, famous among the barns
About the happy yard and singing as the farm was home,
  In the sun that is young once only,
    Time let me play and be
  Golden in the mercy of his means,
And green and golden I was huntsman and herdsman, the calves
Sang to my horn, the foxes on the hills barked clear and cold,
    And the sabbath rang slowly
  In the pebbles of the holy streams.

All the sun long it was running, it was lovely, the hay
Fields high as the house, the tunes from the chimneys, it was air
  And playing, lovely and watery
      And fire green as grass.
  And nightly under the simple stars
As I rode to sleep the owls were bearing the farm away,
All the moon long I heard, blessed among stables, the nightjars
  Flying with the ricks, and the horses
      Flashing into the dark.

And then to awake, and the farm, like a wanderer white
With the dew, come back, the cock on his shoulder: it was all
        Shining, it was Adam and maiden,
                The sky gathered again
        And the sun grew round that very day.
So it must have been after the birth of the simple light
In the first, spinning place, the spellbound horses walking warm
        Out of the whinnying green stable
                On to the fields of praise.

And honoured among foxes and pheasants by the gay house
Under the new made clouds and happy as the heart was long,
        In the sun born over and over,
                I ran my heedless ways,
        My wishes raced through the house high lay
And nothing I cared, at my sky blue trades, that time allows
In all his tuneful turning so few and such morning songs
        Before the children green and golden
                Follow him out of grace,

Nothing I cared, in the lamb white days, that time would take me
Up to the swallow thronged loft by the shadow of my hand,
        In the moon that is always rising,
                Nor that riding to sleep
        I should hear him fly with the high fields
And wake to the farm forever fled from the childless land.
Oh as I was young and easy in the mercy of his means,
                Time held me green and dying
        Though I sang in my chains like the sea.

Over Sir John's Hill

Over Sir John's hill,
The hawk on fire hangs still;
In a hoisted cloud, at drop of dusk, he pulls to his claws
And gallows, up the rays of his eyes the small birds of the bay
And the shrill child's play
Wars
Of the sparrows and such who swansing, dusk, in wrangling hedges.
And blithely they squawk
To fiery tyburn over the wrestle of elms until
The flash the noosed hawk
Crashes, and slowly the fishing holy stalking heron
In the river Towy below bows his tilted headstone.

Flash, and the plumes crack,
And a black cap of Jack-
Daws Sir John's just hill dons, and again the gulled birds hare
To the hawk on fire, the halter height, over Towy's fins,
In a whack of wind.
There
Where the elegiac fisherbird stabs and paddles
In the pebbly dab-filled
Shallow and sedge, and 'dilly dilly,' calls the loft hawk,
'Come and be killed,'
I open the leaves of the water at a passage
Of psalms and shadows among the pincered sandcrabs prancing

And read, in a shell,
Death clear as a buoy's bell:
All praise of the hawk on fire in hawk-eyed dusk be sung,
When his viperish fuse hangs looped with flames under the brand
Wing, and blest shall
Young
Green chickens of the bay and bushes cluck, 'dilly dilly,
Come let us die.'
We grieve as the blithe birds, never again, leave shingle and elm,
The heron and I,
I young Aesop fabling to the near night by the dingle
Of eels, saint heron hymning in the shell-hung distant

Crystal harbour vale
Where the sea cobbles sail,
And wharves of water where the walls dance and the white cranes stilt.
It is the heron and I, under judging Sir John's elmed
Hill, tell-tale the knelled
Guilt
Of the led-astray birds whom God, for their breast of whistles,
Have mercy on,
God in his whirlwind silence save, who marks the sparrows hail,
For their souls' song.
Now the heron grieves in the weeded verge. Through windows
Of dusk and water I see the tilting whispering

Heron, mirrored, go,
As the snapt feathers snow,
Fishing in the tear of the Towy. Only a hoot owl
Hollows, a grassblade blown in cupped hands, in the looted elms
And no green cocks or hens
Shout
Now on Sir John's hill. The heron, ankling the scaly
Lowlands of the waves,

Makes all the music; and I who hear the tune of the slow,
Wear-willow river, grave,
Before the lunge of the night, the notes on this time-shaken
Stone for the sake of the souls of the slain birds sailing.

Lament

When I was a windy boy and a bit
And the black spit of the chapel fold,
(Sighed the old ram rod, dying of women),
I tiptoed shy in the gooseberry wood,
The rude owl cried like a telltale tit,
I skipped in a blush as the big girls rolled
Ninepin down on the donkeys' common,
And on seesaw sunday nights I wooed
Whoever I would with my wicked eyes,
The whole of the moon I could love and leave
All the green leaved little weddings' wives
In the coal black bush and let them grieve.

When I was a gusty man and a half
And the black beast of the beetles' pews,
(Sighed the old ram rod, dying of bitches),
Not a boy and a bit in the wick-
Dipping moon and drunk as a new dropped calf,
I whistled all night in the twisted flues,
Midwives grew in the midnight ditches,
And the sizzling beds of the town cried, Quick!—
Whenever I dove in a breast high shoal,
Wherever I ramped in the clover quilts,
Whatsoever I did in the coal—
Black night, I left my quivering prints.

When I was a man you could call a man
And the black cross of the holy house,
(Sighed the old ram rod, dying of welcome),
Brandy and ripe in my bright, bass prime,
No springtailed tom in the red hot town
With every simmering woman his mouse
But a hillocky bull in the swelter
Of summer come in his great good time
To the sultry, biding herds, I said,
Oh, time enough when the blood creeps cold,
And I lie down but to sleep in bed,
For my sulking, skulking, coal black soul!

When I was a half of the man I was
And serve me right as the preachers warn,
(Sighed the old ram rod, dying of downfall),
No flailing calf or cat in a flame
Or hickory bull in milky grass
But a black sheep with a crumpled horn,
At last the soul from its foul mousehole
Slung pouting out when the limp time came;
And I gave my soul a blind, slashed eye,
Gristle and rind, and a roarers' life,
And I shoved it into the coal black sky
To find a woman's soul for a wife.

Now I am a man no more no more
And a black reward for a roaring life,
(Sighed the old ram rod, dying of strangers),
Tidy and cursed in my dove cooed room
I lie down thin and hear the good bells jaw—
For, oh, my soul found a sunday wife
In the coal black sky and she bore angels!
Harpies around me out of her womb!
Chastity prays for me, piety sings,
Innocence sweetens my last black breath,
Modesty hides my thighs in her wings,
And all the deadly virtues plague my death!

Gwendolyn Brooks (1917-)

She was born in Topeka, Kansas, but has spent most of her life in Chicago —teaching in colleges, giving poetry readings, bringing up two children, and gaining a growing recognition as a poet. In 1950 she won the Pulitzer prize. She has also had several Guggenheims fellowships, and a number of honorary degrees. When Carl Sandburg died, she was named poet laureate of Illinois.

There seems to have been a shift in her life and writing around 1967. Although she has never denied her blackness, she was not a militant. From 1967 on she had more contact with younger blacks, and she made a trip to Africa. About this time she left Harper & Row, which had up to then published all her work, and became associated with the Broadside Press, which is devoted to the work of minorities. Now she seems more interested in speaking to blacks, in exploring the black experience. She insists, as she did in 1972, that the new black "is understood by no white. Not the wise white; not the schooled white; not the kind white." Her autobiography, *Report from Part One,* published in 1972, is helpful in revealing the changes in her.

Brooks has a strong lyric sense, though she can also handle satire—witness "Lovers of the Poor." Some of her recent work tends toward long narrative poems—*In the Mecca.* She has also written a semi-autobiographical novel, *Maud Martha,* and several delightful books of poetry for children. She stopped teaching in 1971 to have more time for writing, and to work in the black movement.

The Mother

Abortions will not let you forget.
You remember the children you got that you did not get,
The damp small pulps with a little or with no hair,
The singers and workers that never handled the air.
You will never neglect or beat
Them, or silence or buy with a sweet.
You will never wind up the sucking-thumb
Or scuttle off ghosts that come.
You will never leave them, controlling your luscious sigh,
Return for a snack of them, with gobbling mother-eye.

I have heard in the voices of the wind the voices of my dim killed children.
I have contracted. I have eased
My dim dears at the breasts they could never suck.
I have said, Sweets, if I sinned, if I seized
Your luck
And your lives from your unfinished reach,
If I stole your births and your names,
Your straight baby tears and your games,
Your stilted or lovely loves, your tumults, your marriages, aches, and

your deaths,
If I poisoned the beginnings of your breaths,
Believe that even in my deliberateness I was not deliberate.
Though why should I whine,
Whine that the crime was other than mine?—
Since anyhow you are dead.
Or rather, or instead,
You were never made.
But that too, I am afraid,
Is faulty: oh, what shall I say, how is the truth to be said?
You were born, you had body, you died.
It is just that you never giggled or planned or cried.

Believe me, I loved you all.
Believe me, I knew you, though faintly, and I loved, I loved you
All.

When You Have Forgotten Sunday: the Love Story

—And when you have forgotten the bright bedclothes on a Wednesday and a Saturday,
And most especially when you have forgotten Sunday—
When you have forgotten Sunday halves in bed,
Or me sitting on the front-room radiator in the limping afternoon
Looking off down the long street
To nowhere,
Hugged by my plain old wrapper of no-expectation
And nothing-I-have-to-do and I'm-happy-why?
And if-Monday-never-had-to-come—
When you have forgotten that, I say,
And how you swore, if somebody beeped the bell,
And how my heart played hopscotch if the telephone rang;
And how we finally went in to Sunday dinner,
That is to say, went across the front room floor to the ink-spotted table in the southwest corner
To Sunday dinner, which was always chicken and noodles
Or chicken and rice
And salad and rye bread and tea
And chocolate chip cookies—
I say, when you have forgotten that,
When you have forgotten my little presentiment
That the war would be over before they got to you;
And how we finally undressed and whipped out the light and flowed into bed,
And lay loose-limbed for a moment in the week-end
Bright bedclothes,
Then gently folded into each other—

When you have, I say, forgotten all that,
Then you may tell,
Then I may believe
You have forgotten me well.

The Sonnet-Ballad

Oh mother, mother, where is happiness?
They took my lover's tallness off to war,
Left me lamenting. Now I cannot guess
What I can use an empty heart-cup for.
He won't be coming back here any more.
Some day the war will end, but, oh, I knew
When he went walking grandly out that door
That my sweet love would have to be untrue.
Would have to be untrue. Would have to court
Coquettish death, whose impudent and strange
Possessive arms and beauty (of a sort)
Can make a hard man hesitate—and change.
And he will be the one to stammer, "Yes."
Oh mother, mother, where is happiness?

In Honor of David Anderson Brooks, My Father

JULY 30, 1883—NOVEMBER 21, 1959

A dryness is upon the house
My father loved and tended.
Beyond his firm and sculptured door
His light and lease have ended.

He walks the valleys, now—replies
To sun and wind forever.
No more the cramping chamber's chill,
No more the hindering fever.

Now out upon the wide clean air
My father's soul revives,
All innocent of self-interest
And the fear that strikes and strives.

He who was Goodness, Gentleness,
And Dignity is free,
Translates to public Love
Old private charity.

The Bean Eaters

They eat beans mostly, this old yellow pair.
Dinner is a casual affair.
Plain chipware on a plain and creaking wood,
Tin flatware.

Two who are Mostly Good.
Two who have lived their day,
But keep on putting on their clothes
And putting things away.

And remembering . . .
Remembering, with twinklings and twinges,
As they lean over the beans in their rented back room that is full of beads and receipts and dolls and cloths, tobacco crumbs, vases and fringes.

A Lovely Love

LILLIAN'S

Let it be alleys. Let it be a hall
Whose janitor javelins epithet and thought
To cheapen hyacinth darkness that we sought
And played we found, rot, make the petals fall.
Let it be stairways, and a splintery box
Where you have thrown me, scraped me with your kiss,
Have honed me, have released me after this
Cavern kindness, smiled away our shocks.
That is the birthright of our lovely love
In swaddling clothes. Not like that Other one.
Not lit by any fondling star above.
Not found by any wise men, either. Run.
People are coming. They must not catch us here
Definitionless in this strict atmosphere.

Bronzeville Woman in a Red Hat

HIRES OUT TO
MRS. MILES

I

They had never had one in the house before.
The strangeness of it all. Like unleashing
A lion, really. Poised

To pounce. A puma. A panther. A black
Bear.
There it stood in the door,
Under a red hat that was rash, but refreshing—
In a tasteless way, of course—across the dull dare,
The semi-assault of that extraordinary blackness.
The slackness
Of that light pink mouth told little. The eyes told of heavy care. . . .
But that was neither here nor there,
And nothing to a wage-paying mistress as should
Be getting her due whether life had been good
For her slave, or bad.
There it stood
In the door. They had never had
One in the house before.

But the Irishwoman had left!
A message had come.
Something about a murder at home.
A daughter's husband—"berserk," that was the phrase:
The dear man had "gone berserk"
And short work—
With a hammer—had been made
Of this daughter and her nights and days.
The Irishwoman (underpaid,
Mrs. Miles remembered with smiles),
Who was a perfect jewel, a red-faced trump,
A good old sort, a baker
Of rum cake, a maker
Of Mustard, would never return.
Mrs. Miles had begged the bewitched woman
To finish, at least, the biscuit blending,
To tarry till the curry was done,
To show some concern
For the burning soup, to attend to the tending
Of the tossed salad. "Inhuman,"
Patsy Houlihan had called Mrs. Miles.
"Inhuman." And "a fool."
And "a cool
One."
The Alert Agency had leafed through its files—
On short notice could offer
Only this dusky duffer
That now made its way to her kitchen and sat on her kitchen stool.

II

Her creamy child kissed by the black maid! square on the mouth!
World yelled, world writhed, world turned to light and rolled
Into her kitchen, nearly knocked her down.

Quotations, of course, from baby books were great
Ready armor; (but her animal distress
Wore, too and under, a subtler metal dress,
Inheritance of approximately hate).
Say baby shrieked to see his finger bleed,
Wished human humoring—there was a kind
Of unintimate love, a love more of the mind
To order the nebulousness of that need.
—This was the way to put it, this the relief.
This sprayed a honey upon marvelous grime.
This told it possible to postpone the reef.
Fashioned a huggable darling out of crime.
Made monster personable in personal sight
By cracking mirrors down the personal night.
Disgust crawled through her as she chased the theme.
She, quite supposing purity despoiled,
Committed to sourness, disordered, soiled,
Went in to pry the ordure from the cream.
Cooing, "Come." (Come out of the cannibal wilderness,
Dirt, dark, into the sun and bloomful air.
Return to freshness of your right world, wear
Sweetness again. Be done with beast, duress.)

Child with continuing cling issued his No in final fire,
Kissed back the colored maid,
Not wise enough to freeze or be afraid.
Conscious of kindness, easy creature bond.
Love had been handy and rapid to respond.

Heat at the hairline, heat between the bowels,
Examining seeming coarse unnatural scene,
She saw all things except herself serene:
Child, big black woman, pretty kitchen towels.

The Ballad of Rudolph Reed

Rudolph Reed was oaken.
His wife was oaken too.
And his two good girls and his good little man
Oakened as they grew.

"I am not hungry for berries.
I am not hungry for bread.
But hungry hungry for a house
Where at night a man in bed

"May never hear the plaster
Stir as if in pain.
May never hear the roaches
Falling like fat rain.

"Where never wife and children need
Go blinking through the gloom.
Where every room of many rooms
Will be full of room.

"Oh my home may have its east or west
Or north or south behind it.
All I know is I shall know it,
And fight for it when I find it."

It was in a street of bitter white
That he made his application.
For Rudolph Reed was oakener
Than others in the nation.

The agent's steep and steady stare
Corroded to a grin.
Why, you black old, tough old hell of a man,
Move your family in!

Nary a grin grinned Rudolph Reed,
Nary a curse cursed he,
But moved in his House. With his dark little wife,
And his dark little children three.

A neighbor would *look,* with a yawning eye
That squeezed into a slit.
But the Rudolph Reeds and the children three
Were too joyous to notice it.

For were they not firm in a home of their own
With windows everywhere
And a beautiful banistered stair
And a front yard for flowers and a back yard for grass?

The first night, a rock, big as two fists.
The second, a rock big as three.
But nary a curse cursed Rudolph Reed.
(Though oaken as man could be.)

The third night, a silvery ring of glass.
Patience ached to endure.
But he looked, and lo! small Mabel's blood
Was staining her gaze so pure.

Then up did rise our Rudolph Reed
And pressed the hand of his wife,
And went to the door with a thirty-four
And a beastly butcher knife.

He ran like a mad thing into the night.
And the words in his mouth were stinking.
By the time he had hurt his first white man
He was no longer thinking.

By the time he had hurt his fourth white man
Rudolph Reed was dead.
His neighbors gathered and kicked his corpse.
"Nigger—" his neighbors said.

Small Mabel whimpered all night long,
For calling herself the cause.
Her oak-eyed mother did no thing
But change the bloody gauze.

Malcolm X

FOR DUDLEY RANDALL

Original.
Ragged-round.
Rich-robust.

He had the hawk-man's eyes.
We gasped. We saw the maleness.
The maleness raking out and making guttural the air
and pushing us to walls.

And in a soft and fundamental hour
a sorcery devout and vertical
beguiled the world.

He opened us—
who was a key,

who was a man.

from *Riot*

A riot is the language of the unheard.
—MARTIN LUTHER KING

John Cabot, out of Wilma, once a Wycliffe,

all whitebluerose below his golden hair,
wrapped richly in right linen and right wool,
almost forgot his Jaguar and Lake Bluff;
almost forgot Grandtully (which is The
Best Thing That Ever Happened To Scotch); almost
forgot the sculpture at the Richard Gray
and Distelheim; the kidney pie at Maxim's,
the Grenadine de Boeuf at Maison Henri.

Because the Negroes were coming down the street.

Because the Poor were sweaty and unpretty
(not like Two Dainty Negroes in Winnetka)
and they were coming toward him in rough ranks.
In seas. In windsweep. They were black and loud.
And not detainable. And not discreet.

Gross. Gross. "*Que tu es grossier!*" John Cabot
itched instantly beneath the nourished white
that told his story of glory to the World.
"Don't let It touch me! the blackness! Lord!" he whispered
to any handy angel in the sky.

But, in a thrilling announcement, on It drove
and breathed on him: and touched him. In that breath
the fume of pig foot, chitterling and cheap chili,
malign, mocked John. And, in terrific touch, old
averted doubt jerked forward decently,
cried "Cabot! John! You are a desperate man,
and the desperate die expensively today."

John Cabot went down in the smoke and fire
and broken and blood, and he cried "Lord!
Forgive these nigguhs that know not what they do."

from *The Third Sermon on the Warpland*

Fire.
That is their way of lighting candles in the darkness.
A White Philosopher said
'It is better to light one candle than curse the darkness.'
These candles curse—
inverting the deeps of the darkness.

GUARD HERE, GUNS LOADED.
The young men run.
The children in ritual chatter
scatter upon
their Own and old geography.

The Law comes sirening across the town.

A woman is dead.
Motherwoman.
She lies among the boxes
(that held the haughty hats, the Polish sausages)
in newish, thorough, firm virginity
as rich as fudge is if you've had five pieces.
Not again shall she
partake of steak
on Christmas mornings, nor of nighttime
chicken and wine at Val Gray Ward's
nor say
of Mr. Beetley, Exit Jones, Junk Smith
nor neat New-baby Williams (man-to-many)
"He treat me right."

That was a gut gal.

"We'll do an us!" yells Yancey, a twittering twelve.
"Instead of your deathintheafternoon,
kill'em, bull!
kill'em, bull!"

The Black Philosopher blares
"I tell you, ex*haust*ive black integrity
would assure a blackless America. . . . "
Nine die, Sun-Times will tell
and will tell too
in small black-bordered oblongs *"Rumor? check it at 744-4111."*

An Aspect of Love, Alive in the Ice and Fire

LaBohem Brown

It is the morning of our love.

In a package of minutes there is this We.
How beautiful.
Merry foreigners in our morning,
we laugh, we touch each other,
are responsible props and posts.

A physical light is in the room.

Because the world is at the window
we cannot wonder very long.

You rise. Although
genial, you are in yourself again.
I observe
your direct and respectable stride.
You are direct and self-accepting as a lion
in African velvet. You are level, lean,
remote.

There is a moment in Camaraderie
when interruption is not to be understood.
I cannot bear an interruption.
This is the shining joy;
the time of not-to-end.

On the street we smile.
We go
in different directions
down the imperturbable street.

A. R. Ammons (1926-)

Ammons was born in North Carolina and attended Wake Forest College in that state, graduating with a bachelor of science degree. He served two years in the U.S. naval reserve and did graduate work at Berkeley. He tried being a business executive in the biological glass industry, but from 1964 on he has taught in the English Department at Cornell University. He, too, has been a Guggenheim fellow and has had an American Academy of Arts and Letters traveling fellowship.

He has published a number of volumes of poetry going back to 1955. In 1973 his *Collected Poems* won the National Book Award. His chief interests are the relationship of man to the natural world, the bond between nature and art. His poetry frequently deals with scientific and metaphysical concepts, and he is an exact observer. Many of his poems are reminiscient of William Carlos Williams in the use of short lines frequently arranged in triads. The body of Ammons' work is of very high quality, but it is interesting that few memorable lines, such as a Frost or a Yeats might write, jump out at, or linger with, the reader.

Mountain Liar

The mountains said they were
    tired of lying down
and wanted to know what
    I could do about
getting them off the ground

Well close your eyes I said
    and I'll see if I can
by seeing into your nature
    tell where you've been wronged
What do you think you want to do
    They said Oh fly

My hands are old
    and crippled keep no lyre
but if that is your true desire
    and conforms roughly
with your nature I said
    I don't see why
we shouldn't try
    to see something along that line

Hurry they said and snapped shut
    with rocky sounds their eyes
I closed mine and sure enough
    the whole range flew
gliding on interstellar ice

They shrieked with joy and peeked
as if to see below
but saw me as before there
foolish without my lyre
We haven't budged they said
You wood

Mechanism

Honor a going thing, goldfinch, corporation, tree,
morality: any working order,
animate or inanimate: it

has managed directed balance,
the incoming and outgoing energies are working right,
some energy left to the mechanism,

some ash, enough energy held
to maintain the order in repair,
assure further consumption of entropy,

expending energy to strengthen order:
honor the persisting reactor,
the container of change, the moderator: the yellow

bird flashes black wing-bars
in the new-leaving wild cherry bushes by the bay,
startles the hawk with beauty,

flitting to a branch where
flash vanishes into stillness,
hawk addled by the sudden loss of sight:

honor the chemistries, platelets, hemoglobin kinetics,
the light-sensitive iris, the enzymic intricacies
of control,

the gastric transformations, seed
dissolved to acrid liquors, synthesized into
chirp, vitreous humor, knowledge,

blood compulsion, instinct: honor the
unique genes,
molecules that reproduce themselves, divide into

sets, the nucleic grain transmitted
in slow change through ages of rising and falling form,
some cells set aside for the special work, mind

or perception rising into orders of courtship,
territorial rights, mind rising
from the physical chemistries

to guarantee that genes will be exchanged, male
and female met, the satisfactions cloaking a deeper
racial satisfaction:

heat kept by a feathered skin:
the living alembic, body heat maintained (bunsen
burner under the flask)

so the chemistries can proceed, reaction rates
interdependent, self-adjusting, with optimum
efficiency—the vessel firm, the flame

staying: isolated, contained reactions! the precise and
necessary worked out of random, reproducible,
the handiwork redeemed from chance, while the

goldfinch, unconscious of the billion operations
that stay its form, flashes, chirping (not a
great songster) in the bay cherry bushes wild of leaf.

Open

Exuberance: joy to the last
pained loss
and hunger of air:
life open, not decided on,
though decided in death:

the mind cannot be
rid
while it works
of remembered genitals
beautiful, dank, pliant,

of canyons, brush hills, pastures, streets,
unities and divisions,
meetings,

exact remembrance of liquid buttocks,
navel, ellipse of hand,

magnified territories of going down
and rising,
the thin tracing saliva line,

joy's configurations:

serendipity: the unexpected,
the
possible, the unembodied,
unevented:

the sun will burst: death
is certain: the future limited
nevertheless is
limitless: the white knotted

groin,
the finger describing
entrances!

the dark, warm with glowing awareness, the
hot dis-
missals of desire
until the last last tear of pain:

until the end nothing ends, lust
forward, rushing;
pillars of ice wet-bright in melt,
warm

with always-yielding joy: yes
yes
yes, the loose mouths hiss in the mornings of death.

Christmas Eve

When cold, I huddle up, foetal, cross
arms:
but in summer, sprawl:

secret is plain old
surface area,
decreased in winter, retaining: in summer no
limbs touching—
radiating:
everything is physical:

chemistry is physical:
electrical noumenal mind
is:
(I declare!)

put up Christmas tree this afternoon:
    fell
asleep in big chair: woke up at
3:12 and it
  was snowing outside, was white!

Christmas Eve tonight: Joseph
is looking for a place:
Mary smiles but
    her blood is singing:

    she will have to lie down:
  hay is warm:
some inns keep only
the public room warm: Mary

is thinking, Nice time
    to lie down,
good time to be brought down by this necessity:

I better get busy
and put the lights on—can't find
  extension cord:
Phyllis will be home, will say, The
tree doesn't have any lights!
I have tiny winking lights, too:
    she will like
them: she went to see her mother:

my mother is dead: she is
deep in the ground, changed: if she
rises, dust will blow all over the place and
  she will stand there shining,
smiling: she will feel good:
she will want
to go home and fix supper: first she
    will hug me:

an actual womb bore Christ,
divinity into the world:
  I hope there are births to lie down to
back
to divinity
since we all must die away from here:

I better look for the cord:
we're going to
    the Plaza for dinner:
tonight, a buffet: tomorrow there, we'll
  have a big Christmas
dinner:

before I fell asleep, somebody
phoned, a Mr. Powell: he asked
if I wanted to
sell my land
in Mays Landing: I don't know:
I have several pieces, wonder
if he wants them all,
wonder what I ought to quote:

earth: so many acres of earth:
own:
how we own who are owned! well,
anyway, he won't care
about that—said he would
call back Monday: I will
tell him something then:
it's nearly Christmas, now:
they are all going into the city:
some have sent ahead for reservations:
the inns are filling up:

Christ was born
in a hay barn among the warm cows and the
donkeys kneeling down: with Him divinity
swept into the flesh
and made it real.

Still

I said I will find what is lowly
and put the roots of my identity
down there:
each day I'll wake up

and find the lowly nearby,
a handy focus and reminder,
a ready measure of my significance,
the voice by which I would be heard,
the wills, the kinds of selfishness
I could
freely adopt as my own:

but though I have looked everywhere,
I can find nothing
to give myself to:
everything is

magnificent with existence, is in
surfeit of glory:
nothing is diminished,
nothing has been diminished for me:

I said what is more lowly than the grass:
    ah, underneath,
    a ground-crust of dry-burnt moss:
    I looked at it closely
and said this can be my habitat: but
nestling in I
found
    below the brown exterior
    green mechanisms beyond intellect
awaiting resurrection in rain: so I got up

and ran saying there is nothing lowly in the universe:
I found a beggar:
he had stumps for legs: nobody was paying
him any attention: everybody went on by:
    I nestled in and found his life:
there, love shook his body like a devastation:
I said
    though I have looked everywhere
    I can find nothing lowly
    in the universe:

I whirled through transfigurations up and down,
transfigurations of size and shape and place:
    at one sudden point came still,
    stood in wonder:
moss, beggar, weed, tick, pine, self, magnificent
    with being!

Belief

for JFK

1

drums gather and humble us beyond escape,
propound the single, falling fact:
time, suspended between memory and present,
hangs unmeasured, empty

2

erect,
disciplined by cadence into direction, the soldier
obeys the forms of rumor:

the riderless horse,
restive with the pressure of held flight,
tosses the hung bit,
worries the soldier's tameless arm—
sidling, prances the energy out

3

ahead, unalterable, the fact proceeds,
and the bit holds:
the fire-needle bites,
training the head on course

4

the light, determined rattle
of the caisson
breaking into sunlight
through the crystal black ribbons of trees!
the slack traces,
weightlessness at the shoulders of horses!

5

if we could break free
and run this knowledge out,
burst this energy of grief
through a hundred countrysides!
if bleak through the black night
we could outrun
this knowledge into a different morning!

6

belief, light as a drumrattle,
touches us and lifts us up to tears.

Zone

I spent the day
differentiating
and wound up
with nothing
whole to keep:

tree came apart from tree,
oak from maple, oak
from oak, leaf from leaf,
mesophyll cell

from cell
and toward dark
I got lost between
cytoplasm's grains
and vacuoles:

the next day began
otherwise: tree
became plant, plant
and animal became
life: life & rock,
matter: that
took up most of
the morning: after
noon, matter began
to pulse, shoot, to
vanish in and out of
energy and

energy's invisible
swirls confused, surpassed
me: from that edge
I turned back,
strict with limitation,
to my world's
bitter acorns
and sweet branch water.

Poetics

I look for the way
things will turn
out spiralling from a center,
the shape
things will take to come forth in

so that the birch tree white
touched black at branches
will stand out
wind-glittering
totally its apparent self:

I look for the forms
things want to come as

from what black wells of possibility,
how a thing will
unfold:

not the shape on paper—though
that, too—but the
uninterfering means on paper:

not so much looking for the shape
as being available
to any shape that may be
summoning itself
through me
from the self not mine but ours.

Guitar Recitativos

1

I know you love me, baby
I know it by the way you carry on around here certain times of the day
    & night
I can make the distinction between the willing and the unrefusable
That's not what I'm talking about
That's not what I need
What I mean is could you just peel me a few of those grapes over there
I want to lie here cool and accumulate . . .
Oh about half a bunch
That's what I need
        —flick out those little seed
—Just drop 'em in here one at a time
I'm not going anyplace, baby, not today
Relax—sneak the skin off a few of those grapes for me, will you?

2

Baby, you been stomping round on my toes so long
They breaking out in black and blue hyacinths,
Well-knit forget-me-nots
Geraniums are flopping out over the tops of my shoes
tendril leaves coming out along the edges of my shoelaces

Gladioli are steering out of the small of my back
  strumming their cool stalks up my spine
Zinnias radiating from the crock of my neck
and petunias swinging down bells from my earlobes
All this stomping around on me you been doing, baby,
I'm gonna break out in a colorful reaction
I'm gonna wade right through you
  with the thorns of all these big red roses

3

I can tell you what I think of your beauty, baby,
You have it, it's keen and fast, there's this
glittery sword whipping about your head all day
and, baby, you make people snap—you condescend

and a surprised little hearth splatters or you turn your
cold head away and a tiny freeze kills a few
cells in some man's brain—I mean, baby, you
may be kind but your beauty sweetie is such

many a man would run himself through for
hating your guts every minute that he died for you

4

I'm tired of the you-and-me thing
I am for more research into the nature of the amorous bond
the discovery of catalysts for speeding-up, wearing out, and getting it
    over with
or for slowling it down to allow long intervals of looseness

Baby, there are times when the mixture becomes immiscible
and other times we get so stirred up I can't tell
whether I'm you or me
and then I have this fear of a surprising reaction in which
we both turn into something else

powdery or gaseous or slightly metallic
What I mean is this whole relationship is, lacking further
knowledge, risky: white there's still time, why
don't you get yourself together and I'll

get myself together and then we'll sort of shy out
of each other's gravitational field, unstring the
electromagnetism and then sort of just drop this
whole orientation baby

5

You come in and I turn on:
freon purrs and the
refrigerator breaks out with hives of ice
The Westinghouse portable electric fan flushes
    my papers all over the room
The waffle-iron whacks down sizzling imaginary waffles
One paper glues iself and billows to the back of the fan
    my nerves nervous as newspapers

I tell you you are a walking calamity
And when you sit down there is hardly less activity
The alarm clock breaks out raging its held cry
and the oven in the kitchen sets itself for broil

I mean the gas-jet in the incinerator bloops on
and frankly the mechanisms in my legs—I hope you
never find out—jerk:
Oh, beauty, beauty is so disturbingly nice.

The Put-Down Come On

You would think I'd be a specialist in contemporary
literature: novels, short stories, books of poetry,
my friends write many of them: I don't read much
and some drinks are too strong for me: my empty-headed

contemplation is still where the ideas of permanence
and transience fuse in a single body, ice, for example,
or a leaf: green pushes white up the slope: a maple
leaf gets the wobbles in a light wind and comes loose

half-ready: where what has always happened and what
has never happened before seem for an instant reconciled:
that takes up most of my time and keeps me uninformed:
but the slope, after maybe a thousand years, may spill

and the ice have a very different look withdrawing into
the lofts of cold: only a little of that kind of
thinking flashes through: but turning the permanent also
into the transient takes up all the time that's left.

The Eternal City

After the explosion or cataclysm, that big
display that does its work but then fails
out with destructions, one is left with the

pieces: at first, they don't look very valuable,
but nothing sizable remnant around for
gathering the senses on, one begins to take
an interest, to sort out, to consider closely
what will do and won't, matters having become
not only small but critical: bulbs may have been

uprooted: they should be eaten if edible, or
got back in the ground: what used to be garages,
even the splinters, should be collected for

fires: some unusually deep holes or cleared
woods may be turned to water supplies or
sudden fields: ruinage is hardly ever a

pretty sight but it must when splendor goes
accept into itself piece by piece all the old
perfect human visions, all the old perfect loves.

Adrienne Rich (1929-)

She was born in Baltimore and educated at Radcliffe. The same year that she graduated from college (1951) she won the Yale Series of Younger Poets contest. In 1953 she married Alfred Conrad. She is the mother of three sons. She has traveled extensively, taught at a number of colleges, among them Swarthmore and Columbia, and has received various honors, such as a Guggenheim award and a Bollingen Foundation grant. She now lives in New York City.

Rich's early poetry has verbal brilliance, but is quite conventional in form. From about 1963 she began to rely much less on rhyme and regular meter and her subject matter became less personal, more concerned with questioning established values, probing what it means to be a woman in our society. During the 1960s she was engaged in antiwar activities and wrote with a fresh urgency. In 1970 her husband died and in a letter written in 1972 she says her goal is "breaking down the artificial barriers between private and public, between Vietnam and the lover's bed, between the deepest images we carry out of our dreams and the most daylight events 'out in the world.' This is the intention and longing behind everything I write."

Landscape of the Star

The silence of the year. This hour the streets
Lie empty, and the clash of bells is scattered
Out to the edge of stars. I heard them tell
Morning's first change and clang the people home
From crèche and scented aisle. Come home, come home,
I heard the bells of Christmas call and die.

This Christmas morning, in the stony streets
Of an unaccustomed city, where the gas
Quivers against the darkly-shuttered walls,
I walk, my breath a veil upon the cold,
No longer sick for home nor hunted down
By faces loved, by gate or sill or tree
That once I used to wreathe in red and silver
Under the splintered incense of the fir.

I think of those inscrutables who toiled,
Heavy and brooding in their camel-train,
Across the blue-wrapped stretches. Home behind,
Kingdoms departed from, the solemn journey
Their only residence: the starlit hour,
The landscape of the star, their time and place.

O to be one of them, and feel the sway
Of rocking cannel through the Judaean sand,—
Ride, wrapped in swathes of damask and of silk,

Hear the faint ring of jewel in silver mesh
Starring the silence of the plain; and hold
With rigid fingers curved as in oblation
The golden jar of myrrh against the knees.

To ride thus, bearing gifts to a strange land,
To a strange King; nor think of fear and envy,
Being so bemused by starlight of one star,
The long unbroken journey, that all questions
Sink like the lesser lights behind the hills;
Think neither of the end is sight, nor all
That lies behind, but dreamlessly to ride,
Traveller at one with travelled countryside.

How else, since for those Magi and their train
The palaces behind have ceased to be
Home, and the home they travel toward is still
But rumor stoking fear in Herod's brain?
What else for them but this, since never more
Can courts and states receive them as they were,
Nor have the trampled earth, the roof of straw
Received the kings as they are yet to be?

The bells are silent, silenced in my mind
As on the dark. I walk, a foreigner,
Upon this night that calls all travellers home,
The prodigal forgiven, and the breach
Mended for this one feast. Yet all are strange
To their own ends, and their beginnings now
Cannot contain them. Once-familiar speech
Babbles in wayward dialect of a dream.

Our gifts shall bring us home: not to beginnings
Nor always to the destination named
Upon our setting-forth. Our gifts compel,
Master our ways and lead us in the end
Where we are most ourselves; whether at last
To Solomon's gaze or Sheba's silken knees
Or winter pastures underneath a star,
Where angels spring like starlight in the trees.

The Trees

The trees inside are moving out into the forest,
the forest that was empty all these days
where no bird could sit
no insect hide

no sun bury its feet in shadow
the forest that was empty all these nights
will be full of trees by morning.

All night the roots work
to disengage themselves from the cracks
in the veranda floor.
The leaves strain toward the glass
small twigs stiff with exertion
long-cramped boughs shuffling under the roof
like newly discharged patients
half-dazed, moving
to the clinic doors.

I sit inside, doors open to the veranda
writing long letters
in which I scarcely mention the departure
of the forest from the house.
The night is fresh, the whole moon shines
in a sky still open
the smell of leaves and lichen
still reaches like a voice into the rooms.
My head is full of whispers
which tomorrow will be silent.

Listen. The glass is breaking.
The trees are stumbling forward
into the night. Winds rush to meet them.
The moon is broken like a mirror,
its pieces flash now in the crown
of the tallest oak.

5:30 A.M.

Birds and periodic blood.
Old recapitulations.
The fox, panting, fire-eyed,
gone to earth in my chest.
How beautiful we are,
he and I, with our auburn
pelts, our trails of blood,
our miracle escapes,
our whiplash panic flogging us on
to new miracles!
They've supplied us with pills
for bleeding, pills for panic.
Wash them down the sink.
This is truth, then:

dull needle groping in the spinal fluid,
weak acid in the bottom of the cup,
foreboding, foreboding.
No one tells the truth about truth,
thats it's what the fox
sees from his scuffled burrow:
dull-jawed, onrushing
killer, being that
inanely single-minded
will have our skins at last.

Continuum

Waking thickheaded by crow's light
I see the suitcase packed
for your early plane; nothing to do
but follow the wristwatch hands
round to the hour. Life is like money
—you said, finishing the brandy from the cracked
plastic bathroom cup last night—
no use except for what you can get with it.
Yet something wants us delivered up
alive, whatever it is,
that causes me to edge the slatted blind
soundlessly up, leaving you
ten minutes' more sleep, while I look
shivering, lucidifying, down
at that street where the poor are already getting started
and that poster streaking the opposite wall
with the blurred face of a singer whose songs
money can't buy nor air contain
someone yet unloved, whose voice
I may never hear, but go on hoping
to hear, tonight, tomorrow, someday,
as I go on hoping to feel
tears of mercy in the of course impersonal rain.

From *Leaflets*

2.

Your face
                    stretched like a mask
                                                            begins to tear
as you speak of Che Guevara

Bolivia, Nanterre
I'm too young to be your mother
you're too young to be my brother

your tears are not political
they are water, burning
as the tears of Telemachus
burned

Over Spanish Harlem the moon
swells up, a fire balloon
fire gnawing the edge
of this crushed-up newspaper

now
the bodies come whirling
coal-black, ash-white
out of torn windows
and the death columns blacken
whispering
Who'd choose this life?

We're fighting for a slash of recognition,
a piercing to the pierced heart.
Tell me what you are going through—

but the attention flickers
and will ficker
a matchflame in poison air
a thread, a hair of light
sum of all answer
to the *Know that I exist!* of all existing things.

Night Watch

And now, outside, the walls
of black flint, eyeless.
How pale is sleep you lie.
Love: my love is just a breath
blown on the pane and dissolved.
Everything, even you,
cries silently for help, the web
of the spider is ripped with rain,
the geese fly on into the black cloud.
What can I do for you?
what can I do for you?
Can the touch of a finger mend
what a finger's toudh has broken?
Blue-eyed now, yellow-haired,

I stand in my old nightmare
beside the track, while you,
and over and over and always you
plod into the deathcars.
Sometimes you smile at me
and I—I smile back at you.
How sweet the odor of the station-master's roses!
How pure, how poster-like the colors of this dream.

I Dream I'm the Death of Orpheus

I am walking rapidly through striations of light and dark thrown under an arcade.

I am a woman in the prime of life, with certain powers
and those powers severely limited
by authorities whose faces I rarely see.
I am a woman in the prime of life
driving her dead poet in a black Rolls-Royce
through a landscape of twilight and thorns.
A woman with a certain mission
which if obeyed to the letter will leave her intact.
A woman with the nerves of a panther
a woman with contacts among Hell's Angels
a woman feeling the fullness of her powers
at the precise moment when she must not use them
a woman sworn to lucidity
who sees through the mayhem, the smoky fires
of these underground streets
her dead poet learning to walk backward against the wind
on the wrong side of the mirror

Our Whole Life

Our whole life a translation
the permissible fibs

and now a knot of lies
eating at itself to get undone

Words bitten thru words

meanings burnt-off like paint
under the blowtorch

All those dead letters
rendered into the oppressor's language

Trying to tell the doctor where it hurts
like the Algerian
who has walked from his village, burning

his whole body a cloud of pain
and there are no words for this

expect himself

A Valediction Forbidding Mourning

My swirling wants. Your frozen lips.
The grammar turned and attacked me.
Themes, written under duress.
Emptiness of the notations.

They gave me a drug that slowed the healing of wounds.

I want you to see this before I leave:
the experience of repetition as death
the failure of criticism to locate the pain
the poster in the bus that said:
my bleeding is under control.

A red plant in a cemetery of plastic wreaths.

A last attempt: the language is a dialect called metaphor.
These images go unglossed: hair, glacier, flashlight.
When I think of a landscape I am thinking of a time.
When I talk of taking a trip I mean forever.
I could say: those mountains have a meaning
but further than that I could not say.

To do something very common, in my own way.

Merced

Fantasies of old age:
they have rounded us up
in a rest-camp for the outworn.
Somewhere is some dustbowl
a barbed-wire cantonment
of low-cost dustcolored prefab
buildings, smelling of shame
and hopeless incontinence
identical clothes of disposable
paper, identical rations
of chemically flavored food

Death in order, by gas,
hypodermics daily
to neutralize despair
So I imagine my world
in my seventieth year alive
and outside the barbed wire
a purposeless exchange
of consciousness for the absence
of pain. We will cal this life.

Yet only last summer I
burned my feet in the sand
of that valley traced by the thread
of the cold quick river Merced
watered by plummets of white
When I swam, my body ached
from the righteous cold
when I lay back floating the jays
flittered from pine to pine
and the shade moved hour by hour
across El Capitan
Our wine cooled in the water
and I watched my sons, half-men
half-children, testing their part
in a world almost archaic
so precious by this time
that merely to step in pure water
or stare into clear air
is to feel a spasm of pain.

For weeks now a rage
has possessed my body, driving
now out upon men and women
now inward upon myself
Walking Amsterdam Avenue
I find myself in tears
without knowing which thought
forced water to my eyes
To speak to another human
becomes a risk
I think of Norman Morrison
the Buddhists of Saigon
the black teacher last week
who put himself to death
to waken guilt in hearts
too numb to get the message
in a world masculinity made
unfit for women or men
Taking off in a plane

I look down at the city
which meant life to me, not death
and think that somewhere there
a cold center, composed
of pieces of human beings
metabolized, restructured
by a process they do not feel
is spreading in our midst
and taking over our minds
a thing that feels neither guilt
nor rage: that is unable
to hate, therefore to love.

Rape

There is a cop who is both prowler and father:
he comes from your block, grew up with your brothers,
had certain ideals.
You hardly know him in his boots and silver badge,
on horseback, one hand touching his gun.

You hardly know him but you have to get to know him:
he has access to machinery that could kill you.
He and his stallion clop like warlords among the trash,
his ideals stand in the air, a frozen cloud
from between his unsmiling lips.

And so, when the time comes, you have to turn to him,
the maniac's sperm still greasing your thighs,
your mind whirling like crazy. You have to confess
to him, you are guilty of the crime
of having been forced.

And you see his blue eyes, the blue eyes of all the family
whom you used to know, grow narrow and glisten,
his hand types out the details
and he wants them all
but the hysteria in your voice pleases him best.

You hardly know him but now he thinks he knows you:
he has taken down your worst moment
on a machine and filed it in a file.
He knows, or thinks he knows, how much you imagined;
he knows, or thinks he knows, what you secretly wanted.

He has access to machinery that could get you put away;
and if, in the sickening light of the precinct,
and if, in the sickening light of the precinct,
your details sound like a portrait of your confessor,
will you swallow, will you deny them, will you lie your way home?

Glossary

accentual verse Verse in which the number of stressed syllables in each line determines the rhythm. The number of unstressed syllabes may vary greatly, as in the Old English *Beowulf*.

alexandrine A line of iambic verse with six feet. May be used in a whole poem, or as an occasional variation of other lines, in particular the pentameter.

allegory A narrative in which persons and objects are identified with a significance existing outside the story. For example, a tale about a plane in which the pilot stands for God, the flight for the journey to heaven, etc.

alliteration The repetition of the initial *stressed* sounds in two or more words. For example, lake / delight. Usually any stressed vowel can alliterate with any other stressed vowel. Systemic alliteration was characteristic of Old English poetry, and has been periodically revived. Alliteration is also used a good deal as an occasional means of acoustic enrichment in a poem.

allusion Reference to some person, event, work of literature, etc., usually of historical or cultural interest. Thus one may say "He is a Hamlet," and suggest a whole cluster of qualities—indecision, morbid introspection, fierce courage.

ambiguity Several valid meanings existing at the same time. Sometimes associated with the *pun,* q.v.

anacrusis A way of varying a meter by adding an extra unstressed syllable at the beginning of the line.

analogy A form of comparison in which something is compared to another thing sharing qualities with it. Thus a passionate lover might be likened to the sun.

anapest A meter in which each foot consists of two unstressed syllables followed by a stressed syllable (⏑ ⏑ ⁄). Most often used for light or fast-verse.

apostrophe Adressing an absent person as though present, or a quality or thing as though it were alive.

approximate rhyme Various kinds of partial rhyme, used for whole poems or as an occasional variation of pure rhyme. See *assonance, consonance, slant rhyme*. See also page 113.

archetypal approach A type of literary criticism (often inspired by Jung). As described by Jung, an archetype is a "primordial image" in the "collective unconscious" of humanity, and frequently finds expression in myths, religions, fantasies, and dreams, as well as in literature. (The works of Joseph Campbell and Jessie Weston are a good introduction to this approach.) Some archetypal themes are death and rebirth, the earthly paradise, the merciless male hero, the *femme fatale*, the scapegoat figure, etc. The use of archetypal themes often seems to give a work of literature a particular kind of resonance and lasting power.

assonance A kind of approximate rhyme in which the stressed vowels are repeated, but the following consonants are not. Example: nose / loaf.

ballad A narrative poem, shorter than an epic, and often of anonymous authorship. Usually very direct in style, impersonal, concerned with such elementary themes as war, unhappy love, and the supernatural. English and Scottish ballads are mostly in four-line stanzas, sometimes with a refrain.

blank verse Unrhymed iambic pentameter. Common in dramatic or meditative poems.

cacophony Dissonant or harsh combinations of sounds. For example, the cluster of consonants in "ne*xt str*eet."

catalexis A metrical variation which consists of omitting the final unstressed syllable in a line of verse. The term is also sometimes loosely applied to omitting initial unstressed syllables.

cesura A pause in a line of verse. Often, though not always, indicated by a punctuation mark.

cliché An expression that has become trite from overuse.

common meter Iambic tetrameter alternating with iambic trimeter. Much used in hymns as well as poetry in general.

conceit An elaborate, extended metaphor. Thus a lover might compare his beloved to a fortress, carefully listing all her methods of defense.

connotation The associations, flavor, or aura of a word, as distinguished from its literal meaning. See *denotation*.

consonance A kind of approximate rhyme in which the consonant before a stressed vowel and all sounds after the vowel rhyme, but the vowel itself does not. For example mate / meet, deceive / save.

couplet A stanza consisting of two lines rhyming with each other. Also, two lines rhyming together and part of a longer form, like the concluding couplet in a Shakespearean sonnet.

criticism The interpretation and evaluation of works of literature. For some of the most important "schools," see *traditional*, *formalistic*, *psychological*, and *archetypal* approaches.

dactyl A metrical foot consisting of a stressed syllable followed by two unstressed syllables (´ ˘ ˘). Usually produces a slow, lingering effect.

denotation The literal or specific meaning of a word. The denotation of *skunk* is a particular animal: the connotation (q.v.) is an unpleasant person —"He's a skunk."

diction Choice of words by the poet. This can help determine the level of formality, the general tone of the poem, etc.

dimeter A line with two metrical feet.

dramatic monologue A poem in which a speaker reveals himself by his words at some dramatic or decisive moment in his life. Several examples are included in the chapter on Browning.

double (duple) meter Meter in which each foot consists of two syllables. For example, *iamb*, *trochee*, q.v.

double rhyme Rhyme in which two syllables rhyme (dreaming / seeming), the last being unstressed. Often called feminine rhyme.

elegy Meditative poem or lamentation, usually for someone dead.

end-stopped line Line of verse with a natural pause at the end, usually indicated by a punctuation mark.

English sonnet See *Shakespearean sonnet*.

enjambment See *run-on line.*

epic Long narrative poem, elevated in tone, usually about the heroes of a people.

euphony Pleasant combination of sounds.

falling meter Meter in which the first syllable of a foot is stressed. See *dactyl, trochee.*

feminine rhyme See *double rhyme.*

figurative language Various ways of using language in a nonliteral fashion. Usually involves some kind of comparison, explicit or implied. For some of the more frequent types, see *allegory, image, metaphor, metonymy, personification, simile, symbol.*

foot Basic "building block" of a metrical line. Usually consists of one stressed syllable, and one or two unstressed ones. The most common feet in English poetry are: *anapest, dactyl, iamb, trochee,* q.v.

formalistic approach A type of literary criticism, associated with the so-called New Critics (Allen Tate, Cleanth Brooks, Robert Penn Warren, John Crowe Ransom, etc). They emphasize that a poem should be studied as an autonomous work of art. The biography and conscious intentions of the poet are not the central considerations. Each poem must "stand on its own feet" and be explored as though its authorship were unknown. Formalistic critics have produced many detailed explications of poem in recent decades.

free verse A loose term for poetry not written in "metrical" lines. Differs from prose by being divided into lines. A sense of rhythm can be created by rhythmic cadences, pauses, repetitive phrases, etc. May be rhymed, but usually rhyme is incidental if used at all.

French forms Various poetic forms created in the Middle Ages and revived in the late Victorian period. All have complicated and strict rhyme schemes. Examples: villanelle, ballade, sestina.

haiku Unrhymed Japanese poem of three lines, with five syllables in first and last, and seven in the middle line.

half rhyme See *approximate rhyme.*

heroic couplet Two lines of iambic pentatmeter rhyming together.

heptameter A seven-foot line of verse.

hexameter A six-foot line of verse.

iamb A metrical foot consisting of an unstressed syllable followed by a stressed syllable (˘ ˊ).

image, imagery Loosely and broadly used, but in general suggests anything in a poem that arouses the senses—sight, taste, sound, and the like. May be combined with other figures of speech, such as the metaphor, as in "My love is a garden of delights."

imagism A poetic movement in England and America between 1909 and 1917. It was a revolt against the often blurred and sentimental poetry of the late nineteenth century. Imagism usually involved free verse, and emphasized the use of common language, freedom to choose any subject for a poem, and a fondness for hard, precise images. As an organized movement, it was short-lived, but its principles have profoundly influenced the course of modern poetry.

imperfect rhyme See *approximate rhyme.*

irony Verbal irony suggests the opposite of what is said, although sometimes without denying the literal meaning of the latter. Dramatic irony is the contrast between a speaker's words and what the author (and reader) know. For example, Oedipus, not knowing he killed his father, vows vengence on the murderer. Irony of situation involves a contrast between an actual situtation and what would be appropriate—for example, an artist seeking to flee the artistic world, and finding his main rival in the hotel next to his.

Italian sonnet See *Petrarchan sonnet.*

lyric Originally, a poem written to be sung to the lyre. Now loosely used for a short poem expressing the feelings and thoughts of a single speaker, usually the poet.

masculine rhyme See *single rhyme.*

mask A role or persona assumed by a poet in a particular poem. For example, a sixty-year old poet may, in a poem, try to enter the thoughts of a teen-age girl and express her feelings, putting his own sensibility strictly aside for the moment. See pages 133-35.

metaphor An implied comparison between two unlike objects. For example, "He is a strong tower." Note the absence of "like."

meter Often used interchangeably with *rhythm*, but the latter is the broader term, and can be applied to prose as well as verse. Strictly, meter in English poetry is a way or organizing a line of poetry by having a certain number of "feet" of a particular kind.

metonymy A figure of speech in which a part represents the whole. For example, "board" as a way of indicating the food as well as the table.

mock-heroic Use of elevated, heroic style for a humble or commonplace subject; the object is usually humor or ridicule.

monometer Line of metrical verse consisting of one foot.

octometer line of metrical verse consisting of eight feet.

ode A poem usually of some length, frequently with a complex stanzaic form, and concerned with a serious or elevated theme.

onomatopoeia Words that more or less sound like what they express. For example, splash, hiss, cock-a-doodle-doo.

orthographical rhyme "Eye rhymes." For example, home / come.

ottava rima Stanza form used by many poets. Consists of eight lines of iambic pentameter, rhyming *abababcc*.

oxymoron A figure of speech in which contradictory terms are combined for wit, emphasis, or paradox. For example, "an honest shoplifter."

paradox A statement that at first glance seems self-contradictory, but which makes sense on another level. For example, G. K. Chesterton's remark that nothing fails like success.

paraphrase A poem rewriten in prose form to bring out the meaning more clearly.

pentameter A five-foot line of verse.

personna See *mask*.

Petrarchan sonnet Also called the Italian sonnet. A fourteen-line poem, introduced into English shortly before the time of Shakespeare. Written in iambic pentameter. First eight lines (the octave) rhyme *abbaabba*. The last six lines (the sestet) usually rhyme *cdcdcd* or *cdecde*, though other schemes are possible.

personification Speaking of lifeless or abstract objects as though they were alive.

phychological approach A type of literary criticism in which psychological insights (often, but not always, Freudian) are applied to the study of literature. This can involve the recognition of psychological processes dramatized in literary works—for example, the Oedipus complex in the relation of Hamlet and his mother. At other times, the psychological critic finds in the psychological circumstances of an author's life an explanation for the kind of writing he did—for example, the prim, bachelor life of a mathematics teacher (Lewis Carroll) inspires a fantasy escape, *Alice in Wonderland.*

pun A play on words, often used for serious purposes in poetry to suggest unsuspected relations. See Donne's poem on page 17 as an example.

pyrrhic A metrical foot consisting of two unstressed syllables (˘ ˘). Sometimes used as a variation for other metrical feet, but of course a whole line cannot be written in pyrrhics.

quatrain A four-line stanza, section of poem, or poem.

refrain A word, phrase, line, or group of lines repeated at regular or irregular intervals in a poem.

rhythm A term often loosely interchanged with *meter*, q.v. Rhythm is the broader term, suggesting the whole cadence and flow of language rather than a strict division into metrical feet.

rhyme In the strict sense, correspondence in the stressed vowels and all following sounds in two or more words—cat / hat, seeing / being, comical / astronomical, etc. There are also many kinds of *approximate rhyme*, q.v.

rime riche Rhyme in which the sounds are identical, but the meanings different. For example, bear / bare.

rime royal Seven-line stanza written in iambic pentameter and rhyming *ababbcc.*

rising meter Meter in which each metrical foot ends on a stressed syllable. See *anapest* and *iamb*.

run-on line A line of verse having no natural pause at the end of the line. Also called enjambment.

scansion Analyzing the metrical pattern of a line of verse.

sentimentality Emotion for the sake of emotion; overdoing it.

Shakespearean sonnet Actually invented by Surrey, and also called the English sonnet. Written in fourteen lines of iambic pentameter, with rhyme scheme of *ababcdcdefefgg*. See also *Petrarchan sonnet*.

simile A comparison involving the use of a work such as *like*. "He is like a strong tower."

single rhyme Rhyme involving only one syllable in each word. For example, rain / pain, defend / bend. Also called masculine rhyme.

slant rhyme A term sometimes applied to a kind of approximate rhyme, in which the stressed vowels do not rhyme, but the following consonants do: frog / big, last / must.

sonnet See *Petrarchan sonnet* and *Shakespearean sonnet*.

Spenserian stanza A nine-line stanza invented by Edmund Spenser and used by many subsequent poets. All the lines are iambic pentameter with the exception of the last, which is iambic hexameter. The rhyme scheme is: *ababbcbcc*.

spondee A metrical foot consisting of two stressed syllables (´ ´). Used as an occasional variation for other feet, though of course a whole line could rarely be written in spondees.

stanza A specific number of lines of verse with a definite metrical pattern of some kind.

stock response Conventional reaction to particular subject matter. An inexperienced reader may automatically respond positively to a mention of mother love or country in a poem and react negatively to a poem dealing with an "unpoetic" subject like the city dump.

stress The force with which a syllable is spoken. Most English words with two or more syllables have one syllable pronounced more vigorously than the others. The contrast between stressed and unstressed syllables is basic to the English system of metrical feet.

syllabic verse A kind of verse in which the sense of rhythm is created by a particular number of syllables in the line, rather than a pattern of stressed and unstressed syllables. The norm in French poetry, syllabic verse is rarer in English, though Marianne Moore, Dylan Thomas, and W. H. Auden have created successful poems using it.

symbol Something that has a broader or deeper meaning than just itself. In Frost's "Stopping by Woods on a Snowy Evening" (page 176) the woods remains a woods, but it also suggests sleep, perhaps death.

synecdoche The use of a part for the whole, the whole for a part, etc. For example, "a hundred winters" instead of "a hundred years," or "the scarlet year" for autumn.

tercet A three-line poem, stanza, or part of a stanza.

terza rima A stanza form, used by Dante and many subsequent poets, in which the first and third lines rhyme, and the second line rhymes with the first and third lines of the next stanza. Thus each stanza is linked to the next.

tetrameter A four-foot line of verse.

texture A term sometimes applied to the individual specific details, images, words, and the like, of a poem, when these are examined *apart* from the overall structure of the poem.

theme The fundamental attitude or idea presented in a poem. Not to be confused with subject matter. For example, Yeats' "Sailing to Byzantium" (page 153) has for its subject the city of Byzantium, but its theme is youth and old age, the body and the spirit, nature and art, etc.

tone The attitude toward the subject matter of a poem, as expressed by the poet or some character created by the poet. It may be light or serious, flippant, whimsical, calm or impassioned, etc.

traditional approach A type of literary criticism in which great attention is paid to historical factors, such as the period when the author lived, the circumstances of his life, the public events and intellectual trends of his period. Often the dominant ideas of the author's work are analyzed in detail. The emphasis is sometimes on the "message" more than on the fine points of aesthetics.

trimeter A three-foot line of metrical verse.

triple meter A metrical foot that has three syllables. See *anapest* and *dactyl.*

triple rhyme Rhyme in which three syllables rhyme. For example, easily / breezily. Most often used in light verse.

trochee Metrical foot consisting of a stressed syllable followed by an unstressed one. (ˊ˘).

vers de société Light verse, usually elegant and witty.

verse Often loosely used as a synonym for poetry, but strictly it applies to a poem in which there is a definite metrical pattern, such as the kind that can be expressed in terms of metrical feet.

Credits and Acknowledgments

A. R. AMMONS. "Mountain Lion," "Mechanism," "Open," "Christmas Eve," "Still," "Belief," "Zone," "Poetics," "Guitar Recitativos," "The Put-Down Come on," "The Eternal City." Reprinted from *Collected Poems,* 1951-1971, by A. R. Ammons. By permission of W.W. Norton & Company, Inc. Copyright © 1972 A. R. Ammons.

W. H. AUDEN. "For the Perpetual Excuse," excerpts from "For the Time Being." Copyright 1944 and renewed 1972 by W.H. Auden. Reprinted from *Collected Longer Poems,* by W.H. Auden, by permission of Random House, Inc. "O Where Are You Going?," "Consider." Copyright 1934 and renewed 1962 by W.H. Auden. Reprinted from *Collected Shorter Poems* 1927-1957, by W.H. Auden, by permission of Random House, Inc. "Schoolchildren," "Musee des Beaux Arts," "In Memory of W.B. Yeats." Copyright 1940 and renewed 1968 by W.H. Auden. Reprinted from *Collected Shorter Poems* 1927-1957, by W.H. Auden, by permission of Random House, Inc. "Macao." Copyright 1945 and renewed 1973 by W. H. Auden. Reprinted from *Collected Shorter Poems* 1927-1957, by W.H. Auden, by permission of Random House, Inc. "An Island Cemetery." Copyright © 1960 by W.H. Auden. Reprinted from *Collected Shorter Poems* 1927-1957, by permission of Random House, Inc. "The Shield of Achilles." Copyright 1952 by W.H. Auden. Reprinted from *Collected Shorter Poems* 1927-1957, by permission of Random House, Inc.

WILLIAM BLAKE. The poems by William Blake are from *The Poetry and Prose of William Blake,* edited by D. V. Erdman. Copyright © 1965 by David V. Erdman and Harold Bloom. Used by permission of Doubleday & Company, Inc.

RICHARD P. BLACKMUR. Passages from *Language as Gesture,* copyright, 1952, by Richard P. Blackmur. Reprinted by permission of Harcourt Brace Jovanovich, Inc.

CLEANTH BROOKS. Passages from "The Language of Paradox" in *The Well Wrought Urn,* copyright, 1947, by Cleanth Brooks. Reprinted by permission of Harcourt Brace Jovanovich, Inc.

GWENDOLYN BROOKS. "Riot," part of "The Third Sermon on the

Warpland," and "An Aspect of Love," from *Riot* by Gwendolyn Brooks, copyright © 1969, by Gwendolyn Brooks. Reprinted by the permission of Broadside Press.

From *The World of Gwendolyn Brooks* by Gwendolyn Brooks: "The Mother," "When you have forgotten Sunday: the love story," Copyright 1945 by Gwendolyn Brooks Blakely; "The Sonnet-ballad," Copyright 1949 by Gwendolyn Brooks Blakely; "In Honor of David Anderson Brooks, My Father," "The Bean Eaters," Copyright © 1959 by Gwendolyn Brooks; "A Lovely Love," "Bronzeville Woman in a Red Hat," "The Ballad of Rudolph Reed," Copyright © 1960 by Gwendolyn Brooks; "Malcolm X," Copyright © 1967 by Gwendolyn Brooks Blakely. All reprinted by permission of Harper & Row, Publishers, Inc.

ROBERT BROWNING. The poems by Browning are based on the text contained in *The Complete Poetical Works of Robert Browning* (edited by Augustine Birrell, new edition with additions; Macmillan, New York, 1915).

JOHN CIARDI. Portions of essay, "Robert Frost: The Way to the Poem," originally published in *The Saturday Review,* April 12, 1958.

STEPHEN CRANE. Poems from *The Poems of Stephen Crane,* edited by Joseph Katz. Copyright © 1966 by Joseph Katz. Published by Cooper Square Publishers, Incorporated, 59 Fourth Avenue, New York, New York 10003.

E. E. CUMMINGS. "in Just-," "the Cambridge ladies who live in furnished souls," "it may not always be so, and i say," Copyright, 1923, 1951, by E. E. Cummings. Reprinted from his volume *Complete Poems* 1913-1962 by permission of Harcourt Brace Jovanovich, Inc. "here is little Effie's head," "i like my body when it is with your," "5 derbies-with-men-in-them smoke Helmar," Copyright, 1925, by E. E. Cummings. Reprinted from his volume *Complete Poems* 1913-1962 by permission of Harcourt Brace Jovanovich, Inc. "jimmie's got a goil," "come, gaze with me upon this dome," Copyright, 1926, by Horace Liveright; copyright, 1954, by E. E. Cummings. Reprinted from *Complete Poems* 1913-1962 by E. E. Cummings by permission of Harcourt Brace Jovanovich, Inc. "the way to hump a cow is not," "my father moved through dooms of love," Copyright, 1940, by E. E. Cummings; copyright, 1968, by Marion Morehouse Cummings. Reprinted from *Complete Poems* 1913-1962 by E. E. Cummings by permission of Harcourt Brace Jovanovich, Inc. "dying is fine) but Death," "when serpents bargain for the right to squirm," "i thank You God for most this amazing," Copyright, 1950, by E. E. Cummings. Reprinted from his volume *Complete Poems* 1913-1962 by permission of Harcourt Brace Jovanovich, Inc. "l(a," © 1958 by E. E. Cummings. Reprinted from his volume *Complete Poems* 1913-1962 by permission of Harcourt Brace Jovanovich, Inc.

EMILY DICKINSON. Poems from *The Complete Poems of Emily Dickinson,* edited by Thomas H. Johnson: "I got so I could hear his name," "Within my Garden, rides a Bird," "My Life had stood—A Loaded Gun," Copyright, 1929, © 1957 by Marl L. Hampson; "After great pain, a formal feeling comes," Copyright 1914, 1942 by Martha Dickinson Bianchi. By permission of Little, Brown and Co.

"I taste a liquor never brewed—," "Wild Nights—Wild Nights!," "There's a certain Slant of Light," "I got so I could hear his name—," "The Soul selects her own Society—," "There came a Day at Summer's Full," "I heard a Fly buzz—when I died—," "Within my Garden, rides a Bird . . . ," "The Way I read a Letter's—this—," "Because I could not stop for Death—," "My Life had stood—a Loaded Gun—," "It is an honorable Thought," "A narrow Fellow in the Grass," "The Bible is an antique Volume—." Reprinted by permission of the publishers and the Trustees of Amherst College from Thomas H. Johnson, Editor, *The Poems of Emily Dickinson,* Cambridge, Mass.: The Belknap Press of Harvard University Press, Copyright, 1951, 1955, by the President and Fellows of Harvard College.

JOHN DONNE. The poems by John Donne are from *The Complete Poetry of John Donne,* edited by John T. Shawcrosse. Copyright © 1967 by Doubleday and Company, Inc. Reprinted by permission of the publisher.

T. S. ELIOT. Harcourt Brace Jovanovich, Inc. "The Love Song of J. Alfred Prufrock," "Morning at the Window," "The Hollow Men," "Journey of the Magi," "Sweeney Among the Nightingales," from *Collected Poems* 1909-1962 by T.S. Eliot, copyright, 1936, by Harcourt Brace Jovanovich, Inc.; copyright © 1963, by T.S. Eliot, Copyright © 1970 by Esme Valerie Eliot. Reprinted by permission of the publishers.

ROBERT FROST. Two lines from "The Death of the Hired Man," "Directive," "Desert Places," "Design," "Neither Far Out Nor In Deep," "Moon Compasses," "A Record Stride," "West-Running Brook," "The Onset," "For Once, Then, Something," "Stopping by Woods on a Snowy Evening," "Out, Out—," "The Oven Bird," "An Old Man's Winter Night," "After Apple-Picking," "Fire and Ice." From *The Poetry of Robert Frost* edited by Edward Connery Lathem. Copyright 1916, 1923, 1928, 1930, 1939, 1947, © 1969 by Holt, Rinehart and Winston, Inc. Copyright 1936, 1944, 1951, © 1956, 1958 by Robert Frost. Copyright © 1964, 1967 by Lesley Frost Ballantine. Reprinted by permission of Holt, Rinehart and Winston, Inc.

ALLEN GINSBERG. "Howl, Part I," and "An Asphodel," from *Howl* *and Other Poems,* by Allen Ginsberg. Copyright © 1956, 1959 by Allen Ginsberg. Reprinted by permission of City Lights Books. Selections from *Kaddish and Other Poems,* Allen Ginsberg. Copyright © 1961 by Allen Ginsberg. Reprinted by permission of City Lights Books "Love Poem on Theme by Whitman," from *Reality Sandwiches,* by Allen Ginsberg. Copyright © 1963 by Allen Ginsberg. Reprinted by permission of City Lights Books. "Patna-Benares Express," "Uptown," "I am a Victim of Telephone," "Cafe in Warsaw," from *Planet News,* by Allen Ginsberg. Copyright © 1968 by Allen Ginsberg. Reprinted by permission of City Lights Books. "Consulting I Ching Smoking Pot Listening to the Fugs Sing Blake," from *Airplane Dreams,* by Allen Ginsberg. Copyright © 1968, 1969, by Allen Ginsberg. Reprinted by permission of City Lights Books.

"The Trembling of the Veil," "Marijuana Notation," and passage from Introduction, from *Empty Mirror* by Allen Ginsberg. Copyright © 1961 by Allen Ginsberg. Reprinted by permission of Corinth Books.

A. E. HOUSMAN. "The Immortal Part," "White in the moon the long road lies," "Bredon Hill," "To an Athlete Dying Young," "When I was One-and-Twenty," "Loveliest of trees, the cherry now." From "A Shropshire Lad"—Authorized Edition—from *The Collected Poems of A.E. Housman.* Copyright 1939, 1940, © 1965 by Holt, Rinehart and Winston, Inc. Copyright © 1967, 1968 by Robert E. Symons. Reprinted by permission of Holt, Rinehart and Winston, Inc. "Delight it is in youth and May," "Easter Hymn," "Parta Quies." From *The Collected Poems of A.E. Housman.* Copyright 1936 by Barclays Bank Ltd. Copyright (c) 1964 by Robert E. Symons. Reprinted by permission of Holt, Rinehart and Winston, Inc. "The First of May," "Now dreary dawns the eastern light," "The fairies break their dances," "The laws of God, the laws of man," "The chestnut casts his flambeaux," "Grenadier," "As I gird on for fighting." From *The Collected Poems of A. E. Housman.* Copyright 1922 by Holt, Rinehart and Winston, Inc. Copyright 1950 by Barclays Bank Ltd. Reprinted by permission of Holt, Rinehart and Winston, Inc.

JOHN KEATS. Poems from *Poetical Works of John Keats* edited by H.W. Garrod, 1956. By permission of The Clarendon Press, Oxford.

ANDREW MARVELL. Poems from *The Poems and Letters of Andrew Marvell* edited by H. M. Margoliouth, Vol. I, 1927. By permission of The Clarendon Press, Oxford.

THE PARIS REVIEW. Excerpts from *Writers at Work:* The Paris Review Interviews, Third Series. Copyright © 1967 by The Paris Review, Inc. All rights reserved. Reprinted by permission of The Viking Press, Inc.

ADRIENNE RICH. "The Trees." Reprinted from *Necessities of Life,* Poems, 1962-1965, by Adrienne Rich. By permission of W.W. Norton & Company, Inc. Copyright © 1966 by W.W. Norton & Company, Inc. "5:30 A. M.," "Continuum," "Leaflets—2," "Night Watch." Reprinted from *Leaflets,* Poems, 1965-1969, by Adrienne Rich. By permission of W.W. Norton & Company, Inc. Copyright © 1969 by W.W. Norton & Company, Inc. "I Dream I'm the Death of Orpheus," "Our Whole Life," "A Valediction Forbidding Mourning." Reprinted from *The Will to Change,* Poems, 1968-1970, by Adrienne Rich. By permission of W.W. Norton & Company, Inc. Copyright © 1971 by W.W. Norton & Company, Inc. "Merced," "Rape." Reprinted from *Diving into the Wreck,* Poems, 1971-1972, by Adrienne Rich. By permission of W.W. Norton & Company, Inc. Copyright © 1973 by W.W. Norton & Company, Inc.

"Landscape of the Star," from *The Diamond Cutters,* by Adrienne Cecile Rich. Copyright, 1952, 1953, 1954, 1955, by Adrienne Rich Conrad. Harper, 1955. Reprinted by permission of Adrienne Rich.

WALLACE STEVENS. Excerpt from "Le Monocle de Mon Oncle," "The Emperor of Ice-Cream," excerpt from "Sunday Morning," "The Show Man," "Anecdote of the Jar," "Peter Quince at the Clavier." Copyright 1923 and renewed 1951 by Wallace Stevens. Reprinted from *The Collected Poems of Wallace Stevens.* Reprinted by permission of Alfred A. Knopf, Inc. "The Idea of Order at Key West," "The Pleasures of Merely Circulating," "Evening Without Angels," Part XXV of "The Man with the Blue Guitar." Copyright 1936 by Wallace Stevens and renewed 1964 by Holly Stevens. Reprinted from *The Collected Poems of Wallace Stevens,* by permission of Alfred A. Knopf, Inc. "To an Old Philosopher in Rome." Copyright 1952 by Wallace Stevens. Reprinted from *The Collected Poems of Wallace Stevens,* by permission of Alfred A. Knopf, Inc. "Angel Surrounded by Paysans." Copyright 1950 by Wallace Stevens. Reprinted from *The Collected Poems of Wallace Stevens,* by permission of Alfred A. Knopf, Inc.

ALLEN TATE. Passages from *Essays of Four Decades* by Allen Tate, published by and reprinted with the permission of the Swallow Press, Inc, © 1969.

DYLAN THOMAS. New Directions Publishing Corp. "Especially When the October Wind," "I see the Boys of summer," "Incarnate Devil," "And death shall have no dominion," "A Refusal to Mourn the Death, by Fire, of a Child in London," "The Hunchback in the Park," "Do not go gentle into that good night," "Fern Hill," "Over Sir John's Hill," "Lament," from *The Poems of Dylan Thomas.* Copyright 1939, 1943, 1946 by New Directions Publishing Corporation, copyright 1952 by Dylan Thomas. Reprinted by permission of New Directions Publishing Corporation.

WILLIAM CARLOS WILLIAMS. Excerpts from William Carlos Williams, *I Wanted to Write a Poem.* Copyright © 1958 by William Carlos Williams. Reprinted by permission of Beacon Press.

Excerpts, from William Carlos Williams, *Paterson.* Copyright 1948, 1949, © 1958 by William Carlos Williams. Reprinted by permission of New Directions Publishing Corporation. "Promenade III," "Complete Destruction," "The Wind Increases," "Dedication for a Plot of Ground," "The Poor," "The Thinker," "The Red Wheelbarrow," from William Carlos Williams, *Collected Earlier Poems.* Copyright 1938 by New Directions Publishing Corporation. Reprinted by permission of New Directions Publishing Corporation. "The Birdsong," "Burning the Christmas Greens," "Io Baccho!," "Rogation Sunday," from William Carlos Williams, *Collected Later Poems.* Copyright 1944, 1948, 1950, © 1963 by William Carlos Williams. Reprinted by permission of New Directions Publishing Corporation. Excerpts from "Asphodel, That Greeny Flower," "Landscape with the Fall of Icarus," "The Stolen Peonies," excerpts from "The Desert Music," "The Descent," from William Carlos Williams, *Pictures from Brueghel and Other Poems.* Copyright © 1954, 1960, 1962 by William Carlos Williams. Reprinted by permission of New Directions Publishing Corporation.

W. B. YEATS. Passage from *A Reader's Guide to William Butler Yeats* by John Unterecker, Copyright © 1959 by John Unterecker. Reprinted with the permission of Farrar, Straus & Giroux, Inc.

Poems from *Collected Poems* by William Butler Yeats. "Long-Legged Fly," "The Circus Animals' Desertion." Copyright © 1940 by Georgia Yeats, renewed 1968 by Bertha Georgie Yeats, Michael Butler Yeats and Anne Yeats. "Easter 1916," "The Second Coming." Copyright © 1924 by Macmillan Publishing Co., Inc., renewed 1952 by Bertha Georgie Yeats. "The Stolen Child." Copyright 1906 by Macmillan Publishing Co., Inc., renewed 1934 by William Butler Yeats. "Adam's Curse." Reprinted with permission of Macmillan Publishing Co., Inc. from *Collected Poems* by William Butler Yeats. Copyright © 1903 by Macmillan Publishing Co., Inc., renewed 1931 by William Butler Yeats. "The Dolls." Reprinted with permission of Macmillan Publishing Co., from *Collected Poems* by William Butler Yeats. Copyright © 1916 by Macmillan Publishing Co., Inc., renewed 1944 by Bertha Georgie Yeats. "Crazy Jane Talks with the Bishop." Reprinted with permission of Macmillan Publishing Co., Inc., from *Collected Poems* by William Butler Yeats. Copyright © 1933 by Macmillan Publishing Co., Inc., renewed 1961 by Bertha Georgia Yeats. "The Lake Isle of Innisfree." Reprinted with permission of Macmillan Publishing Co., Inc., from *Collected Poems* by William Butler

Yeats. Copyright © 1906 by Macmillan Publishing Co., Inc., renewed 1934 by William Butler Yeats. "No Second Troy." Reprinted with permission of Macmillan Publishing Co., Inc., from *Collected Poems* by William Butler Yeats. Copyright © 1912 by Macmillan Publishing Co., Inc., renewed 1940 by Bertha Georgie Yeats. "The Magi." Reprinted with permission of Macmillan Publishing Co., Inc., from *Collected Poems* by William Butler Yeats. Copyright © 1916 by Macmillan Publishing Co., Inc., renewed 1944 by Bertha Georgie Yeats. "The Wild Swans at Coole." Reprinted with permission of Macmillan Publishing Co., Inc. from *Collected Poems* by William Butler Yeats. Copyright © 1919 by Macmillan Publishing Co., Inc., renewed 1947 by Bertha Butler Yeats. "Sailing to Byzantium." Reprinted with permission of Macmillan Publishing Co., Inc. from *Collected Poems* by William Butler Yeats. Copyright © 1928 by Macmillan Publishing Co., Inc., renewed 1956 by Georgie Yeats.

The three lines of poetry on Yeats' tombstone are taken from his "Under Ben Bulben."